W9-BBR-781

ULTIMATE LEADERSHIP

MAXIMIZE YOUR POTENTIAL
and EMPOWER YOUR TEAM

CLASSIC LEADERSHIP COLLECTION

—⁓—

THE 21 IRREFUTABLE LAWS *of* LEADERSHIP
DEVELOPING *the* LEADER WITHIN YOU
THE 17 INDISPUTABLE LAWS *of* TEAMWORK

JOHN C. MAXWELL

THOMAS NELSON
Since 1798

thomasnelson.com

The 21 Irrefutable Laws of Leadership (ISBN 0-7852-7431-6) Copyright © 1998 by Maxwell Motivation, Inc., a Georgia corporation. Scripture quotations noted CEV are from THE CONTEMPORARY ENGLISH VERSION. Copyright © 1991 by the American Bible Society. Used by permission.

Developing the Leader Within You (ISBN 0-7852-6666-6) Copyright © 1993 by Injoy Inc., a Georgia corporation. Scripture quotations are from the NEW KING JAMES VERSION of the Bible. Copyright © 1982 Thomas Nelson, Inc.

The 17 Indisputable Laws of Teamwork (ISBN 0-7852-7434-0) Copyright © 2001 by Maxwell Motivation, Inc., a Georgia corporation. Scripture quotations noted KJV are from the KING JAMES VERSION.

Published in Nashville, Tennessee, by Thomas Nelson, Inc.

Thomas Nelson, Inc. titles may be purchased in bulk for educational, business, fund-raising, or sales promotional use. For information, please e-mail SpecialMarkets@ThomasNelson.com.

ISBN 10: 0-7852-8114-2
ISBN 13: 978-0-7852-8114-6

Printed in the United States of America
07 08 09 10 11 12 QWM 7 6 5 4 3 2 1

CONTENTS
THE 21 IRREFUTABLE LAWS *of* LEADERSHIP

Contents
Developing *the* Leader Within you

Contents
The 17 Indisputable Laws *of* Teamwork

THE 21 IRREFUTABLE
LAWS OF LEADERSHIP

Follow Them and People
Will Follow You

*To the hundreds of thousands of people
to whom I've taught leadership over the years
through conferences and books . . .*

and

*To you—
the person wanting to become a better leader,
because
everything rises and falls on leadership*

FOREWORD

You are going to love this book—whether it is the first leadership book in your collection or the fiftieth—because you can immediately apply the life-changing principles and procedures in your personal, family, and business life. There is no "ivory tower" theory in this book. Instead, it is loaded with unchanging leadership principles confirmed by the real-world experiences of John Maxwell and the many people he writes about.

The 21 Irrefutable Laws of Leadership is a powerful, definitive statement of the timeless laws you simply *must* follow if you want to be a great leader—at home, on the job, in church, or wherever you are called on to lead.

In each chapter, John goes straight to the heart of a profound leadership law, showing you through the successes and failures of others how you can apply the law in your life. And you *can* apply each of the laws. If you're a willing student, you can learn the 21 laws and put them into practice.

What a priceless treasure leadership authority John Maxwell offers as he boils everything he's learned about leadership down into such usable form! Once you apply these leadership laws, you'll notice leaders all around you putting into action (or breaking) the Law of E. F. Hutton, the Law of the Big Mo, and the rest.

I heartily recommend *The 21 Irrefutable Laws of Leadership*. It is helpful and easy to read, yet profound in its depth and clarity. It's loaded with hope, direction, encouragement, and specific procedures. It's principle-based with precise, clear-cut directions to provide you with the necessary tools to fulfill your leadership role.

If you are new to leadership, this book will jump-start your leadership career. If you are an experienced leader with blue-chip credentials, this book will make you an even better leader. It's good—very good.

Zig Ziglar

ACKNOWLEDGMENTS

I'D LIKE TO THANK the many leaders who helped me while I was working on this book. From INJOY: Dick Peterson, Dave Sutherland, Dan Reiland, Tim Elmore, and Dennis Worden. From Thomas Nelson: Rolf Zettersten, Ron Land, Mike Hyatt, Victor Oliver, and Rob Birkhead.

I must say thank you to Brian Hampton, my managing editor at Nelson, for his patience and assistance as we worked through the manuscript.

I also want to thank my assistant, Linda Eggers, whose great heart and incredible service make me a better leader.

Finally, I want to thank Charlie Wetzel, my writer, and his wife, Stephanie. This book would not have been written without their help.

INTRODUCTION

I HAVE THE PRIVILEGE of teaching leadership across the country and around the globe, and I often get the opportunity to talk with people who are attending one of my conferences for a second, third, or even fourth time. At a recent conference here in the United States, a man in his late fifties whom I had met several years before came up and spoke to me during a break. He grabbed my hand and shook it vigorously. "Learning leadership has changed my life," he said. "But I sure wish I had heard you twenty years ago."

"No, you don't," I answered with a chuckle.

"What do you mean?" he said. "I would have achieved so much more! If I had known these leadership principles twenty years ago, I'd be in a totally different place in life. Your leadership laws have fueled my vision. They've given me the desire to learn more about leadership and accomplish my goals. If I'd learned this twenty years ago, I could have done some things that I had never even dreamed possible."

"Maybe you would have," I answered. "But twenty years ago, I wouldn't have been able to teach them to you. It has taken me my entire lifetime to learn and apply the laws of leadership to my life."

As I write this, I am fifty-one years old. I've spent more than thirty years in professional leadership positions. I've founded four companies. And I focus my time and energy on doing what makes a positive impact in the lives of people. But I've also made a lot of mistakes along the way—more than most people I know. Every success and every failure has been an invaluable lesson in what it means to lead.

As I travel and speak to organizations and individuals, people frequently ask me to define the essentials of leadership. "If you were to take everything you've learned about leadership over the years and boil it down into a short list," they ask, "what would it be?"

This book is my answer to that often-asked question. It has taken me a lifetime to learn these 21 Irrefutable Laws of Leadership. My desire is to communicate them to you as simply and clearly as possible. And it sure won't hurt if we have some fun along the way.

One of the most important truths I've learned over the years is this: Leadership is leadership, no matter where you go or what you do. Times change. Technology marches forward. Cultures vary from place to place. But the true principles of leadership are constant—whether you're looking at the citizens of ancient Greece, the Hebrews in the Old Testament, the armies of the last two hundred years, the rulers of modern Europe, the pastors in local churches, or the businesspeople of today's global economy. Leadership principles stand the test of time. They are irrefutable.

As you read the following chapters, I'd like you to keep in mind four ideas:

1. **The laws can be learned.** Some are easier to understand and apply than others, but every one of them can be acquired.

2. **The laws can stand alone.** Each law complements all the others, but you don't need one in order to learn another.

3. **The laws carry consequences with them.** Apply the laws, and people will follow you. Violate or ignore them, and you will not be able to lead others.

4. **These laws are the foundation of leadership.** Once you learn the principles, you have to practice them and apply them to your life.

Whether you are a follower who is just beginning to discover the impact of leadership or a natural leader who already has followers, you can become a better leader. As you read about the laws, you'll recognize that you may already practice some of them effectively. Other laws will expose weaknesses you didn't know you had. But the greater the number of laws you learn, the better leader you will become. Each law is like a tool, ready to be picked up and used to help you achieve your dreams and add value to other people. Pick up even one, and you will become a better leader. Learn them all, and people will gladly follow you.

Now, let's open the toolbox together.

THE LAW OF THE LID

*Leadership Ability Determines
a Person's Level of Effectiveness*

I OFTEN OPEN MY LEADERSHIP conferences by explaining the Law of the Lid because it helps people understand the value of leadership. If you can get a handle on this law, you will see the incredible impact of leadership on every aspect of life. So here it is: Leadership ability is the lid that determines a person's level of effectiveness. The lower an individual's ability to lead, the lower the lid on his potential. The higher the leadership, the greater the effectiveness. To give you an example, if your leadership rates an 8, then your effectiveness can never be greater than a 7. If your leadership is only a 4, then your effectiveness will be no higher than a 3. Your leadership ability—for better or for worse—always determines your effectiveness and the potential impact of your organization.

Let me tell you a story that illustrates the Law of the Lid. In 1930, two young brothers named Dick and Maurice moved from New Hampshire to California in search of the American Dream. They had just gotten out of high school, and they saw few opportunities back home. So they headed straight for Hollywood where they eventually found jobs on a movie studio set.

After a while, their entrepreneurial spirit and interest in the entertainment industry prompted them to open a theater in Glendale, a town about five miles northeast of Hollywood. But despite all their efforts, the brothers just couldn't make the business profitable. In the four years they ran the theater, they weren't able to consistently generate enough money to pay the one hundred dollars a month rent that their landlord required.

A NEW OPPORTUNITY

The brothers' desire for success was strong, so they kept looking for better business opportunities. In 1937, they finally struck on something that worked. They opened a small drive-in restaurant in Pasadena, located just east of Glendale. People in southern California had become very dependent on their cars, and the culture was changing to accommodate that, including its businesses.

Drive-in restaurants were a phenomenon that sprang up in the early thirties, and they were becoming very popular. Rather than being invited into a dining room to eat, customers would drive into a parking lot around a small restaurant, place their orders with carhops, and receive their food on trays right in their cars. The food was served on china plates complete with glassware and metal utensils. It was a timely idea in a society that was becoming faster paced and increasingly mobile.

Dick and Maurice's tiny drive-in restaurant was a great success, and in 1940, they decided to move the operation to San Bernardino, a working-class boomtown fifty miles east of Los Angeles. They built a larger facility and expanded their menu from hot dogs, fries, and shakes to include barbecued beef and pork sandwiches, hamburgers, and other items. Their business exploded. Annual sales reached

$200,000, and the brothers found themselves splitting $50,000 in profits every year—a sum that put them in the town's financial elite.

In 1948, their intuition told them that times were changing, and they made modifications to their restaurant business. They eliminated the carhops and started serving only walk-up customers. And they also streamlined everything. They reduced their menu and focused on selling hamburgers. They eliminated plates, glassware, and metal utensils, switching to paper products instead. They reduced their costs and the prices they charged customers. They also created what they called the Speedy Service System. Their kitchen became like an assembly line, where each person focused on service with speed. Their goal was to fill each customer's order in thirty seconds or less. And they succeeded. By the mid-1950s, annual revenue hit $350,000, and by then, Dick and Maurice split net profits of about $100,000 each year.

Who were these brothers? Back in those days, you could have found out by driving to their small restaurant on the corner of Fourteenth and E Streets in San Bernardino. On the front of the small octagonal building hung a neon sign that said simply McDONALD'S HAMBURGERS. Dick and Maurice McDonald had hit the great American jackpot, and the rest, as they say, is history, right? Wrong. The McDonalds never went any farther because their weak leadership put a lid on their ability to succeed.

THE STORY BEHIND THE STORY

It's true that the McDonald brothers were financially secure. Theirs was one of the most profitable restaurant enterprises in the country, and they felt that they had a hard time spending all the money they made. Their genius was in customer service and kitchen organization. That talent led to the creation of a new system of food and beverage service. In fact, their talent was so widely known in food service circles that people started writing them and visiting from all over the country to learn more about their methods. At one point, they received as many as three hundred calls and letters every month.

That led them to the idea of marketing the McDonald's concept. The idea of franchising restaurants wasn't new. It had been around for several decades. To the McDonald brothers, it looked like a way to make money without having to open another restaurant themselves. In 1952, they got started, but their effort was a dismal failure. The reason was simple. They lacked the leadership necessary to make it effective. Dick and Maurice were good restaurant owners. They understood how to run a business, make their systems efficient, cut costs, and increase profits. They were efficient managers. But they were not leaders. Their thinking patterns clamped a lid down on what they could do and become. At the height of their success, Dick and Maurice found themselves smack-dab against the Law of the Lid.

THE BROTHERS PARTNER WITH A LEADER

In 1954, the brothers hooked up with a man named Ray Kroc who *was* a leader. Kroc had been running a small company he founded, which sold machines for making milk shakes. He knew about McDonald's. Their restaurant was one of his best customers. And as soon as he visited the store, he had a vision for its potential. In his mind he could see the restaurant going nationwide in hundreds of markets. He soon struck a deal with Dick and Maurice, and in 1955, he formed McDonald's System, Inc. (later called the McDonald's Corporation).

Kroc immediately bought the rights to a franchise so that he could use it as a model and prototype to sell other franchises. Then he began to assemble a team and build an organization to make McDonald's a nationwide entity. He recruited and hired the sharpest people he could find, and as his team grew in size and ability, his people developed additional recruits with leadership skill.

In the early years, Kroc sacrificed a lot. Though he was in his midfifties, he worked long hours just as he had when he first got started in business thirty years earlier. He eliminated many frills at home, including his country club membership, which he later said added ten strokes to his golf game. During his first eight years with McDonald's, he took no salary. Not only that, but he personally borrowed money from the bank and against his life insurance to help cover the salaries of a few key leaders he wanted on the team. His sacrifice and his leadership paid off. In 1961 for the sum of $2.7 million, Kroc bought the exclusive rights to McDonald's from the brothers, and he proceeded to turn it into an American institution and global entity. The "lid" in the life and leadership of Ray Kroc was obviously much higher than that of his predecessors.

In the years that Dick and Maurice McDonald had attempted to franchise their food service system, they managed to sell the concept to just fifteen buyers, only ten of whom actually opened restaurants. And even in that small enterprise, their limited leadership and vision were hindrances. For example, when their first franchisee, Neil Fox of Phoenix, told the brothers that he wanted to call his restaurant McDonald's, Dick's response was, "What . . . for? McDonald's means nothing in Phoenix."

On the other hand, the leadership lid in Ray Kroc's life was sky high. Between 1955 and 1959, Kroc succeeded in opening 100 restaurants. Four years after that, there were 500 McDonald's. Today the company has opened more than 21,000 restaurants in no fewer than 100 countries.[1] Leadership ability—or more specifically the lack of leadership ability—was the lid on the McDonald brothers' effectiveness.

SUCCESS WITHOUT LEADERSHIP

I believe that success is within the reach of just about everyone. But I also believe that personal success without leadership ability brings only

> *The higher you want to climb, the more you need leadership. The greater the impact you want to make, the greater your influence needs to be.*

limited effectiveness. A person's impact is only a fraction of what it could be with good leadership. The higher you want to climb, the more you need leadership. The greater the impact you want to make, the greater your influence needs to be. Whatever you will accomplish is restricted by your ability to lead others.

Let me give you a picture of what I mean. Let's say that when it comes to success, you're an 8 (on a scale from 1 to 10). That's pretty good. I think it would be safe to say that the McDonald brothers were in that range. But let's also say that your leadership ability is only a 1. Your level of effectiveness would look like this:

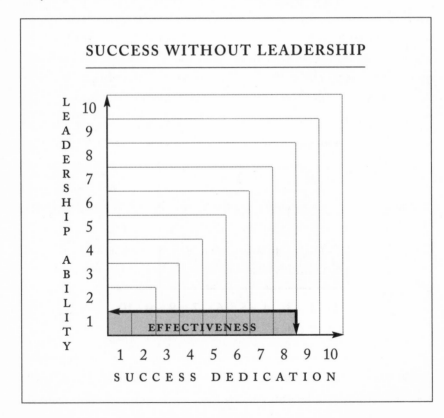

SUCCESS WITHOUT LEADERSHIP

To increase your level of effectiveness, you have a couple of choices. You could work very hard to increase your dedication to success and excellence—to work toward becoming a 10. It's possible that you could make it to that level, though the Law of Diminishing Returns says that the effort it would take to increase those last two points might take more energy than it did to achieve the first eight. If you really killed yourself, you might increase your success by that 25 percent.

But you have another option. Let's say that instead you work hard to increase your level of *leadership*. Over the course of time, you develop yourself as a leader, and eventually, your leadership ability becomes, say, a 6. Visually, the results would look like this:

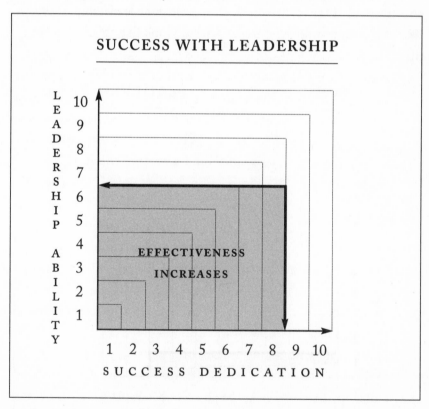

SUCCESS WITH LEADERSHIP

By raising your leadership ability—without increasing your success dedication at all—you can increase your original effectiveness by 500 percent! If you were to raise your leadership to 8, where it matched your success dedication, you would increase your effectiveness by 700 percent! Leadership has a multiplying effect. I've seen its impact over and over again in all kinds of businesses and nonprofit organizations. And that's why I've taught leadership for more than twenty years.

TO CHANGE THE DIRECTION OF THE ORGANIZATION, CHANGE THE LEADER

Leadership ability is always the lid on personal and organizational effectiveness. If the leadership is strong, the lid is high. But if it's not, then the organization is limited. That's why in times of trouble, organizations naturally look for new leadership. When the country is experiencing hard times, it elects a new president. When a company is losing money, it hires a new CEO. When a church is floundering, it searches for a new senior pastor. When a sports team keeps losing, it looks for a new head coach.

> *Personal and organizational effectiveness is proportionate to the strength of leadership.*

The relationship between leadership and effectiveness is evident in sports. For example, if you look at professional sports organizations, the talent on the team is rarely the issue. Just about every team has highly talented players. The leadership provided by the coach—and several key players—makes the difference. To change the effectiveness of the team, lift up the leadership of the coach. That's the Law of the Lid.

A sports team with a long history of leadership and effectiveness is Notre Dame. The school's football teams have won more national championships than any other team in the country. Over the years, the Fighting Irish have won more than three-fourths of all their games (an incredible .759 winning percentage). In fact, two of their former head coaches, Knute Rockne and Frank Leahy, have the highest winning percentages in NCAA history.

Back in the early 1980s, Notre Dame hired Gerry Faust as its head football coach. He was following two great coaches: Ara Parseghian and Dan Devine, both of whom had won national championships during their tenure and both of whom were eventually inducted into the National Football Foundation Hall of Fame. Prior to coming to Notre Dame, Faust had compiled an incredible record of 174-17-2 during his eighteen years as the head coach at Moeller High School. His teams experienced seven undefeated seasons and won six Ohio state titles. Four teams he coached were considered the best in the nation.

But when he arrived at Notre Dame, it didn't take long for people to discover that he was in over his head. As a coach and strategist, he was effective, but he didn't have the leadership ability necessary to make it at the college level. During his five seasons at the university, he compiled a 30-26-1 record and winning percentage of .535, third worst in Notre Dame's one-hundred-plus-year history of college football. Faust coached only one other college team after that, the University of Akron, where he finished with an overall losing record of 43-53-3. He was another casualty of the Law of the Lid.

Wherever you look, you can find smart, talented, successful people who are able to go only so far because of the limitations of their leadership. For example, when Apple got started in the late 1970s, Steve Wozniak was the brains behind the Apple computer. His leadership lid was low, but that was not the case for his partner, Steve Jobs. His lid was so high that he built a world-class organization and gave it a nine-digit value. That's the impact of the Law of the Lid.

A few years ago, I met Don Stephenson, the chairman of Global Hospitality Resources, Inc., of San Diego, California, an international hospitality advisory and consulting firm. Over lunch, I asked him about his organization. Today he primarily does consulting, but back then his company took over the management of hotels and resorts that weren't doing well financially. They oversaw many excellent facilities such as La Costa in southern California.

> *You can find smart, talented, successful people who are able to go only so far because of the limitations of their leadership.*

Don said that whenever they came into an organization to take it over, they always started by doing two things: First, they trained all the staff to improve their level of service to the customers; and second, they fired the leader. When he told me that, I was at first surprised.

"You *always* fire him?" I asked. "Every time?"

"That's right. Every time," he said.

"Don't you talk to the person first—to check him out to see if he's a good leader?" I said.

"No," he answered. "If he'd been a good leader, the organization wouldn't be in the mess it's in."

And I thought to myself, *Of course. It's the Law of the Lid.* To reach the highest level of effectiveness, you have to raise the lid—one way or another.

The good news is that getting rid of the leader isn't the *only* way. Just as I teach in conferences that there is a lid, I also teach that you can raise it—but that's the subject of another law of leadership.

2

THE LAW OF INFLUENCE

The True Measure of Leadership Is Influence—Nothing More, Nothing Less

IF YOU DON'T HAVE INFLUENCE, you will *never* be able to lead others. So how do you measure influence? Here's a story to answer that question. In late summer of 1997, people were jolted by two events that occurred less than a week apart: the deaths of Princess Diana and Mother Teresa. On the surface, the two women could not have been more different. One was a tall, young, glamorous princess from England who circulated in the highest society. The other, a Nobel Peace Prize recipient, was a small, elderly Catholic nun born in Albania, who served the poorest of the poor in Calcutta, India.

What's incredible is that their impact was remarkably similar. In a 1996 poll published by the London *Daily Mail*, Princess Diana and Mother Teresa were voted in first and second places as the world's two most caring people. That's something that doesn't happen unless you have a lot of influence. How did someone like Diana come to be regarded in the same way as Mother Teresa? The answer is that she demonstrated the power of the Law of Influence.

DIANA CAPTURED
THE WORLD'S IMAGINATION

In 1981, Diana became the most talked-about person on the globe when she married Prince Charles of England. Nearly 1 billion people watched Diana's wedding ceremony televised from St. Paul's Cathedral. And since that day, it seemed people never could get enough news about her. People were intrigued with Diana, a commoner who had once been a kindergarten teacher. At first she seemed painfully shy and totally overwhelmed by all the attention she and her new husband were receiving. Early in their marriage, some reports stated that Diana wasn't very happy performing the duties expected of her as a royal princess. However, in time she adjusted to her new role. As she started traveling and representing the royal family around the world at various functions, she quickly made it her goal to serve others and raise funds for numerous charitable causes. And during the process, she built many important relationships—with politicians, organizers of humanitarian causes, entertainers, and heads of state. At first, she was simply a spokesperson and catalyst for fund-raising, but as time went by, her influence increased—and so did her ability to make things happen.

Diana started rallying people to causes such as AIDS research, care for people with leprosy, and a ban on land mines. She was quite influential in bringing that last issue to the attention of the world's leaders. On a visit to the United States just months before her death, she met with members of the Clinton administration to convince them to support the Oslo conference banning the devices. And a few weeks later, they made changes in their position. Patrick Fuller of the British Red Cross said, "The attention she drew to the issue influenced Clinton. She put the issue on the world agenda, there's no doubt about that."[1]

THE EMERGENCE OF A LEADER

In the beginning, Diana's title had merely given her a platform to address others, but she soon became a person of influence in her own right. In 1996 when she was divorced from Prince Charles, she lost her title, but that loss didn't at all diminish her impact on others. Instead, her influence continued to increase while that of her former husband and in-laws declined—despite their royal titles and position. Why? Diana instinctively understood the Law of Influence.

> *"You have achieved excellence as a leader when people will follow you everywhere if only out of curiosity."*
> —*Colin Powell*

Ironically, even in death Diana continued to influence others. When her funeral was broadcast on television and BBC Radio, it was translated into forty-four languages. NBC estimated that the total audience numbered as many as 2.5 billion people—more than twice the number of people who watched her wedding.

THE QUESTION OF LEADERSHIP

Princess Diana has been characterized in many ways. But one word that I've never heard used to describe her is *leader.* Yet that's what she was. Ultimately, she made things happen because she was an influencer, and leadership is influence—nothing more, nothing less.

LEADERSHIP IS NOT . . .

People have so many misconceptions about leadership. When they hear that someone has an impressive title or an assigned leadership position, they assume that he is a leader. *Sometimes* that's true. But titles don't have much value when it comes to leading. True leadership cannot be awarded, appointed, or assigned. It comes only from influence, and that can't be mandated. It must be earned. The only thing a title can buy is a little time—either to increase your level of influence with others or to erase it.

FIVE MYTHS ABOUT LEADERSHIP

There are plenty of misconceptions and myths that people embrace about leaders and leadership. Here are five common ones:

I. THE MANAGEMENT MYTH

A widespread misunderstanding is that leading and managing are one and the same. Up until a few years ago, books that claimed to be on leadership were often really about management. The main difference between the two is that leadership is about influencing people to follow, while management focuses on maintaining systems and processes. As former Chrysler chairman and CEO Lee Iacocca wryly commented, "Sometimes even the best manager is like the little boy with the big dog, waiting to see where the dog wants to go so that he can take him there."

> *The only thing a title can buy is a little time—either to increase your level of influence with others or to erase it.*

The best way to test whether a person can lead rather than just manage is to ask him to create positive change. Managers can maintain direction, but they can't change it. To move people in a new direction, you need influence.

2. THE ENTREPRENEUR MYTH

Frequently, people assume that all salespeople and entrepreneurs are leaders. But that's not always the case. You may remember the

Ronco commercials that appeared on television years ago. They sold items such as the Veg-O-Matic, Pocket Fisherman, and Inside-the-Shell Egg Scrambler. Those products were the brainchildren of an entrepreneur named Ron Popeil. Called the salesman of the century, he has also appeared in numerous infomercials for products such as spray-on relief for baldness and food dehydrating devices.

Popeil is certainly enterprising, innovative, and successful, especially if you measure him by the $300 million in sales his products have earned. But that doesn't make him a leader. People may be buying what he has to sell, but they're not following him. At best, he is able to persuade people for a moment, but he holds no long-term influence with them.

3. THE KNOWLEDGE MYTH

Sir Francis Bacon said, "Knowledge is power." Most people, believing power is the essence of leadership, naturally assume that those who possess knowledge and intelligence are leaders. But that isn't automatically true. You can visit any major university and meet brilliant research scientists and philosophers whose ability to think is so high that it's off the charts, but whose ability to lead is so low that it doesn't even register on the charts. IQ doesn't necessarily equate to leadership.

4. THE PIONEER MYTH

Another misconception is that anyone who is out in front of the crowd is a leader. But being first isn't always the same as leading. For example, Sir Edmund Hillary was the first man to reach the summit of Mount Everest. Since his historic ascent in 1953, many people have "followed" him in achieving that feat. But that doesn't make Hillary a leader. He wasn't even the leader on that particular expedition. John Hunt was. And when Hillary traveled to the South Pole in 1958 as part of the Commonwealth Trans-Antarctic Expedition, he was accompanying another leader, Sir Vivian Fuchs. To be a leader, a person has to not only be out front, but also have people intentionally coming behind him, following his lead, and acting on his vision.

5. THE POSITION MYTH

As mentioned earlier, the greatest misunderstanding about leadership is that people think it is based on position, but it's not. Stanley Huffty affirmed, "It's not the position that makes the leader; it's the leader that makes the position."

Look at what happened several years ago at Cordiant, the advertising agency formerly known as Saatchi & Saatchi. In 1994, institutional investors at Saatchi & Saatchi forced the board of directors to dismiss Maurice Saatchi, the company's CEO. What was the result? Several executives followed him out. So did many of the company's largest accounts, including British Airways and Mars, the candy maker. Saatchi's influence was so great that his departure caused the company's stock to fall immediately from $8⅝ to $4 per share.[2] What happened is a result of the Law of Influence. Saatchi lost his title and position, but he continued to be the leader.

> *"It's not the position that makes the leader; it's the leader that makes the position."*
> —Stanley Huffty

WHO'S THE REAL LEADER?

I personally learned the Law of Influence when I accepted my first job out of college at a small church in rural Indiana. I went in with all the right credentials. I was hired as the senior pastor, which meant that I possessed the position and title of leader in that organization. I had the proper college degree. I had even been ordained. In addition, I had been trained by my father who was an excellent pastor and a very high-profile leader in the denomination. It made for a good-looking résumé—but it didn't make me a leader. At my first board meeting, I quickly found out who was the real leader of that church. (I'll tell you the whole story in the Law of E. F. Hutton.) By the time I took my next position three years later, I had learned the Law of Influence. I recognized that hard work was required to gain influence in any organization and to earn the right to become the leader.

LEADERSHIP IS . . .

Leadership is influence—nothing more, nothing less. When you become a student of leaders, as I am, you recognize people's level of influence in everyday situations all around you. Let me give you an example. In 1997, I moved to Atlanta, Georgia. In that same year, Dan Reeves became the coach of the NFL's Atlanta Falcons. I was glad to hear that. Reeves is an excellent coach and leader. Though he had most recently coached the New York Giants, Reeves made his reputation as the head coach of the Denver Broncos. From 1981 to 1992, he compiled an excellent 117-79-1 record, earned three Super Bowl appearances, and received NFL Coach of the Year honors three times.

Despite Reeves's success in Denver, he didn't always experience smooth sailing. He was known to have had disagreements with quarterback John Elway and assistant coach Mike Shanahan. What was the reason for the problem? It was said that during the 1989 season, Shanahan and Elway sometimes worked on their own offensive game plan, ignoring Reeves's wishes. I don't know if that was true, but if it was, then Shanahan, not Reeves, had developed greater influence with the Denver quarterback. It didn't matter that Reeves held the title and position of head coach. It didn't even matter how good a coach Reeves was. Shanahan had become the more influential leader in the quarterback's life. And leadership is influence.

Shanahan left the Broncos at the end of that season, but he returned in 1995 as the team's head coach. He became in title what he evidently already had been in terms of influence to some of the players: their leader. And that leadership has now paid off. In January of 1998, he led the Denver Broncos franchise and quarterback John Elway to their first Super Bowl victory.

LEADERSHIP WITHOUT LEVERAGE

I admire and respect the leadership of my good friend Bill Hybels, the senior pastor of Willow Creek Community Church in South Barrington, Illinois, the largest church in North America. Bill says he believes that the church is the most leadership-intensive enterprise in society. A lot of businesspeople I know are surprised when they hear that statement, but I think Bill is right. What is the basis of his belief? Positional leadership doesn't work in volunteer organizations. Because a leader doesn't have leverage—or influence—he is ineffective. In other organizations, the person who has position has incredible leverage. In the military, leaders can use rank and, if all else fails, throw people into the brig. In business, bosses have tremendous leverage in the form of salary, benefits, and perks. Most followers are pretty cooperative when their livelihood is at stake.

> "The very essence of all power to influence lies in getting the other person to participate."
> —Harry A. Overstreet

But in voluntary organizations, such as churches, the only thing that works is leadership in its purest form. Leaders have only their influence to aid them. And as Harry A. Overstreet observed, "The very essence of all power to influence lies in getting the other person to participate." Followers in voluntary organizations cannot be forced to get on board. If the leader has no influence with them, then they won't follow. When I recently shared that observation with a group of about

150 CEOs from the automobile industry, I saw lightbulbs going on all over the room. And when I gave them a piece of advice, they really got excited. I'm going to share that same advice with you: If you are a businessperson and you really want to find out whether your people are capable of leading, send them out to volunteer their time in the community. If they can get people to follow them while they're serving at the Red Cross, a United Way shelter, or their local church, then you know that they really do have influence—and leadership ability.

FROM COMMANDER TO PRIVATE
TO COMMANDER IN CHIEF

One of my favorite stories that illustrates the Law of Influence concerns Abraham Lincoln. In 1832, years before he became president, young Lincoln gathered together a group of men to fight in the Black Hawk War. In those days, the person who put together a volunteer company for the militia often became its leader and assumed a commanding rank. In this instance, Lincoln had the rank of captain.

But Lincoln had a problem. He knew nothing about soldiering. He had no prior military experience, and he knew nothing about tactics. He had trouble remembering the simplest military procedures. For example, one day Lincoln was marching a couple of dozen men across a field and needed to guide

> *By the end of his military service, Abraham Lincoln found his rightful place, having achieved the rank of private.*

them through a gate into another field. But he couldn't manage it. Recounting the incident later, Lincoln said, "I could not for the life of me remember the proper word of command for getting my company endwise. Finally, as we came near [the gate] I shouted: 'This company is dismissed for two minutes, when it will fall in again on the other side of the gate.'"[3]

As time went by, Lincoln's level of influence with others in the militia actually *decreased.* While other officers proved themselves and gained rank, Lincoln found himself going in the other direction. He began with the *title and position* of captain, but that did him little good. He couldn't overcome the Law of Influence. By the end of his military service, Abraham Lincoln found his rightful place, having achieved the rank of private.

Fortunately for Lincoln—and for the fate of our country—he overcame his inability to influence others. He followed his time in the military with undistinguished stints in the Illinois state legislature and the U.S. House of Representatives. But over time and with much effort and personal experience, he became a person of remarkable influence and impact.

Here is my favorite leadership proverb: "He who thinks he leads, but has no followers, is only taking a walk." If you can't influence others, they won't follow you. And if they won't follow, you're not a leader. That's the Law of Influence. No matter what anybody else tells you, remember that leadership is influence—nothing more, nothing less.

3

THE LAW OF PROCESS

Leadership Develops Daily, Not in a Day

Anne Scheiber was 101 years old when she died in January of 1995. For years she had lived in a tiny, run-down, rent-controlled studio apartment in Manhattan. The paint on the walls was peeling, and the old bookcases that lined the walls were covered in dust. Rent was four hundred dollars a month.

Scheiber lived on Social Security and a small monthly pension, which she started receiving in 1943 when she retired as an auditor for the Internal Revenue Service. She hadn't done very well at the IRS. More specifically, the agency hadn't done right by her. Despite having a law degree and doing excellent work, she was never promoted. And when she retired at age fifty-one, she was making only $3,150 a year.

"She was treated very, very shabbily," said Benjamin Clark, who knew her as well as anyone did. "She really had to fend for herself in every way. It was really quite a struggle."

Scheiber was the model of thrift. She didn't spend money on herself. She didn't buy new furniture as the old pieces she owned became worn out. She didn't even subscribe to a newspaper. About once a week, she used to go to the public library to read the *Wall Street Journal.*

WINDFALL!

Imagine the surprise of Norman Lamm, the president of Yeshiva University in New York City, when he found out that Anne Scheiber, a little old lady whom he had never heard of—and who had never attended Yeshiva—left nearly her entire estate to the university.

"When I saw the will, it was mind blowing, such an unexpected windfall," said Lamm. "This woman has become a legend overnight."

The estate Anne Scheiber left to Yeshiva University was worth $22 million![1]

How in the world did a spinster who had been retired for fifty years build an eight-figure fortune?

Here's the answer. By the time she retired from the IRS in 1943, Anne Scheiber had managed to save $5,000. She invested that money in stocks. By 1950, she had made enough profit to buy 1,000 shares of Schering-Plough Corporation stock, then valued at $10,000. And she held on to that stock, letting its value build. Today, those original shares have split enough times to produce 128,000 shares, worth $7.5 million.[2]

The secret to Scheiber's success was that she spent most of her life building her worth. Whether her stock's values went up or down, she never sold it off with the thought, *I'm finished building; now it's time to cash out.* She was in for the long haul, the *really* long haul. When she earned dividends—which kept getting larger and larger—she reinvested them. She spent her whole lifetime building. While other older people worry that they may run out of funds before the end of their lives, the longer she lived, the wealthier she became. When it came to finances, Scheiber understood and applied the Law of Process.

LEADERSHIP IS LIKE INVESTING—IT COMPOUNDS

Becoming a leader is a lot like investing successfully in the stock market. If your hope is to make a fortune in a day, you're not going to be successful. What matters most is what you do day by day over the long haul. My friend Tag Short maintains, "The secret of our success is found in our daily agenda." If you continually invest in your leadership development, letting your "assets" compound, the inevitable result is growth over time.

> *Becoming a leader is a lot like investing successfully in the stock market. If your hope is to make a fortune in a day, you're not going to be successful.*

When I teach leadership at conferences, people inevitably ask me whether leaders are born. I always answer, "Yes, of course they are . . . I've yet to meet one that came into the world any other way!" We all laugh, and then I answer the real question—whether leadership is something a person either possesses or doesn't.

Although it's true that some people are born with greater natural gifts than others, the ability to lead is really a collection of skills, nearly all of which can be learned and improved. But that process doesn't happen overnight. Leadership is complicated. It has many facets: respect, experience, emotional strength, people skills, discipline, vision, momentum, timing—the list goes on. As you can see, many factors that come into play in leadership are intangible. That's why leaders require so much seasoning to be effective. That's why only now, at age fifty-one, do I feel that I am truly beginning to understand the many aspects of leadership with clarity.

LEADERS ARE LEARNERS

In a study of ninety top leaders from a variety of fields, leadership experts Warren Bennis and Burt Nanus made a discovery about the relationship between growth and leadership: "It is the capacity to develop and improve their skills that distinguishes leaders from their followers." Successful leaders are learners. And the learning process is ongoing, a result of self-discipline and perseverance. The goal each day must be to get a little better, to build on the previous day's progress.

THE FOUR PHASES OF LEADERSHIP GROWTH

Whether you do or don't have great natural ability for leadership, your development and progress will probably occur according to the following four phases:

PHASE 1—I DON'T KNOW WHAT I DON'T KNOW

Most people fail to recognize the value of leadership. They believe that leadership is only for a few—for the people at the top of the corporate ladder. They have no idea of the opportunities they're passing up when they don't learn to lead. This point was driven home for me when a college president shared with me that only a handful of students signed up for a leadership course offered by the school. Why? Only a few thought of themselves as leaders. If they had known that leadership is influence, and that in the course of each day most individuals usually try to influence at least four other people, their desire might have been sparked to learn more about the subject. It's unfortunate because as long as a person doesn't know what he doesn't know, he doesn't grow.

> *As long as a person doesn't know what he doesn't know, he doesn't grow.*

PHASE 2—I KNOW WHAT I DON'T KNOW

Usually at some point in life, we are placed in a leadership position only to look around and discover that no one is following us.

That's when we realize that we need to *learn* how to lead. And of course, that's when it's possible for the process to start. English Prime Minister Benjamin Disraeli wisely commented, "To be conscious that you are ignorant of the facts is a great step to knowledge."

That's what happened to me when I took my first leadership position in 1969. I had captained sports teams all my life and had been the student government president in college, so I already thought I was a leader. But when I tried to lead people in the real world, I found out the awful truth. That prompted me to start gathering resources and learning from them. I also had another idea: I wrote to the top ten leaders in my field and offered them one hundred dollars for a half hour of their time so that I could ask them questions. (That was quite a sum for me in 1969.) For the next several years, my wife, Margaret, and I planned every vacation around where those people lived. If a great leader in Cleveland said yes to my request, then that year we vacationed in Cleveland so that I could meet him. And my idea really paid off. Those men shared insights with me that I could have learned no other way.

> *"To be conscious that you are ignorant of the facts is a great step to knowledge."*
> —*Benjamin Disraeli*

PHASE 3—I GROW AND KNOW AND IT STARTS TO SHOW

When you recognize your lack of skill and begin the daily discipline of personal growth in leadership, exciting things start to happen.

A while back I was teaching a group of people in Denver, and in the crowd I noticed a really sharp nineteen-year-old named Brian. For a couple of days, I watched as he eagerly took notes. I talked to him a few times during breaks. When I got to the part of the seminar where I teach the Law of Process, I asked Brian to stand up so that I could talk while everyone listened. I said, "Brian, I've been watching you here, and I'm very impressed with how hungry you are to learn and glean and grow. I want to tell you a secret that will change your life." Everyone in the whole auditorium seemed to lean forward.

"I believe that in about twenty years, you can be a *great* leader. I want to encourage you to make yourself a lifelong learner of leadership. Read books, listen to tapes regularly, and keep attending seminars. And whenever you come across a golden nugget of truth or a significant quote, file it away for the future.

"It's not going to be easy," I said. "But in five years, you'll see progress as your influence becomes greater. In ten years you'll develop a competence that makes your leadership highly effective. And in twenty years, when you're only thirty-nine years old, if you've continued to learn and grow, others will likely start asking you to teach

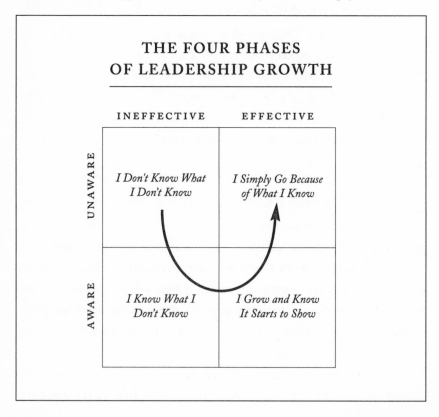

THE FOUR PHASES OF LEADERSHIP GROWTH

	INEFFECTIVE	EFFECTIVE
UNAWARE	*I Don't Know What I Don't Know*	*I Simply Go Because of What I Know*
AWARE	*I Know What I Don't Know*	*I Grow and Know It Starts to Show*

them about leadership. And some will be amazed. They'll look at each other and say, 'How did he suddenly become so wise?'

"Brian, you can be a great leader, but it won't happen in a day. Start paying the price now."

> *"The secret of success in life is for a man to be ready for his time when it comes."*
> —*Benjamin Disraeli*

What's true for Brian is also true for you. Start developing your leadership today, and someday you will experience the effects of the Law of Process.

PHASE 4—I SIMPLY GO BECAUSE OF WHAT I KNOW

When you're in phase 3, you can be pretty effective as a leader, but you have to think about every move you make. However, when you get to phase 4, your ability to lead becomes almost automatic. And that's when the payoff is larger than life. But the only way to get there is to obey the Law of Process and pay the price.

TO LEAD TOMORROW, LEARN TODAY

Leadership is developed daily, not in a day. That is the reality dictated by the Law of Process. Benjamin Disraeli asserted, "The secret of success in life is for a man to be ready for his time when it comes." What a person does on a disciplined, consistent basis gets him ready, no matter what the goal. Basketball legend Larry Bird became an outstanding free-throw shooter by practicing five hundred shots each morning before he went to school. Demosthenes of ancient Greece became the greatest orator by reciting verses with pebbles in his mouth and speaking over the roar of the waves at the seashore—and he did it despite having been born with a speech impairment. The same dedication is required for you to become a great leader.

The good news is that your leadership ability is not static. No matter where you're starting from, you can get better. That's true even for people who have stood on the world stage of leadership. While most presidents of the United States reach their peak while in office, others continue to grow and become better leaders afterward, such as former president Jimmy Carter. Some people questioned his ability to lead while in the White House. But in recent years, Carter's level of influence has continually increased. His high integrity and dedication in serving people through Habitat for Humanity and other organizations have made his influence grow. And now he has been recognized in Mali where he was knighted for his work eradicating Guinea worm disease. People now are truly impressed with his life.

FIGHTING YOUR WAY UP

There is an old saying: Champions don't become champions in the ring—they are merely recognized there. That's true. If you want to see where someone develops into a champion, look at his daily routine. Former heavyweight champ Joe Frazier stated, "You can map out a fight plan or a life plan. But when the action starts, you're down to your reflexes. That's where your road work shows. If you cheated on that in the dark of the morning, you're getting found out now under the bright lights."[3] Boxing is a good analogy for leadership development because it is all about daily preparation. Even if a person has natural talent, he has to prepare and train to become successful.

> *Champions don't become champions in the ring—they are merely recognized there.*

One of this country's greatest leaders was a fan of boxing: President Theodore Roosevelt. In fact, one of his most famous quotes uses a boxing analogy:

It is not the critic who counts, not the man who points out how the strong man stumbled, or where the doer of deeds could have done them better. The credit belongs to the man who is actually in the arena; whose face is marred by dust and sweat and blood; who strives valiantly; who errs and comes short again and again; who knows the great enthusiasms, the great devotions, and spends himself in a worthy cause; who, at best, knows in the end the triumph of high achievement; and who, at the worst, if he fails, at least fails while daring greatly, so that his place shall never be with those cold and timid souls who know neither victory nor defeat.

Roosevelt, a boxer himself, was the ultimate man of action. Not only was he an effective leader, but he was the most flamboyant of all U.S. presidents. British historian Hugh Brogan described him as "the ablest man to sit in the White House since Lincoln; the most vigorous since Jackson; the most bookish since John Quincy Adams."

A MAN OF ACTION

TR (which was Roosevelt's nickname) is remembered as an outspoken man of action and proponent of the vigorous life. While in the White House, he was known for regular boxing and judo sessions, challenging horseback rides, and long, strenuous hikes. A French ambassador who visited Roosevelt used to tell about the time that he accompanied the president on a walk through the woods. When the two men came to the banks of a stream that was too deep to cross by foot, TR stripped off his clothes and expected the dignitary to do the same so that they could swim to the other side. Nothing was an obstacle to Roosevelt.

At different times in his life, Roosevelt was a cowboy in the Wild West, an explorer and big-game hunter, and a rough-riding cavalry officer in the Spanish-American War. His enthusiasm and stamina seemed boundless. As the vice presidential candidate in 1900, he gave 673 speeches and traveled 20,000 miles while campaigning for President McKinley. And years after his presidency, while preparing to deliver a speech in Milwaukee, Roosevelt was shot in the chest by a would-be assassin. With a broken rib and a bullet in his chest, Roosevelt insisted on delivering his one-hour speech before allowing himself to be taken to the hospital.

ROOSEVELT STARTED SLOW

Of all the leaders this nation has ever had, Roosevelt was one of the toughest—both physically and mentally. But he didn't start that way. America's cowboy president was born in Manhattan to a prominent wealthy family. As a child, he was puny and very sickly. He had debilitating asthma, possessed very poor eyesight, and was painfully thin. His parents weren't sure he would survive.

When he was twelve, young Roosevelt's father told him, "You have the mind, but you have not the body, and without the help of the body the mind cannot go as far as it should. You must *make* the body." And make it he did. He lived by the Law of Process.

TR began spending time *every day* building his body as well as his mind, and he did that for the rest of his life. He worked out with weights, hiked, ice-skated, hunted, rowed, rode horseback, and boxed. In later years, Roosevelt assessed his progress, admitting that as a child he was "nervous and timid. Yet," he said, "from reading of the people I admired . . . and from knowing my father, I had a great admiration for men who were fearless and who could hold their own in the world, and I had a great desire to be like them."[4] By the time TR graduated from Harvard, he *was* like them, and he was ready to tackle the world of politics.

NO OVERNIGHT SUCCESS

Roosevelt didn't become a great leader overnight, either. His road to the presidency was one of slow, continual growth. As he served in various positions, ranging from New York City police commissioner to president of the United States, he kept learning and growing. He improved himself, and in time he became a strong leader. That was further evidence that he lived by the Law of Process.

Roosevelt's list of accomplishments is remarkable. Under his leadership, the United States emerged as a world power. He helped the country develop a first-class navy. He saw that the Panama Canal was built. He negotiated peace between Russia and Japan, winning a Nobel Peace Prize in the process. And when people questioned TR's leadership—since he had become president when McKinley was assassinated—he campaigned and was reelected by the largest majority of any president up to his time.

Ever the man of action, when Roosevelt completed his term as president in 1909, he immediately traveled to Africa where he led a scientific expedition sponsored by the Smithsonian Institution. A few years later, in 1913, he co-led a group to explore the uncharted River of Doubt in Brazil. It was a great learning adventure he said he could not pass up. "It was my last chance to be a boy," he later admitted. He was fifty-five years old.

On January 6, 1919, at his home in New York, Theodore Roosevelt died in his sleep. Then Vice President Marshall said, "Death had to take him sleeping, for if Roosevelt had been awake, there would have been a fight." When they removed him from his bed, they found a book under his pillow. Up to the very last, TR was still striving to learn and improve himself. He was still practicing the Law of Process.

If you want to be a leader, the good news is that you can do it. Everyone has the potential, but it isn't accomplished overnight. It requires perseverance. And you absolutely cannot ignore the Law of Process. Leadership doesn't develop in a day. It takes a lifetime.

THE LAW OF NAVIGATION

Anyone Can Steer the Ship, But It
Takes a Leader to Chart the Course

I N 1911, TWO GROUPS of explorers set off on an incredible mission. Though they used different strategies and routes, the leaders of the teams had the same goal: to be the first in history to reach the South Pole. Their stories are life-and-death illustrations of the Law of Navigation.

One of the groups was led by Norwegian explorer Roald Amundsen. Ironically, Amundsen had not originally intended to go to Antarctica. His desire was to be the first man to reach the *North* Pole. But when he discovered that Robert Peary had beaten him there, Amundsen changed his goal and headed toward the other end of the earth. North or south—he knew his planning would pay off.

AMUNDSEN CAREFULLY CHARTED HIS COURSE

Before his team ever set off, Amundsen had painstakingly planned his trip. He studied the methods of the Eskimos and other experienced Arctic travelers and determined that their best course of action would be to transport all their equipment and supplies by dogsled. When he assembled his team, he chose expert skiers and dog handlers. His strategy was simple. The dogs would do most of the work as the group traveled fifteen to twenty miles in a six-hour period each day. That would allow both the dogs and the men plenty of time to rest each day for the following day's travel.

Amundsen's forethought and attention to detail were incredible. He located and stocked supply depots all along the route. That way they would not have to carry every bit of their supplies with them the whole trip. He also equipped his people with the best gear possible. Amundsen had carefully considered every possible aspect of the journey, thought it through, and planned accordingly. And it paid off. The worst problem they experienced on the trip was an infected tooth that one man had to have extracted.

SCOTT VIOLATED THE LAW OF NAVIGATION

The other team of men was led by Robert Falcon Scott, a British naval officer who had previously done some exploring in the Antarctic area. Scott's expedition was the antithesis of Amundsen's. Instead of using dogsleds, Scott decided to use motorized sledges and ponies. Their problems began when the motors on the sledges stopped working only five days into the trip. The ponies didn't fare well either in those frigid temperatures. When they reached the foot of the Transantarctic Mountains, all of the poor animals had to be killed. As a result, the team members themselves ended up hauling the two-hundred-pound sledges. It was arduous work.

Scott hadn't given enough attention to the team's other equipment. Their clothes were so poorly designed that all the men developed frostbite. One team member required an hour every morning just to get his boots onto his swollen, gangrenous feet. And everyone became snowblind because of the inadequate goggles Scott had supplied. On top of everything else, the team was always low on food and water. That was also due to Scott's poor planning. The depots of supplies Scott established were inadequately stocked, too far apart, and often poorly marked, which made them very difficult to find. Because they were continually low on fuel to melt snow, everyone became dehydrated. Making things even worse was Scott's last-minute decision to take along a fifth man, even though they had prepared enough supplies only for four.

After covering a grueling eight hundred miles in ten weeks, Scott's exhausted group finally arrived at the South Pole on January 17, 1912. There they found the Norwegian flag flapping in the wind and a letter from Amundsen. The other well-led team had beaten them to their goal by more than a month!

IF YOU DON'T LIVE BY THE
LAW OF NAVIGATION . . .

As bad as their trip to the Pole was, that isn't the worst part of their story. The trek back was horrific. Scott and his men were starving and suffering from scurvy. But Scott, unable to navigate to the very end, was oblivious to their plight. With time running out and desperately low on food, Scott insisted that they collect thirty pounds of geological specimens to take back—more weight to be carried by the worn-out men.

Their progress became slower and slower. One member of the party sank into a stupor and died. Another, Lawrence Oates, was in terrible shape. The former army officer, who had originally been brought along to take care of the ponies, had frostbite so severe that he had trouble going on. Because he believed he was endangering the team's survival, it's said that he purposely walked out into a blizzard to relieve the group of himself as a liability. Before he left the tent and headed out into the storm, he said, "I am just going outside; I may be some time."

Scott and his final two team members made it only a little farther north before giving up. The return trip had already taken two months, and still they were 150 miles from their base camp. There they died. We know their story only because they spent their last hours writing in their diaries. Some of Scott's last words were these: "We shall die like gentlemen. I think this will show that the Spirit of pluck and power to endure has not passed out of our race."[1] Scott had courage, but not leadership. Because he was unable to live by the Law of Navigation, he and his companions died by it.

> *Because Robert Falcon Scott was unable to live by the Law of Navigation, he and his companions died by it.*

Followers need leaders able to effectively navigate for them. When they're facing life-and-death situations, the necessity is painfully obvious. But, even when consequences aren't as serious, the need is just as great. The truth is that nearly anyone can steer the ship, but it takes a leader to chart the course. That is the Law of Navigation.

NAVIGATORS SEE THE TRIP AHEAD

General Electric chairman Jack Welch asserts, "A good leader remains focused . . . Controlling your direction is better than being controlled by it." Welch is right, but leaders who navigate do even more than control the direction in which they and their people travel. They see the whole trip in their minds before they leave the dock. They have a vision for their destination, they understand what it will take to get there, they know who they'll need on the team to be successful, and they recognize the obstacles long before they appear on the horizon. Leroy Eims, author of *Be the Leader You Were Meant to Be*, writes, "A leader is one who sees more than others see, who sees farther than others see, and who sees before others do."

The larger the organization, the more clearly the leader has to be able to see ahead. That's true because sheer size makes midcourse corrections more difficult. And if there are errors, many more people are affected than when you're traveling alone or with only a few people. The disaster shown in the recent film *Titanic* was a good example of that kind of problem. The crew could not see far enough ahead to avoid the iceberg altogether, and they could not maneuver enough to change course once the object was spotted because of the size of the ship, the largest built at that time. The result was that more than one thousand people lost their lives.

> *"A leader is one who sees more than others see, who sees farther than others see, and who sees before others do."*
> —*Leroy Eims*

WHERE THE LEADER GOES . . .

First-rate navigators always have in mind that other people are depending on them and their ability to chart a good course. I read an observation by James A. Autry in *Life and Work: A Manager's Search for Meaning* that illustrates this idea. He said that occasionally you hear about the crash of four military planes flying together in a formation. The reason for the loss of all four is this: When jet fighters fly in groups of four, one pilot—the leader—designates where the team will fly. The other three planes fly on the leader's wing, watching him and following him wherever he goes. Whatever moves he makes, the rest of his team will make along with him. That's true whether he soars in the clouds or smashes into a mountaintop.

Before leaders take their people on a journey, they go through a process in order to give the trip the best chance of being a success:

NAVIGATORS DRAW ON PAST EXPERIENCE

Every past success and failure can be a source of information and wisdom—if you allow it to be. Successes teach you about yourself and what you're capable of doing with your particular gifts and talents. Failures show what kinds of wrong assumptions you've made and where your methods are flawed. If you fail to learn from your mistakes, you're going to fail again and again. That's why effective navigators start with experience. But they certainly don't end there.

NAVIGATORS LISTEN TO WHAT OTHERS HAVE TO SAY

> *No matter how much you learn from the past, it will never tell you all you need to know for the present.*

No matter how much you learn from the past, it will never tell you all you need to know for the present. That's why top-notch navigators gather information from many sources. They get ideas from members of their leadership team. They talk to the people in their organization to find out what's happening on the grassroots level. And they spend time with leaders from outside the organization who can mentor them.

NAVIGATORS EXAMINE THE CONDITIONS BEFORE MAKING COMMITMENTS

I like action, and my personality prompts me to be spontaneous. On top of that, I have reliable intuition when it comes to leadership. But I'm also conscious of my responsibilities as a leader. So before I make commitments that are going to impact my people, I take stock and thoroughly think things through. Good navigators count the cost *before* making commitments for themselves and others.

NAVIGATORS MAKE SURE THEIR CONCLUSIONS REPRESENT BOTH FAITH AND FACT

Being able to navigate for others requires a leader to possess a positive attitude. You've got to have faith that you can take your people all the way. If you can't confidently make the trip in your mind, you're not going to be able to take it in real life. On the other hand, you also have to be able to see the facts realistically. You can't minimize obstacles or rationalize your challenges. If you don't go in with your eyes wide open, you're going to get blindsided. As Bill Easum observes, "Realistic leaders are objective enough to minimize illusions. They understand that self-deception can cost them their vision." Sometimes it's difficult balancing optimism and realism, intuition and planning, faith and fact. But that's what it takes to be effective as a navigating leader.

> *It's difficult balancing optimism and realism, intuition and planning, faith and fact. But that's what it takes to be effective as a navigating leader.*

A LESSON IN NAVIGATION

I remember the first time I really understood the importance of the Law of Navigation. I was twenty-eight years old, and I was leading Faith Memorial in Lancaster, Ohio, my second church. Before my arrival there in 1972, the church had experienced a decade-long plateau in its growth. But by 1975, our attendance had gone from four hundred to more than one thousand. I knew we could keep growing and reach more people, but only if we built a new auditorium.

> *If the leader can't navigate the people through rough waters, he is liable to sink the ship.*

The good news was that I already had some experience in building and relocation because I had taken my first church through the process. The bad news was that the first one was really small in comparison to the second one. To give you an idea of the difference, the changing room in the nursery in Lancaster was going to be larger than the whole sanctuary in the original building of my first church!

It was going to be a multimillion-dollar project more than twenty times larger than my first one. But even that was not the greatest obstacle. Right before I came on board at Faith Memorial, there had been a huge battle over another building proposal, and the debate had been vocal, divisive, and bitter. For that reason, I knew that I would experience genuine opposition to my leadership for the first time. There were rough waters ahead, and if I as the leader didn't navigate us well, I could sink the ship.

CHARTING THE COURSE
WITH A NAVIGATION STRATEGY

At that time I developed a strategy that I have since used repeatedly in my leadership. I wrote it as an acrostic so that I would always be able to remember it:

Predetermine a Course of Action.
Lay Out Your Goals.
Adjust Your Priorities.
Notify Key Personnel.

Allow Time for Acceptance.
Head into Action.
Expect Problems.
Always Point to the Successes.
Daily Review Your Plan.

That became my blueprint as I prepared to navigate for my people.

Back then, I knew exactly what our course of action needed to be. If we were going to keep growing, we needed to build a new auditorium. I had looked at every possible alternative, and I knew that was our only viable solution. My goal was to design and build the facility, pay for it in ten years, and unify all the people in the process. I also knew our biggest adjustment would come in the area of finances, since it would turn our current budget upside down.

I started preparing for the congregational meeting. I scheduled it a couple of months ahead to give me time to get everything ready. The first thing I did was direct our board members and a group of key financial leaders to conduct a twenty-year analysis of our growth and financial patterns. It covered the previous ten years and projections for the next ten years. Based on that, we determined the requirements of the facility. Then we formulated a ten-year budget that carefully explained how we would handle the financing. I also asked that all of the information we were gathering be put into a twenty-page report that I intended to give to the members of the congregation. I knew that major barriers to successful planning are fear of change, ignorance, uncertainty about the future, and lack of imagination. I was going to do everything I could to prevent those factors from hindering us.

Major barriers to successful planning are fear of change, ignorance, uncertainty about the future, and lack of imagination.

My next step was to notify the key leaders. I started with the ones who had the most influence, meeting with them individually and sometimes in small groups. Over the course of several weeks, I met with about a hundred leaders. I cast the vision for them and fielded their questions. And when I could sense that a person was hesitant about the project, I planned to meet individually with him again. Then I allowed time for the rest of the people to be influenced by those leaders and for acceptance to develop among the congregation.

When the time rolled around for the congregational meeting, we were ready to head into action. I took two hours to present the project to the people. I handed out my twenty-page report with the floor plans, financial analysis, and budgets. I tried to answer every question the people would have before they had a chance to ask it. I also asked some of the most influential people in the congregation to speak.

> *The secret to the Law of Navigation is preparation.*

I had expected some opposition, but when I opened the floor for questions, I was shocked. There were only two questions: One person wanted to know about the placement of the building's water fountains, and the other asked about the number of rest rooms. That was when I knew we had navigated the tricky waters successfully. When it was time for the motion asking everyone to vote, the church's most influential layperson made it. And I had arranged for the leader who had previously opposed building to second the motion. When the final count was tallied, 98 percent of the people had voted in favor.

Once we had navigated through that phase, the rest of the project wasn't difficult. I continually kept the vision in front of the people by giving them good news reports to acknowledge our successes. And I periodically reviewed our plans and their results to make sure we were on track. The course had been charted. All we had to do was steer the ship.

> *It's not the size of the project that determines its acceptance, support, and success. It's the size of the leader.*

That was a wonderful learning experience for me. Above everything else I found out that the secret to the Law of Navigation is preparation. When you prepare well, you convey confidence and trust to the people. Lack of preparation has the opposite effect. You see, it's not the size of the project that determines its acceptance, support, and success. It's the size of the leader. That's why I say that anyone can *steer* the ship, but it takes a leader to chart the course. Leaders who are good navigators are capable of taking their people just about anywhere.

5

THE LAW OF E. F. HUTTON

When the Real Leader Speaks, People Listen

Young, inexperienced leaders often walk confidently into a room full of people only to discover that they have totally misjudged the leadership dynamics of the situation. I know that's happened to me! But when it did, it usually didn't take me very long to recognize my blunder. That was the case when I presided over my very first board meeting as a young leader. It occurred in the first church I led in rural Indiana, right after I graduated from college at age twenty-two. I hadn't been at the church for much more than a month, and I was leading a group of people whose average age was about fifty. Most of the people in the meeting had been at that church longer than I'd been alive.

I went into the meeting with no preconceptions, no agenda—and no clue. I figured that I was the appointed leader and just assumed everyone would follow me because of that. With all the wisdom and knowledge of my two decades of life experience, I opened the meeting and asked whether anyone had an issue to discuss.

There was a brief pause as I looked around the table, and then a man in his sixties named Claude cleared his throat and said, "I've got something."

"Go right ahead, Claude," I said.

"Well," he said, "I've noticed lately that the piano seems to be out of tune when it's played in the service."

"You know, I've noticed the same thing," said one of the other board members.

"I make a motion that we spend the money to get a piano tuner to come out from Louisville and take care of it," said Claude.

"Hey, that's a great idea," everyone at the table started saying.

> *The* real
> *leader holds the*
> *power, not just*
> *the position.*

"I second the motion," said Benny, the board member sitting next to Claude.

"That's great," I said. "Does anybody else have anything?"

"Yep," said Claude, "I noticed the other day that there's a pane of glass in one of the Sunday school rooms that's busted. I've got a piece a glass out at the farm that would fit that. Benny, you're a pretty good glazer. How about you put that glass in."

"Sure, Claude," said Benny, "I'd be glad to."

"Good. There's one other thing," said Claude. "This year's picnic. I was thinking maybe this time we ought to have it down by the lake. I think it would be good for the kids."

"Oh, that would be perfect. What a good idea!" everyone started saying.

"Let's make it official," Benny said.

As everyone nodded agreement, we all waited to see if Claude had anything else to say.

"That's all I've got," said Claude. "Pastor, why don't you close us in prayer." And that's what I did. That was pretty much the whole content of my first board meeting. And it was also the day I realized who the real leader in that church was. I held the position, but

Claude had the power. That's when I discovered the Law of E. F. Hutton.

You've probably heard of E. F. Hutton, the financial services company. Years ago, their motto was, "When E. F. Hutton speaks, people listen." Maybe you remember their old television commercials. The setting was typically a busy restaurant or other public place. Two people would be talking about financial matters, and the first person would repeat something his broker had said concerning a certain investment. The second person would say, "Well, my broker is E. F. Hutton, and E. F. Hutton says . . ." At that point every single person in the bustling restaurant would stop dead in his tracks, turn, and listen to what the man was about to say. That's why I call this leadership truth the Law of E. F. Hutton. Because when the *real* leader speaks, people do listen.

WHAT COULD I DO?

After my first board meeting, I had to determine how I was going to handle the situation in my church. I had several options. For example, I could have insisted on my right to be in charge. I've seen a lot of positional leaders do that over the years. They tell their people something like this: "Hey, wait! I'm the leader. You're supposed to follow me." But that doesn't work. People might be polite to you, but they won't really follow. It's similar to something former British prime minister Margaret Thatcher once said: "Being in power is like being a lady. If you have to tell people you are, you aren't."

> *"Being in power is like being a lady. If you have to tell people you are, you aren't."*
> —*Margaret Thatcher*

Another option would have been to try to push Claude out as the leader. But how do you think that would have turned out? He was more than twice my age, he had lived in that area his whole life, and he was respected by everybody in the community. He was a member of that church before I got there, and everybody knew that he would be there long after I left.

I pursued a third option. By the time the next board meeting was ready to roll around, I had a list of items that I knew needed to be accomplished at the church. So about a week before we were scheduled to meet, I called Claude and asked him if I could come out to the farm and spend some time with him. As we did chores together throughout the day, he and I talked.

"Claude," I said, "you know, I've noticed that the front door on the church is cracked and peeling. It would look terrible to any new people coming to the church for the first time. Do you think we could do something about that?"

"Sure," said Claude, "that would be no problem."

I continued, "I went down into the basement the other day. Did you know there's water down in there? Shoot, there are frogs hopping around down there, tadpoles swimming, and crawdads crawling. What do you think we ought to do?"

"Well, John," Claude said, "I think we ought to have a work day and get that basement all cleaned out."

"That's a great idea," I said. "Would you bring that up at our next board meeting?"

"I sure will."

"There's another thing that's been worrying me," I continued. "Right now we've got only three rooms in the building besides the auditorium. One is being used as a storage room for a bunch of junk. The other two are for Sunday school, but one of those classes has an awful lot of kids and is getting pretty full."

"Don't say another word," said Claude. "We'll get that room all cleaned out."

"Oh, that would be great. Thank you, Claude."

At the next board meeting, when I called for new business, Claude said, "You know, I think it's about time for us to have a work day around here."

"That's a great idea," everyone around the table started saying.

"We'll have it a week from Saturday," said Claude. "I'll bring my truck, and, Benny, you bring yours too. We're going to do some painting, clean out that basement, and get the junk out of that storage room. We need it for a new Sunday school class." Then he turned to one of the board members and said, "And Sister Maxine, you're going to teach it."

> *If you see a disparity between who's leading the* meeting *and who's leading the* people, *then the person running the meeting is not the real leader.*

"I second that," said Benny, and that was it.

From then on, if I wanted to accomplish anything at that church, I just went out to the farm and did chores with Claude. I could always count on him to bring those things before the people, and whenever Claude spoke, people listened.

THE EYES HAVE IT

Once you learn the Law of E. F. Hutton, you'll never have trouble figuring out who the real leader is in just about any situation. For example, go to a meeting with a group of people you've never met before and watch them for five minutes. You'll know who the leader is. When somebody asks a question, who do people watch? Who do they wait to hear? The person they look to is the real leader.

Try it. The next time you're in a meeting, look around you. See if you notice a difference between these two kinds of leaders:

POSITIONAL LEADERS	REAL LEADERS
Speak first	*Speak later*
Need the influence of the real leader to get things done	*Need only their own influence to get things done*
Influence only the other positional leaders	*Influence everyone in the room*

If you see a disparity between who's leading the *meeting* and who's leading the *people,* then the person running the meeting is not the real leader.

> *The real test of leadership isn't where you start out. It's where you end up.*

I have never been the real leader at any job when I started it, other than at the companies I've founded. When I took that first position in Hillham, Indiana, Claude was the leader. In my second church in Ohio, the real leader was a man named Jim. And when I went to Skyline in San Diego, the staff first followed Steve, not me. So if you're starting in a new position and you're not the leader, don't let it bother you. The real test of leadership isn't where you start out. It's where you end up.

WILL THE REAL LEADER PLEASE STAND UP?

Many years ago, there was a game show called *To Tell the Truth.* Here's how it worked. At the opening of the show, three contestants claimed to be the same person. One of them was telling the truth; the other two were actors. A panel of celebrity judges took turns asking the three people questions, and when time was up, each panelist guessed which person was the real truth-teller. Many times, the actors bluffed well enough to fool the panelists and the members of the audience.

When it comes to identifying a real leader, that task can be much easier—if you remember what you're looking for. Don't listen to the claims of the person professing to be the leader. Instead, watch the reactions of the people around him. The proof of leadership is found in the followers.

Think about the reactions certain people get when they speak. When Alan Greenspan speaks before Congress, everybody listens. When he prepares to make a statement on lending rates, the entire financial community stops what it's doing. It's really a lot like the old E. F. Hutton commercials. When Martin Luther King Jr. was alive, he got an incredible amount of respect. No matter where or when he spoke, people— black and white—listened. Today, Billy

> *The proof of leadership is found in the followers.*

Graham gets a similar kind of respect because of his unquestionable integrity and lifetime of service. For nearly fifty years, his advice has been heeded by world leaders. Every president of the United States since Harry Truman has sought his leadership and wise counsel.

The Law of E. F. Hutton reveals itself in just about every kind of situation. I read a story about former NBA player Larry Bird that illustrates it well. During the final seconds of an especially tense game, Boston Celtics coach K. C. Jones called a time-out. As he gathered the players together at courtside, he diagrammed a play, only to have Bird say, "Get the ball out to me and get everyone out of my way."

Jones responded, "I'm the coach, and I'll call the plays!" Then he turned to the other players and said, "Get the ball to Larry and get out of his way."[1] It just shows that when the real leader speaks, people listen.

PEOPLE BECOME REAL LEADERS BECAUSE OF . . .

How do the real leaders *become* the real leaders within groups? As I explained in the chapter on the Law of Process, leadership doesn't develop in just a day. Neither does a person's recognition as a leader. Over the course of time, seven key areas reveal themselves in leader's lives that cause them to step forward as leaders:

1. CHARACTER—WHO THEY ARE

True leadership always begins with the inner person. That's why someone like Billy Graham is able to draw more and more followers to him as time goes by. People can sense the depth of his character.

2. RELATIONSHIPS—WHO THEY KNOW

You're a leader only if you have followers, and that always requires the development of relationships—the deeper the relationships, the stronger the potential for leadership. Each time I entered a new leadership position, I immediately started building relationships. Build enough of the right kinds of relationships with the right people, and you can become the real leader in an organization.

3. KNOWLEDGE—WHAT THEY KNOW

Information is vital to a leader. You need a grasp of the facts, an understanding of the factors involved, and a vision for the future. Knowledge alone won't make someone a leader, but without it, he can't become one. I always spent a lot of time doing homework before I tried to take the lead in an organization.

4. INTUITION—WHAT THEY FEEL

Leadership requires more than just a command of data. It demands an ability to deal with numerous intangibles (as I explain in the chapter on the Law of Intuition).

5. EXPERIENCE—WHERE THEY'VE BEEN

The greater the challenges you've faced in the past, the more likely followers are to give you a chance. Experience doesn't guarantee credibility, but it encourages people to give you a chance to prove that you are capable.

6. PAST SUCCESS—WHAT THEY'VE DONE

Nothing speaks to followers like a good track record. When I went to my first church, I had no track record. I couldn't point to past successes to help people believe in me. But by the time I went to my second church, I had a few. Every time I extended myself, took a risk, and succeeded, followers had another reason to trust my leadership ability—and to listen to what I had to say.

7. ABILITY—WHAT THEY CAN DO

The bottom line for followers is what a leader is capable of. Ultimately, that's the reason people will listen to you and acknowledge you as their leader. As soon as they no longer believe you can deliver, they will stop listening.

WHEN SHE SPOKE . . .

Once you have a handle on the Law of E. F. Hutton, you understand that people listen to what someone has to say not necessarily because of the truth being communicated in the message, but because of their respect for the speaker.

I was reminded of this again recently when I read something about Mother Teresa. When most people think about her they envision a frail little woman dedicated to serving the poorest of the poor. That she was. But she was

> *People listen not necessarily because of the truth being communicated in the message, but because of their respect for the speaker.*

also a real leader. Lucinda Vardey, who worked with Mother Teresa on the book *The Simple Path*, described the nun as "the quintessential, energetic entrepreneur, who has perceived a need and done something about it, built an organization against all odds, formulated its constitution, and sent out branches all over the world."

The organization Mother Teresa founded and led is called the Missionaries of Charity. While other vocational orders in the Catholic Church declined, hers grew rapidly, reaching more than four thousand members during her lifetime (not including numerous volunteers). Under her direction, her followers served in twenty-five countries on five continents. In Calcutta alone, she established a children's home, a center for people with leprosy, a home for people who were dying and destitute, and a home for people suffering with tuberculosis or mental disorders. That kind of organizational building can be accomplished only by a true leader.

Author and former presidential speechwriter Peggy Noonan wrote about a speech Mother Teresa gave at the National Prayer Breakfast in 1994. Noonan said,

> The Washington establishment was there, plus a few thousand born-again Christians, orthodox Catholics, and Jews. Mother Teresa spoke of God, of love, of families. She said we must love one another and care for one another. There were great purrs of agreement.
>
> But as the speech continued, it became more pointed. She spoke of unhappy parents in old people's homes who are "hurt because they are forgotten." She asked, "Are we willing to give until it hurts in order to be with our families, or do we put our own interests first?"
>
> The baby boomers in the audience began to shift in their seats. And she continued. "I feel that the greatest destroyer of peace today is abortion," she said, and told them why, in uncom-

promising terms. For about 1.3 seconds there was silence, then applause swept the room. But not everyone clapped; the President and First Lady, the Vice President and Mrs. Gore looked like seated statues at Madame Tussaud's moving not a muscle. Mother Teresa didn't stop there either. When she was finished, there was almost no one she hadn't offended.[2]

If just about any other person in the world had made those statements, people's reactions would have been openly hostile. They would have booed, jeered, or stormed out. But the speaker was Mother Teresa. She was probably the most respected person on the planet at that time. So everyone listened to what she had to say, even though many of them violently disagreed with it. In fact, *every time* that Mother Teresa spoke, people listened. Why? She was a real leader, and when the real leader speaks, people listen.

So I must ask you this: How do people react when you communicate? When you speak, do people listen—I mean *really* listen? Or do they wait to hear what someone else has to say before they act? You can find out a lot about your level of leadership if you have the courage to ask and answer that question. That's the power of the Law of E. F. Hutton.

6

THE LAW OF SOLID GROUND

Trust Is the Foundation of Leadership

I PERSONALLY LEARNED THE power of the Law of Solid Ground in the fall of 1989. It happened during a very busy time when I was the senior pastor at Skyline Church in San Diego. Every year, we created and performed a major Christmas production. It was a really big deal. The cast included more than 300 people. The staging was elaborate—on the level of most professional productions. Each year more than 25,000 people saw the show, and it had become a San Diego tradition, having been produced annually for more than two decades.

That year the fall season was very hectic for me. We had several new programs starting at the church. Preparations for the Christmas show were in full swing. In addition, I was doing quite a bit of speaking and traveling around the country. And because I was so busy, I let my choleric nature get the better of me and made a big mistake. I very quickly made three major decisions and implemented them without providing the right kind of leadership. In one week, I changed some components of the Christmas show, I permanently discontinued our Sunday evening service, and I fired a staff member.

IT WASN'T THE DECISIONS—
IT WAS THE LEADERSHIP

What's interesting is that none of my three decisions was wrong. The change in the Christmas program was beneficial. The Sunday evening service, though enjoyed by some of the older members of the congregation, wasn't building the church or serving a need that wasn't already being met elsewhere. And the particular staff member I fired had to go, and it was important that I not delay in dismissing him.

My mistake was the way I made those three decisions. Because everything in the church was going so well, I thought I could act on the decisions without taking everyone through the deliberate steps needed to process them. Ordinarily, I would gather my leaders, cast vision for them, answer questions, and guide them through the issues. Then I would give them time to exert their influence with the next level of leaders in the church. And finally, once the timing was right, I would make a general announcement to all, letting them know about the decisions, giving them plenty of reassurance, and encouraging them to be a part of the new vision. But I didn't do any of those things, and I should have known better.

THE RESULT WAS MISTRUST

It wasn't long afterward that I began to sense unrest among the people. I also heard some rumblings. At first, my attitude was that everyone should get over it and move on. But then I realized that the problem wasn't them. It was me. I had handled things badly. And on top of that, my attitude wasn't very positive—not good when you're the guy who wrote a book called *The Winning Attitude!* That's when

I realized that I had broken the Law of Solid Ground. For the first time in my life, my people didn't completely trust me.

As soon as I realized I was wrong, I publicly apologized to my people and asked for their forgiveness. Your people know when you make mistakes. The real question is whether you're going to 'fess up. If you do, you can often quickly regain their trust. That's what happened with me once I apologized. And from then on, I made sure to do things right. I learned firsthand that when it comes to leadership, you just can't take shortcuts, no matter how long you've been leading your people.

> *When it comes to leadership, you just can't take shortcuts, no matter how long you've been leading your people.*

It didn't take long for me to get back onto solid ground with everyone. As I've explained in *Developing the Leader Within You,* a leader's history of successes and failures makes a big difference in his credibility. It's a little like earning and spending pocket change. Each time you make a good leadership decision, it puts change into your pocket. Each time you make a poor one, you have to pay out some of your change to the people.

Every leader has a certain amount of change in his pocket when he starts in a new leadership position. From then on, he either builds up his change or pays it out. If he makes one bad decision after another, he keeps paying out change. Then one day, after making one last bad decision, he is going to reach into his pocket and realize he is out of change. It doesn't even matter if the blunder was big or small. When you're out of change, you're out as the leader.

A leader who keeps making good decisions and keeps recording wins for the organization builds up his change. Then even if he makes a huge blunder, he can still have plenty of change left over. That's the kind of history I had at Skyline, which is why I was able to rebuild trust with the people very quickly.

TRUST IS THE FOUNDATION OF LEADERSHIP

Trust is the foundation of leadership. To build trust, a leader must exemplify these qualities: competence, connection, and character. People will forgive occasional mistakes based on ability, especially if they can see that you're still growing as a leader. But they won't trust someone who has slips in character. In that area, even occasional lapses are lethal. All effective leaders know this truth. PepsiCo chairman and CEO Craig Weatherup acknowledges, "People will tolerate honest mistakes, but if you violate their trust you will find it very difficult to ever regain their confidence. That is one reason that you need to treat trust as your most precious asset. You may fool your boss but you can never fool your colleagues or subordinates."

> *To build trust, a leader must exemplify competence, connection, and character.*

General H. Norman Schwarzkopf points to the significance of character: "Leadership is a potent combination of strategy and character. But if you must be without one, be without strategy." Character and leadership credibility always go hand in hand. Anthony Harrigan, president of the U.S. Business and Industrial Council, said,

> The role of character always has been the key factor in the rise and fall of nations. And one can be sure that America is no exception to this rule of history. We won't survive as a country because we are smarter or more sophisticated but because we are—we hope—stronger inwardly. In short, character is the only effective bulwark against internal and external forces that lead to a country's disintegration or collapse.

Character makes trust possible. And trust makes leadership possible. That is the Law of Solid Ground.

CHARACTER COMMUNICATES

Whenever you lead people, it's as if they consent to take a journey with you. The way that trip is going to turn out is predicted by your character. With good character, the longer the trip is, the better it seems. But if your character is flawed, the longer the trip is, the worse it gets. Why? Because no one enjoys spending time with someone he doesn't trust.

Character communicates many things to followers:

CHARACTER COMMUNICATES CONSISTENCY

Leaders without inner strength can't be counted on day after day because their ability to perform changes constantly. NBA great Jerry West commented, "You can't get too much done in life if you only work on the days when you feel good." If your people don't know what to expect from you as a leader, at some point they won't look to you for leadership.

Think about what happened in the late 1980s. Several high-profile Christian leaders stumbled and fell due to moral issues. That

> *Character makes trust possible. And trust makes leadership possible. That is the Law of Solid Ground.*

lack of consistency compromised their ability to lead their people. In fact, it gave a black eye to every pastor across the nation because it caused people to become suspicious of all church leaders, regardless of their personal track records. The flawed character of those fallen leaders destroyed the foundation for their leadership.

When I think of leaders who epitomize consistency of character, the first person who comes to mind is Billy Graham. Regardless of personal religious beliefs, everybody trusts him. Why? Because he has modeled high character for more than half a century. He lives out his values every day. He never makes a commitment unless he is going to keep it. And he goes out of his way to personify integrity.

CHARACTER COMMUNICATES POTENTIAL

John Morley observed, "No man can climb out beyond the limitations of his own character." That's especially true when it comes to leadership. Take, for instance, the case of NHL coach Mike Keenan. As of mid-1997, he had a noteworthy record of professional hockey victories: the fifth greatest number of regular-season wins, the third greatest number of play-off victories, six division titles, four NHL finals appearances, and one Stanley Cup.

> *"No man can climb out beyond the limitations of his own character."*
> *—John Morley*

Yet despite those commendable credentials, Keenan was unable to stay with a single team for any length of time. In eleven and a half seasons, he coached four different teams. And after his stint with the fourth team—the St. Louis Blues—he was unable to land a job for a long time. Why? Sportswriter E. M. Swift said of Keenan, "The reluctance to hire Keenan is *easily* explicable. Everywhere he has been, he has alienated players and management."[1] Evidently, his players didn't trust him. Neither did the owners, who were benefiting from seeing their teams win. It seems he kept violating the Law of Solid Ground.

Craig Weatherup explains, "You don't build trust by talking about it. You build it by achieving results, always with integrity and in a manner that shows real personal regard for the people with whom you work."[2] When a leader's character is strong, people trust him, and they trust in his ability to release their potential. That not only gives followers hope for the future, but it also promotes a strong belief in themselves and their organization.

CHARACTER COMMUNICATES RESPECT

When you don't have strength within, you can't earn respect without. And respect is absolutely essential for lasting leadership. How do leaders earn respect? By making sound decisions, admitting their mistakes, and putting what's best for their followers and the organization ahead of their personal agendas.

Several years ago, a movie was made about the Fifty-fourth Massachusetts Infantry regiment and its colonel, Robert Gould Shaw. The film was called *Glory,* and though some of its plot was fictionalized, the Civil War story of Shaw's journey with his men—and of the respect he earned from them—was real.

The movie recounted the formation of this first unit in the Union army composed of African-American soldiers. Shaw, a white officer, took command of the regiment, oversaw recruiting, selected the (white) officers, equipped the men, and trained them as soldiers. He drove them hard, knowing that their performance in battle would either vindicate or condemn the value of black people as soldiers and citizens in the minds of many white Northerners. In the process, both the soldiers and Shaw earned one another's respect.

> *How do leaders earn respect? By making sound decisions, admitting their mistakes, and putting what's best for their followers and the organization ahead of their personal agendas.*

A few months after their training was complete, the men of the Fifty-fourth got the opportunity to prove themselves in the Union assault on Confederate Fort Wagner in South Carolina. Shaw's biographer Russell Duncan said of the attack: "With a final admonition to 'prove yourselves men,' Shaw positioned himself in front and ordered, 'forward.' Years later, one soldier remembered that the regiment fought hard because Shaw was in front, not behind."

Almost half of the six hundred men from the Fifty-fourth who fought that day were wounded, captured, or killed. Though they fought valiantly, they were unable to take Fort Wagner. And Shaw, who had courageously led his men to the top of the fort's parapet in the first assault, was killed along with his men.

Shaw's actions on that final day solidified the respect his men already had for him. Two weeks after the battle, Albanus Fisher, a sergeant in the Fifty-fourth, said, "I still feel more Eager for the struggle than I ever yet have, for I now wish to have Revenge for our galant Curnel [*sic*]."[3] J. R. Miller once observed, "The only thing that walks back from the tomb with the mourners and refuses to be buried is the character of a man. This is true. What a man is survives him. It can never be buried." Shaw's character, strong to the last, had communicated a level of respect to his men that lived beyond him.

> *"The only thing that walks back from the tomb with the mourners and refuses to be buried is the character of a man. This is true. What a man is survives him. It can never be buried."*
> —*J. R. Miller*

A leader's good character builds trust among his followers. But when a leader breaks trust, he forfeits his ability to lead. That's the Law of Solid Ground. I was again reminded of this while listening to a lesson taught by my friend Bill Hybels. Four times a year, he and I teach a seminar called Leading and Communicating to Change Lives. Bill was conducting a session titled "Lessons from a Leadership Nightmare," and he shared observations and insights on some of the leadership mistakes made by Robert McNamara and the Johnson administration during the Vietnam War: the administration's inability to prioritize multiple challenges, its acceptance of faulty assumptions, and Johnson's failure to face serious staff conflicts. But in my opinion, the greatest insight Bill shared during that talk concerned the failure of American leaders, including McNamara, to face and publicly admit the terrible mistakes they had made concerning the war in Vietnam. Their actions broke trust with the American people, and because of that, they violated the Law of Solid Ground. The United States has been suffering from the repercussions ever since.

AN INHERITED POLICY BECOMES
A LEADERSHIP-SHATTERING PROBLEM

Vietnam was already at war when President Kennedy and Robert McNamara, his secretary of defense, took office in January of 1961. The Vietnam region had been a battleground for decades, and the United States got involved in the mid-1950s when President Eisenhower sent a small number of U.S. troops to Vietnam as advisors. When Kennedy took office, he continued Eisenhower's policy. It was always his intention to let the South Vietnamese fight and win their own war, but over time, the United States became increasingly involved. Before the war was over, more than half a million American troops at a time served in Vietnam.

If you remember those war years, you may be surprised to know that American support for the war was very strong even as the number of troops being sent overseas rapidly increased and the casualties mounted. By 1966, more than two hundred thousand Americans had been sent to Vietnam, yet two-thirds of all Americans surveyed by Louis Harris believed that Vietnam was the place where the United States should "stand and fight communism." And most people expressed the belief that the U.S. should stay until the fight was finished.

FIRST TRUST, THEN SUPPORT

But support didn't continue for long. The Vietnam War was being handled very badly. On top of that, our leaders continued the war even after they realized that we couldn't win it. But the worst mistake of all was that McNamara and President Johnson weren't honest with the American people about it. That broke the Law of Solid Ground, and it ultimately destroyed the administration's leadership.

In his book *In Retrospect*, McNamara recounts that he repeatedly minimized American losses and told only half-truths about the war. For example, he says, "Upon my return to Washington [from Saigon] on December 21, [1963,] I was less than candid when I reported to the press . . . I said, 'We observed the results of a very substantial increase in Vietcong activity' (true); but I then added, 'We reviewed the plans of the South Vietnamese and we have every reason to believe they will be successful' (an overstatement at best)."

For a while, nobody questioned McNamara's statements because there was no reason to mistrust the country's leadership. But in time, people recognized that his words and the facts weren't matching up. And that's when the American public began to lose faith. Years later, McNamara admitted his failure: "We of the Kennedy and Johnson administrations who participated in the decisions on Vietnam acted according to what we thought were the principles and traditions of this nation. We made our decisions in light of those values. Yet we were wrong, terribly wrong."[4]

BY THEN, IT WAS TOO LATE

Many would argue that McNamara's admission came thirty years and fifty-eight thousand lives too late. The cost of Vietnam was high, and not just in human lives. As the American people's trust in their leaders eroded, so did their willingness to follow them. Protests led to open rebellion and to societywide turmoil. The era that had begun with the hope and idealism characterized by John F. Kennedy ultimately ended with the mistrust and cynicism associated with Richard Nixon.

Whenever a leader breaks the Law of Solid Ground, he pays a price in his leadership. McNamara and President Johnson lost the trust of the American people, and their ability to lead suffered as a result. Eventually, McNamara resigned as secretary of defense. Johnson, the consummate politician, recognized his weakened position, and he didn't run for reelection. But the repercussions of broken trust didn't end there. The American people's distrust for politicians has continued to this day, and it is still growing.

No leader can break trust with his people and expect to keep influencing them. Trust is the foundation of leadership. Violate the Law of Solid Ground, and you're through as a leader.

THE LAW OF RESPECT

People Naturally Follow Leaders
Stronger Than Themselves

I F YOU HAD SEEN HER, your first reaction might not have been respect. She wasn't a very impressive-looking woman—just a little over five feet tall, in her late thirties, with dark brown weathered skin. She couldn't read or write. The clothes she wore were coarse and worn. When she smiled, people could see that her top two front teeth were missing.

She lived alone. The story was that she had abandoned her husband when she was twenty-nine. She gave him no warning. One day he woke up, and she was gone. She talked to him only once after that, years later, and she never mentioned his name again afterward.

Her employment was intermittent. Most of the time she took domestic jobs in small hotels: scrubbing floors, making up rooms, and cooking. But just about every spring and fall she would disappear from her place of employment, come back broke, and work again to scrape together what little money she could. When she was present on the job, she worked hard and seemed physically tough, but she also was known to have bouts where she would suddenly fall asleep—

some coming in the middle of a conversation. She attributed her affliction to a blow to the head she had taken during a teenage fight.

Who would respect a woman like that? The answer is the more than three hundred slaves who followed her to freedom out of the South—they recognized and respected her leadership. So did just about every abolitionist in New England. The year was 1857. The woman's name was Harriet Tubman.

A LEADER BY ANY OTHER NAME

While she was only in her thirties, Harriet Tubman came to be called Moses because of her ability to go into the land of captivity and bring so many of her people out of slavery's bondage. Tubman started life as a slave. She was born in 1820 and grew up in the farmland of Maryland. When she was thirteen, she received the blow to her head that troubled her all her life. She was in a store, and a white overseer demanded her assistance so that he could beat an escaping slave. When she refused and blocked the overseer's way, the man threw a two-pound weight that hit Tubman in the head. She nearly died, and her recovery took months.

At age twenty-four, she married John Tubman, a free black man. But when she talked to him about escaping to freedom in the North, he wouldn't hear of it. He said that if she tried to leave, he'd turn her in. When she resolved to take her chances and go north in 1849, she did so alone, without a word to him. Her first biographer, Sarah Bradford, said that Tubman told her: "I had reasoned this out in my mind: there was one of two things I had a *right* to, liberty or death. If I could not have one, I would have the other, for no man should take me alive. I should fight for my liberty as my strength lasted, and when the time came for me to go, the Lord would let them take me."

Tubman made her way to Philadelphia, Pennsylvania, via the Underground Railroad, a secret network of free blacks, white abolitionists, and Quakers who helped escaping slaves on the run. Though free herself, she vowed to return to Maryland and bring her family out. In 1850, she made her first return trip as an Underground Railroad "conductor"—someone who retrieved and guided out slaves with the assistance of sympathizers along the way.

A LEADER OF STEEL

Each summer and winter, Tubman worked as a domestic, scraping together the funds she needed to make return trips to the South. And every spring and fall, she risked her life by going south and returning with more people. She was fearless, and her leadership was unshakable. It was extremely dangerous work, and when people in her charge wavered, she was strong as steel. Tubman knew escaped slaves who returned would be beaten and tortured until they gave information about those who had helped them. So she never allowed any people she was guiding to give up. "Dead folks tell no tales," she would tell a faint-hearted slave as she put a loaded pistol to his head. "You go on or die!"

Between 1850 and 1860, Harriet Tubman guided out more than three hundred people, including many of her own family members. She made nineteen trips in all and was very proud of the fact that she never once lost a single person under her care. "I never ran my train off the track," she said, "and I never lost a passenger." Southern whites put a $12,000 price on her head—a fortune. Southern blacks simply called her Moses. By the start of the Civil War, she had brought more people out of slavery than any other American in history—black or white, male or female.

INCREASING RESPECT

Tubman's reputation and influence commanded respect, and not just among slaves who dreamed of gaining their freedom. Influential

Northerners of both races sought her out. She spoke at rallies and in homes throughout Philadelphia, Pennsylvania; Boston, Massachusetts; St. Catharines, Canada; and Auburn, New York, where she eventually settled. People of prominence sought her out, such as Senator William Seward, who later became Abraham Lincoln's secretary of state, and outspoken abolitionist and former slave Frederick Douglass. Tubman's advice and leadership were also requested by John Brown, the famed revolutionary abolitionist. Brown always referred to the former slave as "General Tubman," and he was quoted as saying she "was a better officer than most whom he had seen, and could command an army as successfully as she had led her small parties of fugitives."[1] That is the essence of the Law of Respect.

A TEST OF LEADERSHIP

Harriet Tubman would appear to be an unlikely candidate for leadership because the deck was certainly stacked against her. She was uneducated. She lived in a culture that didn't respect African-Americans. And she labored in a country where women didn't have the right to vote yet. Despite her circumstances, she became an incredible leader. The reason is simple: People naturally follow leaders stronger than themselves. Everyone who came in contact with her recognized her strong leadership ability and felt compelled to follow her. That's how the Law of Respect works.

> *When people respect someone as a person, they admire her. When they respect her as a friend, they love her. When they respect her as a leader, they* **follow** *her.*

IT'S NOT A GUESSING GAME

People don't follow others by accident. They follow individuals whose leadership they respect. Someone who is an 8 in leadership (on a scale from 1 to 10, with 10 being the strongest) doesn't go out and look for a 6 to follow—he naturally follows a 9 or 10. The less skilled follow the more highly skilled and gifted. Occasionally, a strong leader may choose to follow someone weaker than himself. But when that happens, it's for a reason. For example, the stronger leader may do it out of respect for the person's office or past accomplishments. Or he may be following the chain of command. In general, though, followers are attracted to people who are better leaders than themselves. That is the Law of Respect.

> *The more leadership ability a person has, the more quickly he recognizes leadership—or its lack—in others.*

When people get together for the first time as a group, take a look at what happens. As they start interacting, the leaders in the group immediately take charge. They think in terms of the direction they desire to go and who they want to take with them. At first, people may make tentative moves in several different directions, but after the people get to know one another, it doesn't take long for them to recognize the strongest leaders and to follow them.

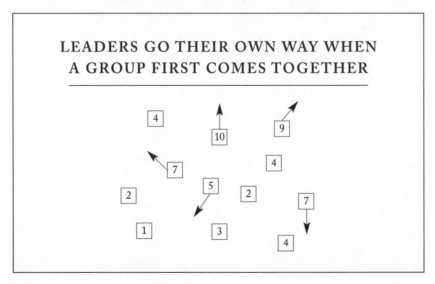

LEADERS GO THEIR OWN WAY WHEN A GROUP FIRST COMES TOGETHER

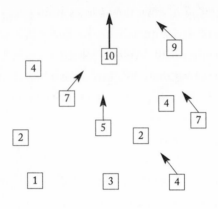

SOON PEOPLE CHANGE DIRECTION TO FOLLOW THE STRONGEST LEADERS

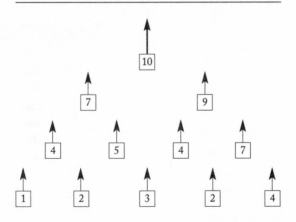

PEOPLE NATURALLY ALIGN THEMSELVES AND FOLLOW LEADERS STRONGER THAN THEMSELVES

Usually the more leadership ability a person has, the more quickly he recognizes leadership—or its lack—in others. In time, people in the group get on board and follow the strongest leaders. Either that or they leave the group and pursue their own agenda.

I remember hearing a story that shows how people come to follow stronger leaders. It happened in the early 1970s when Hall of Fame basketball center Bill Walton joined Coach John Wooden's UCLA team. As a young man, Walton wore a beard. It has been said that the coach told him his players were not allowed to have facial hair. Walton, attempting to assert his independence, said that he would not shave off his beard. Wooden's no-nonsense response was, "We'll miss you, Bill." Needless to say, Walton shaved the beard.

A RESPECTED LEADER STEPS DOWN

In October of 1997, college basketball saw the retirement of another great leader, someone who engendered respect as he spent more than thirty years of his life pouring himself into others. His name is Dean Smith, and he was the head basketball coach of the University of North Carolina. He compiled a remarkable record while leading the Tar Heels and is considered one of the best to coach at any level. In thirty-two years as head coach at North Carolina, he won 879 games, more than any other coach in college basketball's history. His teams recorded 27 consecutive 20-win seasons. They won thirteen Atlantic Coast Conference titles, played in eleven Final Fours, and won two national championships.

The respect Smith has earned among his peers is tremendous. When he scheduled the press conference to announce his retirement, people such as John Thompson, head coach of

> "The leader must know, must know he knows, and must be able to make it abundantly clear to those about him that he knows."
> —Clarence B. Randall

Georgetown, whom Smith beat for the national championship in 1982, and former player Larry Brown, who now coaches the Philadelphia 76ers, came to show their support. Michael Hooker, the chancellor of the University of North Carolina, gave Smith an open invitation to do just about anything he wanted at the school in the coming years. Even the president of the United States called to honor Smith.

THOSE CLOSEST TO HIM
RESPECTED SMITH THE MOST

But the Law of Respect can be best seen in Smith's career by looking at the way his players interacted with him. They respected him for many reasons. He taught them much, about basketball as well as life. He pushed them to achieve academically, with nearly every player earning a degree. He made them winners. And he showed them incredible loyalty and respect. Charlie Scott, who played for Smith and graduated from North Carolina in 1970, advanced to play pro basketball and then went on to work as marketing director for Champion Products. Concerning his time with Smith, he said,

> As one of the first black college athletes in the ACC, I experienced many difficult moments during my time at North Carolina, but Coach Smith was always there for me. On one occasion, as we walked off the court following a game at South Carolina, one of their fans called me a "big black baboon." Two assistants had to hold Coach Smith back from going after the guy. It was the first time I had ever seen Coach Smith visibly upset, and I was shocked. But more than anything else, I was proud of him.[2]

During his time at North Carolina, Smith made quite an impact. His leadership not only won games and the respect of his players, but also helped produce a remarkable forty-nine men who went on to play professional basketball. Included in that list are greats such as Bob McAdoo, James Worthy, and of course, Michael Jordan—not only one of the best players ever to dribble a basketball, but also a fine leader in his own right.

James Jordan, Michael's father, credited Smith and his leadership for a lot of his son's success. Before a play-off game in Chicago in 1993, the elder Jordan observed:

> People underestimate the program that Dean Smith runs. He helped Michael realize his athletic ability and hone it. But more important than that, he built character in Michael that took him through his career. I don't think Michael was privileged to any more teaching than anyone else. He had the personality to go with the teaching, and at Carolina he was able to blend the two of them together. That's the only way I can look at it, and I think that's what made Michael the player he became.[3]

In recent years, Michael Jordan has been adamant about his desire to play for only one coach—Phil Jackson, the man he believes is the best in the business. It makes sense. A leader like Jordan wants to follow a strong leader. That's the Law of Respect. It's just possible that Jordan's desire got its seed when the young North Carolinian, still developing, was being led and mentored by his strong coach, Dean Smith.

HOW MANY WILL FOLLOW?

There are many ways to measure a follower's respect for his leader, but perhaps the greatest test of respect comes when a leader creates major change in an organization. I experienced this test in 1997 when I moved my company, INJOY, from San Diego, California, to

Atlanta, Georgia. I made the decision to move in early 1996 while I was on a cruise in China with my wife, Margaret. As we discussed the move and our expectations, I began weighing my influence with my core leaders. After mentally reviewing my personal history with each leader and the strength of my leadership with them, I estimated

> *The greatest test of respect comes when a leader creates major change in an organization.*

that about 50 percent of them would be willing to uproot themselves and make the move across country with me and the organization. And Margaret agreed with my assessment.

A few months later, after INJOY president Dick Peterson and I had worked through all the preliminaries of the move, I began the task of approaching my leaders individually to tell them about the decision to go to Atlanta. And one after another, the leaders told me they wanted to take the trip. I had expected about half to go. Imagine how delighted I was when I discovered that every single one of my core leaders was going with me—100 percent.

About a year has passed since we made the move, and all of those top leaders are still working with me in Atlanta. Why did so many make the trip? I know one of the reasons is that those leaders are difference makers and want to be part of the vision of our organization. Another is that I've invested a lot of time and energy in my relationships with them, adding value to their lives. But there is another, more important one. The reasons I've named wouldn't have been enough if I had been a weaker leader. Because I've spent my whole life developing my leadership skills, that has made it possible for me to lead other strong leaders. People who are 9s and 10s don't follow a 7. That's just the way leadership works. That's the secret of the Law of Respect.

THE LAW OF INTUITION

*Leaders Evaluate Everything
with a Leadership Bias*

D O YOU REMEMBER the old television show *Dragnet?* If you do, then you probably know the phrase that Jack Webb made famous in it: "Just the facts, ma'am, just the facts." Of all the laws of leadership, the Law of Intuition is probably the most difficult to understand. Why? Because it depends on so much more than *just the facts.* The Law of Intuition is based on facts *plus* instinct and other intangible factors. And the reality is that leadership intuition is often the factor that separates the greatest leaders from the merely good ones. Let me recount a conversation I had several years ago with a staff member named Tim Elmore. It will give you some insight into the Law of Intuition.

THE BEST LEADERS READ AND RESPOND

It occurred when we lived in San Diego, and three players were competing on the Chargers football team for the starting quarter-back's position. Tim asked me who I thought would secure the job, and without hesitation, I said, "Stan Humphries."

"Really?" replied Tim. "I didn't think he had a chance. He's not all that big, and they say he doesn't have a strong work ethic in the weight room. He doesn't even really look like a quarterback."

"That doesn't matter," I said. "He's a better leader. Watch Stan play, and you'll see that he has the ability to read just about any situation, call the right play, and pull it off. He's the one who'll get the job." And Stan did get the job. He was so good that he was able to lead a fairly weak San Diego team to the Super Bowl in 1995.

All professional quarterbacks have physical talent. At the pro level the differences in physical ability really aren't that significant. What makes one man a third-string backup and another a Hall of Famer is intuition. The great ones can see things others can't, make changes, and move forward before others know what's happening.

IT'S INFORMED INTUITION

Several years ago I learned a lot about how quarterbacks are trained to think when I was invited to visit the University of Southern California by Coach Larry Smith. He asked me to speak to the Trojans football team before a big game. While I was there, I also visited their offensive war room. On chalkboards covering every wall, the coaches had mapped out every possible situation their team could be in—according to down, yardage, and place on the field. And for every situation, the coaches had mapped out a specific play designed to succeed, based on their years of experience and their intuitive knowledge of the game. Together those plays constituted the approach and bias they would take into the game in order to win it. The three USC quarterbacks had to memorize every one of those plays. The night before the game, I watched as the coaches fired one situ-

A leader has to read the situation and know instinctively what play to call.

ation after another at those three young men, requiring them to tell which play was the right one to be called.

After they were finished, I noticed that the offensive coordinator headed for a cot in the war room, and I said, "Aren't you going home to get some sleep?"

"No," he said. "I always spend Friday night here to make sure that *I* know all the plays too."

"Yeah, but you've got all of them written down on that sheet that you'll carry with you tomorrow on the sidelines," I said. "Why don't you just use that?"

"I can't rely on that," he answered, "there isn't time. You see, by the time the ball carrier's knee touches the ground, I have to know what play to call next. There's no time to fumble around deciding what to do." It was his job to put the coaching staff's intuition into action in an instant.

LEADERSHIP IS THEIR BIAS

The kind of informed intuition that coaches and quarterbacks have on game day is similar to what leaders exhibit. Leaders see everything with a leadership bias, and as a result, they instinctively, almost automatically, know what to do. You can see this read-and-react instinct in all great leaders. For example, look at the career of U.S. Army General H. Norman Schwarzkopf. Time after time, he was assigned commands that others avoided, but he was able to turn the situations around as the result of his exceptional leadership intuition and ability to act.

> *Schwarzkopf was repeatedly able to turn bad situations around as the result of his exceptional leadership intuition.*

When Schwarzkopf had been in the army seventeen years, he finally got his chance to command a battalion. It occurred in

December 1969 during his second tour of Vietnam as a lieutenant colonel. The command, which nobody wanted, was of the First Battalion of the Sixth Infantry, called the "First of the Sixth." But because the group had such a horrible reputation, it was nicknamed the "worst of the Sixth." Confirming this was the fact that as he took command, Schwarzkopf was told that the battalion had just flunked an annual inspection. They had scored an abysmal sixteen out of one hundred points. He had only thirty days to whip his men into shape.

SEEING THROUGH A LEADERSHIP LENS

After the change-in-command ceremony, Schwarzkopf met the outgoing commander, who told him, "This is for you," handing him a bottle of Scotch. "You're gonna need it. Well, I hope you do better than I did. I tried to lead as best I could, but this is a lousy battalion. It's got lousy morale. It's got a lousy mission. Good luck to you." And with that, he left.

Schwarzkopf's intuition told him that he faced a terrible situation, but it was even worse than he had expected. His predecessor hadn't known the first thing about leadership. The man had never ventured outside the safety of the base camp to inspect his troops. And the results were appalling. The entire battalion was in chaos. The officers were indifferent, the most basic military security procedures weren't being followed, and soldiers were dying needlessly. The departing commander was right: It was a lousy battalion with lousy morale. But he didn't say that it was his fault. Based on Schwarzkopf's description, it's obvious that the previous commander had displayed no ability to read the situation, and he had failed his people as a leader.

During the next few weeks, Schwarzkopf's intuition kicked in, and he took action. He implemented military procedures, retrained the troops, developed his leaders, and gave the men direction and a sense of purpose. When it was time for the thirty-day inspection, they achieved a passing score. And the men started to think to themselves, *Hey, we can do it right. We can be a success. We're not the "worst of the Sixth" anymore.* As a result, fewer men died, morale rose, and the battalion started to become effective in its mission. Schwarzkopf's leadership was so strong and the turnaround was so effective that just a few months after he took it over, his battalion was selected to perform more difficult missions—the kind that could be carried out only by a disciplined, well-led group with strong morale.

ANOTHER LEADERSHIP CHALLENGE

Later in his career, Schwarzkopf got the opportunity to command a brigade. Once again, he accepted a post that others didn't want, and he followed someone who I believe was another poor leader. The unit was the First Reconnaissance/Commando Brigade of the Ninth Infantry at Fort Lewis, but people called it the "circus brigade" because of the way the previous commander had run it.

Schwarzkopf's leadership intuition told him that the people he commanded were good. The real problem was that their priorities were all wrong. He immediately rallied his officers, set new priorities, and empowered them to retrain their people to get back on track. As he implemented changes, his vision for them was clear in his mind. He wanted them to be ready for battle.

The unit began improving. A weaker leader might have been afraid to push the troops while they were regaining their confidence, but Schwarzkopf's intuition told him

> *People need a goal to galvanize them.*

that his people needed a goal to galvanize them. So he found one: the desert maneuvers scheduled for the following summer.

Schwarzkopf received his commander's commitment to let the

men of the First represent the division in the exercises, and then he threw himself into preparing his people to fulfill that mission. And when the maneuvers came around that summer, Schwarzkopf's three battalions went up against *thirteen* marine battalions and performed so successfully that the marine commander, a two-star general, refused to speak to Schwarzkopf when the exercises were finished.

HOW LEADERS THINK

Because of their intuition, leaders evaluate everything with a leadership bias. Some people are born with great leadership intuition. Others have to work hard to develop and hone it. But either way it evolves, the result is a combination of natural ability and learned skills. This informed intuition causes leadership issues to jump out. The best way to describe this bias is an ability to get a handle on intangible factors, understand them, and work with them to accomplish leadership goals.

Intuition helps leaders become readers of the numerous intangibles of leadership:

LEADERS ARE READERS OF THEIR SITUATION

In all kinds of circumstances, they capture details that elude others. For example, when I was the senior pastor of Skyline, my church in San Diego, there were times when I was required to travel for long periods of time. Often when I returned after being gone for ten to fourteen days, I could tell something was going on. I could feel it. And usually in an hour or so of talking with staff and getting the pulse of what was going on, I'd be able to track it down.

> *Natural ability and learned skills create an informed intuition that makes leadership issues jump out at leaders.*

LEADERS ARE READERS OF TRENDS

Everything that happens around us does so in the context of a bigger picture. Leaders have the ability to step back from what's happening at the moment and see not only where they and their people have gone, but also where they are headed in the future. It's as if they can smell change in the wind.

LEADERS ARE READERS OF THEIR RESOURCES

A major difference between achievers and leaders is the way they see resources. Successful individuals think in terms of what they can do. Successful leaders, on the other hand, see every situation in terms of available resources: money, raw materials, technology and, most important, people. They never forget that people are their greatest asset.

> *Leaders who want to succeed maximize every asset and resource they have for the benefit of their organization.*

LEADERS ARE READERS OF PEOPLE

President Lyndon Johnson once said that when you walk into a room, if you can't tell who's for you and who's against you, you don't belong in politics. That statement also applies to leadership. Intuitive leaders can sense what's happening among people and almost instantly know their hopes, fears, and concerns.

LEADERS ARE READERS OF THEMSELVES

Finally, good leaders develop the ability to read themselves—their strengths, skills, weaknesses, and current state of mind. They recognize the truth of what James Russell Lovell said: "No one can produce great things who is not thoroughly sincere in dealing with himself."

WHAT YOU SEE
RESULTS FROM WHO YOU ARE

How was Schwarzkopf able to turn around difficult assignments again and again? The answer lies in the Law of Intuition. Other officers had the benefit of the same training in soldiering and tactics. And they all had access to the same resources, so that wasn't the answer. Schwarzkopf wasn't necessarily smarter than his counterparts, either. What he brought to the table was strong leadership intuition. He saw everything with a leadership bias.

Who you are dictates what you see. If you've seen the movie *The Great Outdoors*, you may remember a scene that illustrates this idea perfectly. In the movie, John Candy plays Chet, a man vacationing with his family at a small lake community in the woods. He is unexpectedly visited by his sister-in-law and her husband, Roman

> *Who you are dictates what you see.*

(played by Dan Aykroyd), who is kind of a shady character. As the two men sit on the porch of their cabin overlooking the lake and miles of beautiful forest, they start to talk. And Roman, who sees himself as a wheeler-dealer, shares his vision with Chet: "I'll tell you what I see when I look out there . . . I see the underdeveloped resources of northern Minnesota, Wisconsin, and Michigan. I see a syndicated development consortium exploiting over a billion and a half dollars in forest products. I see a paper mill and—if the strategic metals are there—a mining operation; a green belt between the condos on the lake and a waste management facility . . . Now I ask you, what do you see?"

"I, uh, I just see trees," answers Chet.

"Well," says Roman, "nobody ever accused you of having a grand vision."

Chet saw trees because he was there to enjoy the scenery. Roman saw opportunity because he was a businessman whose desire was to make money. How you see the world around you is determined by who you are.

THREE LEVELS OF LEADERSHIP INTUITION

Just about everyone is capable of developing a degree of leadership intuition, though we don't all start off at the same place. I've found that all people fit into three major intuition levels:

1. THOSE WHO NATURALLY SEE IT

Some people are born with exceptional leadership gifts. They instinctively understand people and know how to move them from point A to point B. Even when they're kids, they act as leaders. Watch them on the playground, and you can see everyone is following them. People with natural leadership intuition can build upon it and become world-class leaders of the highest caliber. This natural ability is often the difference between a 9 (an excellent leader) and a 10 (a world-class leader).

2. THOSE WHO ARE NURTURED TO SEE IT

Not everyone starts off with great instincts, but whatever abilities people have can be nurtured and developed. The ability to think like a leader is *informed* intuition. Even someone who doesn't start off as a natural leader can become an excellent one. People who don't develop their intuition are condemned to be blindsided in their leadership for the rest of their lives.

3. THOSE WHO WILL NEVER SEE IT

I believe nearly everyone is capable of developing leadership skills and intuition. But occasionally, I run across someone who doesn't seem to have a leadership bone in his body *and* who has no interest in developing the skills necessary to lead. Those people will never think like anything but followers.

LEADERS SOLVE PROBLEMS
USING THE LAW OF INTUITION

Whenever leaders find themselves facing a problem, they automatically measure it—and begin solving it—using the Law of Intuition. They evaluate everything with a leadership bias. For example, you can see where leadership intuition came into play recently at Apple Computer. Just about everybody knows the success story of Apple. The company was created in 1976 by Steve Jobs and Steve Wozniak in Jobs's father's garage. Just four years later, the business went public, opening at twenty-two dollars a share and selling 4.6 million shares. It made more than forty employees and investors millionaires overnight.

> *Whenever leaders find themselves facing a problem, they automatically measure it—and begin solving it—using the Law of Intuition.*

But Apple's story isn't all positive. Since those early years, Apple's success, stock value, and ability to capture customers have fluctuated wildly. Jobs left Apple in 1985, having been pushed out in a battle with CEO John Sculley, the former Pepsi president whom Jobs had recruited in 1983. Sculley was followed by Michael Spindler in 1993 and then Gilbert Amelio in 1996. None of them was able to reestablish Apple's previous success. In its glory days, Apple had sold 14.6 percent of all personal computers in the United States. By 1997, sales were depressed to 3.5 percent. That was when Apple again looked to the leadership of its original founder, Steve Jobs, for help. The failing company believed he could save it.

REINVENTING APPLE

Jobs intuitively reviewed the situation and immediately took action. He knew that improvement was impossible without a change in leadership, so he quickly dismissed all but two of the previous board members and installed new ones. Executive leadership also experienced positive change at his hands.

Once new leaders were in place, he looked at the company's focus. Jobs wanted to get back to the basics of what Apple had always done best: use its individuality to create products that made a difference. Jobs said, "We've reviewed the road map of new products and axed more than 70% of the projects, keeping the 30% that were gems. Plus we're adding new ones that are a whole new paradigm of looking at computers." He also sensed a problem with the company's marketing, so he fired the ad agency and held a competition for the account among three firms.[1]

None of those actions was especially surprising. But Jobs also did something that really showed the Law of Intuition in action.

> *Improvement is impossible without a change in leadership.*

He made a leadership decision that went absolutely against the grain of Apple's previous thinking. It was an incredible intuitive leadership leap. Jobs created a strategic alliance with the man whom Apple employees considered to be their archenemy—Bill Gates. Jobs explained, "I called Bill and said Microsoft and Apple should work more closely together, but we have this issue to resolve, this intellectual-property dispute. Let's resolve it."

They negotiated a deal quickly, which settled Apple's lawsuit against Microsoft. Gates promised to pay off Apple and invest $150 million in nonvoting stock. That cleared the way for future partnership and brought much-needed capital to the company. It was something only an intuitive leader would have done. Not surprisingly, when Jobs announced the new alliance to a meeting of the Apple faithful, they booed. But on Wall Street, Apple stock value immediately soared 33 percent to $26.31.[2]

Apple looks as if it's turning around. Prior to Jobs's return, the company had posted net quarterly losses the previous year totaling more than $1 billion. However, in the first fiscal quarter of 1998, Apple finally recorded a net profit of $47 million. In the long run, it's hard to know whether the company will ever recapture its former success. But at least it now has a fighting chance.

> *Leadership is more art than science.*

Leadership is really more art than science. The principles of leadership are constant, but the application changes with every leader and every situation. That's why it requires intuition. Without it, you can get blindsided, and that's one of the worst things that can happen to a leader. If you want to lead long, you've got to obey the Law of Intuition.

9

THE LAW OF MAGNETISM

Who You Are Is Who You Attract

Effective leaders are always on the lookout for good people. I think each of us carries around a mental list of what kind of people we would like to have in our organization. Think about it. Do you know who you're looking for right now? What is your profile of perfect employees? What qualities do these people possess? Do you want them to be aggressive and entrepreneurial? Are you looking for leaders? Do you care whether they are in their twenties, forties, or sixties? Stop right now, take a moment, and make a list of the qualities you'd like to see in the people on your team. Find a pencil or pen, and do it now before you read any farther.

MY PEOPLE WOULD HAVE THESE QUALITIES

_____   _____
_____   _____
_____   _____
_____   _____

_____

_____ _____

_____ _____

_____ _____

_____ _____

Now, what will determine whether the people you want are the people you get, whether they will possess the qualities you desire? You may be surprised by the answer. Believe it or not, who you get is not determined by what you *want*. It's determined by who you *are*. Go back to the list you just made, and next to each characteristic you identified, check to see if you possess that quality. For example, if you wrote that you would like "great leaders" and you are an excellent leader, that's a match. Put a check by it. But if your leadership is no better than average, put an X and write "only average leader" next to it. If you wrote that you want people who are "entrepreneurial" and you possess that quality, put a check. Otherwise, mark it with an X, and so on. Now review the whole list.

> *Who you get is not determined by what you* want. *It's determined by who you* are.

If you see a whole bunch of Xs, then you're in trouble because the people you describe are not the type who will want to follow you. In most situations, you draw people to you who possess the same qualities you do. That's the Law of Magnetism: Who you are is who you attract.

FROM MUSICIANSHIP TO LEADERSHIP

When I was a kid, my mother used to tell me that birds of a feather flock together. I thought that was a wise saying when I was spending time with my older brother, Larry, and playing ball. He was a good athlete, so I figured that made me one too. As I grew up, I think I instinctively recognized that good students spent time with good students, people who only wanted to play stuck together, and so on. But I don't think I *really* understood the impact of the Law of Magnetism until I moved to San Diego, California, and became the leader of my last church.

My predecessor at Skyline Church was Dr. Orval Butcher. He is a wonderful man with many fine qualities. One of his best is his musicianship. He plays piano and has a beautiful Irish tenor voice, even today in his eighties. At the time I arrived in 1981, Skyline had a solid reputation for fine music. It was nationally known for its out-standing musical productions. In fact, the church was filled with tal-ented musicians and vocalists. And in the twenty-seven years Dr. Butcher led the church, only two music directors worked for him—an unbelievable track record. (In comparison, during my fourteen years there, I employed five people in that capacity.)

Why were there so many exceptional musicians at Skyline? The answer lies in the Law of Magnetism. People with musical talent were naturally attracted to Dr. Butcher. They respected him and understood him. They shared his motivation and values. They were on the same page with him. In contrast, I *enjoy* music, but I am not a musician. It's funny, but when I interviewed for the position at Skyline, one of the first questions they asked me was whether I could sing. They were very disappointed when I told them no.

After I came on board at the church, the number of new musi-cians declined quickly. We still had more than our share, because Dr. Butcher had created momentum and a wonderful legacy in that area. But do you know what kind of people started coming instead? Leaders. By the time I left Skyline, not only was the church filled with hundreds of excellent leaders, but the church had also equipped and sent out hundreds of men and women as leaders during the time I was there. The reason was the Law of Magnetism. Our organization became a magnet for people with leadership ability.

PEOPLE LIKE YOU WILL SEEK YOU OUT

Of course, it is possible for a leader to go out and recruit people unlike himself. Good leaders know that one secret to success is to staff their weaknesses. That way they can focus and function in their areas of strength while others take care of the important matters that would otherwise be neglected. But it's crucial to recognize that people who are different will not naturally be attracted to you. Leaders draw people who are like themselves.

> *It is possible for a leader to go out and recruit people unlike himself, but those are not the people he will naturally attract.*

For example, think about the NFL's Dallas Cowboys. In the sixties and seventies, the Cowboys' image was squeaky clean. Tex Schramm was the president and general manager of the team, and Tom Landry was the coach. Players were men like Roger Staubach, called "Captain Comeback," a family man with strong values similar to those of Tom Landry. In those days, the Cowboys were called "America's team." They were one of the most popular groups of athletes around the country. And they were respected not only because of the talent and character of the individuals associated with the organization, but also because of their incredible ability to work together as a team. As they developed a winning tradition in Dallas, they continued to attract more winners.

But for the past ten years, the Dallas Cowboys have been a very different kind of team. They have changed, and their image has too. Instead of working together as a team, they sometimes appear to be a loosely associated group of individuals who are in the game solely for their own benefit. (Unfortunately, because the country has also changed, they could still be called "America's team.") Various players, such as wide receiver Michael Irvin, have been on the wrong side of the law. Even Coach Barry Switzer found himself in trouble several times, such as when he tried to take a loaded gun through the security gate at an airport. Why has the complexion of the team changed so drastically? It's the Law of Magnetism. In 1989 the Cowboys' ownership changed. The new owner, Jerry Jones, is an individualist and something of a maverick. He had no qualms about going out and signing his own deals with shoe and soft drink companies despite the fact that all the NFL teams had already signed a collective endorsement contract with a competitor.

It's little wonder that the Cowboys don't enjoy the reputation they once had, even with their recent Super Bowl victories. Al McGuire, former head basketball coach of Marquette University, once said, "A team should be an extension of the coach's personality. My teams were arrogant and obnoxious." I say that teams cannot be anything *but* an extension of the coach's personality. Fortunately, Dallas just brought on board a new coach, Chan Gailey. He is a good leader with strong character and values. If he is given enough time and authority, he may be able to attract enough additional people like himself to turn the Cowboys around. Then the Law of Magnetism will be able to work *for* Dallas, but it won't happen overnight.

WHERE DO THEY MATCH UP?

Maybe you've started thinking about the people that you have attracted in your organization. You might say to yourself, "Wait a minute. I can name twenty things that make my people different from me." And my response would be, "Of course, you can." But the people who are drawn to you probably have more similarities than differences, especially in a few key areas. Take a look at the following characteristics. You will probably find

> *If you think your people are negative, then you better check your attitude.*

that you and the people who follow you share common ground in several of these key areas:

ATTITUDE

Rarely have I seen positive and negative people attracted to one another. People who view life as a series of opportunities and exciting challenges don't want to hear others talk about how bad things are all the time. I know that's true for me. I can't think of a single negative person in my organizations. And if you were to talk to my four company presidents and all my top managers, you'd find that every one of them is an especially positive person.

GENERATION

People tend to attract others of roughly the same age. My top leaders are a good example. Three of my four company presidents are only one or two years different in age from me. And that same pattern can be seen in other areas of my companies, such as among some managers at INJOY. For instance, Kevin Small, who heads the seminar marketing area, is a sharp, aggressive young man in his twenties. Can you guess what kind of people are attracted to him? Most of them are sharp and aggressive and in their twenties. Who you are is who you attract.

BACKGROUND

In the chapter on the Law of Process, I wrote about Theodore Roosevelt. One of his memorable accomplishments is his daring charge up San Juan Hill with the Rough Riders during the Spanish-American War. Roosevelt personally recruited that all-volunteer cavalry company, and it was said to be a remarkably peculiar group of people. It was comprised primarily of two types of men: wealthy aristocrats from the Northeast and cowboys from the Wild West. Why? Because TR was an aristocratic-born, Harvard-educated New Yorker who turned himself into a real-life cowboy and big-game hunter in the Dakotas of the West. He was a strong and genuine leader in both worlds, and as a result, he attracted both kinds of people.

VALUES

People are attracted to leaders whose values are similar to their own. Think about the people who flocked to President John F. Kennedy after he was elected in 1960. He was a young idealist who wanted to change the world, and he attracted people with a similar profile. When he formed the Peace Corps and called people to service, saying, "Ask not what your country can do for you; ask what you can do for your country," thousands of young, idealistic people stepped forward to answer the challenge.

It doesn't matter whether the shared values are positive or negative. Either way, the attraction is equally strong. Think about someone like Adolf Hitler. He was a very strong leader (as you can judge by his level of influence). But his values were rotten to the core. What kinds of people did he attract? Leaders with similar values: Hermann Goering, founder of the Gestapo; Joseph Goebbels, a bitter anti-Semite who ran Hitler's propaganda machine; Reinhard Heydrich, second in command of the Nazi secret police, who ordered mass executions of Nazi opponents; and Heinrich Himmler, chief of the SS and director of the Gestapo who initiated the systematic execution of Jews. They were all strong leaders, and they were all utterly evil men. The Law of Magnetism is powerful. Whatever character you possess you will likely find in the people who follow you.

LIFE EXPERIENCE

Life experience is another area of attraction for people. For example, anytime I speak to a new audience, I can tell within thirty seconds what kind of speaker they are used to hearing. If they regularly listen to gifted and energetic communicators, they are a sharp and responsive audience. You can see it in their faces. Their sense of expectation is high, their body language is positive, and when you get ready to speak, they have paper and pencil ready to take notes. But if people are used to a poor communicator, I find that they just check out mentally.

LEADERSHIP ABILITY

Finally, the people you attract will have leadership ability similar to your own. As I said in discussing the Law of Respect, people naturally follow leaders stronger than themselves. But you also have to factor in the Law of Magnetism, which states that who you are is who you attract. What that means is that if you are a 7 when it comes to leadership, you are more likely to draw 5s and 6s to you than 2s and 3s. The leaders you attract will be similar in style and ability to you.

HISTORY CHANGES COURSE

A vivid example of the Law of Magnetism can be seen among the military leaders of the Civil War. When the Southern states seceded, there were questions about which side many of the generals would fight for. Robert E. Lee was considered the best general in the nation, and President Lincoln actually offered him command of the Union army. But Lee would never consider fighting against his native Virginia. He declined the offer and joined the Confederacy—and the best generals in the land followed him.

> *The better leader you are, the better leaders you will attract.*

If Lee had chosen to lead an army for the Union instead, many other good generals would have followed him north. As a result, the war probably would have been much shorter. It might have lasted two years instead of five—and hundreds of thousands of lives would have been saved. It just goes to show you that the better leader you are, the better leaders you will attract. And that has an incredible impact on everything you do.

How do the people you are currently attracting to your organization or department look to you? Are they the strong, capable potential leaders you desire? Or could they be better? Remember, their quality does not ultimately depend on a hiring process, a human resources department, or even what you consider to be the quality of your area's applicant pool. It depends on you. Who you are is who you attract. That is the Law of Magnetism.

> *If you think the people you attract could be better, then it's time for you to improve yourself.*

THE LAW OF CONNECTION

*Leaders Touch a Heart Before
They Ask for a Hand*

I LOVE COMMUNICATING. It's one of the joys of my life and one of my passions. Although I've spent more than thirty years speaking professionally, I'm always looking for ways to grow and keep improving in that area. That's why I try to see first-rate communicators in person when I get the chance. For instance, I made a trip to San Jose, California, to see an event sponsored by the local chamber of commerce. Speaking that day was an all-star cast of communicators: Mark Russell, who used humor so effectively; Mario Cuomo, who infused passion into everything he said; the brilliant Malcolm Forbes, whose insight made every subject he talked about seem brand new; and Colin Powell, whose confidence gave everyone in the audience security and hope. Every one of those communicators was strong and was able to develop an incredible rapport with the audience. But as good as they were, none was as good as my favorite. Head and shoulders above the rest stood Elizabeth Dole.

THE AUDIENCE'S BEST FRIEND

No doubt you've heard of Elizabeth Dole. She is a lawyer by trade, was a cabinet member in the Reagan and Bush administrations, and is now the president of the American Red Cross. She is a marvelous communicator. Her particular gift, which she demonstrated in San Jose that day, was making me and everyone else in her audience feel as though she was really our friend. She made me glad I was there. The bottom line is that she really knows how to connect with people.

In 1996, she demonstrated that ability to the whole country when she spoke at the Republican National Convention. If you watched it on television, you know what I'm talking about. When Elizabeth Dole walked out into the audience that night, they felt that she was their best friend. She was able to develop an amazing connection with them. I also felt that connection, even though I was sitting in my living room at home watching her on television. Once she finished her talk, I would have followed her anywhere.

BOB NEVER MADE THE CONNECTION

Also speaking at that convention was Bob Dole, Elizabeth's husband—not surprising since he was the Republican nominee for the presidential race. Anyone who watched would have observed a remarkable difference between the communication abilities of the two speakers. Where Elizabeth was warm and approachable, Bob appeared stern and distant. Throughout the campaign, he never seemed to be able to connect with the people.

Many factors come into play in the election of a president of the United States, but not least among them is the ability of a candidate to connect with his audience. A lot has been written about the Kennedy-Nixon debates of the 1960 election. One of the reasons Kennedy succeeded was that he was able to make the television audience feel connected to him. The same kind of connection developed between Ronald Reagan and his audiences. And in the 1992 election, Bill Clinton worked extremely hard to develop a sense of connection with the American people—to do it he even appeared on the talk show *Arsenio* and played the saxophone.

I believe Bob Dole is a good man. But I also know he never connected with the people. Ironically, after the presidential race was over, he appeared on *Saturday Night Live,* a show that made fun of him during the entire campaign, implying that he was humorless and out of touch. On the show Dole came across as relaxed, approachable, and able to make fun of himself. And he was a hit with the audience. I can't help wondering what might have happened if he had done more of that early in the campaign.

THE HEART COMES FIRST

Effective leaders know that you first have to touch people's hearts before you ask them for a hand. That is the Law of Connection. All great communicators recognize this truth and act on it almost instinctively. You can't move people to action unless you first move them with emotion. The heart comes before the head.

An outstanding orator and African-American leader of the nineteenth century was Frederick Douglass. It's said that he had a remarkable ability to connect with people and move their hearts when he spoke. Historian Lerone Bennett said of Douglass, "He could make people *laugh* at a slave owner preaching the duties of Christian obedience; could make them *see* the humiliation of a Black maiden ravished by a brutal slave owner; could make them *hear* the sobs of a mother separated from her child. Through

> *You can't move people to action unless you first move them with emotion. The heart comes before the head.*

him, people could cry, curse, and *feel;* through him they could *live* slavery."

PUBLIC AND PRIVATE CONNECTION

Connecting with people isn't something that needs to happen only when a leader is communicating to groups of people. It needs to happen with individuals. The stronger the relationship and connection between individuals, the more likely the follower will want to help the leader. That is one of the most important principles I've taught my staff over the years. My staff at Skyline used to groan every time I would say, "People don't care how much you know until they know

> *The stronger the relationship and connection between individuals, the more likely the follower will want to help the leader.*

how much you know," but they also knew that it was true. You develop credibility with people when you connect with them and show that you genuinely want to help them.

The greatest leaders are able to connect on both levels: with individuals and with an audience. A perfect example was Ronald Reagan. His ability to develop rapport with an audience is reflected in the nickname he received as president: the Great Communi-

cator. But he also had the ability to touch the hearts of the individuals close to him. Former Reagan speechwriter Peggy Noonan said that when the president used to return to the White House from long trips and the staff heard his helicopter landing on the lawn, everyone would stop working, and staff member Donna Elliott would say, "Daddy's home!" It was an indication of the affection his people felt for him.

You don't need the charisma of Ronald Reagan to connect with people. You will sometimes discover the ability to connect with people where you would least expect to find it. I was reminded of that recently as I read about the funeral of Sonny Bono. Though he had succeeded in recent years in the world of politics, having served as the mayor of Palm Springs and a member of the U.S. House of Representatives, most people remember Bono from his show business days. He was hard to take seriously. He wore outrageous clothes. He was always the butt of then wife Cher's jokes, and he couldn't sing. But the man knew how to connect with others. At his funeral, House Speaker Newt Gingrich said of Bono:

> You looked at him and thought to yourself: "This can't be a famous person." He smiled, he said something, then you thought to yourself: "This can't be a serious person." Four jokes and two stories later you were pouring your heart out to him, he was helping you solve a problem and you began to realize this is a very hard-working, very thoughtful man who covered up a great deal of his abilities with his wonderful sense of humor and his desire to make you bigger than him so he could serve you, which would then make it easier for you to do something the two of you needed to do together.[1]

Bono understood the Law of Connection. He won people over before he enlisted their help. He knew that you have to touch a heart before you ask for a hand.

CONNECT WITH PEOPLE ONE AT A TIME

A key to connecting with others is recognizing that even in a group, you have to relate to people as individuals. General Norman Schwarzkopf remarked, "I have seen competent leaders who stood in front of a platoon and all they saw was a platoon. But great leaders stand in front of a platoon and see it as 44 individuals, each of whom has aspirations, each of whom wants to live, each of whom wants to do good."[2]

> *To connect with people in a group, relate to them as individuals.*

I've had the opportunity to speak to some wonderful audiences during the course of my career. The largest have been in stadiums where 60,000 to 70,000 people were in attendance. Some of my colleagues who also speak for a living have asked me, "How in the world do you speak to that many people?" The secret is simple. I don't try to talk to the thousands. I focus on talking to one person. That's the only way to connect with people.

IT'S THE LEADER'S JOB

Some leaders have problems with the Law of Connection because they believe that connecting is the responsibility of followers. That is especially true of positional leaders. They often think, *I'm the boss. I have the position. These are my employees. Let them come to me.* But successful leaders who obey the Law of Connection are always initiators. They take the first step with others and then make the effort to continue building relationships. That's not always easy, but it's important to the success of the organization. A leader has to do it, no matter how many obstacles there might be.

I learned this lesson in 1972 when I was faced with a very difficult situation. I was moving to Lancaster, Ohio, where I would be taking over the leadership of a church. Before I accepted the position, I found out from a friend that the church had just gone through a big battle related to a building project. Heading up one of the factions was the number one influencer in the church, a man named Jim Butz who was the elected lay leader of the congregation. And I also heard that Jim had a reputation for being negative and something of a maverick. He liked to use his influence to move the people in directions that didn't always help the organization.

Because the previous senior pastor had butted heads with Jim more than a few times, I knew my best chance for being successful in leadership there was to make a connection with Jim. So the first thing I did when I got there was to make an appointment to meet him in my office.

Jim was a big man. He was about six feet four inches tall and weighed about 250 pounds—the kind of guy who could go bear hunting with nothing but a switch. He was very intimidating, and he was about sixty-five years old. I, on the other hand, was only twenty-five. When he came in, I said, "Jim, I know you're the influencer in this church, and I want you to know that I've decided I'm going to do everything in my power to build a good relationship with you. I'd like to meet with you every Tuesday for lunch at the Holiday Inn to talk through issues. While I'm the leader here, I'll never take any decision to the people without first discussing it with you. I really want to work with you.

"But I also want you to know that I've heard you're a very negative person," I said,

> *It's the leader's job to initiate connection with the people.*

"and that you like to fight battles. If you decide to work against me, I'll guess we'll just have to be on opposite sides. And because you have so much influence, I know you'll win most of the time in the beginning. But I'm going to develop relationships with people and draw new people to this church, and someday, I'll have greater influence than you.

"But I don't want to battle you," I continued. "You're sixty-five years old right now. Let's say you've got another ten to fifteen years of good health and productivity ahead of you. If you want, you can make these years your very best and make your life count. We can do a lot of great things together at this church, but the decision is yours."

When I finished, Jim didn't say a word. He got up from his seat, walked into the hall, and stopped to take a drink at the water fountain. I followed him out and waited. After a long time, he stood up straight and turned around. When he did, I could see that tears were rolling down his cheeks. And then he gave me a great big bear hug and said, "You can count on me to be on your side."

And Jim did get on my side. As it turned out, he did live about another ten years, and because he was willing to help me, we accomplished some positive things together at that church. But it never would have happened if I hadn't had the courage to try to make a connection with him that first day in my office.

THE TOUGHER THE CHALLENGE,
THE GREATER THE CONNECTION

Never underestimate the power of building relationships with people before asking them to follow you. If you've ever studied the lives of notable military commanders, you have probably noticed that the best ones practiced the Law of Connection. I once read that during World War I in France, General Douglas MacArthur told a battalion commander before a daring charge, "Major, when the signal comes to go over the top, I want you to go first, before your men. If you do, they'll follow." Then MacArthur removed the Distinguished Service Cross from his uniform and pinned it on the major. He had, in effect, awarded him for heroism before asking him to exhibit it. And of course, the major led his men, they followed him over the top, and they achieved their objective.

Not all military examples of the Law of Connection are quite so dramatic. For example, it's said that Napoleon made it a practice to know every one of his officers by name and to remember where they lived and which battles they had fought with him. Robert E. Lee was known to visit the men in their campsites the night before any major battle. Often he met the next day's challenges without having slept. More recently, I read about how Norman Schwarzkopf often found ways of connecting with his troops. On Christmas in 1990 during the

Persian Gulf War, he spent the day among the men and women who were so far away from their families. In his autobiography, he says,

> I started at Lockheed Village . . . Some [troops] had already sat down to dinner, though it was only noon, because they were eating in shifts. I shook a lot of hands. Next I went back out to the Escan Village, where there were three huge mess halls in tents. At the first a long line of troops stretched out the entryway. I shook hands with everyone in the line, went behind the serving counter to greet the cooks and helpers, and worked my way through the mess hall, hitting every table, wishing everyone Merry Christmas. Then I went into the second and third dining facilities and did the same thing. I came back to the first mess tent and repeated the exercise, because by this time there was an entirely new set of faces. Then I sat down with some of the troops and had my dinner. In the course of four hours, I must have shaken four thousand hands.[3]

> *It may sound corny, but it's really true: People don't care how much you know until they know how much you care.*

Schwarzkopf didn't have to do that, but he did. He used one of the most effective methods for connecting with others, something I call walking slowly through the crowd. It may sound corny, but it's really true: People don't care how much you know until they know how much you care.

THE RESULT OF CONNECTION

When a leader has done the work to connect with his people, you can see it in the way the organization functions. Among employees there are incredible loyalty and a strong work ethic. The vision of the leader becomes the aspiration of the people. The impact is incredible.

You can also see the results in other ways. On Boss's Day in 1994, a full-page ad appeared in *USA Today*. It was contracted and paid for by the employees of Southwest Airlines, and it was addressed to Herb Kelleher, the company's CEO:

Thanks, Herb

For remembering every one of our names.

For supporting the Ronald McDonald House.

For helping load baggage on Thanksgiving.

For giving everyone a kiss (and we mean everyone).

For listening.

For running the only profitable major airline.

For singing at our holiday party.

For singing only once a year.

For letting us wear shorts and sneakers to work.

For golfing at The LUV Classic with only one club.

For outtalking Sam Donaldson.

For riding your Harley Davidson into Southwest Headquarters.

For being a friend, not just a boss.

Happy Boss's Day from Each One of Your 16,000 Employees[4]

A display of affection like that occurs only when a leader has worked hard to connect with his people.

Don't ever underestimate the importance of building relational bridges between yourself and the people you lead. There's an old saying: To lead yourself, use your head; to lead others, use your heart. That's the nature of the Law of Connection. Always touch a person's heart before you ask him for a hand.

> *To lead yourself, use your head; to lead others, use your heart.*

THE LAW OF THE INNER CIRCLE

*A Leader's Potential Is Determined
by Those Closest to Him*

IN 1981, I RECEIVED a marvelous offer. I was working as an executive director at Wesleyan World Headquarters when I was given the opportunity to become the leader of the largest church in the Wesleyan denomination. The name of the church was Skyline, and it was located in the San Diego, California, area.

The church had a great history. It had been founded in the 1950s by a wonderful man named Orval Butcher, and he was retiring after serving there for twenty-seven years. Dr. Butcher had touched the lives of thousands of people with his leadership, and the church had a strong, nationally recognized reputation. It was a good church, but it did have one problem. It had not grown in years. After making it to a little more than one thousand members, it had reached a plateau.

The first time I flew out to talk with the board, I knew that Skyline was the place I was supposed to be. I immediately called and told my wife, Margaret, that we should start packing and preparing for a move. And as soon as they offered me the job, off we went with our two kids to San Diego.

> *Every leader's potential is determined by the people closest to him. No matter what I did with that staff, they would never be able to take the organization to the place we needed to go.*

As we drove across the country, I began thinking about the task ahead. I was really looking forward to the challenge of taking Skyline to a new level. After we arrived, I met with each of the staff members to assess individual abilities. Almost immediately I discovered why the church had flat-lined. The staff were good people, but they weren't strong leaders. No matter what I did with them, they would never be able to take the organization to the place we needed to go. You see, every leader's potential is determined by the people closest to him. If those people are strong, then the leader can make a huge impact. If they are weak, he can't. That is the Law of the Inner Circle.

THREE PHASES TO NEW GROWTH

The task that lay ahead of me was clear. I needed to remove the weak leaders I possessed and bring in better ones. That was the only way I would be able to turn the situation around. Mentally, I divided the people into three groups according to their ability to lead and deliver results. The first group I wanted to deal with was the bottom third, the staff contributing least to the organization. I knew I could dismiss them right away because the impact of their departure could be nothing but positive. I immediately replaced them with the best people I could find.

I then began working on the middle third. One by one, as I found good leaders from outside the organization, I brought them in and let go the weakest of the existing staff. It took me another year to process out the old middle group. By the end of three years, I had completely cleaned house, leaving only two on staff out of the original group. And because the inner circle had gone to a new level, the organization was able to go to a new level. On the new staff, even the weakest of the new people were stronger than all the old ones I had let go.

The staff continued to grow in strength. I developed the people to make them better leaders. And anytime a staff member left, I searched for someone even better as a replacement. As a result, the impact on Skyline was incredible. Almost as soon as I made the initial staff changes in 1981, we started growing again. In fewer than ten years, the church became three times the size it had been when I started. And the annual budget, which was $800,000 when I arrived, grew to more than $5 million a year.

> *When you have the right staff, potential skyrockets.*

The growth and success we experienced at Skyline were due to the Law of the Inner Circle. When we had the right staff, our potential skyrocketed. And in 1995 when I left, other leaders from

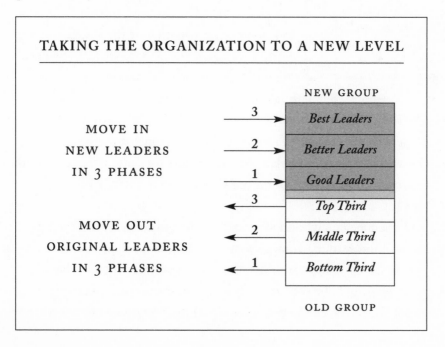

TAKING THE ORGANIZATION TO A NEW LEVEL

NEW GROUP

MOVE IN
NEW LEADERS
IN 3 PHASES

3 →	*Best Leaders*
2 →	*Better Leaders*
1 →	*Good Leaders*

MOVE OUT
ORIGINAL LEADERS
IN 3 PHASES

← 3	*Top Third*
← 2	*Middle Third*
← 1	*Bottom Third*

OLD GROUP

around the country sought to hire my key staff members for their own organizations. They recognized the power of the Law of the Inner Circle and wanted to hire the very best they could find to boost their potential.

EVERY ORGANIZATION HAS AN INNER CIRCLE

Look at an organization in just about any profession and you can see the Law of the Inner Circle at work. For example, in 1997 baseball's Florida Marlins assembled an awesome group of players together as a team. What was the result? They won the World Series. But once their championship season was over, they began dismantling the team. It was a "fire sale" similar to the one that the San Diego Padres management held in the early 1990s before their team was sold. The result in Florida will be the same as it was in San Diego. Without their key players, their inner circle, the Marlins will fall into the ranks of the mediocre. The potential of the leader—along with the potential of the whole organization—is determined by those closest to him.

> *There are no Lone Ranger leaders. Think about it: If you're alone, you're not leading anybody, are you?*

Knowing what I do about the impact of the Law of the Inner Circle, I am amazed when I meet people who continue to hold up the Lone Ranger as their model for leadership. One of the best illustrations of how unrealistic that ideal of leadership really is can be found in *American Spirit* by Lawrence Miller:

> Problems are always solved in the same way. The Lone Ranger and his faithful Indian companion . . . come riding into town. The Lone Ranger, with his mask and mysterious identity, background, and life-style, never becomes intimate with those whom he will help. His power is partly in his mystique. Within ten

minutes the Lone Ranger has understood the problem, identified who the bad guys are, and has set out to catch them. He quickly outwits the bad guys, draws his gun, and has them behind bars. And then there was always that wonderful scene at the end [where] the helpless victims are standing in front of their ranch or in the town square marveling at how wonderful it is now that they have been saved.[1]

That's baloney. There are no Lone Ranger leaders. Think about it: If you're alone, you're not *leading* anybody, are you?

Leadership expert Warren Bennis was right when he maintained, "The leader finds greatness in the group, and he or she helps the members find it in themselves."[2] Think of any highly effective leader, and you will find someone who surrounded himself with a strong inner circle. My friend Joseph Fisher reminded me of that as he talked about the impact of evangelist Billy Graham. His success has come as the result of a fantastic inner circle: Ruth Bell Graham, Grady Wilson, Cliff Barrows, and George Beverly Shea. They made him better than he ever would have been alone. You could say the same thing of two-term President Ronald Reagan. He was successful because he surrounded himself with good people.

THE BEST DON'T ALWAYS DO THE BEST

At a conference where I was teaching the Law of the Inner Circle, a man named Ashley Randall of Woodbine, Georgia, came up to me during a break and said, "John, you're right about the power of association with good people. I bicycle a lot, and I follow the world-class racers. In endurance bicycle races like the Tour de France, the winner is almost always the person who is racing with the strongest team. They aren't the first to finish every day, but they are always in the first pack to finish each day.

"I've also found that to be true myself," he said. "I've competed in a couple of triathlons, and I can testify that I swim, bike, and run better on the day of the race than I do any other day of training. It's because I am surrounded by people who are swimming, biking, and running at a higher level and doing it with me."

You can tell when a leader has mastered the Law of the Inner Circle. For example, Jack Welch, chairman and CEO of General Electric, doesn't leave to chance the formation of the top inner circles within his organization. Since assuming leadership of GE in 1981, he has personally given his okay to every general manager's circle of executives—that's five hundred positions in all.

THE VALUE OF RAISING UP THE
RIGHT PEOPLE IN YOUR INNER CIRCLE

Under the best circumstances, a leader should try to raise up people for his inner circle from within his organization. Of course, that's not always possible, as my story from Skyline shows. But you can't beat the satisfaction and rewards of bringing up men and women from the "farm team."

Hewlett-Packard manager Ned Barnholt believes there are three groups of people in an organization when it comes to their response to leadership and its impact: (1) those who get it almost immediately and they're off and running with it; (2) those who are skeptical and not sure what to do with it; and (3) another third who start out negative and hope it will go away. "I used to spend most of my time with those who were the most negative," says Barnholt, "trying to convince them to change. Now I spend my time with the people in the first [group]. I'm investing in my best assets"[3] That attitude pays rich dividends in the future.

You may be wondering where you should be spending your time in your organization. You should try to bring five types of people into your inner circle. All of them can add tremendous value to you and your organization.

1. POTENTIAL VALUE—THOSE WHO RAISE UP THEMSELVES

The first ability that every leader must have is the ability to lead and motivate himself. Always keep your eyes open for people with potential.

2. POSITIVE VALUE—THOSE WHO RAISE MORALE IN THE ORGANIZATION

Here is an old poem by Ella Wheeler Wilcox that my mother used to recite to me:

> There are two kinds of people on earth today,
> Just two kinds of people, no more, I say.
> Not the good and the bad, for 'tis well understood
> That the good are half-bad and the bad are half-good.
> No! The two kinds of people on earth I mean
> Are the people who lift and the people who lean.

People who are able to lift up others and boost the morale in an organization are invaluable, and they are always a tremendous asset to a leader's inner circle.

3. PERSONAL VALUE—THOSE WHO RAISE UP THE LEADER

A friend once told me, "It's lonely at the top, so you had better know why you're there." It's true that leaders carry a heavy load. When you're out front, you can be an easy target. But you don't have to go it alone. That's why I say, "It's lonely at the top, so you'd better take someone with you." Who could be better than

> *It's lonely at the top, so you'd better take someone with you.*

someone who lifts you up, not as a yes-man, but as a solid supporter and friend? Solomon of ancient Israel recognized this truth: "As iron sharpens iron, friends sharpen the minds of each other."[4] Seek for your inner circle people who help you improve.

4. PRODUCTION VALUE—THOSE WHO RAISE UP OTHERS

Radio comedian Fred Allen said about television host Ed Sullivan, "He'll be around as long as other people have talent." Though he said it as a joke, there was a lot of wisdom in his comment. Sullivan had an eye for talent and was a master at attracting talented people to his show. Many stand-up comics and musical groups who became famous in the 1960s can trace the beginning of their success back to an appearance on the *Ed Sullivan Show*. For your inner circle, value people capable of raising up others.

5. PROVEN VALUE—THOSE WHO RAISE UP PEOPLE WHO RAISE UP OTHER PEOPLE

The greatest value to any leader is someone who can raise up other leaders. That produces multigenerational leadership. (The power of this can be seen in the Law of Explosive Growth.)

NEVER STOP IMPROVING YOUR INNER CIRCLE

In my book *Developing the Leader Within You*, I wrote about how I reviewed my life when I turned forty. I had the desire to keep going to a higher level and to make a greater impact, but I realized that I had leveraged my time as much as I possibly could, and it would have been impossible to sharpen the focus on my priorities any more than it already was. In other words, I could not work harder *or* smarter. That left me only one choice: learning to work through others. That's the day I truly understood the Law of the Inner Circle. Since then, I have been committed to continually developing my inner circle. I hire the best staff I can find, develop them as much as I can, and hand off everything I possibly can.

In 1994, I discovered one of the key members of my inner circle. At the time, INJOY Stewardship Services (ISS), the second company I founded, was about two years old, and it wasn't doing all that well. It was succeeding in fulfilling its mission of capital campaign consulting, but it wasn't growing fast enough, and as a result, it was losing money. It needed a really good leader. Dick Peterson, the president of my first company, already had his hands full with INJOY. And I didn't have the time to lead it myself, with my heavy speaking schedule, a church of 3,500 (including a staff of forty), and a family with two kids in high school.

> *Hire the best staff you can find, develop them as much as you can, and hand off everything you possibly can to them.*

At that time, Dick and I decided to go to Seattle to seek advice from Dave Sutherland, an IBM executive with a remarkable marketing background, an intuitive leadership ability, and one of the finest strategic minds I've ever encountered. I already knew Dave casually, and he had some experience interacting with ISS, so he was willing to sit down and talk to me as a favor to a friend. Several weeks prior to the meeting, I filled him in on everything I thought he needed to know, and I asked him to think about what he would do if he were the one trying to take the company to the next level.

As we sat down in my hotel room in Seattle, he started to lay out an incredible strategy for ISS. He believed in our mission because we had helped his church and pastor earlier that year. And he knew exactly what it would take to move the company to the next level. After about thirty minutes, that's when it hit me. *Dave is the guy who can do it.*

"Dave," I said, "I want to hire *you* to run ISS." Dave ignored me and kept communicating the plan to me. About an hour later, I told him again, "Dave, I want to hire you." Again, he ignored me and kept telling Dick and me his plan. Finally, after we had been at it about four hours, I told him again. I said, "Dave, didn't you hear me? I'm telling you that I want to hire you to be the president of ISS. Why are you ignoring me?"

At that point, he finally took my request seriously. I realized that I didn't have much to offer Dave. He was one of the top guys in the country for IBM in its marketing area. And all I had was a small company and a dream. But because of the Law of the Inner Circle, I knew that my potential and that of my organizations would skyrocket if Dave became a part of my team. When I offered to give him my ISS salary if he came on board, he finally realized how serious I was. And though it meant taking a big pay cut, Dave took the job.

Today, ISS is the fastest growing company of its type and the second largest capital campaign consulting firm in the United States. It has gone to a whole new level, thanks to Dave Sutherland. And not only that, Dave brings his strategic thinking and marketing savvy to the table for all four of my companies.

Dave Sutherland is only one of a dozen or so key players that I've added to my inner circle. I've been strategically building that group for more than ten years—ever since my fortieth birthday. Dave is joined by INJOY President Dick Peterson and longtime colleagues Dan Reiland and Tim Elmore, who feel like my right and left hands when it comes to creating resources for leaders. The three of them have been with me for well over a decade. Other more recent additions include Ron McManus and Chris Fryer, my other two company presidents. My assistant, Linda Eggers, does the impossible with my calendar and organizational needs every day, while Charlie Wetzel, my writer, makes it possible for me to keep producing books despite my demanding schedule. Up-and-coming leaders like young managers Dave Johnson, Kevin Small, and Larry Figueroa are also helping INJOY make an incredible impact. And of course, I can't forget my good buddy Jim Dornan, my brother, Larry Maxwell, and my best friend in the whole world, Margaret, my wife.

Lee Iacocca says that success comes not from what you know, but from who you know and how you present yourself to each of those people. There is a lot of truth in that. I must say that I'm blessed with an incredible team. But I'm not finished yet. I'll continue building and adding good people for another decade and longer. You see, I know I have more potential that I haven't yet reached, and if I want someday to get there, I've got to surround myself with the best people possible. That's the only way it will ever happen. That's the Law of the Inner Circle.

THE LAW OF EMPOWERMENT

Only Secure Leaders Give Power to Others

Just about everybody has heard of Henry Ford. He was the revolutionary innovator in the automobile industry and a legend in American business history. In 1903, he cofounded the Ford Motor Company with the belief that the future of the automobile lay in putting it within the reach of the average American. Ford said,

> I will build a motorcar for the multitude. It will be large enough for the family but small enough for the individual to run and care for. It will be constructed of the best materials, by the best men to be hired, after the simplest designs that modern engineering can devise. But it will be so low in price that no man making a good salary will be unable to own one—and enjoy with his family the blessings of hours of pleasure in God's great open spaces.

Henry Ford carried out that vision with the Model T, and it changed the face of twentieth-century American life. By 1914,

Ford was producing nearly 50 percent of all automobiles in the United States. The Ford Motor Company looked like an American success story.

A LESS-KNOWN CHAPTER OF THE STORY

However, all of Ford's story is not about positive achievement, and one of the reasons was that he didn't embrace the Law of Empowerment. Henry Ford was so in love with his Model T that he never wanted to change or improve it—nor did he want anyone else to tinker with it. One day when a group of his designers surprised him by presenting him with the prototype of an improved model, Ford ripped its doors off the hinges and proceeded to destroy the car with his bare hands.

For almost twenty years, the Ford Motor Company offered only one design, the Model T, which Ford had personally developed. It wasn't until 1927 that he finally—grudgingly—agreed to offer a new car to the public. The company produced the Model A, but it was incredibly far behind its competitors in technical innovations. Despite its early head start and the incredible lead over its competitors, the Ford Motor Company's market share kept shrinking. By 1931, it was down to only 28 percent.

Henry Ford was the antithesis of an empowering leader. He always seemed to undermine his leaders and look over the shoulders of his people. He even created a sociological department within Ford Motor Company to check up on his employees and direct their private lives. And as time went by, he became more and more eccentric. He once went into his accounting office and tossed the company's books into the street, saying, "Just put all the money we take in in [*sic*] a big barrel and when a shipment of material comes in reach into the barrel and take out enough money to pay for it." He also devoted more and more of his time and money to pet projects, such as growing and experimenting with hundreds of varieties of soybeans.

Perhaps Ford's most peculiar dealings were with his executives, especially his son Edsel. The younger Ford had worked at the company since he was a boy. As Henry became more eccentric, Edsel worked harder to keep the company going. If it weren't for Edsel, the Ford Motor Company probably would have gone out of business in the 1930s. Henry eventually gave Edsel the presidency of the company and publicly said that Ford Motor Company's future looked bright with his leadership. Yet at the same time he undermined him and backed other leaders within the organization. Anytime a promising leader rose up in the company, Henry tore him down. As a result, the company kept losing its best executives. The few who stayed did so because of Edsel. They figured that someday old Henry would die, and Edsel would finally take over and set things right. But that's not what happened. In 1943, Edsel died at age forty-nine.

ANOTHER HENRY FORD

Edsel's oldest son, the twenty-six-year-old Henry Ford II, quickly left the navy so that he could return to Dearborn, Michigan, and take over the company. At first, he faced opposition from his grandfather's entrenched followers. But within two years, he gathered the support of several key people, received the backing of the board of directors (his mother controlled 41 percent of Ford Motor Company's stock), and convinced his grandfather to step down so that he could become president in his place.

Young Henry was taking over a company that hadn't made a profit in fifteen years. At that time, it was losing $1 million *a day!* The young president knew he was in over his head, so he began looking for leaders. Fortunately, the first group actually approached him. It was a team of ten men, headed by Colonel Charles "Tex" Thornton, who had decided they wanted to work together following their service at the War Department during World War II. Their contribution to Ford Motor Company was substantial. In the years to come, the group produced six company vice presidents and two presidents.

The second influx of leadership came with the entrance of Ernie Breech, an experienced General Motors executive and the former president of Bendix Aviation. Young Henry hired him to be Ford's executive vice president. Although Breech held a position second to Henry's, the expectation was that he would take command and turn the company around. And he did. Breech quickly brought in more than 150 outstanding executives from General Motors, and by 1949, Ford Motor Company was on a roll again. In that year, the company sold more than a million Fords, Mercurys, and Lincolns—the best sales since the Model A.

WHO'S THE BOSS?

If Henry Ford II had lived by the Law of Empowerment, the Ford Motor Company might have grown enough to eventually overtake General Motors and become the number one car company again. But only secure leaders are able to give power to others. Henry felt threatened. The success of Tex Thornton, Ernie Breech, and Lewis Crusoe, a legendary GM executive Breech had brought into the company, made Henry worry about his own place at Ford. His position was based not on influence but on his name and his family's control of company stock.

So Henry began pitting one top executive against another. He would invite Thornton to his office and encourage him to criticize fellow executive Crusoe. After a while, Crusoe got fed up with Thornton's insubordination and demanded that Breech fire him, which he did. Then Ford started backing Crusoe, who worked for Breech. Ford biographers Peter Collier and David Horowitz described the second Henry Ford's method this way:

Henry's instinct for survival manifested itself as craftiness combined with a kind of weakness. He had endowed Crusoe with the power to do virtually what ever he wished. By withdrawing his grace from Breech and bestowing it on his lieutenant, he had made antagonists of the two men most vital to Ford's success. While Henry had lost confidence in Breech, however, he had left him officially in charge because this increased his own maneuverability. And, as Crusoe's official superior, Breech could be useful if Henry wanted to keep Crusoe in check.[1]

> *"The best executive is the one who has sense enough to pick good men to do what he wants done, and self-restraint enough to keep from meddling with them while they do it."*
> —*Theodore Roosevelt*

This became a pattern in the leadership of Henry Ford II. Anytime an executive gained power and influence, Henry undercut the person's authority by moving him to a position with less clout, supporting the executive's subordinates, or publicly humiliating him. This continued all the days Henry II was at Ford. As one Ford president, Lee Iacocca, commented after leaving the company, "Henry Ford, as I would learn firsthand, had a nasty habit of getting rid of strong leaders."

IF YOU CAN'T LEAD 'EM . . .

Iacocca said that Henry Ford II once described his leadership philosophy to him, years before Iacocca himself became its target. Ford said, "If a guy works for you, don't let him get too comfortable. Don't let him get cozy or set in his ways. Always do the opposite of what he expects. Keep your people anxious and off-balance."[2]

Both Henry Fords failed to abide by the Law of Empowerment. Rather than finding leaders, building them up, giving them resources, authority, and responsibility, and then turning them loose to achieve, they alternately encouraged and undermined their best people because of their own insecurity. But if you want to be successful as a leader, you have to be an empowerer. Theodore Roosevelt realized that, "the best executive is the one who has sense enough to pick good men to do what he wants done, and the self-restraint enough to keep from meddling with them while they do it."

BARRIERS TO EMPOWERMENT

Leadership analysts Lynne McFarland, Larry Senn, and John Childress affirm that "the empowerment leadership model shifts away from 'position power' where all people are given leadership roles so they can contribute to their fullest capacity."[3] Only empowered people can reach their potential. When a leader can't or won't empower others, he creates barriers within the organization that people cannot overcome. If the barriers remain long enough, then the people give up, or they move to another organization where they can maximize their potential.

> *The people's capacity to achieve is determined by their leader's ability to empower.*

Why do some leaders violate the Law of Empowerment? Consider some common reasons:

DESIRE FOR JOB SECURITY

The number one enemy of empowerment is the desire for job security. A weak leader worries that if he helps subordinates, he will become dispensable. But the truth is that the only way to make yourself indispensable is to make yourself dispensable. In other words, if you are able to continually empower others and help them develop so that they become capable of taking over your job, you will become so valuable to the organization that you become indispensable. That's a paradox of the Law of Empowerment.

> *The only way to make yourself indispensable is to make yourself dispensable.*

RESISTANCE TO CHANGE

Nobel Prize–winning author John Steinbeck asserted, "It is the nature of man as he grows older to protest against change, particularly change for the better." By its very nature, empowerment brings constant change because it encourages people to grow and innovate. Change is the price of progress.

LACK OF SELF-WORTH

Many people gain their personal value and esteem from their work or position. Threaten to change either of them, and you threaten their self-worth. On the other hand, author Buck Rogers says, "To those who have confidence in themselves, change is a stimulus because they believe one person can make a difference and influence what goes on around them. These people are the doers and motivators." They are also the empowerers.

LEADING BY LIFTING UP OTHERS

Only secure leaders are able to give themselves away. Mark Twain once remarked that great things can happen when you don't care who gets the credit. But you can take that a step farther. I believe the greatest things happen *only* when you give others the credit. That's the Law of Empowerment in action. One-time vice presidential candidate Admiral James B. Stockdale declared, "Leadership must be based on goodwill . . . It means obvious and wholehearted commitment to helping followers . . . What we need for leaders are men of heart who are so helpful that they, in effect, do away with the need of their jobs.

But leaders like that are never out of a job, never out of followers. Strange as it sounds, great leaders gain authority by giving it away."

One of the greatest leaders of this nation was truly gifted at giving his power and authority to others. His name was Abraham Lincoln. The depth of Lincoln's security as a leader can be seen in the selection of his cabinet. Most presidents pick like-minded allies. But not Lincoln. At a time of turmoil for the country when disparate voices were many, Lincoln brought together a group of leaders who would unify his party and bring strength through diversity and mutual challenge. One Lincoln biographer said this of his method:

> *The greatest things happen only when you give others the credit.*

For a President to select a political rival for a cabinet post was not unprecedented; but deliberately to surround himself with all of his disappointed antagonists seemed to be courting disaster. It was a mark of his sincere intentions that Lincoln wanted the advice of men as strong as himself or stronger. That he entertained no fear of being crushed or overridden by such men revealed either surpassing naïveté or a tranquil confidence in his powers of leadership.[4]

Lincoln lived the Law of Empowerment. His security enabled him to give his power away.

FINDING STRONG LEADERS TO EMPOWER

Lincoln's ability to empower played a major role in his relationship with his generals during the Civil War. In the beginning, he had trouble finding worthy recipients of his confidence. When the Southern states seceded, the finest generals in the land went south to serve the Confederacy. But Lincoln never lost hope, nor did he neglect to give his leaders power and freedom, even when that strategy had failed with previous generals.

For example, in June of 1863, Lincoln put the command of the Army of the Potomac into the hands of General George G. Meade. Lincoln hoped that he would do a better job than had preceding generals Ambrose E. Burnside and Joseph Hooker. Within hours of Meade's appointment, Lincoln sent a courier to him. The president's message, in part, said,

> Considering the circumstances, no one ever received a more important command; and I cannot doubt that you will fully justify the confidence which the Government has reposed in you. You will not be hampered by any minute instructions from these headquarters. Your army is free to act as you may deem proper under the circumstances as they arise . . . All forces within the sphere of your operations will be held subject to your orders.[5]

As it turned out, Meade's first significant challenge came as he commanded the army at a small Pennsylvania town named Gettysburg. It was a test he passed with authority. In the end, though, Meade was not the general who would make full use of the power Lincoln offered. It took Ulysses S. Grant to turn the war around. But Meade stopped Lee's army when it counted, and he prevented the Confederate general from moving on Washington.

Lincoln's use of the Law of Empowerment was as consistent as Henry Ford's habit of breaking it. Even when his generals performed poorly, Lincoln took the blame. Lincoln expert Donald T. Phillips acknowledged, "Throughout the war Lincoln continued to accept public responsibility for battles lost or opportunities missed."[6]

> *To push people down, you have to go down with them.*

Lincoln was able to stand strongly during the war and continually give power to others because of his rock-solid security.

THE POWER OF EMPOWERMENT

A key to empowering others is high belief in people. I feel I've been fortunate because believing in others has always been very easy for me. I recently received a note from the one person, outside my family, whom I have worked hardest to empower. His name is Dan Reiland. He was my executive pastor when I was at Skyline, and today he is the vice president for leadership development at INJOY. Dan wrote,

John,

The ultimate in mentoring has come to pass. I am being asked to teach on the topic of empowerment! I can do this only because you first empowered me. The day is still crystal clear in my mind when you took a risk and chose me as your Executive Pastor. You trusted me with significant responsibility, the day to day leadership of the staff and ministries of your church. You released me with authority . . . You believed in me—perhaps more than I believed in myself. You demonstrated your faith and confidence in me in such a way that I could tap into your belief, and eventually it became my own . . .

I am so very grateful for your life-changing impact on my life. Saying thank you hardly touches it. "I love and appreciate you" is better. Perhaps the best way I can show my gratitude is to pass on the gift you have given me to other leaders in my life.

Dan

I am grateful to Dan for all he has done for me, and I believe he has returned to me much more than I have given to him. And I've genuinely enjoyed the time I've spent with Dan helping him grow. The truth is that empowerment is powerful—not only for the person being developed, but also for the mentor. Enlarging others makes you larger. Dan has made me better than I am, not just because he helped me achieve much more than I could have done on my own, but also because the whole process made me a better leader. That is the impact of the Law of Empowerment.

13

THE LAW OF REPRODUCTION

It Takes a Leader to Raise Up a Leader

This year in my leadership conferences, I've been taking time to conduct an informal poll to find out what prompted the men and women who attend to become leaders. The results of the survey are as follows:

HOW THEY BECAME LEADERS

Natural Gifting	10 percent
Result of Crisis	5 percent
Influence of Another Leader	85 percent

If you've ever given much thought to the origins of leadership, then you're probably not surprised by those figures. It's true that a few people step into leadership because their organization experiences a crisis, and they are compelled to do something about it. Another small group is comprised of people with such great natural gifting and instincts that they are able to navigate their way into leadership on their own. But more than four out of five of all the leaders that you ever meet will have emerged as leaders because of the impact made on them by established leaders who mentored them. That happens because of the Law of Reproduction: It takes a leader to raise up a leader.

MANY FOLLOW IN THEIR FOOTSTEPS

Of the people I surveyed, about one-third are leaders in the business world and two-thirds are leaders in churches. But the responses will be similar in just about any field. For instance, you will find the Law of Reproduction at work in professional football. Let me ask you this: Did you know that the development and mentoring of half of the head coaches in the NFL (in 1998) can be traced to two outstanding former pro football leaders—Bill Walsh and Tom Landry? Ten current NFL head coaches spent a year or longer working for three-time Super Bowl–champion Bill Walsh or for one of the top assistants he trained. And five NFL coaches have a direct or indirect mentoring connection with two-time Super Bowl–winner Tom Landry or one of the men he trained.

Just about every successful coach in the NFL has spent time working with another strong leader who helped to teach and model for him. In addition to the ones with a Walsh or Landry connection, there are other NFL examples: Dave Wannstedt worked for two-time Super Bowl–champion Jimmy Johnson, and head coaches Bill Cowher and Tony Dungy spent significant time working with Marty Schottenheimer of the Kansas City Chiefs. It takes a leader to raise up a leader.

SOME DO IT, SOME DON'T

In the chapter on the Law of Respect, I explained that people naturally follow leaders stronger than themselves. In the same way, only leaders

CURRENT NFL HEAD COACHES TRACED TO THE LEADERSHIP OF 49ERS COACH BILL WALSH

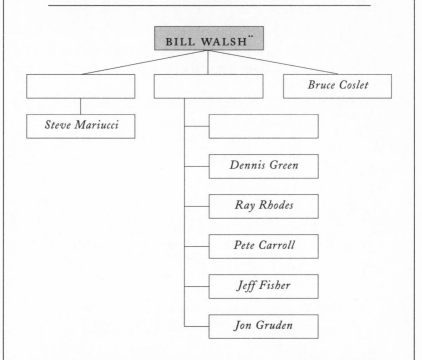

CURRENT NFL HEAD COACHES TRACED TO THE LEADERSHIP OF COWBOYS COACH TOM LANDRY

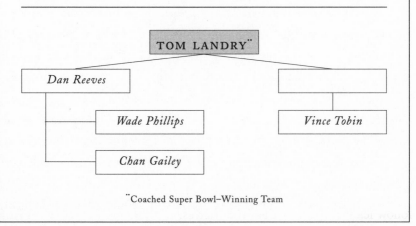

"Coached Super Bowl–Winning Team

are capable of developing other leaders. People cannot give to others what they themselves do not possess. Followers simply cannot develop leaders. But just because a person is a leader, it does not necessarily mean that he will raise up other leaders. For every Bill Walsh, George Seifert, or Tom Landry, there is a Vince Lombardi—a person who is a great coach and leader in his own right, but who doesn't raise up other great coaches to follow in his footsteps.

> *People cannot give to others what they themselves do not possess. Followers simply cannot develop leaders.*

Why don't all leaders develop others? There are many reasons. Sometimes they just don't recognize the tremendous *value* of developing leaders. (I'll talk more about that value in the chapter on the Law of Explosive Growth.) Others may focus so much attention on their followers and give them so much that they don't have anything left for their key staff. I suspect that was the case with Vince Lombardi. For other leaders the real problem may be insecurity. Remember what the Law of Empowerment teaches: Only secure leaders give power to others.

As a kid, did you ever play follow the leader? I know I did. Even then I wanted to be the leader. Do you remember what you had to do to stay in front in that game? You purposely tried to get your followers to make mistakes. That's what sent them to the back of the line. The same thing was true when playing the game of horse on the basketball court. You made your shots so hard that others couldn't possibly duplicate them. And if you were like me, you had a special home-court, failsafe shot that no other kid could make, and you used it to put the game away. The problem with the old follow-the-leader games is that to win, you had to make the other guy lose. That's opposite of the way you raise up leaders.

Last year as I conducted a leadership conference in Jakarta,

Indonesia, I taught the Law of Reproduction and talked about the follow-the-leader game. I asked a volunteer to come up so that I could show visually what happens when a leader tries to keep others down instead of raising them up. I had the volunteer stand in front of me, and I put my hands on his shoulders. Then I began pushing him down. The lower I wanted to push him, the more I had to bend down to do it. The lower I wanted him to go, the lower I had to go. That's the same way it is in leadership: to keep others down, you have to go down with them.

RAISING UP GIANT KILLERS

One of my favorite stories that illustrates the Law of Reproduction is about David of ancient Israel. Just about everyone has heard the story of David and Goliath. When the armies of the Philistines faced off against King Saul and the people of Israel, Goliath, a large, powerful professional warrior, laid out a challenge. He said he'd fight Israel's greatest champion in a winner-take-all battle. And who stepped forward to accept the challenge? Not Saul, the mighty king, or any of his seasoned veterans. David, a lowly shepherd boy, stood to face him, and using a sling, he hurled a rock at Goliath, knocked him out, and then cut the big warrior's head off with Goliath's own sword.

We all identify with a story like that because we like to cheer for the underdog. But many people don't know the rest of the story. David grew up to be a warrior and eventually became king. But along the way, he raised up a group of great warriors who were called his "mighty men." No fewer than five of them also became giant killers, just like their leader. Had Saul, the previous king, done that? No. It took a person who had done it himself. And just as it takes a giant killer to produce other giant killers, it takes a leader to raise up other leaders.

WE TEACH WHAT WE KNOW—
WE REPRODUCE WHAT WE ARE

I was very fortunate growing up because I lived in the household of a leader: my father, Melvin Maxwell. Every day of my early life, I learned lessons about working with people, understanding priorities, developing myself through a personal growth plan, and paying the price of leadership. Some of what I learned came from his teaching. But even more of it came from being around him, watching him interact with others, and learning how he thought. As a result, by the time I went to college, I already had pretty good intuition and understood leadership better than most of my peers did. Since then, I've continued to learn about leadership. And I've sought out great leaders to mentor me so that I can keep learning.

> *Just as it takes a giant killer to produce other giant killers, it takes a leader to raise up other leaders.*

If you want to continue developing as a leader, you should do the same. Spend time with the best leaders you can find. If you're just starting out, you may want to spend time with people in your field so that you can master the basics of your profession. But once you have that foundation, learn leadership from people in many professions. I've learned from businesspeople, pastors, politicians, generals, ballplayers, entrepreneurs—you name it. No matter what the profession, the principles of leadership remain the same.

Not everyone understands that immediately. For example, several years ago when I told my brother, Larry, that I was going to start spending more time teaching leadership in the corporate world, he was a little skeptical. Larry is a natural businessman. He achieved financial independence in real estate by the time he was in his twenties, and he sits on several corporate boards and is a trustee of one university. But he wasn't sure if businesspeople would be receptive to learning leadership from someone with a pastoral background. But I knew that leadership is leadership; the principles apply no matter where you are. And sure enough, when I started teaching leadership to organizations such as Sam's Club, Wal-Mart, Mary Kay, and Baillie Lumber—and the people saw that the principles worked—they kept asking for more. Why would such big companies seek advice from someone who leads four small companies? Because they understand the Law of Reproduction. They know that it takes a leader to raise up other leaders—no matter the field.

TAKE THE NEXT STEP

The only way you will be able to develop other leaders is to become a better leader yourself. If you've already taken those first steps, you are to be commended. You're in a position to begin raising up other leaders. As you get started, keep in mind that leaders who develop leaders . . .

SEE THE BIG PICTURE

Every effective leadership mentor makes the development of leaders one of his highest priorities in life. He knows that the potential of the organization depends on the growth of its leadership. The more leaders there are, the greater its chance of success.

ATTRACT POTENTIAL LEADERS

You've probably heard the Ross Perot quote: "Leaders don't flock. You have to find them one at a time." That's true. But as the Law of Magnetism also suggests, if you first develop your leadership qualities, you will be capable of attracting people with leadership potential. When you do that and also earn their respect, you will get the opportunity to develop them into better leaders.

CREATE AN EAGLE ENVIRONMENT

An environment where leadership is valued and taught becomes an asset to a leadership mentor. It not only attracts "eagles," but it also helps them learn to fly. An eagle environment is one where the leader casts a vision, offers incentives, encourages creativity, allows risks, and provides accountability. Do that long enough with enough people, and you'll develop a leadership culture where eagles begin to flock.

THE IMPACT CARRIES OVER

Once you understand the Law of Reproduction, you recognize its incredible impact on an organization. If a company has poor leaders, what little leadership it has will only get worse. If a company has strong leaders—and they are reproducing themselves—then the leadership just keeps getting better and better.

Occasionally, a company will emerge where the leadership is so strong and the development process is so deliberate that the impact not only drives that organization to the highest level, but it also over-flows into other businesses. That is the case at General Electric, led by chairman Jack Welch. GE has become one of the best-run companies in the world, and it keeps developing leader upon leader. In fact, the company has *lost* more leaders capable of running organizations than most other good companies are able to produce in their lifetimes. Scan this list of CEOs who once worked at GE:

> William Anders, *General Dynamics*
> Norman P. Blake Jr., *USF&G*
> Larry A. Bossidy, *Allied-Signal Inc.*
> Michael J. Emmi, *Systems and Computer Technology*
> Stanley C. Gault, *Rubbermaid Inc.*, and later,
>   *Goodyear Tire and Rubber Corp.*

Fred Garry, *late chief executive of Rohr Inc.*
Robert Goldsmith, *former chief executive, Rohr Inc.*
Glen Hiner, *Owens Corning Fiberglass*
Clyde Keaton, *Clean Harbors*
Chuck Lillis, *MediaOne Group*
  (formerly *U.S. West Media Group*)
Michael Lockhart, *General Signal Corp.*
Daniel McClaughlin, *Equifax*
Richard Miller, *Wang Laboratories*
George Schofield, *Zurn Industries*
Roger Shipke, *Ryland Group Inc.*
Harry C. Stonecipher, *Sunstrand,* and later,
  McDonnell Douglas Corp.
John M. Trani, *Stanley Works*
Walter Williams, *Rubbermaid*
Thomas Vanderslice, *president of GTE,* then *CEO for*
  Apollo Computer, and then *CEO of M/A Com,*
  which produces microwave components
Alva O. Way, *American Express Co.*

Just as in the world of pro football, the ability of many leaders can be traced to a common source. How was General Electric able to produce so many outstanding leaders? First, leadership development is one of the company's highest priorities. It spends more than $500 million a year on training and develops leaders at its own institute in Crotonville, often called "the Harvard of corporate America."[1] But even more important than that is the fact that the company is run by a great leader, Jack Welch.

It all starts at the top because it takes a leader to raise up another leader. Followers can't do it. Neither can institutional programs. It takes one to know one, show one, and grow one. That's the Law of Reproduction.

14

THE LAW OF BUY-IN

People Buy Into the Leader, Then the Vision

I N THE FALL OF 1997, a few members of my staff and I had the opportunity to travel to India and teach four leadership conferences. India is an amazing country, full of contradictions. It's a place of beauty with warm and generous people, yet at the same time millions and millions of its inhabitants live in the worst poverty imaginable. It was there that I was reminded of the Law of Buy-In.

I'll never forget when our plane landed in Delhi. Exiting the airport, I felt as if we had been transported to another planet. There were crowds everywhere. People on bicycles, in cars, on camels and elephants. People on the streets, some sleeping right on the sidewalks. Animals roamed free, no matter where we were. And everything was in motion. As we drove along the main street toward our hotel, I also noticed something else. Banners. Wherever we looked, we could see banners celebrating India's fifty years of liberty, along with huge pictures of one man: Mahatma Gandhi.

Today, people take for granted that Gandhi was a great leader. But the story of his leadership is a marvelous study in the Law of Buy-In.

Mohandas K. Gandhi, called Mahatma (which means "great soul"), was educated in London. After finishing his education in law, he traveled back to India and then to South Africa. There he worked for twenty years as a barrister and political activist. And in that time he developed as a leader, fighting for the rights of Indians and other minorities who were oppressed and discriminated against by South Africa's apartheid government.

By the time he returned to India in 1914, Gandhi was very well known and highly respected among his countrymen. Over the next several years, as he led protests and strikes around the country, people rallied to him and looked to him more and more for leadership. In 1920—a mere six years after returning to India—he was elected president of the All India Home Rule League.

The most remarkable thing about Gandhi isn't that he became their leader, but that he was able to change the people's vision for obtaining freedom. Before he began leading them, the people used violence in an effort to achieve their goals. For years riots against the British establishment had been common. But Gandhi's vision for change in India was based on nonviolent civil disobedience. He once said, "Nonviolence is the greatest force at the disposal of mankind. It is mightier than the mightiest weapon of destruction devised by the ingenuity of man."

Gandhi challenged the people to meet oppression with peaceful disobedience and noncooperation. Even when the British military massacred more than one thousand people at Amritsar in 1919, Gandhi called the people to stand, but without fighting back. Rallying everyone to his way of thinking wasn't easy. But because the people had come to buy into him as their leader, they embraced his vision. And then they followed him faithfully. He asked them not to fight, and eventually, they stopped fighting. When he called for everyone to burn foreign-made clothes and start wearing nothing but home-spun material, millions of people started doing it. When he decided that a March to the Sea to protest the Salt Act would be their rallying point for civil disobedience against the British, the nation's leaders followed him the two hundred miles to the city of Dandi, where they were arrested by government representatives.

> *The leader finds the dream and then the people. The people find the leader and then the dream.*

Their struggle for independence was slow and painful, but Gandhi's leadership was strong enough to deliver on the promise of his vision. In 1947, India gained home rule. Because the people had bought into Gandhi, they accepted his vision. And once they had embraced the vision, they were able to carry it out. That's how the Law of Buy-In works. The leader finds the dream and then the people. The people find the leader, and then the dream.

DON'T PUT THE CART FIRST

When I teach leadership seminars, I field a lot of questions about vision. Invariably someone will come up to me during a break, give me a brief description of an evolving vision, and ask me, "Do you think my people will buy into my vision?" My response is always the same: "First tell me this. Do your people buy into you?"

You see, many people who approach the area of vision in leadership have it all backward. They believe that if the cause is good enough, people will automatically buy into it and follow. But that's not how leadership really works. People don't at first follow worthy causes. They follow worthy leaders who promote worthwhile causes. People buy into the leader first, then the leader's vision. Having an understanding of that changes your whole approach to leading people.

For the person who attends one of my conferences and asks whether his people will follow, the question really becomes, "Have I given my people reasons to buy into me?" If his answer is yes, they will gladly buy into his vision. But if he has not built his credibility with his people, it really doesn't matter how great a vision he has.

> *People don't at first follow worthy causes. They follow worthy leaders who promote worthwhile causes.*

Not long ago I was reading an article in *Business Week* that profiled entrepreneurs who partner with venture capitalists in the computer industry. Silicon Valley in California is evidently full of people who work in the computer industry for a while and then try to start their own companies. Every day hundreds of them are buzzing around trying to find investors so that they can get their ideas and enterprises off the ground. Many are unsuccessful. But if an entrepreneur succeeds once, then he finds it pretty easy to find money the next time around. Many times, the investors aren't even interested in finding out what the entrepreneur's vision is. If they've bought into the person, then they readily accept the ideas.

For example, software entrepreneur Judith Estrin and her partner have founded two companies over the years. She said that funding her first company took six months and countless presentations, even though she had a viable idea and believed in it 100 percent. But the start-up of her second company happened almost overnight. It took only two phone calls that lasted mere minutes for her to land $5 million in backing. When the word got out that she was starting her second company, people were dying to give her even more money. She said, "We had venture capitalists calling us and begging us to take their money."[1] Why had everything changed so drastically for her? Because of the Law of Buy-In. People had bought into her, so they were ready to buy into whatever vision she offered, sight unseen.

YOU ARE THE MESSAGE

Every message that people receive is filtered through the messenger who delivers it. If you consider the messenger to be credible, then you believe the message has value. That's one of the reasons actors and athletes are hired as promoters of products. People buy Nike shoes because they have bought into Michael Jordan, not necessarily because of the quality of the shoes. The same is true when actors promote causes. Have the actors being employed suddenly become experts in the cause they're promoting? Usually not. But that doesn't matter. People want to listen to Charlton Heston as he speaks for the NRA, not because they believe he is an expert in the field of hunting or guns, but because they believe in him as a

> *People want to go along with people they get along with.*

person and because he has credibility as an actor. Once people have bought into someone, they are willing to give his vision a chance. People want to go along with people they get along with.

IT'S NOT AN EITHER/OR PROPOSITION

You cannot separate the leader from the cause he promotes. It cannot be done, no matter how hard you try. It's not an either/or proposition. The two always go together. Take a look at the following table. It shows how people react to a leader and his vision under different circumstances:

LEADER +	VISION =	RESULT
Don't Buy In	*Don't Buy In*	*Get Another Leader*
Don't Buy In	*Buy In*	*Get Another Leader*
Buy In	*Don't Buy In*	*Get Another Vision*
Buy In	*Buy In*	*Get Behind the Leader*

WHEN FOLLOWERS DON'T LIKE THE LEADER OR THE VISION, THEY LOOK FOR ANOTHER LEADER

It's easy to understand the reaction of people when they don't like the leader or the vision. They don't follow. But they also do something else: They start looking for another leader. It's a no-win situation.

WHEN FOLLOWERS DON'T LIKE THE LEADER BUT THEY DO LIKE THE VISION, THEY STILL LOOK FOR ANOTHER LEADER

You may be surprised by this. Even though people may think a cause is good, if they don't like the leader, they will go out and find another one. That's one reason that coaches change teams so often in professional sports. The vision for any team always stays the same: Everyone wants to win a championship. But the players don't always believe in their leader. And when they don't, what happens? The owners don't fire all of the players. They fire the leader and bring in someone they hope the players will buy into.

WHEN FOLLOWERS LIKE THE LEADER BUT NOT THE VISION, THEY CHANGE THE VISION

Even when people don't like a leader's vision, if they've already bought into him, they will keep following him. You often see this response in politics. For example, in the past, the National Organization of Women (NOW) has spoken out strongly against sexual harassment. But recently when Paula Jones accused President Clinton of sexually harassing her, NOW continued to support him. Why? It's not because the members suddenly think sexual harassment is acceptable. They have chosen to put their agenda on hold in order to keep supporting the leader they've already bought into.

When followers don't agree with their leader's vision, they react in many ways. Sometimes they work to convince their leader to change his vision. Sometimes they abandon their point of view and adopt his. Other times they find a compromise. But as long as they still buy into the leader, they won't out-and-out reject him. They will keep following.

WHEN FOLLOWERS LIKE THE LEADER AND THE VISION, THEY WILL GET BEHIND BOTH

They will follow their leader no matter how bad conditions get or how much the odds are stacked against them. That's why the Indian people in Gandhi's day refused to fight back as soldiers mowed them down. That's what inspired the U.S. space program to fulfill John F. Kennedy's vision and put a man on the moon. That's the reason people continued to have hope and keep alive the dream of Martin Luther King Jr., even after he was gunned down. That's what continues to inspire followers to keep running the race, even when they feel they've hit the wall and given everything they've got.

As a leader, having a great vision and a worthy cause is not enough to get people to follow you. First you have to become a better leader; you must get your people to buy into *you*. That is the price you have to pay if you want your vision to have a chance of becoming a reality.

BUYING TIME FOR PEOPLE TO BUY IN

If in the past you tried to get your people to act on your vision but were unable to make it happen, you probably came up against the Law of Buy-In, maybe without even knowing it. I first recognized the importance of the Law of Buy-In in 1972 when I accepted my second leadership position. In the chapter on the Law of Navigation, I mentioned that after I had been at that church several years, I took them through a multimillion-dollar construction program in which we built a new auditorium. But when I first got there, that was not the direction that the congregation had wanted to go.

The week before I arrived at my new church, more than 65 percent of the members had voted in favor of building a new activity center. Now, I had done some homework on that church, and I knew coming in that its future growth and success depended not on a new activity center, but on a new auditorium. My vision for the years ahead was absolutely clear to me. But I couldn't walk in and say, "Forget the decision you just made and all the agonizing you did to make it. Follow me instead." I needed to buy some time to build my credibility with the people.

I arranged for a committee to make a thorough study of all the issues involved with the activity center project. I told the members, "If we're going to invest this kind of time and money, we have to be sure about it. I must have information on every possible issue related to it." That seemed fair enough to everyone, and off the committee went to work. For the next year, the group would come back to me every month or so and report on the information gathered. And each time I'd praise their work and ask several questions that would prompt them to do more research.

In the meantime, I worked hard to build my credibility with the people. I forged relationships with the leaders in the church. I answered everybody's questions so that they could understand me and how I thought as a leader. I shared my ideas, hopes, and dreams for the work we were doing. And I started to produce growth in the organization. That, more than anything else, gave the people confidence in me and my ability.

After about six months, the people started to see that the church was changing and beginning to move in a new direction. In a year, the building committee decided that the activity center was not in the church's best interest, and they recommended that we not build it. In another year, the people had reached consensus: The key to the future was the building of a new auditorium. And when the time came, 98 percent of the people voted yes on the issue, and off we went.

When I arrived at that church, I could have tried to push my vision and agenda on the people. I was just as sure that it was the right thing to do in 1972 as I was two years later when we implemented it. But if I had approached it in that way, I wouldn't have succeeded in helping those people get where they needed to go. And in the process I would have undermined my ability to lead them.

As a leader, you don't earn any points for failing in a noble cause. You don't get credit for being "right." Your success is measured by your ability to actually take the people where they need to go. But you can do that only if the people first buy into you as a leader. That's the reality of the Law of Buy-In.

15

THE LAW OF VICTORY

Leaders Find a Way for the Team to Win

HAVE YOU EVER THOUGHT about what separates the leaders who achieve victory from those who suffer defeat? What does it take to be a winner? It's hard to put a finger on the quality that separates a winner from a loser. Every leadership situation is different. Every crisis has its own challenges. But I think that victorious leaders share an inability to accept defeat. The alternative to winning seems totally unacceptable to them, so they figure out what must be done to achieve victory, and then they go after it with everything at their disposal.

> *Victorious leaders feel the alternative to winning is totally unacceptable, so they figure out what must be done to achieve victory, and then they go after it with everything at their disposal.*

I'm a Civil War buff, and I was reading an old book that reminded me of the importance of the Law of Victory. It discussed the differences between the presidents of the Union and the Confederacy: Abraham Lincoln and Jefferson Davis. I've talked quite a bit about

Lincoln throughout *The 21 Irrefutable Laws of Leadership* because he was such a remarkable leader. Lincoln never forgot that the nation's victory was his highest priority, ahead of his pride, reputation, and personal comfort. He surrounded himself with the best leaders possible, empowered his generals, and was never afraid to give others the credit for the victories the Union gained. For example, following General Grant's victory at Vicksburg, Lincoln sent a letter to him saying, "I never had any faith, except the general hope that you knew better than I . . . I now wish to make the personal acknowledgment that you were right and I was wrong."

Jefferson Davis, on the other hand, never seemed to make victory his priority. When he should have been thinking like a revolutionary, he worked like a bureaucrat. When he should have been delegating authority and decision making to his generals—the best in the land—he spent his time micromanaging them. And worst of all, he was more concerned with being right than with winning the war. Historian David M. Potter says of Davis, "He used an excessive share of his energy in contentious and even litigious argument to prove he was right. He seemed to feel that if he were right that was enough; that it was more important to vindicate his own rectitude than to get results."[1] Davis violated the Law of Victory, and as a consequence, his people suffered a devastating defeat.

THESE LEADERS PURSUED VICTORY

Crisis seems to bring out the best—and the worst—in leaders. During World War II, two outstanding leaders who practiced the Law of Victory emerged for the Allies: British Prime Minister Winston Churchill and U.S. President Franklin Roosevelt. They prevented Adolf Hitler from crushing Europe and remaking it according to his own vision.

On his side of the Atlantic Ocean, Winston Churchill inspired the British people to resist Hitler. Long before he became prime minister in 1940, Churchill spoke out against the Nazis. He seemed like the lone critic in 1932 when he warned, "Do not delude yourselves . . . Do not believe that all Germany is asking for is equal status . . . They are looking for weapons and when they have them believe me they will ask for the return of lost territories or colonies."

Churchill continued to speak out against the Nazis. And when Hitler annexed Austria in 1938, Churchill said to members of the House of Commons:

> For five years I have talked to the House on these matters—not with very great success. I have watched this famous island descending incontinently, fecklessly, the stairway which leads to a dark gulf . . . Now is the time at last to rouse the nation. Perhaps it is the last time it can be roused with a chance of preventing war, or with a chance of coming through with victory should our effort to prevent war fail.

Unfortunately, Prime Minister Neville Chamberlain and the other leaders of Great Britain did not make a stand against Hitler. And more of Europe fell to the Nazis.

By mid-1940, most of Europe was under Germany's thumb. But then something happened that might have changed the history of the free world. The leadership of England fell to Winston Churchill. He refused to buckle under the Nazis' threats. For more than a year, Great Britain stood alone facing the threat of German invasion. When Hitler indicated that he wanted to make a deal with England, Churchill defied him. When Germany began bombing England, the British stood strong. And all the while, Churchill looked for a way to gain victory.

CHURCHILL WOULD ACCEPT NOTHING LESS

Time after time, Churchill rallied the British people. It began with his first speech after becoming prime minister:

> We have before us an ordeal of the most grievous kind. We have before us many, many long months of struggle and of suffering. You ask what is our policy? I will say: It is to wage war, by sea, land and air, with all our might and with all the strength that God can give us; to wage war against a monstrous tyranny, never surpassed in the dark, lamentable catalogue of human crime. That is our policy. You ask, What is our aim? I answer in one word: Victory—victory at all costs, victory in spite of all terror, victory, however long and hard the road may be; for without victory, there is no survival.[2]

Meanwhile, Churchill did everything in his power to prevail. He deployed troops in the Mediterranean against Mussolini's forces. Although he hated communism, he allied himself with Stalin and the Soviets, sending them aid even when Great Britain's supplies were threatened and its survival hung in the balance. And he developed his personal relationship with Franklin Roosevelt. Though the president of the United States was reluctant to enter the war, Churchill worked to build his relationship with him, hoping to change it from one of friendship and mutual respect to a full-fledged war alliance. In time his efforts paid off. On the day the Japanese bombed Pearl Harbor, ushering the United States into the war, Churchill said to himself, "So we have won after all."

> *"What is our aim? I answer in one word: Victory—victory at all costs, victory in spite of all terror, victory, however long and hard the road may be; for without victory, there is no survival."*
> —*Winston Churchill*

ANOTHER LEADER DEDICATED TO VICTORY

Prior to December 1941, Franklin Roosevelt had already been practicing the Law of Victory for decades. In fact, it is a hallmark of his entire life. He had found a way to achieve political victory while winning over polio. When he was elected president and became responsible for pulling the American people out of the Great Depression, it was just another impossible situation that he learned how to fight through. And fight he did. Through the 1930s, the country was slowly recovering.

By the time the Nazis were battling in Europe, the stakes were high. Pulitzer Prize–winning historian Arthur Schlesinger Jr., noted, "The Second World War found democracy fighting for its life. By 1941, there were only a dozen or so democratic states left on earth. But great leadership emerged in time to rally the democratic cause." The team of Roosevelt and Churchill provided that leadership like a one-two punch. Just as the prime minister had rallied England, the president brought together the American people and united them in a common cause as no one ever had before or has since.

To those two leaders, victory was the only option. If they had accepted anything less, the world would be a very different place today. Schlesinger says, "Take a look at our present world. It is manifestly not Adolf Hitler's world. His Thousand-Year Reich turned out to have a brief and bloody run of a dozen years. It is manifestly not Joseph Stalin's world. That ghastly world self-destructed before our eyes. Nor is it Winston Churchill's world . . . The world we live in is Franklin Roosevelt's world."[3] Without Churchill and England, all of Europe would have fallen. Without Roosevelt and the United States, it might never have been reclaimed for freedom. But not even an Adolf Hitler and the army of the Third Reich could stand against two leaders dedicated to the Law of Victory.

GREAT LEADERS FIND A WAY TO WIN

When the pressure is on, great leaders are at their best. Whatever is inside them comes to the surface and works for or against them. Just a few years ago, Nelson Mandela was elected president of South Africa. It was a huge victory for the people of that country, but it was a long time coming. The road to that victory was paved with twenty-seven years of Mandela's own life spent in prison. Along the way, he did whatever it took to bring victory one step closer. He joined the African National Congress, which became an outlawed organization. He staged peaceful protests. He went underground and traveled overseas to try to enlist support. When he needed to, he stood trial and accepted a prison sentence, with dignity and courage. And when the time was right, he negotiated changes in the government with

> *When the pressure is on, great leaders are at their best. Whatever is inside them comes to the surface.*

F. W. de Klerk. Today he is working to bring lasting victory by trying to bring healing to the country. Mandela describes himself as "an ordinary man who had become a leader because of extraordinary circumstances."[4] I say he is a leader made extraordinary because of the strength of his character and his dedication to the Law of Victory.

YOU CAN SEE IT EVERY DAY

You can readily see the Law of Victory in action at sporting events. In other areas of life, leaders do most of their work behind the scenes, and you never get to see it. But at a ball game, you can actually watch a leader as he works to achieve victory. And when the final buzzer sounds or the last out is recorded, you know exactly who won and why. Games have immediate and measurable outcomes.

When I want to see the Law of Victory in action, I go to a game and watch someone such as basketball's Michael Jordan. He is an awesome athlete, but he is also an exceptional leader. He lives and breathes the Law of Victory every day. When the game is on the line, Jordan finds a way for the team to win. His biographer, Mitchell Krugel, says that Jordan's tenacity and passion for victory are evident in every part of his life. He even shows it in practice when the Bulls scrimmage. Krugel explains,

> At Bulls' practices, the starters were known as the white team. The second five wore red. [Former Bulls' coach] Loughery had Jordan playing with the white team from his first day. With Jordan and [teammate] Woolridge, the white team easily rolled up leads of 8-1 or 7-4 in games to 11. The loser of these games always had to run extra wind sprints after practice. It was about that time of the scrimmage that Loughery would switch Jordan to the red team. And the red team would wind up winning more often than not.[5]

Early in his career, Jordan relied heavily on his personal talent and efforts to win games. But as he has matured, he has turned his attention more to being a leader and making the whole team play better. Jordan thinks that many people have overlooked that. He once said, "That's what everybody looks at when I miss a game. Can they win without me? . . . Why doesn't anybody ask why or what it is I contribute that makes a difference? I bet nobody would ever say they miss my leadership or my ability to make my teammates better." Yet that is exactly what he provides. Leaders always find a way for the team to win.

Not long ago Michael Jordan did a commercial for Nike in which he recounted some of his failures: "I've missed over 9,000 shots in my career, lost over 300 games. Twenty-six times I took the game-winning shot and missed." I read an interview with Jordan soon after the commercial first aired where a reporter asked Jordan whether he had really missed that many shots. Jordan's response was revealing: "I have no idea." People may be disappointed by that comment, but it offers insight into his personality. Michael Jordan is not dwelling on his past mistakes. What's important to him is what he can do right now to lead his team to victory.

IT DOESN'T MATTER
WHAT "GAME" THEY'RE IN

There are a lot of great athletes in the game of basketball today. But flashy individual play doesn't always bring victory. What's needed more than anything else is leadership. The greatest players of the past had more than individual talent, though that was definitely present. A player such as Boston center Bill Russell, for example, measured his play by whether it helped the whole team play better. And the result was a remarkable eleven NBA titles. Lakers guard Magic Johnson, who was named NBA Most Valuable Player (MVP) three times and won five championships, was an outstanding scorer, but his greatest contribution was his ability to run the team and get the ball into the hands of his teammates. Larry Bird, who made things happen for the Celtics in the 1980s, is remarkable because he exemplified the Law of Victory not only as a player, but also later as the head coach of the Indiana Pacers. When he was playing in Boston, he was named Rookie of the Year, became the MVP three times, and led his team to three NBA championships. In his first year with the Pacers, he was named NBA Coach of the Year after leading his team to its best-winning percentage in the franchise's history.

Good leaders find a way for their teams to win. That's the Law of Victory. Their particular sport is irrelevant. Michael Jordan, Magic Johnson, and Larry Bird did it in the NBA. John Elway did it in football, leading his team to more fourth-quarter victories than any other quarterback in NFL history. Pelé did it in soccer, winning an unprecedented three World Cups for Brazil. Leaders find a way for the team to succeed.

THREE COMPONENTS OF VICTORY

Whether you're looking at a sports team, an army, a business, or a nonprofit organization, victory is possible as long as you have three components:

1. UNITY OF VISION

Teams succeed only when the players have a unified vision, no matter how much talent or potential there is. A team doesn't win the championship if its players have different agendas. That's true in professional sports. It's true in business. It's true in churches.

> *A team doesn't win the championship if its players have different agendas.*

I learned this lesson in high school when I was a junior on the varsity basketball team. We had a very talented group of kids, and we had been picked to win the state championship. But we had a problem. The juniors and seniors on the team refused to work together. It got so bad that the coach eventually gave up trying to get us to play together and divided us into two different squads for our games. In the end the team had miserable results. Why? We didn't share a common vision.

2. DIVERSITY OF SKILLS

It almost goes without saying that the team needs diversity of skills. Can you imagine a whole hockey team of goalies? Or a football team of quarterbacks? It doesn't make sense. In the same way, organizations require diverse talents to succeed, each player taking his part.

3. A LEADER DEDICATED TO VICTORY AND RAISING
PLAYERS TO THEIR POTENTIAL

It's true that having good players with diverse skills is important.

> *"You've got to have great athletes to win, I don't care who the coach is. You can't win without good athletes, but you can lose with them. This is where coaching makes the difference."*
> —*Lou Holtz*

As former Notre Dame head football coach Lou Holtz says, "You've got to have great athletes to win, I don't care who the coach is. You can't win without good athletes, but you can lose with them. This is where coaching makes the difference." In other words, you also require leadership to achieve victory. Unity of vision doesn't happen spontaneously. The right players with the proper diversity of talent don't come together on their own. It takes a leader to make those things happen, and it takes a leader to provide the motivation, empowerment, and direction required to win.

THE LAW OF VICTORY IS HIS BUSINESS

One of the most noteworthy success stories I've come across recently is that of Southwest Airlines and Herb Kelleher, whom I mentioned in the chapter on the Law of Connection. Their story is an admirable example of the Law of Victory in action. Today Southwest looks like a powerhouse that has everything going for it. In the routes where it flies, it dominates the market. The company is on a steady growth curve, and its stock performs extremely well. In fact, it is the only U.S. airline that has earned a profit every year since 1973. Employees love working there. Turnover is extremely low, and the company is considered to have the most productive workforce in the industry. And it's extremely popular with customers; Southwest gets consistently superior customer service ratings.

Given Southwest's current position, you wouldn't suspect that its start-up was anything but smooth. It's a testament to the Law of Victory that the company even exists today. The airline was begun in 1967 by Rollin King, owner of a small commuter air service in Texas; John Parker, a banker; and Herb Kelleher, an attorney. But it took them four years to get their first plane off the ground. As soon as the company incorporated, Braniff, Trans Texas, and Continental Airlines all tried to put it out of business. And they almost succeeded. One court battle followed another, and one man, more than any other, made the fight his own: Herb Kelleher. When their start-up capital was gone, and they seemed to be defeated, the board wanted to give up. However, Kelleher said, "Let's go one more round with them. I will continue to represent the company in court, and I'll postpone any legal fees and pay every cent of the court costs out of my own pocket." Finally when their case made it to the Texas Supreme Court, they won, and they were at last able to put their planes in the air.

Once it got going, Southwest hired experienced airline leader Lamar Muse as its new CEO. He, in turn, hired the best executives available. And as other airlines kept trying to put them out of business, Kelleher and Muse kept fighting—in court and in the marketplace. When they had trouble filling their planes going to and from Houston, Southwest began flying into Houston's Hobby Airport, which was more accessible to commuters because of its proximity to downtown. When all the major carriers moved to the newly created Dallas–Fort Worth Airport, Southwest kept flying into convenient Love Field. When the airline had to sell one of its four planes to survive, the executives figured out a way for their planes to remain on the ground no longer than an amazingly short ten minutes between flights. That way Southwest could maintain routes and schedules. And when they couldn't figure out any other way to fill their planes, they pioneered peak and off-peak pricing, giving leisure travelers a huge break in the cost of fares.

Through it all, Kelleher kept fighting and helped keep Southwest alive. In 1978, seven years after he helped put the company's first small fleet of planes into the air, he became chairman of the company. In 1982, he was made president and CEO. Today he continues to fight and find ways for the company to win. And look at the success:

SOUTHWEST AIRLINES YESTERDAY AND TODAY

	1971	1997
Size of fleet	4	262
Employees at year-end	195	23,974
Customers carried	108,000	50,399,960
Cities served	3	51
Trips flown	6,051	786,288
Stockholders' equity	$3.3 million	$2.0 billion
Total assets	$22 million	$4.2 billion

Southwest's Vice President of Administration Colleen Barrett sums it up: "The warrior mentality, the very fight to survive is truly what created our culture."[6] What Kelleher and Southwest have is not just a will to survive, but a will to win. Leaders who practice the Law of Victory believe that anything less than success is unacceptable. And they have no Plan B. That keeps them fighting.

> *Leaders who practice the Law of Victory have no Plan B. That keeps them fighting.*

What is your level of expectation when it comes to succeeding for your organization? How dedicated are you to winning your "game"? Are you going to have the Law of Victory in your corner as you fight, or when times get difficult, are you going to throw in the towel? Your answer to that question may determine whether you fail or succeed as a leader.

THE LAW OF THE BIG MO

Momentum Is a Leader's Best Friend

ALL LEADERS FACE THE challenge of creating change in an organization. The key is momentum—what I call the Big Mo. Just as every sailor knows that you can't steer a ship that isn't moving forward, strong leaders understand that to change direction, you first have to create forward progress—and that takes the Law of the Big Mo.

I saw a movie several years ago called *Stand and Deliver*. Maybe you've seen it too. It's about a real-life teacher named Jaime Escalante who worked at Garfield High School in East Los Angeles, California. The movie focused on Escalante's ability to teach, but the real story is actually a study in the Law of the Big Mo.

Teaching, motivating, and leading were in Jaime Escalante's blood, even from the time of his youth in his native Bolivia. He started tutoring kids when he was in elementary school, and he began his career as a physics teacher before he finished his college degree. He quickly became known as his city's finest teacher. When he was in his thirties, Escalante and his family immigrated to the United

States. He worked several years in a restaurant, and then at Russell Electronics. Though he could have pursued a promising career at Russell, he went back to school and earned a second bachelor's degree so that he could teach in the United States. Escalante's burning desire was to make a difference in people's lives.

At age forty-three, he was hired by Garfield High School to teach computer science. But when he arrived at Garfield on the first day of class, he found that there was no funding for computers. And because his degree was in mathematics, he would be teaching basic math. Disappointed, he went in search of his first class, hoping that his dream of making a difference wasn't slipping through his fingers.

FIGHTING A TIDAL WAVE OF NEGATIVE MOMENTUM

The change from computers to math turned out to be the least of Escalante's problems. The school, which had been quiet during his summertime interview, was now in chaos. Discipline was nonexistent. Fights seemed to break out continually. Trash and graffiti were everywhere. Students—and even outsiders from the neighborhood—roamed all over the campus throughout the day. Escalante discovered that Alex Avilez, the school's liberal principal, was actually *encouraging* gang recognition on campus. Avilez had decided that student gang members needed validation and more opportunities to identify with the school. So he encouraged eighteen different gangs to put up their *placas* (signs with the gang's symbol) in various places on campus to serve as meeting areas for them. It was a teacher's worst nightmare. How in the world was Escalante going to make a difference under those conditions?

Almost daily he thought of quitting. But his passion for teaching and his dedication to improving the lives of his students wouldn't allow him to give up. Yet at the same time Escalante knew that the students were doomed if the school didn't change. They were all sliding backward fast, and they needed something to move them forward.

The break came as a result of what looked like a major setback: When administrators were informed that the school was in danger of losing its accreditation, the district removed Principal Avilez and replaced him with a better leader, Paul Possemato. He immediately cleaned up the school, discouraged gang activity, and chased outsiders from the campus. Though he was at the school only two years, the principal saved Garfield from losing its accreditation, and he stopped the negative momentum the school had experienced.

IT TAKES A LEADER TO GET THINGS STARTED

The movie *Stand and Deliver* made it look as though Escalante was the one who came up with the idea of preparing students to take an advanced placement (AP) exam. The reality was that a few AP tests were already being given on campus. Each year several students took tests for Spanish. And occasionally, one or two would attempt a test in physics or history. But the problem was that the school didn't have a leader with vision to take up the cause. That's where Escalante came into play. He believed that he and the school could make a positive impact on his students' lives, and the way to start the ball rolling was to challenge the school's best and brightest with an AP calculus test.

SMALL BEGINNINGS

In the fall of 1978, Escalante organized the first calculus class. Rounding up every possible candidate who might be able to handle the course from Garfield's 3,500 student population, he was able to find only fourteen students. In the first few classes, he laid out the work it would take for them to prepare for the AP calculus test at the end of the year.

By the end of the second week of school, he had lost seven students—half the class. Even the ones who stayed were not well prepared for calculus. And by late spring, he was down to only five students. All of them took the AP test in May, but only two passed.

Escalante was disappointed, but he refused to give up, especially since he had made some progress. He knew that if he could give some of the students a few wins, build their confidence, and give them hope, he could move them forward. If he could just build some momentum, things at the school could turn around.

TWO KEYS:
PREPARATION AND MOTIVATION

Escalante recognized that he could succeed only if his students were effectively inspired and properly prepared. Motivation would not be a problem because the calculus teacher was gifted in that area. He read his students masterfully and always knew exactly what to do with them. If they needed motivation, he'd give them extra homework or challenge one of the school's athletes to a handball match. (Escalante never lost!) If they needed encouragement, he'd take them out to McDonald's as a reward. If they got lazy, he'd inspire, amaze, amuse, and even intimidate them. And all along the way, he modeled hard work, dedication to excellence, and what he called *ganas*—desire.

> *Leaders always find a way to make things happen.*

Getting his students prepared was more difficult. He introduced more algebra and trigonometry to students in the lower-level classes, and he got some of his colleagues to do the same. He also started to rally support for a summer program to teach advanced math. And in time, the students improved.

IT STARTS WITH A LITTLE PROGRESS

In the fall, Escalante put together another calculus class, this time with nine students. At the end of the year, eight took the test and six passed. He was making progress. Word of his success spread, and in the fall of 1980, his calculus class numbered fifteen. When they all took the test at the end of the year, fourteen students passed. The steps forward weren't huge, but Escalante could see that the program was building momentum.

The next group of students, numbering eighteen, was the subject of the movie *Stand and Deliver*. Like their predecessors, they worked very hard to learn calculus, many coming to school at 7:00 A.M. every day—a full hour and a half before school started. And often they stayed until 5:00, 6:00, or 7:00 P.M. When they took the test in May, they felt that they had done well.

MOMENTUM BREAKER?

But then there was a problem, one that threatened to destroy the fledgling program and stop cold the momentum Escalante had been working hard to build over the past several years. A grader for the Educational Testing Service (ETS), which administered the AP exams, found some similarities on several of the tests the students had taken. That led to an investigation of fourteen of the eighteen Garfield students who took the test. The testers accused Escalante's students of cheating.

Resolving the investigation was a bureaucratic nightmare. The only way for the students to receive the college credit they wanted so desperately was to retake the test, but the students were indignant and felt retesting was an admission of guilt. Escalante tried to intervene, but the bureaucrats at ETS refused to talk with him. Henry Gradillas, who was then the principal, also tried to get the testing service to reverse its decision but was unsuccessful. They were at an impasse.

Finally, the students agreed to retake the test—even though they had been out of school and hadn't studied for three months. What were the results? Every single student passed. Escalante's pass rate for the year was 100 percent.

NO—MOMENTUM MAKER

What could have killed the momentum Escalante had built at Garfield turned into a real momentum builder. Students at the school became more confident, and people within the community rallied around Escalante and his program. And the publicity surrounding the test gave a push of momentum that made it possible for East Los Angeles College to start a summer program that Escalante wanted for his students.

After that, the math program exploded. In 1983, the number of students passing the AP calculus exam almost doubled, from 18 to 31. The next year it doubled again, the number reaching 63. And it continued growing. In 1987, 129 students took the test, with 85 of them receiving college credit. Garfield High School in East Los Angeles, once considered the sinkhole of the district, produced 27 percent of all passing AP calculus test scores by Mexican-Americans in the entire United States.

THE MOMENTUM EXPLOSION

The benefits of the Law of the Big Mo were felt by all of Garfield High School's students. The school started offering classes to prepare students for other AP exams. In time, Garfield held regular AP classes in Spanish, calculus, history, European history, biology, physics, French, government, and computer science.

In 1987, nine years after Escalante spearheaded the program, Garfield students took more than 325 AP examinations. Most incredibly, Garfield had a waiting list of more than four hundred students from areas outside its boundaries wanting to enroll. The school that was once the laughingstock of the district and that had almost lost its accreditation had become one of the top three inner-city schools in the entire nation![1] That's the power of the Law of the Big Mo.

ONLY A LEADER CAN CREATE MOMENTUM

It takes a leader to create momentum. Followers catch it. And managers are able to continue it once it has begun. But *creating* it requires someone who can motivate others, not who needs to be motivated. Harry Truman once said, "If you can't stand the heat, get out

> *If you can't make some heat, get out of the kitchen.*

of the kitchen." But for leaders, that statement should be changed to read, "If you can't *make* some heat, get out of the kitchen."

TRUTHS ABOUT MOMENTUM

Momentum really is a leader's best friend. Sometimes it's the only difference between losing and winning. That's why in basketball games, for instance, when the opposing team scores a lot of unanswered points and starts to develop too much momentum, a good coach will call a time-out. He knows that if the other team's momentum gets too strong, his team is likely to lose the game.

Momentum also makes a huge difference in organizations. When you have no momentum, even the simplest tasks can seem to be insurmountable problems. But when you have momentum on your side, the future looks bright, obstacles appear small, and trouble seems temporary.

MOMENTUM MAKES LEADERS LOOK BETTER THAN THEY ARE

When leaders have momentum on their side, people think they're geniuses. They look past shortcomings. They forget about the mistakes the leaders have made. Momentum changes people's perspective of leaders.

MOMENTUM HELPS FOLLOWERS PERFORM BETTER THAN THEY ARE

When leadership is strong and there is momentum in an organization, people are motivated and inspired to perform at higher levels. They become effective beyond their hopes and expectations.

> *With enough momentum, nearly any kind of change is possible.*

If you remember the 1980 U.S. Olympic hockey team, you know what I'm talking about. The team was good, but not good enough to win the gold medal. Yet that's what the Americans did. Why? Because leading up to the championship game, they won game after game against very tough teams. They gained so much momentum that they performed beyond their capabilities. And after they beat the Russians, nothing could stop them from coming home with the gold medal.

MOMENTUM IS EASIER TO STEER THAN TO START

Have you ever been waterskiing? If you have, you know that it's harder to get up on the water than it is to steer once you're up there. Think about the first time you skied. Before you got up, the boat was dragging you along, and you probably thought your arms were going to give way as the water flooded against your chest and into your face. For a moment, you might have believed you couldn't hold on to the tow rope any longer. But then the force of the water drove your skis up onto the surface, and off you went. At that point, you were able to make a turn with only a subtle shift of weight from one foot to another. That's the way the momentum of leadership works. Getting started is a struggle, but once you're moving forward, you can really start to do some amazing things.

MOMENTUM IS THE MOST POWERFUL CHANGE AGENT

With enough momentum, nearly any kind of change is possible. That was true for Garfield High School, considered by many people to be a place with no hope, and it's true for any other organization. Momentum puts victory within reach.

MY GREATEST MOMENTUM CHALLENGE

As a leader, my greatest fight for momentum occurred at Skyline, my third church. I arrived there as the senior pastor in 1981, and as the church started growing, it didn't take me long to recognize that we would need to relocate to sustain our growth.

At first, I thought that wouldn't be a problem. A relocation that size isn't easy, but we were in a good position for the move. We had started to develop momentum, having doubled in size from one thousand to more than two thousand in attendance. Through my application of the Law of the Inner Circle, we had an exceptional staff in place. Morale among the people was very high. And I also had the advantage of having led both of my previous churches through building projects. But I failed to take into account the depth of San Diego's bureaucracy and California's environmental protection laws.

When I was the pastor at my first church in Indiana, we had gone through a rapid period of growth and decided to relocate. After the decision was made to construct a new building, a member of the church donated a plot of land, and we started building within a few weeks. In less than nine months, we had built a new facility and moved in.

Things couldn't have been more different in California. We started the relocation process in 1984. Because of local politics, neighborhood concerns, and environmental red tape, what appeared to be a three-year project dragged out for more than three times that long. As it turned out, it took us eleven years *just to get the zoning and building permits approved.* I wasn't the leader anymore when the project finally received approval. Jim Garlow, who followed me as the senior pastor at the church, accomplished that along with a fine team of laypeople.

The greatest challenge of my life as a leader was sustaining momentum during those last five years at Skyline. The people at most churches facing similar circumstances would have given up, and before long, their churches would have shrunk in size. But not Skyline. What saved us? The answer can be found in the Law of the Big Mo. I did everything possible during those years to build momentum. I continually kept the vision for the relocation in front of the people. We made it a habit to focus on what we *could* do rather than on what we couldn't, and we often celebrated our victories, no matter how small. Meanwhile, we made progress in areas where we could. We improved our small groups, making them very strong, and we continually focused on developing leaders. It kept us going. The momentum we built was so strong that even that eleven-year obstacle couldn't stop us.

If your desire is to do great things with your organization, never overlook the power of momentum. It truly is the leader's best friend. If you can develop it, you can do almost anything. That's the power of the Big Mo.

17

THE LAW OF PRIORITIES

*Leaders Understand That Activity Is
Not Necessarily Accomplishment*

L EADERS NEVER GROW to a point where they no longer need to
prioritize. It's something that good leaders keep doing, whether
they're leading a small group, pastoring a church, running a small business, or leading a billion-dollar corporation. I was reminded of that last
year when I moved my companies from San
Diego, California, to Atlanta, Georgia.

I used to think that I would live the rest of
my life in San Diego. It's a gorgeous city with
one of the best climates in the world. It's ten
minutes from the beach and two hours from
the ski slopes. It has culture, professional
sporting teams, and fine restaurants. And I
could play golf there year-round. Why would
I ever want to leave a place like that?

> *"A leader
> is the one who
> climbs the tallest
> tree, surveys the
> entire situation,
> and yells,
> 'Wrong jungle!'"*
> —Stephen Covey

But then one day I sat down and started to reevaluate my priorities. I fly a tremendous amount because of my speaking engagements
and consulting work. I realized that because I lived in San Diego, I

was spending too much time traveling just to various airline hubs in order to make connections. So I asked Linda, my assistant, to figure out exactly how much time I was doing that. What I discovered shocked even me. In 1996, I had spent twenty-seven *days* traveling back and forth just between San Diego and Dallas to make flight connections. That's when I decided to look into moving INJOY and my other companies to an airline hub. Stephen Covey remarked, "A leader is the one who climbs the tallest tree, surveys the entire situation, and yells, 'Wrong jungle!'" I felt a little like that when I realized what we were about to do.

We finally settled on Atlanta as the ideal location. First, it was a major airline hub. From there I would be able to reach 80 percent of the United States with a two-hour flight. That would give me a lot of extra time in the coming years. Second, the area is beautiful, and it offers excellent cultural, recreational, and entertainment opportunities. Finally, my people moving from California would be able to enjoy a good standard of living. The move was quite an undertaking, but it went smoothly thanks to the hard work and strong leadership of the people who work for me.

THE THREE Rs

Immediately after our move to Atlanta, I also set aside some time to reevaluate my personal priorities. For the last several years, my schedule has gotten heavier and heavier. And the size of our organizations has grown. Four years ago, we had fewer than twenty employees. Now we have more than one hundred. But just because we're doing more doesn't automatically mean that we're being successful and accomplishing our mission. For that, you have to look to the Law of Priorities.

For the last ten years, I've used two guidelines to help me measure my activity and determine my priorities. The first is the Pareto

Principle. I've often taught it to people at leadership conferences over the years, and I also explain it in my book *Developing the Leader Within You.* The idea is this: If you focus your attention on the activities that rank in the top 20 percent in terms of importance, you will have an 80 percent return on your effort. For example, if you have ten employees, you should give 80 percent of your time and attention to your best two people. If you have one hundred customers, the top twenty will provide you with 80 percent of your business. If your to-do list has ten items on it, the two most important ones will give you an 80 percent return on your time. If you haven't already observed this phenomenon, test it and you'll see that it really works out.

> *"There are many things that will catch my eye, but there are only a few things that will catch my heart."*
> —*Tim Redmond*

The second guideline is the three Rs. No, they're not reading, writing, and 'rithmetic. My three Rs are requirement, return, and reward. To be effective, leaders must order their lives according to these three questions:

I. WHAT IS REQUIRED?

We're all accountable to somebody—an employer, a board of directors, our stockholders, or someone else. For that reason, your list of priorities must always begin with what is required of you. Anything required that's not necessary for you to do personally should be delegated or eliminated.

2. WHAT GIVES THE GREATEST RETURN?

As a leader, you should spend most of your time working in your areas of greatest strength. If something can be done 80 percent as well by someone else in your organization, delegate it. If a responsibility could *potentially* meet that standard, then develop a person to handle it.

3. WHAT BRINGS THE GREATEST REWARD?

Tim Redmond admitted, "There are many things that will catch my eye, but there are only a few things that will catch my heart." The things that bring the greatest personal reward are the fire lighters in a leader's life. Nothing energizes a person the way passion does.

REORDERING PRIORITIES

My most important priority after the move to Atlanta was to carve out more time for my family. So I discussed that issue with my wife, Margaret, and we came to an agreement concerning what our time would look like. Then I brought together the four presidents of my organizations and several other key players to help me review my other priorities and determine how I would spend my time in the coming year. As we talked through the issues, they shared their needs with me, and I shared my vision with them. Together, we confirmed the amount of time I would give each of my four key priority areas. Here's what we came up with:

AREA	TIME ALLOTTED
1. Leadership	19 percent
2. Communicating	38 percent
3. Creating	31 percent
4. Networking	12 percent

I am passionate about each of these four areas. All of them are absolutely necessary for the growth and health of the organizations, and they bring the highest return for my time. So far these guidelines seem to be serving the companies and me well. But every year we will revisit them and take a hard look at how effective we're being. Activity is not necessarily accomplishment. If we want to continue to be effective, we have to work according to the Law of Priorities.

PRIORITIES WERE THE
NAME OF HIS GAME

Examine the life of any great leader, and you will see him putting priorities into action. Every time Norman Schwarzkopf assumed a new command, he didn't just rely on his leadership intuition; he also reexamined the unit's priorities. When Lee Iacocca took over Chrysler, the first thing he did was to reorder its priorities. When explorer Roald Amundsen succeeded in taking his team to the South Pole and back, it was due, in part, to his ability to set right priorities.

Successful leaders live according to the Law of Priorities. They recognize that activity is not necessarily accomplishment. But the best leaders seem to be able to get the Law of Priorities to work for them by satisfying multiple priorities with each activity. This actually enables them to increase their focus while reducing their number of actions.

A leader who was a master at that was one of my idols: John Wooden, the former head basketball coach of the UCLA Bruins. He is called the Wizard of Westwood because the amazing feats he accomplished in the world of college sports were so incredible that they seemed to be magical.

Evidence of Wooden's ability to make the Law of Priorities work for him could be seen in the way he approached basketball practice. Wooden claimed that he learned some of his methods from watching Frank Leahy, the great former Notre Dame football head coach. He said, "I often went to his [Leahy's] practices and observed how he broke them up into periods. Then I would go home and analyze why he did things certain ways. As a player, I realized there was a great deal of time wasted. Leahy's concepts reinforced my ideas and helped in the ultimate development of what I do now."

EVERYTHING HAD A PURPOSE
BASED ON PRIORITIES

Friends who have been in the military tell me that they often had to hurry up and wait. That seems to be the way some coaches work too. Their players are asked to work their hearts out one minute and then to stand around doing nothing the next. But that's not the way Wooden worked. He orchestrated every moment of practice and planned each activity with specific purposes in mind.

Every year, Wooden determined a list of overall priorities for the team, based on observations from the previous season. Those items might include objectives such as, "Build confidence in Drollinger and Irgovich," or "Use 3 on 2 continuity drill at least three times a week." Usually, he had about a dozen or so items that he wanted to work on throughout the season. But Wooden also reviewed his agenda for his teams every day. Each morning, he and an assistant would meticulously plan the day's practice. They usually spent two hours strategizing for a practice that might not even last that long. He drew ideas from notes jotted on three-by-five cards that he always carried with him. He planned every drill, minute by minute, and recorded the information in a notebook prior to practice. Wooden once boasted that if you asked what his team was doing on a specific date at three o'clock in 1963, he could tell you precisely what drill his team was running.

Wooden always maintained his focus, and he found ways for his players to do the same thing. His special talent was for addressing several priority areas at once. For example, to help players work on their free throws—something that many of them found tedious—Wooden instituted a free-throw shooting policy during scrimmages that would encourage them to concentrate and improve instead of just marking time. The sooner a sidelined player made a set number of shots, the sooner he could get back into action. And Wooden continually changed the number of shots required by the guards, forwards, and centers so that team members rotated in and out at different rates. That way everyone, regardless of position or starting status, got experience playing, a critical priority for Wooden's development of total teamwork.

The most remarkable aspect about John Wooden—and the most telling about his ability to focus on his priorities—is that he never scouted opposing teams. Instead, he focused on getting his players to reach *their* potential. And he addressed those things through practice and personal interaction with the players. It was never his goal to win championships or even to beat the other team. His desire was to get each person to play to his potential and to put the best possible team on the floor. And of course, Wooden's results were incredible. In more than forty years of coaching, he had only *one* losing season—his first. And he led his UCLA teams to four undefeated seasons and a record ten NCAA championships.[1] No other college team has ever come close. Wooden is a great leader. He just might be the finest man to coach in any sport. Why? Because every day he lived by the Law of Priorities.

REFOCUSING ON A WORLDWIDE SCALE

One of the most effective leaders today when it comes to the Law of Priorities is Jack Welch, chairman and CEO of General Electric, whom I mentioned in discussing the Law of Reproduction. When Welch assumed leadership of GE in 1981, it was a good company. It had a ninety-year history, the company stock traded at $4 per share, and the company was worth about $12 billion, eleventh best on the stock market. It was a huge, diverse company that included 350 strategic businesses. But Welch believed the company could become better. What was his strategy? He used the Law of Priorities.

Within a few months of taking over the company, he began what he called the hardware revolution. It changed the entire profile and focus of the company. Welch said,

> To the hundreds of businesses and product lines that made up the company we applied a single criterion: can they be number 1 or number 2 at whatever they do in the world marketplace? Of the 348 businesses or product lines that could not, we closed some and divested others. Their sale brought in almost $10 billion. We invested $18 billion in the ones that remained and further strengthened them with $17 billion worth of acquisitions.
>
> What remained [in 1989], aside from a few relatively small supporting operations, are 14 world-class businesses . . . all well positioned for the '90s . . . each one either first or second in the world market in which it participates.[2]

Welch's strong leadership and ability to focus have paid incredible dividends. Since he took over, GE's stock has experienced a 2 to 1 split four times. And it trades at more than $80 per share as I write this. The company is currently ranked as the nation's most admired company according to *Fortune,* and it has recently become the most valuable company in the world, with a market capitalization of more than $250 billion.

What has made GE one of the best companies in the world? Jack Welch's ability to use the Law of Priorities in his leadership. He never mistook activity for accomplishment. He knew that the greatest success comes only when you focus your people on what really matters.

Take some time to reassess your leadership priorities. Like GE in the early '80s, are you spread out all over the place? Or are you focused on the few things that bring the highest reward? If you aren't living by the Law of Priorities, you might be spinning your wheels.

18

THE LAW OF SACRIFICE

A Leader Must Give Up to Go Up

ONE OF THE MOST incredible turnarounds in American business history dramatically demonstrates the Law of Sacrifice. It happened at the Chrysler Corporation in the early 1980s. Chrysler was in a mess, despite a prior history of success. The company has been around since the mid-1920s, when Walter Chrysler reorganized the Maxwell and Chalmers Motor Car Companies and gave the business his name. In 1928, he bought out Dodge and Plymouth, and by 1940, the year he died, he had the second largest auto company in the world, ahead of Ford, the pioneer of the industry, and behind only General Motors. It was a tremendous success story. At one point, Chrysler had captured 25 percent of the entire domestic automobile market.

The company remained fairly strong through the 1960s. A hallmark of its cars was innovative engineering. For example, Chrysler engineers designed the first electronic ignition for cars, the first hydraulic brakes, and the first under-the-hood computer. And in the 1960s, its cars were also known for high performance, with models such as the Barracuda, the Dodge Daytona, and the Plymouth Road Runner—called by some the ultimate street racer.

A DEVASTATING DOWNTURN

But by the 1970s, the company was declining rapidly. In 1978, its market share was down from 25 percent to a puny 11 percent. And things were getting worse. The organization was headed for bankruptcy. Then in November 1978, Chrysler brought aboard a new leader. His name was Lee Iacocca. He was a seasoned car man who had worked his way up through the ranks at Ford. Though educated as an engineer, he had voluntarily started his career in sales for Ford in Pennsylvania in the 1940s and eventually earned his way to headquarters in Dearborn, Michigan. While there, he led teams who created groundbreaking automobiles such as the Lincoln Continental Mark III and the legendary Mustang, one of the most popular cars in history.

In 1970, Iacocca became the president of the Ford Motor Company, the highest leadership position possible under Chairman Henry Ford II. In all, Iacocca worked for Ford for thirty-two years. And when he left in 1978, the company was earning record profits, having made $1.8 billion in *each* of his last two years running the business. Though the separation wasn't pleasant, between the severance package he received and the stock he had acquired while at Ford, Iacocca was in a position where he would never have to work again. But he was only fifty-four years old when he left Ford, and he knew he still had a lot to offer an organization.

LEADER TO THE RESCUE

Chrysler's invitation for him to come on board presented him with the opportunity—and the challenge—of a lifetime. John Riccardo, then chairman of the board for Chrysler, recognized that the company needed strong leadership to survive, something he could not adequately provide. According to Iacocca, Riccardo knew that he was in over his head, so he wanted to bring in the former Ford man as president of Chrysler. In turn, Riccardo would step aside in less than two years so that Iacocca could become chairman and CEO. John Riccardo was willing to sacrifice himself for the good of the company. As a result, Iacocca would have the chance to realize a lifelong dream: becoming the top man at one of the Big Three.

IACOCCA GAVE UP TO GO UP

Iacocca accepted the job, but it also started him down his own road of personal sacrifice. The first came in his finances. The salary he accepted at Chrysler was a little over half of what he had earned as the president of Ford. The next sacrifice came in his family life. At Ford, Iacocca had always prided himself on the fact that he worked hard from Monday to Friday, but he always set aside Saturday, Sunday, and most Friday nights for his family. And when he came home from work at the end of the day, he left his troubles at the office.

> *The Law of Sacrifice says you have to give up to go up.*

But to lead Chrysler, he had to work almost around the clock. On top of that, when he got home, he couldn't sleep. Iacocca later described the company as having been run like a small grocery store, despite its size. There were no viable financial systems or controls in place, production and supply methods were a mess, products were poorly built, and nearly all of the divisions were run by turf-minded vice presidents who refused to work as a team. Morale was abysmal throughout the company, customer loyalty was the worst in the business, and the company continued to lose money.

WHEN ALL ELSE FAILS,
MAKE ANOTHER SACRIFICE

Iacocca understood that successful leaders have to maintain an attitude of sacrifice in order to turn around an organization. They have to be willing to do what it takes to go to the next level. Iacocca fired thirty-three of the thirty-five vice presidents during a three-year period. Yet things continued to worsen. The country was experiencing a terrible recession, and interest rates were the highest they had ever been. Then oil prices skyrocketed when the shah of Iran was deposed in early 1979. Chrysler's market share fell to a weak 8 percent. Despite all Iacocca's work, it seemed as if the Law of Sacrifice wasn't working.

> *The Law of Sacrifice maintains that one sacrifice seldom brings success.*

Iacocca worked harder to rebuild the company by bringing in the very best leaders in the business, many of whom had retired from Ford. He cut every expense he could and built on the company's strengths, but those measures weren't enough to lift up the company. Chrysler was headed for bankruptcy. Iacocca had to face the greatest personal sacrifice of all: He would go to the American government with his proverbial hat in his hand for loan guarantees.

At Ford, Iacocca had developed a reputation for being highly critical of any government involvement in business. So when he approached Congress for help, no one spoke very kindly about him. Iacocca later discussed that episode:

> In the minds of Congress and the media, we had sinned. We had missed the market, and we deserved to be punished.
>
> And punished we were. During the congressional hearings, we were held up before the entire world as living examples of

everything that was wrong with American industry. We were humiliated on the editorial pages for not having the decency to give up and die gracefully . . . Our wives and kids were the butt of jokes in shopping malls and schools. It was a far higher price to pay than just closing the doors and walking away. It was personal. It was pointed. And it was painful.

Swallowing his pride was a heroic sacrifice for Iacocca, one that many top corporate executives never would have made. But it was a price he had to pay to save the company.

At least one sacrifice he made at that time received positive press: Iacocca reduced his own salary to one dollar a year. At the time he said, "Leadership means setting an example. When you find yourself in a position of leadership, people follow your every move." He followed that action with requests for others to make sacrifices. He asked Chrysler's top executives to take a 10 percent pay cut. Then he asked for—and received—concessions from the unions and the banks that were working with the automaker. For Chrysler to succeed, they would all make sacrifices together. And succeed they did. By 1982, Chrysler generated an operating profit of $925 million, the best in its history. And in 1983, the company was able to repay its loans.[1]

Chrysler has continued to succeed and grow. The company has fought its way back, and today it has a combined U.S. and Canadian market share of more than 16 percent—double what it was in the early years when Iacocca took over. He has since retired, but his leadership put Chrysler back on the map. Why? Because he modeled the Law of Sacrifice.

> *"Leadership means setting an example. When you find yourself in a position of leadership, people follow your every move."*
> *—Lee Iacocca*

THE HEART OF LEADERSHIP

What was true for Lee Iacocca is true for any leader. You have to give up to go up. Many people today want to climb up the corporate ladder because they believe that freedom and power are the prizes waiting at the top. They don't realize that the true nature of leadership is really sacrifice.

Most people will acknowledge that sacrifices are necessary fairly early in a leadership career. People give up many things in order to gain potential opportunities. For example, Tom Murphy began working for General Motors in 1937. But he almost refused the first position he was offered with the company because the one-hundred-dollars-a-month salary barely covered his expenses. Despite his misgivings, he took the job anyway, thinking the opportunity was worth the sacrifice. He was right. Murphy eventually became General Motors' chairman of the board.

COUNTING THE COST OF LEADERSHIP

Sacrifice is a constant in leadership. It is an ongoing process, not a one-time payment. When I look back at my career, I recognize that there has always been a cost involved in moving forward. That's been true for me in the area of finances with every career change I've made except one. When I accepted my first job, our family income decreased since my position paid little and my wife, Margaret, had to give up her job as a schoolteacher for me to take it. When I accepted a director's job at denominational headquarters in Marion, Indiana, I once again took a pay cut. After I interviewed for my third pastoral position, I accepted the position from the board without knowing what the

> *Sacrifice is an ongoing process, not a one-time payment.*

salary would be. (It was lower.) When some board members expressed their surprise, I told them that if I did the job well, the salary would take care of itself. And in 1995 when I finally left the church after a twenty-six-year career so that I could teach leadership full-time, I gave up a salary altogether. Anytime you know that the step is right, don't hesitate to make a sacrifice.

YOU'VE GOT TO GIVE UP TO GO UP

Leaders who want to rise have to do more than take an occasional cut in pay. They have to give up their rights. As my friend Gerald Brooks says, "When you become a leader, you lose the right to think about yourself." For every person, the nature of the sacrifice may be different. For example, Iacocca's greatest sacrifices came late in his career. In the case of someone like former South African president F. W. de Klerk, who worked to dismantle apartheid in his country, the cost was his career itself. The circumstances may change from person to person, but the principle doesn't. Leadership means sacrifice.

> *"When you become a leader, you lose the right to think about yourself."*
> —Gerald Brooks

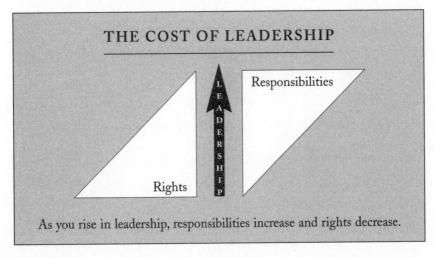

THE COST OF LEADERSHIP

Responsibilities

Rights

LEADERSHIP

As you rise in leadership, responsibilities increase and rights decrease.

Leaders give up to go up. That's true of every leader regardless of profession. Talk to any leader, and you will find that he has made repeated sacrifices. Usually, the higher that leader has climbed, the greater the sacrifices he has made. Effective leaders sacrifice much that is good in order to dedicate themselves to what is best. That's the way the Law of Sacrifice works. Digital Chairman and Chief Executive Robert Palmer said in an interview, "In my model of management, there's very little wiggle room. If you want a management job, then you have to accept the responsibility and accountability that goes with it."[2] He is really talking about the cost of leadership.

If leaders have to give up to go up, then they have to give up even more to stay up. Have you ever considered how infrequently teams have back-to-back championship seasons? The reason is simple: If a leader can take a team to the championship game and win it, he often assumes he can duplicate the results the next year without making changes. He becomes reluctant to make additional sacrifices in the off-season. But what gets a team to the top isn't what keeps it there. The only way to stay up is to give up even more. Leadership success requires continual change, improvement, and sacrifice. Philosopher-poet Ralph Waldo Emerson offered this option: "For everything you have missed, you have gained something else; and for everything you gain, you lose something."

> *If leaders have to give up to go up, then they have to give up even more to stay up.*

THE HIGHER YOU GO, THE MORE YOU GIVE UP

Who is the most powerful leader in the world? I'd say it's the president of the United States. More than any other single person, his actions and words make an impact on people, not just in our country, but around the globe. Think about what he must give up to reach the office of president and then to hold that office. His time is no longer his own. He is scrutinized constantly. His family is under tremendous pressure. And as a matter of course, he must make decisions that can cost thousands of people their lives. Even after he leaves office, he will spend the rest of his life in the company of Secret Service agents who protect him from bodily harm.

> "For everything you have missed, you have gained something else; and for everything you gain, you lose something."
> —Ralph Waldo Emerson

The Law of Sacrifice demands that the greater the leader, the more he must give up. Think about someone like Martin Luther King Jr. His wife, Coretta Scott King, remarked in *My Life with Martin Luther King, Jr.*, "Day and night our phone would ring, and someone would pour out a string of obscene epithets . . . Frequently the calls ended with a threat to kill us if we didn't get out of town. But in spite of all the danger, the chaos of our private lives, I felt inspired, almost elated."

While pursuing his course of leadership during the civil rights movement, King was arrested and jailed on many occasions. He was stoned, stabbed, and physically attacked. His house was bombed. Yet his vision—and his influence—continued to increase. Ultimately, he sacrificed everything he had. But what he gave up he parted with willingly. In his last speech, delivered the night before his assassination in Memphis, he said,

> I don't know what will happen to me now. We've got some difficult days ahead. But it doesn't matter to me now. Because I've been to the mountaintop. I won't mind. Like anybody else, I would like to live a long life. Longevity has its place. But I'm not concerned about that now. I just want to do God's will. And He's allowed me to go up to the mountain. And I've looked over and

I've seen the Promised Land. I may not get there with you, but I want you to know tonight that we, as a people, will get to the Promised Land. So I'm happy tonight . . . I'm not fearing any man. "Mine eyes have seen the glory of the coming of the Lord."[3]

The next day he paid the ultimate price of sacrifice. King's impact was profound. He influenced millions of people to peacefully stand up against a system and society that fought to exclude them.

> *The higher the level of leadership people want to reach, the greater the sacrifices they will have to make.*

What successful people find to be true becomes even clearer to them when they become leaders. There is no success without sacrifice. The higher the level of leadership you want to reach, the greater the sacrifices you will have to make. To go up, you have to give up. That is the true nature of leadership. That is the Law of Sacrifice.

19

THE LAW OF TIMING

When to Lead Is As Important As
What to Do and Where to Go

THE LAW OF TIMING gave him the chance to become president of the United States. It was a volatile time in the nation's history. Everyone was worn out from the war in Vietnam and the disgrace of Watergate. The people were discouraged and demoralized. And they were especially skeptical of anyone who had *any* connection with Washington government. While campaigning for office, this future president, who had never served in Washington, said about himself, "I have been accused of being an outsider. I plead guilty. Unfortunately, the vast majority of Americans . . . are also outsiders."[1] That person was Jimmy Carter.

THE TIMING WAS RIGHT FOR AN OUTSIDER

When you understand the Law of Timing, you see why Jimmy Carter was elected president of the United States in 1976. In fact, Carter's life and career are characterized by one well-timed move after another. A graduate of Annapolis, Carter had intended to spend his career in the U.S. Navy, but when his father unexpectedly died in 1953, he returned to Plains, Georgia, to take over the family business. In only a few years, he became a strong, respected businessman and a leader in the community.

In 1962, times were changing. The old political machine in Georgia with its corrupt methods of electing officials was beginning to crumble, and Carter decided to run for the Georgia senate. Carter recognized that for the first time in history, a person who was not part of the old system had a chance of being elected to office. But he faced a huge battle. The entrenched political bosses were still fighting to maintain control of their turf. One corrupt leader openly intimidated voters in his district and falsified voting records. As a result, Carter lost the primary. But he refused to quit without a battle. He fought the results of the primary and appealed to a superior court judge to have the voting process reviewed. When the results were overturned, Carter was able to stay on the ticket, and he went on to win the election. Then in 1970, he successfully ran for governor. Once again, he recognized that the timing was right for a relative newcomer to challenge the established political machine.

NONLEADERS CAN'T ALWAYS SEE IT

What Carter did next was almost unthinkable. He decided to run for president of the United States. Here was a man whose entire career as an elected politician consisted of one term in the Georgia senate and one term as the state's governor. His experience was minimal, and he had no presence on the national scene. Carter was such an unknown that when he appeared on the television show *What's My Line?* in 1973 while governor, the panelists didn't know him and couldn't guess his profession.

When Carter first threw his hat into the ring for the presidency, people in the media ignored him. They figured that a little-known ex-governor from the South with no Washington experience had no kind of chance to obtain the Democratic nomination, much less achieve the presidency. But Carter was undaunted. He and a few key associates had recognized that the timing would be right for him in 1976, and they met to talk about it. Carter biographer Peter G. Bourne, who attended the meeting, said that he saw "a unique, open opportunity for an outsider to run for the presidency." Carter saw it, too; he knew that it was a now-or-never proposition.

Carter made his candidacy for president official in December of 1975, a year after finishing his term as governor. The reaction of people across the nation was painfully indifferent. Bourne reported,

> Most journalists seemed not to grasp the profound social and political currents affecting the country. The impact of Vietnam, Watergate, the change in race relations in the South, and especially the profound opening up of the political process seemed largely ignored, and candidates were examined only within the context of the old political paradigm.[2]

The Law of Timing showed that it was the right time for an outsider to run, and Carter was everything that recent presidents had not been: He held no public office while campaigning, having finished his term as governor in 1974. He was not a lawyer by profession. He was a vocal proponent of his Christian faith. And unlike the people who had previously held the nation's highest office, he had not been a part of Washington politics as a congressman, senator, vice president, or cabinet member. His was a fresh face with a different approach to government, something the American people desperately wanted. I believe that at no other time—either before or since—would Jimmy Carter have been elected. Remarkably, on January 20, 1977, James Earl Carter was inaugurated as thirty-ninth president of the United States.

However, timing was not always Jimmy Carter's friend. When the 1980 election rolled around, it killed his chances for reelection. The country was experiencing as many problems as it ever had. The economy was a mess: Americans faced double-digit inflation, record-high oil prices, and skyrocketing mortgage rates. There were also numerous foreign policy problems, including the Soviet invasion of Afghanistan and, of course, the long captivity of the American hostages in Iran. A botched rescue attempt to free the captives further worked against Carter. After the returns came in on the night of the election, Carter found that he had won only an abysmal 49 electoral votes to Ronald Reagan's 489. It was a devastating defeat. The Law of Timing is a double-edged sword. Just as it served to elect Carter president in 1976, it worked against him four years later.

TIMING IS EVERYTHING

Great leaders recognize that *when* to lead is as important as what to do and where to go. Every time a leader makes a move, there are really only four outcomes that can result:

I. THE WRONG ACTION AT THE WRONG TIME LEADS TO DISASTER

A leader who takes the wrong action at the wrong time is sure to suffer negative repercussions. When U.S. forces attempted to rescue the Iranian-held hostages during the Carter administration, it was an example of the wrong action at the wrong time. Prior to the decision to try the rescue, Secretary of State Cyrus Vance had argued that the plan was flawed. He believed something would go wrong. Unfortunately, he was right. Several helicopters experienced mechanical problems, one got lost in a sandstorm, and another crashed into a transport plane, killing eight servicemen. Peter

Bourne described it as "a combination of bad luck and military ineptitude." It could be described only as a disaster. It was an exercise in bad timing, and as much as anything else, it signaled the end of Carter's chances to be reelected.

2. THE RIGHT ACTION AT THE WRONG TIME BRINGS RESISTANCE

It's one thing to figure out *what* needs to be done; it's another to understand *when* to make a move. I remember an example of this kind of bad timing from my leadership experience. In the early 1980s, I tried to start a small group program at Skyline, my church in San Diego. It was the right thing to do, but it failed miserably. Why? The timing was wrong. We hadn't recognized that we had developed too few leaders to support the launch. But six years later, when we tried again, the program was very successful. It was all a matter of timing.

> *If a leader repeatedly shows poor judgment, even in little things, people start to think that having him as the leader is the real mistake.*

3. THE WRONG ACTION AT THE RIGHT TIME IS A MISTAKE

For about a decade, various colleagues of mine tried to talk me into doing a radio program. For a long time I resisted the idea. But a couple of years ago, I recognized that the time was right. So we created a program called *Growing Today*. However, there was one problem: the format. I wanted to get materials into the hands of people to help them, but I was determined not to accept donations from the public. The solution, I thought, was to air a growth-oriented program and depend on product sales to support it. We found out that it was a mistake. That type of show could not break even. Radio was right, but the type of show was wrong. The Law of Timing had spoken again.

4. THE RIGHT ACTION AT THE RIGHT TIME
RESULTS IN SUCCESS

When leaders do the right things at the right time, success is almost inevitable. People, principles, and processes converge to make an incredible impact. And the results touch not only the leader but also the followers and the whole organization.

THE RESULTS OF TIMING

ACTION

Wrong Action Wrong Time *Disaster*	Right Action Wrong Time *Resistance*
Wrong Action Right Time *Mistake*	Right Action Right Time *Success*

TIMING

When the right leader and the right timing come together, incredible things happen. Think about the life of Winston Churchill.

> When the right leader and the right timing come together, incredible things happen.

It wasn't until he was in his sixties that he became prime minister of England. A soldier, writer, and statesman, he had spent his life leading others, but only during the Second World War was the timing right for him to emerge as a great leader. And once the war was over, the people who had rallied around him dismissed him.

During his eightieth birthday address to Parliament on November 30, 1954, Churchill reflected on his role in Great Britain's leadership: "I have never accepted what many people have kindly said—namely that I inspired the nation. Their will was resolute and remorseless, and as it proved, unconquerable. It fell to me to express it. It was the nation and the race dwelling all round the globe that had the lion's heart. I had the luck to be called upon to give the roar."[3]

Churchill's contribution really had nothing to do with luck, but it had a lot to do with timing. He understood the impact that timing can have on a person's life. Another time he described it like this: "There comes a special moment in everyone's life, a moment for which that person was born. That special opportunity, when he seizes it, will fulfill his mission—a mission for which he is uniquely qualified. In that moment, he finds greatness. It is his finest hour."

THE CRUCIBLE OF WAR
DISPLAYS THE LAW OF TIMING

Churchill's experience shows that the Law of Timing becomes especially obvious during times of war. You could see it at work in the 1991 Gulf War with Iraq. In the early stages of Desert Shield, the big concern was to get enough troops and equipment into place to effectively defend Saudi Arabia. If Iraq attacked before the defenders arrived, another country would be lost to Saddam Hussein's aggression.

Then the goal was to deploy enough forces to win decisively against the Iraqis. The coalition forces bided their time and waged a successful air campaign before launching Desert Storm to push Iraq out of Kuwait. And the proof of their good timing can be seen in the results: While Iraq suffered tens of thousands of casualties and had more than sixty thousand soldiers captured, the United States and its allies lost fewer than 150 troops and had only forty-one prisoners taken by Iraqi forces.

One of the reasons war shows the Law of Timing so clearly is that the consequences are so dramatic and immediate. If you look back at any major battle, you'll be able to see the critical importance of timing. The Battle of Gettysburg during the American Civil War is a prime example.

The stage was set for the conflict when Confederate General Robert E. Lee took the Army of Northern Virginia into Pennsylvania in late June of 1863. It was the third year of the war, and both nations were growing weary of the conflict. Lee's actions had three goals: (1) draw the Union army out of Virginia, (2) resupply his troops using Pennsylvania's resources, and (3) bring the fighting to the heart of enemy territory, hoping to thereby precipitate an end to the conflict.

The general's strategy was to move on Harrisburg, Pennsylvania, in an attempt to prod the Union army—last known to be in Virginia—into a hasty and unwanted action. Several days prior to the battle, Lee told General Trimble,

> Our army is in good spirits, not overfatigued, and can be concentrated on any one point in twenty-four hours or less. I have not yet heard that the enemy have crossed the Potomac, and am waiting to hear from General Stuart. When they hear where we are, they will make forced marches . . . They will come up . . . broken down from hunger and hard marching, strung out on a long line and much demoralized, when they come into Pennsylvania. I shall throw an overwhelming force on their advance, crush it, follow up the success, drive one corps back on another, and by successive repulses and surprises, before they can concentrate, create a panic and virtually destroy the army.[4]

Lee was trying to seize the opportunity for overwhelming victory. He didn't know until the morning of July 1 that the Union army had already moved north. By then some of its forces were already engaging Confederate troops on the Chambersburg Road west of Gettysburg. That development disrupted Lee's strategy and ruined his timing.

Lee's first instinct was to hold back and wait for his army's full strength to assemble before forcing a major engagement. But always conscious of the Law of Timing, he recognized when his troops had a sudden advantage. As Lee watched from a nearby ridge, he saw that Federal troops were being routed and retreating. Confederate forces had an opportunity to seize the high ground of Cemetery Hill, defended only by a few Union infantry reserves and artillery. If they could capture and control that position, Lee reasoned, they would control the whole area. It would be the key to a Confederate victory and possibly bring an end to the war.

TIMING MISSED, OPPORTUNITY GONE

But the South did not secure that hill. Though it was still early in the day and the time was ripe to execute an effective attack, Confederate General R. S. Ewell, who was in position to take the hill, simply watched instead of engaging the enemy. And the opportunity slipped away. By the next morning, Union troops had reinforced their previous positions, and the South's chance was gone. The Northern and Southern armies fought for two more days, but in the end, Lee's forces suffered defeat, having lost about 33,000 of his 76,300 men to injury or death.[5] Their only choice was to retreat and make their way back to Virginia.

ANOTHER OPPORTUNITY LOST

After the South's defeat, Lee expected the Union forces under the leadership of General Meade to immediately pursue a counterattack and utterly destroy his reeling army. That was also the expectation of

Abraham Lincoln after he received the news of the Union's victory. Anxious to make the most of the Law of Timing, Lincoln sent a communication from Washington, D.C., to Meade via General Halleck on July 7, 1863. In it, Halleck said,

> I have received from the President the following note, which I respectfully communicate.
>
> "We have certain information that Vicksburg surrendered to General Grant on the 4th of July. Now, if General Meade can complete his work so gloriously prosecuted thus far by the literal or substantial destruction of Lee's army, the rebellion will be over."[6]

Lincoln recognized that the timing was right for an action that could end the war. But just as the Southern forces did not seize the moment for victory when it was available, neither did their Northern counterparts. Meade took his time following up his victory at Gettysburg, and he didn't pursue Lee aggressively enough. When he announced his goal, saying he would "drive from our soil every vestige of the presence of the invader," Lincoln's response was, "My God, is that all?" Lincoln knew he was seeing the Union's chance slip away.

The Law of Timing had been violated. On July 14, what remained of the Army of Northern Virginia crossed over the Potomac, escaping destruction. Lincoln was appalled that the Union had missed a chance to end the war. Later he said that Meade's efforts had reminded him of "an old woman trying to shoo her geese across a creek."[7]

In the end, both armies had missed their best opportunity to achieve victory. Instead, the fighting continued for almost two more years, and hundreds of thousands more troops died. Leaders from both sides had known what to do to achieve victory, but they failed to follow through at the critical moment.

Reading a situation and knowing what to do are not enough to make you succeed in leadership. Only the right action *at the right time* will bring success. Anything else exacts a high price. That's the Law of Timing.

20

THE LAW OF EXPLOSIVE GROWTH

To Add Growth, Lead Followers—
To Multiply, Lead Leaders

I N 1984 AT AGE TWENTY-TWO, John Schnatter started his own business. He began by selling pizzas out of a converted broom closet at Mick's Tavern, a lounge that was co-owned by his father. Although he was just a kid, he had a tremendous amount of vision, drive, and energy—enough to make his tiny pizza stand into a success. The next year, he opened his first store next door to Mick's in Jeffersonville, Indiana. He named the place Papa John's. For the next several years, Schnatter worked hard to build the company. In time, he opened additional stores, and later he began selling franchises. By the beginning of 1991, he had 46 stores. That in itself is a success story. But what happened during the next couple of years is even better.

In 1991 and 1992, Papa John's turned a huge corner. By the end of 1991, the number of stores more than doubled to 110 units. By the end of 1992, they had doubled again to 220. And the growth has continued dramatically. In early 1998, that number surpassed 1,600. What made the company suddenly experience such an incredible period of rapid expansion? The answer can be found in the Law of Explosive Growth.

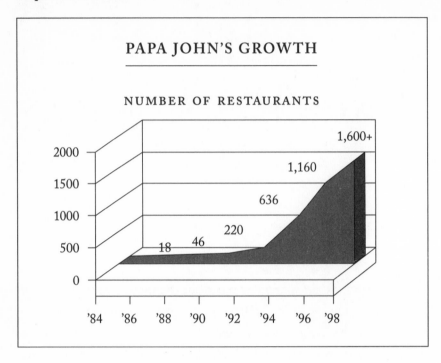

PAPA JOHN'S GROWTH

NUMBER OF RESTAURANTS

Schnatter had always hired good people for his staff, but in the early years he was really the sole leader and primary driving force behind the business's success. Back in the 1980s, he didn't dedicate much time to developing other strong leaders. "It's taking a lot of growing on my part," says Schnatter of Papa John's success. "Between 26 and 32 [years old], the hardest thing was I had a lot of John Schnatters around me [people with great potential who needed to be mentored]. They needed a lot of coaching, and I was so busy developing myself, trying to get myself to the next level, I didn't develop those people. As a result, I lost them. It's my job to build the people who are going to build

> "It's my job to build the people who are going to build the company."
> —John Schnatter

the company. That's going to be much harder for me than the first 1,200 stores."[1]

THE KEY TO GROWTH IS LEADERSHIP

In the early 1990s, Schnatter began thinking about what it would take to really grow the company. The key was leadership. He had already begun to grow as a leader personally. His having made significant progress in his leadership development was opening the door for him to attract better leaders to the company and to give them the time they needed. That's when he started recruiting some of the people who currently lead the company, including Wade Oney, now the company's chief operating officer. Wade had worked for Domino's Pizza for fourteen years, and John believed he was one of the reasons that company had been so successful. When Wade left Domino's, John immediately asked him to be a part of the Papa John's Pizza team.

Schnatter had already built a company capable of creating a taste-tempting pizza—and earning a healthy profit in the process. (Their per store sales average is higher than that of Pizza Hut, Domino's, or Little Caesar's.) Their goal was to build a bigger company. Together, they started talking about what it would take to be capable of opening four hundred to five hundred new restaurants a year. And that's when they focused their attention on developing leaders so that they could take the company to the next level. Says Oney, "The reason we're successful in the marketplace is our focus on quality and our desire to keep things simple. The reason we're successful as a company is our good people."

Since the early 1990s, Schnatter and Oney have developed a top-rate team of leaders who are helping the company experience explosive growth, people such as Blaine Hurst, Papa John's president and vice chairman; Drucilla "Dru" Milby, the CFO; Robert Waddell, president of Papa John's Food Service; and Hart Boesel, who heads up franchise operations.

Papa John's growth has been phenomenal in an industry that was thought to be glutted with competitors a decade ago. In 1997, they opened more than 350 new restaurants. In 1998, they expect the number to be more than 400. And they are also implementing plans to launch Papa John's internationally. They don't plan to stop growing until they are the largest seller of pizza in the world.

"The challenge now," explains Oney, "is developing the next leaders. The company's in great shape financially. [Acquiring] real estate is always a battle, but we can succeed there. And the economy is never a deterrent when you offer customers a good value. The key is to develop leaders. You do that by building up people."

LEADER'S MATH BRINGS EXPLOSIVE GROWTH

John Schnatter and Wade Oney have succeeded because they have practiced the Law of Explosive Growth. Any leader who does that makes the shift from follower's math to what I call leader's math.

> *Any leader who practiced the Law of Explosive Growth makes the shift from follower's math to leader's math.*

Here's how it works. Leaders who develop followers grow their organization only one person at a time. But leaders who develop leaders multiply their growth, because for every leader they develop, they also receive all of that leader's followers. Add ten followers to your organization, and you have the power of ten people. Add ten leaders to your organization, and you have the power of ten leaders times all the followers and leaders *they* influence. That's the difference between addition and multiplication. It's like growing your organization by teams instead of by individuals. The better the leaders you develop, the greater the quality and quantity of followers.

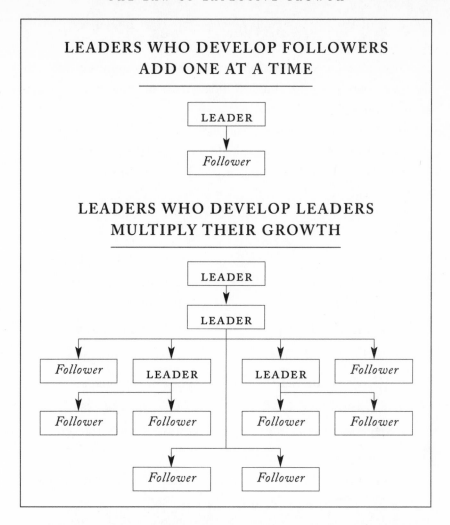

To go to the highest level, you have to develop leaders of leaders. My friend Dale Galloway asserts that "some leaders want to make followers. I want to make leaders. Not only do I want to make leaders, but I want to make leaders of leaders. And then leaders of leaders of leaders." Once you are able to follow that pattern, there is almost no limit to the growth of your organization. That's why I say to add growth, lead followers, but to muliply growth, lead leaders. That's the Law of Explosive Growth.

A DIFFERENT FOCUS

Becoming a leader who develops leaders requires an entirely different focus and attitude from those of a developer of followers. Consider some of the differences:

LEADERS WHO DEVELOP FOLLOWERS	LEADERS WHO DEVELOP LEADERS
Need to be needed	Want to be succeeded
Focus on weaknesses	Focus on strengths
Develop the bottom 20 percent	Develop the top 20 percent
Treat their people the same for "fairness"	Treat their leaders as individuals for impact
Hoard power	Give power away
Spend time with others	Invest time in others
Grow by addition	Grow by multiplication
Impact only people they touch personally	Impact people far beyond their own reach

Developing leaders is difficult because potential leaders are harder to find and attract. They're also harder to hold on to once you find them because unlike followers, they are energetic and entrepreneurial, and they tend to want to go their own way. Developing leaders is also hard work. Leadership development isn't an add-water-and-stir proposition. It takes time, energy, and resources.

A LEADER DEVELOPED FROM AFAR

I've made the development of leaders my focus in life for the last twenty years. The impact on my organizations has always been very rewarding. But in the last ten years, I've also had the incredible privilege of seeing it impact other leaders and their organizations. That's happened because many of the leaders I've helped develop over the last decade work in organizations other than my own. As a result, I'm occasionally surprised to find someone I've developed without even knowing it. That's what happened when I held a conference overseas last fall.

As I mentioned in previous chapters, I sometimes teach leadership outside the United States. Over the years, I've held conferences in Australia, Brazil, Canada, India, Indonesia, Korea, New Zealand, Nigeria, and South Africa. In addition, my books have been translated into more than twenty languages, and my tapes are distributed to countries all over the globe. So I know my leadership principles have traveled far. But I was still pleasantly surprised when I traveled to India last fall, met David Mohan for the first time in the city of Madras, and heard his remarkable story.

Pastor Mohan leads the largest Christian church in all of India. I traveled there to teach leadership to a group of about two thousand pastors. When I arrived, he greeted me like a long-lost friend. I was running late that morning, our plane having been delayed five hours prior to our arrival, so he and I didn't have much time to talk before the conference began. As I taught leadership, he sat on the front row soaking up everything I said. When I taught the Law of Priorities and the Pareto Principle, I saw that he gathered his top leaders around him to make sure they understood all that I was communicating. And occasionally, as I introduced another principle that is part of my foundational teachings on leadership, he seemed to anticipate what I was about to say.

When we finished the conference, he warmly thanked me and insisted on driving me to the airport. As we made the long drive, he told me his story. He said that he was originally scheduled to be in Pittsburgh, Pennsylvania, during this conference, but when he heard that I was coming, he changed his plans because he wanted to meet me. Seven years earlier, his church had been comprised of about seven hundred people. That is a good-sized church, especially in India. But he wanted to reach more people and make a greater impact on his area. And he recognized that to do it, he needed to start developing leaders among his people.

Around that time, someone told him about my books and tapes on leadership. For the next seven years, he was like a sponge, reading my books, listening to my tapes, and soaking up everything he could learn about leadership. And he was also developing people into strong leaders. As he grew, so did his team of leaders. As they grew, so did his church. By the time I visited in the fall of 1997, fourteen thousand people were attending the church's services every weekend. Not only that, but one out of every ten people in his church has been trained and developed as a leader. And he was thanking *me* for help I'd unknowingly given him.

> *The only way to experience an explosive level of growth is to do the math —leader's math.*

I felt humbled by what he told me; I also felt incredibly encouraged. I started wondering how many other men and women were out there that I had never met who had learned about leadership and were making a greater impact on people as a result. Meeting him and hearing his story underlined my commitment to continue teaching leadership.

I don't know where you are in your journey of leadership development. You may be working on your leadership growth, or you may already be a highly developed leader. No matter where you are, I know one thing: You will go to the highest level only if you begin developing leaders instead of followers. Leaders who develop leaders experience an incredible multiplication effect in their organizations that can be achieved in no other way—not by increasing resources, reducing costs, increasing profit margins, analyzing systems, implementing quality management procedures, or doing anything else. The only way to experience an explosive level of growth is to do the math—leader's math. That's the incredible power of the Law of Explosive Growth.

21

THE LAW OF LEGACY

*A Leader's Lasting Value Is
Measured by Succession*

I N 1997, ONE OF the finest business leaders in the world died. His name was Roberto Goizueta, and he was the chairman and chief executive of the Coca-Cola Company. In a speech he gave to the Executives' Club of Chicago a few months before he died, Goizueta made this statement: "A billion hours ago, human life appeared on Earth. A billion minutes ago, Christianity emerged. A billion seconds ago, the Beatles performed on 'The Ed Sullivan Show.' A billion Coca-Colas ago . . . was yesterday morning. And the question we are asking ourselves now is, 'What must we do to make a billion Coca-Colas ago this morning?'"

Making Coca-Cola the best company in the world was Goizueta's lifelong quest, one he was still pursuing diligently when he suddenly, unexpectedly died. Companies that lose a CEO often go into turmoil, especially if his departure is unexpected, as Goizueta's was. Shortly before his death, Goizueta said in an interview with the *Atlanta Journal-Constitution* that retirement was "not on my radar screen. As long as I'm having the fun I'm having, as long as I have the energy necessary, as long as I'm not keeping people from their day in the sun, and as long as the board wants me to stay on, I will stay on." Just months after the interview, he was diagnosed with cancer. Six weeks later, he was dead.

Upon Goizueta's death, former president Jimmy Carter observed, "Perhaps no other corporate leader in modern times has so beautifully exemplified the American dream. He believed that in America, all things are possible. He lived that dream. And because of his extraordinary leadership skills, he helped thousands of others realize their dreams as well."

GOIZUETA'S LEGACY

The legacy left to the company by Goizueta is incredible. When he took over Coca-Cola in 1981, the company's value was $4 billion. Under Goizueta's leadership, it rose to $150 billion. That's an increase in value of more than 3,500 percent! Coca-Cola became the second most valuable corporation in America, ahead of the car makers, the oil companies, Microsoft, Wal-Mart, and all the rest. The only company more valuable was General Electric. Many of Coke's stockholders became millionaires many times over. Emory University in Atlanta, whose portfolio contains a large block of Coca-Cola stock, now has an endowment comparable to that of Harvard.

But high stock value wasn't the most significant thing Goizueta gave to the Coca-Cola company. Instead it was the way he lived the Law of Legacy. When the CEO's death was announced, there was no panic among Coca-Cola stockholders. Paine Webber analyst Emanuel Goldman said that Goizueta "prepared the company for his not being there as well as any executive I've ever seen."

How did he do it? First, by making the company as strong as he possibly could. Second, by preparing a successor for the top position named Douglas Ivester. Mickey H. Gramig, writer for the *Atlanta*

Constitution, reported, "Unlike some companies, which face a crisis when the top executive leaves or dies, Coca-Cola is expected to retain its status as one of the world's most admired corporations. Goizueta had groomed Ivester to follow his footsteps since the Georgia native's 1994 appointment to the company's No. 2 post. And as an indication of how strongly Wall Street felt about Coca-Cola's footings, the company's stock barely rippled six weeks ago when Goizueta was diagnosed with lung cancer."[1]

Doug Ivester, an accountant by training, started his career with Coca-Cola in 1979 as the assistant controller. Four years later, he was named chief financial officer. He was known for his exceptional financial creativity, and he was a major force in Goizueta's ability to revolutionize the company's approach to investment and the handling of debt. By 1989, Goizueta must have decided that Ivester had untapped potential, because he moved him out of his strictly financial role and sent him to Europe to obtain operating and international experience. A year later, Goizueta brought him back and named him president of Coca-Cola USA, where he oversaw expenditures and marketing. From there he continued to groom Ivester, and in 1994, there could be no doubt that Ivester would follow Goizueta into the top position. Goizueta made him president and chief operating officer.

What Roberto Goizueta did was very unusual. Few chief executives of companies today develop strong leaders and groom them to take over the organization. John S. Wood, a consultant at Egon Zehnder International Inc., has noted that "companies have not in the recent past been investing as heavily in bringing people up. If they're not able to grow them, they have to go get them." So why was Roberto Goizueta different? He was a product of the Law of Legacy.

Roberto Goizueta was born in Cuba and educated at Yale, where he earned a degree in chemical engineering. When he returned to Havana in 1954, he answered a newspaper ad for a bilingual chemist.

The company hiring turned out to be Coca-Cola. By 1966, he had become vice president of technical research and development at the company's headquarters in Atlanta. He was the youngest man ever to hold such a position in the company. But in the early 1970s,

> "Leadership is one of the things you cannot delegate. You either exercise it, or you abdicate it."
> —Robert Goizueta

something even more important happened. Robert W. Woodruff, the patriarch of Coca-Cola, took Goizueta under his wing and began developing him. In 1975, Goizueta became the executive vice president of the company's technical division and took on other corporate responsibilities, such as overseeing legal affairs. And in 1980, with Woodruff's blessing, Goizueta became president and chief operating officer. One year later he was the chairman and chief executive. The reason Goizueta so confidently selected, developed, and groomed a successor in the 1990s is that he was building on the legacy that he had received in the 1970s.

LEADERS WHO LEAVE
A LEGACY OF SUCCESSION . . .

Goizueta once said, "Leadership is one of the things you cannot delegate. You either exercise it, or you abdicate it." I believe there is a third choice: You pass it on to your successor. That's a choice Goizueta exercised. Leaders who practice the Law of Legacy are rare. But the ones who do leave a legacy of succession for their organization by doing the following:

LEAD THE ORGANIZATION WITH A "LONG VIEW"

Just about anybody can make an organization look good for a moment—by launching a flashy new program or product, drawing crowds to a big event, or slashing the budget to boost the bottom line. But leaders who leave a legacy take a different approach. They lead with tomorrow as well as today in mind. That's what Goizueta did. He planned to keep leading as long as he was effective, yet he prepared his successor anyway. He always looked out for the best interests of the organization and its stockholders.

> *Just as in sports a coach needs a team of good players to win, an organization needs a team of good leaders to succeed.*

CREATE A LEADERSHIP CULTURE

The most stable companies have strong leaders at every level of the organization. The only way to develop such widespread leadership is to make developing leaders a part of your culture. That is a strong part of Coca-Cola's legacy. How many other successful companies do you know about that have had a succession of leaders come up within the ranks of their own organization?

PAY THE PRICE TODAY TO ASSURE SUCCESS TOMORROW

There is no success without sacrifice. Each organization is unique, and that dictates what the price will be. But any leader who wants to help his organization must be willing to pay that price to ensure lasting success.

VALUE TEAM LEADERSHIP ABOVE INDIVIDUAL LEADERSHIP

No matter how good he is, no leader can do it all alone. Just as in sports a coach needs a team of good players to win, an organization needs a team of good *leaders* to succeed. The larger the organization, the stronger, larger, and deeper the team of leaders needs to be.

WALK AWAY FROM THE ORGANIZATION WITH INTEGRITY

In the case of Coca-Cola, the leader didn't get the opportunity to walk away because he died an untimely death. But if he had lived, I believe Goizueta would have done just that. When it's a leader's time to leave the organization, he has got to be willing to walk away and let his successor do his own thing. Meddling only hurts him and the organization.

A LEGACY OF SUCCESSION

I mentioned in the chapter on the Law of Buy-In that in the fall of 1997, I went to India with a handful of leaders from my nonprofit organization EQUIP. While we were there, I wanted to visit the headquarters of Mother Teresa. It's a plain concrete block building located in Calcutta, which the people there call the Mother House.

As I stood outside the doors preparing to go in, I thought about how no one could tell by looking at it that this modest place had been the home base of such an effective leader. We walked through a foyer and into a central patio that was open to the sky. Our goal was to visit Mother Teresa's tomb, which is located in the facility's dining room. But when we got there, we found out that the room was in use and we would not be allowed to go in until the ceremony that was being performed was over.

We could see a group of about forty to fifty nuns seated, all dressed in the familiar habit that Mother Teresa had worn.

"What's going on in there?" I asked a nun passing by.

She smiled. "Today we are taking forty-five new members into our order," she said and then hurried away into another part of the building.

Since we were already running late and soon had to catch a plane, we couldn't stay. We looked around briefly and then left. As I walked out of the compound, through an alley, and out among the throngs of people, I thought to myself, *Mother Teresa would have been proud*. She was gone, but her legacy was continuing. She had made an impact on the world, and she had developed leaders who were carrying on her vision. And it looks as though they will continue influencing people for generations to come. Mother Teresa's life is a great example of the Law of Legacy.

FEW LEADERS PASS IT ON

Max Dupree, author of *Leadership Is an Art*, declared, "Succession is one of the key responsibilities of leadership." Yet of all the laws of leadership, the Law of Legacy is the one that the fewest leaders seem to learn. Achievement comes to someone when he is able to do great things for himself. Success comes when he empowers followers to do great things *with* him. Significance comes when he develops leaders to do great things *for* him. But a legacy is created only when a person puts his organization into the position to do great things *without* him.

> *A legacy is created only when a person puts his organization into the position to do great things without him.*

I learned the Law of Legacy the hard way. Because the church grew so much while I was in my first leadership position in Hillham, Indiana, I thought I was a success. When I began there, we had only three people in attendance. For three years, I built up that church, reached out to the community, and influenced many people's lives. When I left, our average attendance was in the high two hundreds, and our record was more than three hundred people. I had programs in place, and everything looked rosy to me. I thought I had really done something significant.

When I had been at my second church for about eighteen months, I had lunch with a friend I hadn't seen in a while, and he had just spent some time in Hillham. I asked him about how things were going back there, and I was surprised to hear his answer.

"Not too good," he answered.

"Really?" I said. "Why? Things were going great when I left. What's wrong?"

"Well," he said, "it's kind of fallen off. Some of the programs you got started kind of petered out. The church is running only about a hundred people. It might get even smaller before it's all over."

That really bothered me. A leader hates to see something that he put his sweat, blood, and tears into starting to fail. At first, I got ticked off at the leader who followed me. But then it hit me. If I had done a really good job there, it wouldn't matter what kind of leader followed me, good or bad. The fault was really mine. I hadn't set up the organization to succeed after I left. It was the first time I realized the significance of the Law of Legacy.

PARADIGM SHIFT

After that, I started to look at leadership in a whole new way. Every leader eventually leaves his organization—one way or another. He may change jobs, get promoted, or retire. And even if a person refuses to retire, he is going to die. That made me realize that part of my job as a leader was to start preparing my people and organization for what inevitably lies ahead. That prompted me to change my focus from leading followers to developing leaders. My lasting value, like that of any leader, would be measured by my ability to give the organization a smooth succession.

My best personal succession story concerns my departure from Skyline Church. When I first arrived there in 1981, I made one of my primary goals the identification and development of leaders because I knew that our success depended on it. Over the fourteen years I was there, my staff and I developed literally hundreds of outstanding leaders, both volunteers and staff.

The development of so many leaders put the church in a good position to succeed, but that alone wasn't enough. In many businesses and nonprofit organizations, the leader is in a position to develop and groom a successor. That wasn't something I was able to do at Skyline.

The local board of administration would select someone to succeed me, and I would not drive that process. The most I would be able to do was give them any information I knew about the potential candidates with whom I was acquainted. But there were other things I *could* do, such as preparing the people and the organization for the arrival of their new leader. I wanted to set that person up to succeed as much as I could.

THE SUCCESS CONTINUES

One of my greatest joys in life is knowing that Skyline is stronger now than when I left in 1995. Jim Garlow, who succeeded me as the senior pastor, is doing a wonderful job there. The church's attendance has increased, finances have improved, and best of all, the building and relocation program is going forward after a decade of delays. In the fall of 1997, Jim asked me to come back to Skyline and speak at a fund-raising banquet for the next phase of the building project, and I was delighted to honor his request.

They staged the event at the San Diego Convention Center, located on the city's beautiful bay. They really did a first-class job of everything, and about 4,100 people attended. My wife, Margaret, and I really enjoyed the chance to see and talk with so many of our old friends. And of course, I felt privileged to be the evening's keynote speaker. It was quite a celebration—and quite a success. People pledged more than $7.8 million toward the building of the church's new facility.

As soon as I finished speaking, Margaret and I slipped out of the ballroom. We wanted the night to belong to Jim, since he was now the leader of Skyline. Because of that, we knew it would be best if we made a quick exit before the program was over. Descending the stairs, I grabbed her hand and gave it a squeeze.

"Margaret," I said, "wasn't it an awesome night?"

"Oh, it was great," she said. "I think Jim was really pleased."

"I think you're right," I said. "You know what was the best part for me? Knowing that what we started all those years ago is going to continue." As we left the convention center behind us, I felt that our final chapter with Skyline was finished, and it had a very happy ending. It's like my friend Chris Musgrove says, "Success is not measured by what you're leaving to, but by what you are leaving behind."

When all is said and done, your ability as a leader will not be judged by what you achieved personally or even by what your team accomplished during your tenure. You will be judged by how well your people and your organization did after you were gone. You will be gauged according to the Law of Legacy. Your lasting value will be measured by succession.

CONCLUSION

*Everything Rises and
Falls on Leadership*

WELL, THERE YOU have them—the 21 Irrefutable Laws of Leadership. Learn them, take them to heart, and apply them to your life. If you follow them, people will follow you.

I've been teaching leadership for two and a half decades now, and during those years I've told the people I've trained something that I'm now going to say to you: Everything rises and falls on leadership. Most people don't believe me when I say that, but it's true. The more you try to do in life, the more you will find that leadership makes the difference. Any endeavor you can undertake that involves other people will live or die depending on leadership. As you work to build your organization, remember this:

- Personnel determine the potential of the organization.
- Relationships determine the morale of the organization.
- Structure determines the size of the organization.
- Vision determines the direction of the organization.
- Leadership determines the success of the organization.

I wish you success. Pursue your dreams. Desire excellence. Become the person you were created to be. And accomplish all that you were put on this earth to do. Leadership will help you to do that. Learn to lead—not just for yourself, but for the people who follow behind you. And as you reach the highest levels, don't forget to take others with you to be the leaders of tomorrow.

NOTES

CHAPTER 1

1. John F. Love, *McDonald's: Behind the Arches* (New York: Bantam Books, 1986).

CHAPTER 2

1. Quoted at www.abcnews.com on 4 February 1998.
2. Thomas A. Stewart, "Brain Power: Who Owns It . . . How They Profit from It," *Fortune*, 17 March 1997, 105–6.
3. Paul F. Boller, Jr., *Presidential Anecdotes* (New York: Penguin Books, 1981), 129.

CHAPTER 3

1. Sharon E. Epperson, "Death and the Maven," *Time*, 18 December 1995.
2. James K. Glassman, "An Old Lady's Lesson: Patience Usually Pays," *Washington Post*, 17 December 1995, H01.
3. "The Champ," *Reader's Digest*, January 1972, 109.
4. Milton Meltzer, *Theodore Roosevelt and His America* (New York: Franklin Watts, 1994).

CHAPTER 4

1. *Forbes.*

CHAPTER 5

1. Bruce Nash and Allan Zullo, *The Sports Hall of Shame.*
2. Peggy Noonan, *Time* 15 September 1997.

CHAPTER 6

1. E. M. Swift, "Odd Man Out," *Sports Illustrated*, 92–96.
2. Robert Shaw, "Tough Trust," *Leader to Leader* (winter 1997), 46–54.
3. Russell Duncan, *Blue-Eyed Child of Fortune* (Athens: University of Georgia Press, 1992), 52–54.
4. Robert S. McNamara with Brian VanDeMark, *In Retrospect: The Tragedy and Lessons of Vietnam* (New York: Times Books, 1995).

CHAPTER 7

1. M. W. Taylor, *Harriet Tubman* (New York: Chelsea House Publishers, 1991).
2. Alexander Wolff, "Tales Out of School," *Sports Illustrated*, 20 October 1997, 64.
3. Mitchell Krugel, *Jordan: The Man, His Words, His Life* (New York: St. Martin's Press, 1994), 39.

CHAPTER 8

1. Cathy Booth, "Steve's Job: Restart Apple," *Time*, 18 August 1997, 28–34.
2. Michael Krantz, "If You Can't Beat 'Em," *Time*, 18 August 1997, 35–37.

CHAPTER 10

1. Quoted in Atlanta *Journal-Constitution*, 9 January 1998.
2. H. Norman Schwarzkopf, "Lessons in Leadership," Vol. 12, no. 5.
3. H. Norman Schwarzkopf and Peter Petre, *It Doesn't Take a Hero* (New York: Bantam Books, 1992).
4. Kevin and Jackie Freiberg, *Nuts! Southwest Airlines' Crazy Recipe for Business* (New York: Broadway Books, 1996), 224.

CHAPTER 11

1. Lawrence Miller, *American Spirit: Visions of a New Corporate Culture.*
2. Warren Bennis, *Scarce Organizing Genius: The Secrets of Creative Collaboration.*
3. Judith M. Bardwick, *In Praise of Good Business* (New York: John Wiley and Sons, 1988).
4. Prov. 27:17 CEV.

CHAPTER 12

1. Peter Collier and David Horowitz, *The Fords: An American Epic* (New York: Summit Books, 1987).
2. Lee Iacocca and William Novak, *Iacocca: An Autobiography* (New York: Bantam Books, 1984).
3. Lynne Joy McFarland, John R. Childress, and Larry E. Senn, *21st Century Leadership: Dialogues with 100 Top Leaders* (Leadership Press, 1993).
4. Benjamin P. Thomas, *Abraham Lincoln: A Biography* (New York: Modern Library, 1968), 235.
5. Richard Wheeler, *Witness to Gettysburg* (New York: Harper and Row, 1987).
6. Donald T. Phillips, *Lincoln on Leadership: Executive Strategies for Tough Times* (New York: Warner Books, 1992), 103–4.

CHAPTER 13

1. Janet Lowe, *Jack Welch Speaks: Wisdom from the World's Greatest Business Leader* (New York: John Wiley and Sons, 1998).

CHAPTER 14

1. Otis Port, "Love Among the Digerati," *Business Week*, 25 August 1997, 102.

CHAPTER 15

1. David M. Potter, *Jefferson Davis and the Political Factors in Confederate Defeat.*
2. James C. Humes, *The Wit and Wisdom of Winston Churchill* (New York: Harper Perennial, 1994).
3. Arthur Schlesinger Jr., "Franklin Delano Roosevelt," *Time*, 13 April 1998.
4. Andre Brink, "Nelson Mandela," *Time*, 13 April 1998.
5. Mitchell Krugel, *Jordan: The Man, His Words, His Life* (New York: St. Martin's Press, 1994), 41.
6. Kevin and Jackie Freiberg, *Nuts! Southwest Airlines' Crazy Recipe for Business and Personal Success* (New York: Broadway Books, 1996).

CHAPTER 16

1. Jay Mathews, *Escalante: The Best Teacher in America* (New York: Henry Holt, 1988).

CHAPTER 17

1. John Wooden and Jack Tobin, *They Call Me Coach* (Chicago: Contemporary Books, 1988).
2. Janet C. Lowe, *Jack Welch Speaks: Wisdom from the World's Greatest Business Leader* (New York: John Wiley and Sons, 1998).

CHAPTER 18

1. Lee Iacocca and William Novak, *Iacocca: An Autobiography* (New York: Bantam Books, 1984).
2. Hillary Margolis, "A Whole New Set of Glitches for Digital's Robert Palmer," *Fortune,* 19 August 1996, 193–94.
3. David Wallechinsky, *The Twentieth Century* (Boston: Little, Brown, 1995), 155.

CHAPTER 19

1. Paul F. Boller Jr., *Presidential Anecdotes* (New York: Penguin Books, 1981), 340.
2. Peter G. Bourne, *Jimmy Carter: A Comprehensive Biography from Plains to Postpresidency* (New York: Scribner, 1997).
3. Daniel B. Baker, *Power Quotes* (Detroit: Visible Ink Press, 1992), 337.
4. Douglas Southall Freeman, *Lee: An Abridgement in One Volume* (New York: Charles Scribner's Sons, 1961), 319.
5. Samuel P. Bates, *The Battle of Gettysburg* (Philadelphia: T. H. Davis and Company, 1875), 198–99.
6. Ibid.
7. Richard Wheeler, *Witness to Gettysburg* (New York: Harper and Row, 1987).

CHAPTER 20

1. Rajan Chaudhry, "Dough Boy," *Chain Leader,* April 1997.

CHAPTER 21

1. Mickey H. Gramig, *Atlanta Constitution,* 10 November 1997.

DEVELOPING
the LEADER
WITHIN YOU

This book is dedicated to the man I most admire.
A friend whose touch warmed me;
A mentor whose wisdom guided me;
An encourager whose words lifted me;
A leader I love to follow . . .
My father,
Melvin Maxwell

INTRODUCTION

I t was a moment I will never forget. I was lecturing on the subject of leadership and we had just taken a fifteen-minute break. A man named Bob rushed up to me and said, "You have saved my career! Thank you so much." As he turned to walk away, I stopped him and asked, "How have I 'saved' your career?" He replied, "I'm fifty-three years old and for the last seventeen years I have been in a position that demands leadership. Up until recently I have struggled, acutely aware of my lack of leadership skills and success. Last year I attended your leadership seminar and learned principles that I immediately began applying in my work situation. And it happened. People began to follow my direction—slowly at first, but now quite readily. I had plenty of experience but no expertise. Thanks for making me a leader!"

Testimonials like Bob's have encouraged me to devote much of my time to developing leaders. It is the reason why I hold leadership seminars in the United States and other countries about ten times a year. It is the reason for this book.

What you are about to read is a culmination of skills learned in twenty years of leading people. For more than twenty years I have taught these leadership principles and watched with great satisfaction as men and women have become more effective in leading others. Now I have the opportunity to share them with you.

THE KEY TO SUCCESS IN AN ENDEAVOR IS THE ABILITY TO LEAD OTHERS SUCCESSFULLY.

Everything rises and falls on leadership. Whenever I make that statement the listeners are tempted to change it to, "Almost everything rises and falls on leadership." Most people have a desire to look for the exception instead of the desire to become exceptional.

Right now you lead at a certain skill level. For the sake of teaching this principle, let's say that on a scale of 1 to 10, your leadership skills reach the level of 6. This is what I know: The effectiveness of your work will never rise above your ability to lead and influence others. You cannot produce consistently on a level higher than your leadership. In other words, your leadership skills determine the level of your success—and the success of those who work around you.

Recently I read these words in Newsweek magazine from the president of Hyatt Hotels: "If there is anything I have learned in my 27 years in the service industry, it is this: 99 percent of all employees want to do a good job. How they perform is simply a reflection of the one for whom they work."[1]

This humorous story underscores the importance of effective leadership: During a sales meeting, the manager was berating the sales staff for their dismally low sales figures. "I've had just about enough of poor performance and excuses," he said. "If you can't do the job, perhaps there are other sales people out there who would jump at the chance to sell the worthy products that each of you has the privilege to represent." Then, pointing to a newly recruited, retired pro-football player, he said, "If a football team isn't winning, what happens? The players are replaced. Right?"

The question hung heavy for a few seconds; then the ex-football player answered, "Actually, sir, if the whole team was having trouble, we usually got a new coach."[2]

LEADERSHIP CAN BE TAUGHT.

Leadership is not an exclusive club for those who were "born with it."

The traits that are the raw materials of leadership can be acquired. Link them up with desire and nothing can keep you from becoming a leader. This book will supply the leadership principles. You must supply the desire.

Leonard Ravenhill in "The Last Days Newsletter" tells about a group of tourists who were visiting a picturesque village. As they walked by an old man sitting beside a fence, one tourist asked in a patronizing way, "Were any great men born in this village?"

The old man replied, "Nope, only babies."

Leadership is developed, not discovered. The truly "born leader" will always emerge; but, to stay on top, natural leadership characteristics must be developed. In working with thousands of people desirous of becoming leaders, I have discovered they all fit in one of four categories or levels of leadership:

THE LEADING LEADER:

- Is born with leadership qualities.
- Has seen leadership modeled throughout life.
- Has learned added leadership through training.
- Has self-discipline to become a great leader.

Note: Three out of four of these qualities are acquired.

THE LEARNED LEADER:

- Has seen leadership modeled most of life.
- Has learned leadership through training.
- Has self-discipline to be a great leader.

Note: All three qualities are acquired.

THE LATENT LEADER:

- Has just recently seen leadership modeled.

- Is learning to be a leader through training.
- Has self-discipline to become a good leader.

Note: All three qualities are acquired.

THE LIMITED LEADER:

- Has little or no exposure to leaders.
- Has little or no exposure to leadership training.
- Has desire to become a leader.

Note: All three can be acquired.

THERE ARE VERY FEW LEADERSHIP BOOKS; MOST DEAL WITH MANAGEMENT.

There seems to be a great deal of confusion over the difference between "leadership" and "management."

John W. Gardner, former Secretary of the U.S. Department of Health, Education, and Welfare, who directed a leadership study project in Washington, D.C., has pinpointed five characteristics that set "leader managers" apart from "run-of-the-mill managers":

1. Leader managers are long-term thinkers who see beyond the day's crisis and the quarterly report.

2. Leader managers' interests in their companies do not stop with the units they head. They want to know how all of the company's departments affect one another, and they are constantly reaching beyond their specific areas of influence.

3. Leader managers put heavy emphasis on vision, values, and motivation.

4. Leader managers have strong political skills to cope with conflicting requirements of multiple constituents.

5. Leader managers don't accept the status quo.[3]

Management is the process of assuring that the program and objectives of the organization are implemented. Leadership, on the other hand, has to do with casting vision and motivating people.

"People don't want to be managed. They want to be lead. Whoever heard of a world manager? World leader, yes. Education leader, yes. Political leader. Religious leader. Scout leader. Community leader. Labor leader. Business leader. Yes. They lead. They don't manage. The carrot always wins over the stick. Ask your horse. You can lead your horse to water, but you can't manage him to drink. If you want to manage somebody, manage yourself. Do that well and you'll be ready to stop managing and start leading."[4]

- Knowing how to do a job is the accomplishment of labor.
- Showing others is the accomplishment of a teacher.
- Making sure the work is done by others is the accomplishment of a manager.
- Inspiring others to do better work is the accomplishment of a leader.

My desire is that you be able to accomplish the work of a leader. This book is dedicated to that goal. While you read this book and begin applying these leadership principles, please be reminded of Bruce Larson. In his book *Wind and Fire*, Larson points out some interesting facts about Sandhill cranes: "These large birds, who fly great distances across continents, have three remarkable qualities. First, they rotate leadership. No one bird stays out in front all the time. Second, they choose leaders who can handle the turbulence.

And then, all during the time one bird is leading, the rest are honking their affirmation."

Hopefully you will learn enough about leadership to take your place at the front of the pack. While you are making that attempt, I will be honking affirmation to you with great pride and inner satisfaction.

In every age there comes a time when leadership must come forth to meet the needs of the hour. Therefore, there is no potential leader who does not find his or her time. Read this book and be ready to seize your moment!

—John C. Maxwell

THE DEFINITION OF LEADERSHIP:
INFLUENCE

E veryone talks about it; few understand it. Most people want it; few achieve it. There are over fifty definitions and descriptions of it in my personal files. What is this intriguing subject we call "leadership"?

Perhaps because most of us want to be leaders we become emotionally involved when trying to define leadership. Or, perhaps because we know one, we try to copy his or her behavior and describe leadership as a personality. Ask ten people to define leadership and you'll probably receive ten different answers. After more than five decades of observing leadership within my family and many years of developing my own leadership potential, I have come to this conclusion: *Leadership is influence.* That's it. Nothing more; nothing less. My favorite leadership proverb is: He who thinketh he leadeth and hath no one following him is only taking a walk.

James C. Georges, of the ParTraining Corporation, said it quite effectively in a recent interview with *Executive Communications*: "What is leadership? Remove for a moment the moral issues behind it, and there is only one definition: *Leadership is the ability to obtain followers.*

"Hitler was a leader and so was Jim Jones. Jesus of Nazareth, Martin Luther King, Jr., Winston Churchill, and John F. Kennedy all were leaders. While their value systems and management abilities were very different, each had followers.

"Once you define leadership as the ability to get followers, you work backward from that point of reference to figure out how to lead."[1]

Therein lies the problem. Most people define leadership a the ability to achieve a position, not to get followers. Therefore, they go after a position, rank, or title and upon their arrival think they have become a leader. This type of thinking creates two common problems: Those who possess the "status" of a leader often experience the frustration of few followers, and those who lack the proper titles may not see themselves as leaders and therefore don't develop their leadership skills.

My goal with this book is to help you accept leadership as influence (that is, the ability to get followers), and then work backward from that point to help you learn how to lead. Each chapter is designed to place in your hand another principle that will assist your leadership development. This first chapter is designed to expand the level of your influence.

INSIGHTS ABOUT INFLUENCE

EVERYONE INFLUENCES SOMEONE.

Sociologists tell us that even the most introverted individual will influence ten thousand other people during his or her lifetime! This amazing statistic was shared with me by my associate Tim Elmore. Tim and I concluded that each one of us is both influencing and being influenced by others. That means that all of us are leading in some areas, while in other areas we are being led. No one is excluded from being a leader or a follower. Realizing your potential as a leader is your responsibility. In any given situation with any given group there is a prominent influencer. Let me illustrate. The mother may be the dominant influencer over a child in the morning before school begins. Mom may choose what to eat and what to wear. The child who is influenced before school may become the influencer of other children once school begins. Dad and Mom may meet at a restaurant for lunch and both be influenced by the waiter who suggests the house specialty. The time dinner is served in the evening may be set because of either the husband's or wife's work schedule.

The prominent leader of any group is quite easily discovered. Just observe the people as they gather. If an issue is to be decided, who is the person whose opinion seems most valuable? Who is the one others watch the most when the issue is being discussed? Who is the one with whom people quickly agree? Most importantly, who is the one the others follow? Answers to these questions will help you discern who the real leader is in a particular group.

WE NEVER KNOW WHO OR HOW MUCH WE INFLUENCE.

The most effective way to understand the power of influence is to think of the times you have been touched by the influence of a person or an event. Big events leave marks on all our lives and memories. For example, ask a couple of people born prior to 1930 what they were doing when they heard that Pearl Harbor had been bombed, and they will describe in detail their feelings and surroundings when they heard the terrible news. Ask someone born before 1955 to describe what he or she was doing when the news that John F. Kennedy had been shot was broadcast. Again, you will find no loss for words. A similar response occurs with the younger generation when asked about the day the Challenger blew up. These were big events that touched everyone.

Think also of the little things or people who influenced you in a powerful way. In reflecting on my own life, I think of the influence of a camp I attended as a youth and how it helped determine my career choice. I think of my seventh grade teacher, Glen Leatherwood . . . the bubble lights on our Christmas tree that gave me the "Christmas feeling" every year . . . the affirming note I received from a professor in college . . . The list is endless. Life consists of influencers who daily find us vulnerable to their impressions and, therefore, have helped mold us into the persons we are. J. R. Miller said it well: "There have been meetings of only a moment which have left impressions for life, for eternity. No one can understand that mysterious thing we call influence . . . yet . . . everyone of us continually exerts influence, either to heal, to bless, to leave marks of beauty; or to wound, to hurt, to poison, to stain other lives."[2]

This truth also sobers me when I realize my influence as a father. A friend gave me a plaque with this poem on it. Now it sits on my desk:

The Little Chap Who Follows Me

A careful man I want to be,
A little fellow follows me;
I do not dare to go astray
For fear he'll go the self-same way.

I cannot once escape his eyes.
Whate'er he sees me do he tries.
Like ME he says he's going to be—
That little chap who follows me.

I must remember as I go
Through summer suns and winter snows,
I am building for the years to be—
That little chap who follows me.

THE BEST INVESTMENT IN THE FUTURE IS A PROPER INFLUENCE TODAY.

The issue is not whether you influence someone. What needs to be settled is what kind of an influencer will you be? Will you grow into your leadership skills? In the book *Leaders*, Bennis and Nanus say, "The truth is that leadership opportunities are plentiful and within reach of most people."[3]

You must believe that! The rest of this chapter is committed to helping you make a difference tomorrow by becoming a better leader today.

INFLUENCE IS A SKILL THAT CAN BE DEVELOPED.

Robert Dilenschneider, the CEO of Hill and Knowlton, a worldwide public relations agency, is one of the nation's major influence brokers. He skillfully weaves his persuasive magic in the global arena where governments and megacorporations meet. He wrote a book entitled *Power and Influence*, in which he shares the idea of the "power triangle" to help leaders get ahead. He says, "The three components of this triangle are communication, recognition, and influence. You start to communicate effectively. This leads to recognition and recognition in turn leads to influence."[4]

We can increase our influence and our leadership potential. Out of this conviction I have developed a teaching tool to assist others in understanding their levels of leadership so they can increase their levels of influence (see chart on page 13).

THE FIVE LEVELS OF LEADERSHIP

LEVEL 1: POSITION

This is the basic entry level of leadership. The only influence you have is that which comes with a title. People who stay at this level get into territorial rights, protocol, tradition, and organizational charts. These things are not negative unless they become the basis for authority and influence, but they are poor substitutes for leadership skills.

A person may be "in control" because he has been appointed to a position. In that position he may have authority. But real leadership is more than having authority; it is more than having the technical training and following the proper procedures. Real leadership is being the person others will gladly and confidently follow. A real leader knows the difference between being the boss and being a leader, as illustrated by the following:

The boss drives his workers; the leader coaches them.

The boss depends upon authority; the leader on goodwill.

253

The boss inspires fear; the leader inspires enthusiasm.

The boss says "I"; the leader, "we."

The boss fixes the blame for the breakdown; the leader fixes the breakdown.

The boss knows how it I done; the leader shows how.

The boss says "go"; the leader says "let's go!"

Characteristics of a "Positional Leader."

Security is based on title, not talent. The story is told of a private in World War I who shouted on the battlefield, "Put out that match!" only to find to his chagrin that the offender was General "Black Jack" Pershing. When the private, who feared severe punishment, tried to stammer out his apology, General Pershing patted him on the back and said, "That's all right, son. Just be glad I'm not a second lieutenant." The point should be clear. The higher the person's level of true ability and the resulting influence, the more secure and confident he becomes.

This level is often gained by appointment. All other levels are gained by ability. Leo Durocher was coaching at first base in an exhibition game the Giants were playing at West Point. One noisy cadet kept shouting at Leo and doing his best to upset him.

"Hey, Durocher," he hollered. "How did a little squirt like you get into the major leagues?"

Leo shouted back, "My Congressman appointed me!"[5]

People will not follow a positional leader beyond his stated authority. They will only do what they have to do when they are required to do it. Low morale is always present. When the leader lacks confidence, the followers lack commitment. They are like the little boy who was asked by Billy Graham how to find the nearest post office. When the lad told him, Dr. Graham thanked him and said, "If you'll come to the convention center this evening you can hear me telling everyone how to get to heaven."

"I don't think I'll be there," the boy replied. "You don't even know your way to the post office."

Positional leaders have more difficulty working with volunteers, white collar workers, and younger people. Volunteers don't have to work in the organization so there is no monetary leverage that a positional leader can use to make them respond. White collar workers are used to participating in decision-making and resent dictatorial leadership. Baby boomers in particular are unimpressed with symbols of authority.

Most of us have been taught that leadership is a position. Frustration rises within us when we get out into the real world and find that few people follow us because of our titles. Our joy and success in leading others depend on our abilities to keep climbing the levels of leadership.

LEVEL 2: PERMISSION

Fred Smith says, "Leadership is getting people to work for you when they are not obligated."[6] That will only happen when you climb to the second level of influence. People don't care how much you know until they know how much you care. Leadership begins with the heart, not the head. It flourishes with a meaningful relationship, not more regulation.

Leaders on the "position" level often lead by intimidation. They are like the chickens that Norwegian psychologist T. Schjelderup-Ebbe studied in developing the "pecking order" principle that today is used to describe all types of social gatherings.

Schjelderup-Ebbe found that in any flock one hen usually dominates all the others. She can peck any other without being pecked in return. Second comes a hen that pecks all but the top hen, and the rest are arranged in descending hierarchy, ending in one hapless hen that is pecked by all and can peck no one.

In contrast to this a person on the "permission" level will lead by interrelationships. The agenda is not the pecking order but people development. On this level, time, energy, and focus are placed on the individual's needs and desires. A wonderful illustration of why it's so critical to put people and their needs first is found in the story of Henry Ford in Amitai Etzioni's book, *Modern Organizations*:

"He made a perfect car, the Model T, that ended the need for any other car. He was totally product-oriented. He wanted to fill the world with Model T cars. But when people started coming to him and saying, 'Mr. Ford, we'd like a different color car,' he remarked, 'You can have any color you want as long as it's black.' And that's when the decline started."

People who are unable to build solid, lasting relationships will soon discover that they are unable to sustain long, effective leadership. (Chapter 7 of this book, "Developing Your Most Appreciable Asset: *People*," will deal more extensively with this subject.) Needless to say, you can love people without leading them, but you cannot lead people without loving them.

One day one of my staff members, Dan Reiland, shared an insight with me that I have never forgotten: "If level 1, *Position*, is the door to leadership, then level 2, *Permission*, is the foundation."

Caution! Don't try to skip a level. The most often skipped level is 2, *Permission*. For example, a husband goes from level 1, *Position*, a wedding day title, to level 3, *Production*. He becomes a great provider for the family, but in the process he neglects the essential relationships that hold a family together. The family disintegrates and so does the husband's business. Relationships involve a process that provides the glue and much of the staying power for long-term, consistent production.

LEVEL 3: PRODUCTION

On this level things begin to happen, good things. Profit increases. Morale is high. Turnover is low. Needs are being met. Goals are being realized. Accompanying this growth is the "big mo"—momentum. Leading and influencing others is fun. Problems are solved with minimum effort. Fresh statistics are shared on a regular basis with the people who undergird the growth of the organization. Everyone is results-oriented. In fact, results are the main reason for the activity.

This is a major difference between levels 2 and 3. On the "relationship" level, people get together just to get together. There is no other objective. On the "results" level, people come together to accomplish a purpose. They like to get together to get together, but they love to get together to accomplish something. In other words, they are results-oriented.

They are like a character played by Jack Nicholson who, while in a restaurant in a famous scene from the movie *Five Easy Pieces*, is told he cannot get a side-order of toast. He comes up with an imaginative solution. First, he orders a chicken salad sandwich on toast, Then he instructs the waitress: "No mayonnaise, but butter . . . and hold the chicken."

One of my favorite stories is about a newly hired traveling salesman who sent his first sales report to the home office. It stunned the brass in the sales department because it was obvious that the new salesman was ignorant! This is what he wrote: "I seen this outfit which they ain't never bot a dim's worth of nothin from us and I sole them some goods. I'm now goin to Chicawgo."

Before the man could be given the heave-ho by the sales manager, along came this letter from Chicago: "I cum hear and sole them haff a millyon."

Fearful if he did, and afraid if he didn't fire the ignorant salesman, the sales manager dumped the problem in the lap of the president. The following morning, the ivory-towered sales department members were amazed to see posted on the bulletin board above the two letters written by the ignorant salesman this memo from the president: "We ben spendin two much time trying to spel instead of trying to sel. Let's watch those sails. I want everybody should read these letters from Gooch who is on the rode doin a grate job for us and you should go out and do like he done."

Obviously, any sales manager would prefer to have a salesman who can both sell and spell. However, many people have produced great results who were not "qualified."

LEVEL 4: PEOPLE DEVELOPMENT

How do you spot a leader? According to Robert Townsend, they come in all sizes, ages, shapes, and conditions. Some are poor administrators, while some are not overly bright. There is a clue: Since some people are mediocre, the true leader can be recognized because somehow his people consistently demonstrate superior performances.

A leader is great, not because of his or her power, but because of his or her ability to empower others. Success without a successor is failure. A worker's main responsibility is developing others to do the work (see chapter 7).

Loyalty to the leader reaches its highest peak when the follower has personally grown through the mentorship of the leader. Note the progression: At level 2, the follower loves the leader; at level 3, the follower admires the leader; at level 4, the follower is loyal to the leader. Why? You win people's hearts by helping them grow personally.

One of the key players on my staff is Sheryl Fleisher. When she first joined the team she was not a people person. I began to work closely with her until she truly became a people person. Today she successfully develops others. There is a bond of loyalty that Sheryl gives to my leadership, and we both know the reason. My time invested with her brought a positive change. She will never forget what I have done for her. Interestingly her time invested in the lives of others has greatly helped me. I will never forget what she has done for me, either.

The core of leaders who surround you should all be people you have personally touched or helped to develop in some way. When that happens, love and loyalty will be exhibited by those closest to you and by those who are touched by your key leaders.

There is, however, a potential problem of moving up the levels of influence as a leader and becoming comfortable with the group of people you have developed around you. You may not realize that many new people view you as a "position" leader because you have had no contact with them. The following suggestions will help you become a people developer:

Walk slowly though the crowd. Have some way of keeping in touch with everyone. When I was a pastor, I did this in my congregation of 5,000 by:

- Learning names through the pictorial church directory.

- Making communication cards available to the congregation and reading the cards as they are turned in (about 250 were received weekly).

- Reading every interview form of a membership applicant.

- Reading and replying to letters that are sent to me.

- Visiting one social event of each Sunday school class each year.

Develop key leaders. I systematically meet with and teach those who are influencers within the organization. They in turn pass on to others what I have given them.

LEVEL 5: PERSONHOOD

Little time will be spent discussing this level since most of us have not yet arrived at it. Only a lifetime of proven leadership will allow us to sit at level 5 and reap the rewards that are eternally satisfying. I do this—some day I want to sit atop this level. It's achievable.

CLIMBING THE STEPS OF LEADERSHIP

Here are some additional insights on the leadership-levels process:

THE HIGHER YOU GO, THE LONGER IT TAKES.

Each time there is a change in your job or you join a new circle of friends, you start on the lowest level and begin to work yourself up the steps.

THE HIGHER YOU GO, THE HIGHER THE LEVEL OF COMMITMENT.

This increase in commitment is a two-way street. Greater commitment is demanded not only from you, but from the other individuals involved. When either the leader or the follower is unwilling to make the sacrifices a new level demands, influence will begin to decrease.

THE HIGHER YOU GO, THE EASIER IT IS TO LEAD.

Notice the progression from level two through level four. The focus goes from liking you to liking what you do for the common interest of all concerned to liking what you do for them personally. Each level climbed by the leader and the followers adds another reason why people will want to follow.

THE HIGHER YOU GO, THE GREATER THE GROWTH.

Growth can only occur when effective change takes place. Change will become easier as you climb the levels of leadership. As you rise, other people will allow and even assist you in making needed changes.

YOU NEVER LEAVE THE BASE LEVEL.

Each level stands upon the previous one and will crumble if the lower level is neglected. For example, if you move from a permission (relationships) level to a production (results) level and stop caring for the people who are following you and helping you produce, they might begin to develop a feeling of being used. As you move up in the levels, the deeper and more solid your leadership will be with a person or group of people.

THE FIVE LEVELS OF LEADERSHIP

5
PERSONHOOD

RESPECT
People follow
because of who
you are and what
you represent.

NOTE: This step
is reserved for
leaders who
have spent years
growing people
and organizations.
Few make it. Those
who do are bigger
than life.

4
PEOPLE
DEVELOPMENT

REPRODUCTION
People follow
because of what
you have done for
them.

NOTE: This is where long-
range growth occurs. Your
commitment to developing
leaders will insure ongoing
growth to the organization
and to people. Do whatever
you can to achieve and
stay on this level.

3
PRODUCTION

RESULTS
People follow
because of what
you have done for
the organization.

NOTE: This is where success is sensed
by most people. They like you and
what you are doing. Problems are
fixed with very little effort because
of momentum.

2
PERMISSION

RELATIONSHIPS
People follow
because they
want to.

NOTE: People will follow you beyond your stated
authority. This level allows work to be fun.
Caution: Staying too long on this level without
rising will cause highly motivated people to
become restless.

1
POSITION

RIGHTS
People follow
because they
have to.

NOTE: Your influence will not extend beyond the lines of
your job description. The longer you stay here, the higher
the turnover and the lower the morale.

IF YOU ARE LEADING A GROUP OF PEOPLE, YOU WILL NOT BE ON THE SAME LEVEL WITH EVERYONE.

Not every person will respond the same way to your leadership.

FOR YOUR LEADERSHIP TO REMAIN EFFECTIVE, IT IS ESSENTIAL THAT YOU TAKE THE OTHER INFLUENCERS WITHIN THE GROUP WITH YOU TO THE HIGHER LEVELS.

The collective influence of you and the other leaders will bring the rest along. If this does not happen, divided interest and loyalty will occur within the group.

CONCLUSIONS OF INFLUENCE

We now have a blueprint to help us understand influence and how to increase it. The blueprint indicates that in order to get to the top, you must do two things:

KNOW WHAT LEVEL YOU ARE ON AT THIS MOMENT.

Since you will be on different levels with different people, you need to know which people are on which level. If the biggest influencers within the organization are on the highest levels and are supportive of you, then your success in leading others will be attainable. If the best influencers are on the highest levels and not supportive, then problems will soon arise.

KNOW AND APPLY THE QUALITIES NEEDED TO BE SUCCESSFUL AT EACH LEVEL.

Listed below are some characteristics that must be exhibited with excellence before advancement to the next level is possible.

Level 1: Position/Rights

- Know your job description thoroughly.
- Be aware of the history of the organization.
- Relate the organization's history to the people of the organization (in other words, be a team player).
- Accept responsibility.
- Do your job with consistent excellence.
- Do more than expected.
- Offer creative ideas for change and improvement.

Level 2: Permission/Relationship

- Possess a genuine love for people.
- Make those who work with you more successful.
- See through other people's eyes.
- Love people more than procedures.
- Do "win-win" or don't do it.
- Include others in your journey.
- Deal wisely with difficult people.

Level 3: Production/Results

- Initiate and accept responsibility for growth.
- Develop and follow a statement of purpose.
- Make your job description and energy an integral part of the statement of purpose.
- Develop accountability for results, beginning with yourself.

- Know and do the things that give a high return.
- Communicate the strategy and vision of the organization.
- Become a change-agent and understand timing.
- Make the difficult decisions that will make a difference.

Level 4: People Development/Reproduction

- Realize that people are your most valuable asset.
- Place a priority on developing people.
- Be a model for others to follow.
- Pour your leadership efforts into the top 20 percent of your people.
- Expose key leaders to growth opportunities.
- Be able to attract other winners/producers to the common goal.
- Surround yourself with an inner core that complements your leadership.

Level 5: Personhood/Respect

- Your followers are loyal and sacrificial.
- You have spent years mentoring and molding leaders.
- You have become a statesman/consultant, and are sought out by others.
- Your greatest joy comes from watching others grow and develop.
- You transcend the organization.

Everyone is a leader because everyone influences someone. Not everyone will become a great leader, but everyone can become a better leader. Now, only two questions must be answered: "Will you unleash your leadership potential?" and "Will you use your leadership skills to better mankind?" This book was written to help you do both.

My Influence

My life shall touch a dozen lives
Before this day is done.
Leave countless marks of good or ill,
E'er sets the evening sun.

This, the wish I always wish,
The prayer I always pray;
Lord, may my life help others lives
It touches by the way.[7]

ACTION STEPS TO UNLEASH YOUR LEADERSHIP POTENTIAL

REVIEW:

1. Leadership is _____.

2. The five levels of leadership are:
   (1)_____
   (2)_____
   (3)_____
   (4)_____
   (5)_____

3. What level am I currently on with most people?

   _____

4. What level am I currently on with other influencers?

   _____

RESPOND:

1. List the five top influencers in your organization.

    (a) What level of influence are you on with them?

    (b) What level of influence are they on with others?

2. Spend one hour a month with the top five influencers, individually, building a relationship with them.

3. Spend two hours a month with the top influencers as a group, developing them. Spend one of the two hours reviewing a chapter in this book. Spend the other hour doing a project together that enhances the organization.

4. Review the characteristics of each of the five levels of leadership and pick out three that you are weak in and need to develop.
   (1)
   (2)
   (3)

=====

THE KEY TO LEADERSHIP:
PRIORITIES

Recently, while attending a conference, I heard a speaker say, "There are two things that are most difficult to get people to do: to think and to do things in order of importance." He went on to say that these two things are the difference between a professional and an amateur.

I also believe that thinking ahead and prioritizing responsibilities marks the major differences between a leader and a follower, because:

- Practical people know how to get what they want.
- Philosophers know what they ought to want.
- Leaders know how to get what they ought to want.

Success can be defined as *the progressive realization of a predetermined goal*. This definition tells us that the discipline to prioritize and the ability to work toward a stated goal are essential to a leader's success. In fact, I believe they are the key to leadership.

Many years ago, while working toward a business degree, I learned about the Pareto Principle. It is commonly called the 20/80 principle. Although I received little information about this principle at the time, I began applying it to

> Success is the progressive realization of a predetermined goal.

The Pareto Principle

20 percent of your priorities will give you 80 percent
of your production.

IF

you spend your time, energy, money, and personnel
on the top 20 percent of your priorities.

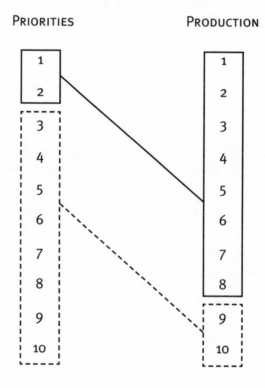

PRIORITIES   PRODUCTION

my life. Twenty years later I find it a most useful tool for determining priorities for any person's life or for any organization.

THE PARETO PRINCIPLE
THE 20/80 PRINCIPLE

The solid lines on the illustration of the 20/80 Principle on page 20 represent a person or organization that spends time, energy, money, and personnel on the most important priorities. The result is a four-fold return in productivity. The dotted lines represent a person or organization that spends time, energy, money, and personnel on the lesser priorities. The result is a very small return.

EXAMPLES OF THE PARETO PRINCIPLE:

TIME   20 percent of our time produces 80 percent of the results.

COUNSELING   20 percent of the people take up 80 percent of our time.

PRODUCTS   20 percent of the products bring in 80 percent of the profit.

READING   20 percent of the book contains 80 percent of the content.

JOB   20 percent of our work gives us 80 percent of our satisfaction.

SPEECH   20 percent of the presentation produces 80 percent of the impact.

DONATIONS   20 percent of the people will give 80 percent of the money.

LEADERSHIP   20 percent of the people will make 80 percent of the decisions.

PICNIC   20 percent of the people will eat 80 percent of the food!

Every leader needs to understand the Pareto Principle in the area of people oversight and leadership. For example, 20 percent of the people in an organization will be responsible for 80 percent of the company's success. The following strategy will enable a leader to increase the productivity of an organization.

1. Determine which people are the top 20 percent producers.

2. Spend 80 percent of your "people time" with the top 20 percent.

3. Spend 80 percent of your personal developmental dollars on the top 20 percent.

4. Determine what 20 percent of the work gives 80 percent of the return and train an assistant to do the 80 percent less effective work. This "frees up" the producer to do what he/she does best.

5. Ask the top 20 percent to do on-the-job training for the next 20 percent.

Remember, we teach what we know; we reproduce what we are. Like begats like.

I teach this principle at leadership conferences. I am often asked, "How do I identify the top 20 percent influencers/producers in my organization?" I suggest that you make a list of everyone in your company or department. Then ask yourself this question about each individual: "If this person takes a negative action against me or withdraws his or her support from me, what will the impact likely be?"

> Efficiency is the foundation for survival. Effectiveness is the foundation for success.

If you won't be able to function, then put a check mark next to that name. If the person can help you or hurt you, but cannot make or break you in terms of your ability to get important things done, then don't put a check mark next to that name. When you get through making the check marks, you will have marked between 15 and 20 percent of the names. Those are the vital relationships that need to be developed and given the proper amount of resources needed to grow the organization.

It's Not How Hard You Work;
It's How Smart You Work.

A man was told that if he worked the very hardest he could he would become rich. The hardest work he knew was digging holes, so he set about digging great holes in his backyard. He didn't get rich; he only got a backache. He worked hard but he worked without any priorities.

ORGANIZE OR AGONIZE.

The ability to juggle three or four high priority projects successfully is a must for every leader. A life in which anything goes will ultimately be a life in which nothing goes.

Prioritize Assignments

High Importance/High Urgency: Tackle these projects first.

High Importance/Low Urgency: Set deadlines for completion and get these projects worked into your daily routine.

Low Importance/High Urgency: Find quick, efficient ways to get this work done without much personal involvement. If possible, delegate it to a "can do" assistant.

Low Importance/Low Urgency: This is busy or repetitious work such as filing. Stack it up and do it in one-half hour segments every week; get somebody else to do it; or don't do it at all. Before putting off until tomorrow something you can do today, study it clearly. Maybe you can postpone it indefinitely.

PARETO

DATE_____

PHONE CALLS TO MAKE	COMP		PERSONAL NOTES	COMP
1._____	☐		1._____	☐
2._____	☐		2._____	☐
3._____	☐		3._____	☐
4._____	☐		4._____	☐

_____ 20/80 TIME _____

ORDER OF
PRIORITY TIME ALLOWED DESCRIPTION—LIST OF THINGS TO DO <u>NOW</u> COMPLETED
(HIGH IMPORTANCE; HIGH URGENCY)

1._____ ☐

2._____ ☐

3._____ ☐

4._____ ☐

5._____ ☐

6._____ ☐

7._____ ☐

8._____ ☐

9._____ ☐

10._____ ☐

LIST OF THINGS TO DO
(HIGH IMPORTANCE; LOW URGENCY)

			LIST OF THINGS TO DELEGATE (LOW IMPORTANCE; HIGH URGENCY)		
1._____	☐		1._____	☐	
2._____	☐		2._____	☐	
3._____	☐		3._____	☐	
4._____	☐		4._____	☐	
5._____	☐		5._____	☐	
6._____	☐		6._____	☐	
7._____	☐		7._____	☐	
8._____	☐		8._____	☐	

A few years ago I was teaching the 20/80 principle at a conference in Boston. A few weeks later my friend, John Bowen, sent me a tablet of paper that he designed from the lecture. I have used it for my own prioritizing ever since. Perhaps it will have value to you, too (see pg. 24).

Choose Or Lose.

Every person is either an initiator or a reactor when it comes to planning. An example is our calendar. The question is not, "Will my calendar be full?" but "Who will fill my calendar?" If we are leaders of others, the question is not, "Will I see people?" but "Who will I see?" My observation is that leaders tend to initiate and followers tend to react. Note the difference.

LEADERS	FOLLOWERS
Initiate	React
Lead; pick up phone and make contact	Listen; wait for phone to ring
Spend time planning; anticipate problems	Spend time living day-to-day; react to problems
Invest time with people	Spend time with people
Fill the calendar by priorities	Fill the calendar by requests.

EVALUATE OR STALEMATE.

A veteran of many years of decision-making gave me this short, simple advice: Decide what to do and do it; decide what not to do and don't do it. Evaluation of priorities, however, is not quite that simple. Many times they are not black or white, but many tones of gray. I have found that the last thing one knows is what to put first.

The following questions will assist your priority process:

What is required of me? A leader can give up anything except final responsibility. The question that must always be answered before accepting a new job is "What is required of me?" In other words, what do I have to do that no one but me can do? Whatever those things are, they must be put high on the priority list. Failure to do them will cause you to be among the unemployed. There will be many responsibilities of the levels under your position, but only a few that require you to be the one and only one who can do them. Distinguish between what you have to do and what can be delegated to someone else.

Take a minute and list what is required of you in your job (by priority, if possible).

1.

2.

3.

4.

What gives me the greatest return? The effort expended should approximate the results expected. A question I must continually ask myself is, "Am I doing what I do best and receiving a good return for the organization?" Three common problems in many organizations are:

- Abuse: Too few employees are doing too much.
- Disuse: Too many employees are doing too little.
- Misuse: Too many employees are doing the wrong things.

Bo Jackson played defensive end for his high school football team. He was good, but he didn't lead his team to a championship. In fact they finished the season with three wins and seven losses. At Auburn University, when all three running backs were injured, Bo's coach asked him to fill in "until the regulars are healthy again." Bo was apprehensive, but he did it. The rest is history. This is an excellent example of fulfilling the "return" questions.

Take a minute and list what gives you the greatest return on your job.

1.

2.

3.

4.

What is most rewarding? Life is too short not to be fun. Our best work takes place when we enjoy it. Some time ago I spoke at a leaders' conference where I attempted to teach this principle. The title of my lecture was, "Take This Job and Love It." I encouraged the audience to find something they liked to do so much they would gladly do it for nothing. Then I suggested they learn to do it so well that people would be happy to pay them for it. Andy Granatelli said that when you are making a success of something, it's not work. It's a way of life. You enjoy yourself because you are making your contribution to the world. I believe that! Take a minute and write down what is most satisfying in your job.

1.

2.

3.

4.

Success in your work will be greatly increased if the 3 R's (Requirements/Return/Reward) are similar. In other words, if the requirements of my job are the same as my strengths that give me the highest return and doing those things brings me great pleasure, then I will be successful if I act on my priorities.

PRIORITY PRINCIPLES

PRIORITIES NEVER "STAY PUT."

Priorities continually shift and demand attention. H. Ross Perot said, "Anything that is excellent or praiseworthy moment-by-moment on the cutting edge must be constantly fought for." Well-placed priorities always sit on "the edge."

To keep priorities in place:

- Evaluate: Every month review the 3 R/s (Requirements/Return/ Reward)

- Eliminate: Ask yourself, "What am I doing that can be done by someone else?"

- Estimate: What are the top projects you are doing this month and how long will they take?

PRINCIPLE: YOU CANNOT OVERESTIMATE THE UNIMPORTANCE OF PRACTICALLY EVERYTHING.

I love this principle. It's a little exaggerated but needs to be said. William James said that the art of being wise is the "art of knowing what to overlook." The petty and the mundane steal much of our time. Too many are living for the wrong things.

> You cannot overestimate the unimportance of practically everything.

Dr. Anthony Campolo tells about a sociological study in which fifty people over the age of ninety-five were asked one question: "If you could live your life over again, what would you do differently?" It was an open-ended question, and a multiplicity of answers constantly reemerged and dominated the results of the study. These three answers were:

- If I had it to do over again, I would reflect more.
- If I had it to do over again, I would risk more.

- If I had it to do over again, I would do more things that would live on after I am dead.

A young concert violinist was asked the secret of her success. She replied, "Planned neglect." Then she explained, "When I was in school, there were many things that demanded my time. When I went to my room after breakfast, I made my bed, straightened the room, dusted the floor, and did whatever else came to my attention. Then I hurried to my violin practice. I found I wasn't progressing as I thought I should, so I reversed things. Until my practice period was completed, I deliberately neglected everything else. That program of planned neglect, I believe, accounts for my success."[1]

THE GOOD IS THE ENEMY OF THE BEST.

Most people can prioritize when faced with right or wrong issue. The challenge arises when we are faced with two good choices. Now what should we do? What if both choices fall comfortably into the requirements, return, and reward of our work?

How to Break the Tie Between Two Good Options

- Ask your overseer or coworkers their preference.
- Can one of the options be handled by someone else? If so, pass it on and work on the one only you can do.
- Which option would be of more benefit to the customer? Too many times we are like the merchant who was so intent on trying to keep the store clean that he would never unlock the front door. The real reason for running the store is to have customers come in, not to clean it up!
- Make your decision based on the purpose of the organization.

A lighthouse keeper who worked on a rocky stretch of coastline received his new supply of oil once a month to keep the light burning.

Not being far from shore, he had frequent guests. One night a woman from the village begged some oil to keep her family warm. Another time a father asked for some to use in his lamp. Another needed some to lubricate a wheel. Since all the requests seemed legitimate, the lighthouse keeper tried to please everyone and grant the requests of all. Toward the end of the month he noticed the supply of oil was very low. Soon it was gone, and the beacon went out. That night several ships were wrecked and lives were lost. When the authorities investigated, the man was very repentant. To his excuses and pleading their reply was, "You were given oil for one purpose—to keep that light burning!"

YOU CAN'T HAVE IT ALL.

When my son, Joel Porter, was younger, every time we entered a store, I would say to him, "You can't have it all." Like many people, he had a hard time eliminating things in his life. Ninety-five percent of achieving anything is knowing what you want. Many years ago I read this poem by William H. Hinson:

> He who seeks one thing, and but one,
> May hope to achieve it before life is done.
> But he who seeks all things wherever he goes
> Must reap around him in whatever he sows
> A harvest of barren regret.

A group of people were preparing for an ascent to the top of Mont Blanc in the Alps in France. On the evening before the climb, a French guide outlined the main prerequisite for success. He said, "To reach the top, you must carry only equipment necessary for climbing. You must leave behind all unnecessary accessories. It's a difficult climb."

A young Englishman disagreed and the next morning showed up with a rather heavy, brightly colored blanket, some large pieces of cheese, a bottle of wine, a couple of cameras with several lenses hanging around his neck, and some bars of chocolate. The guide said, "You'll never make it with that. You can only take the bare necessities to make the climb."

But strong-willed as he was, the Englishman set off on his own in front of the group to prove to them he could do it. The group then followed under the direction of the guide, each one carrying just the bare necessities. On the way up to the summit of Mont Blanc, they began to notice certain things someone had left along the way. First, they encountered a brightly colored blanket, then some pieces of cheese, a bottle of wine, camera equipment, and some chocolate bars. Finally when they reached the top, they discovered the Englishman. Wisely along the way he had jettisoned everything unnecessary.

TOO MANY PRIORITIES PARALYZE US.

Every one of us has looked at our desks filled with memos and papers, heard the phone ringing, and watched the door open all at the same time! Remember the "frozen feeling" that came over you?

William H. Hinson tells us why animal trainers carry a stool when they go into a cage of lions. They have their whips, of course, and their pistols are at their sides. But invariably they also carry a stool. Hinson says it is the most important tool of the trainer. He holds the stool by the back and thrusts the legs toward the face of the wild animal. Those who know maintain that the animal tries to focus on all four legs at once. In the attempt to focus on all four, a kind of paralysis overwhelms the animal, and it becomes tame, weak, and disabled because its attention is fragmented. (Now we will have more empathy for the lions.)

One day, Sheryl, one of our most productive staff members, came to see me. She looked exhausted. I learned that she was overloaded. Her "to do" list was getting too long. I asked her to list all her projects. We prioritized them together. I can still see the look of relief on her face as the load began to lift.

If you are overloaded with work, list the priorities on a separate sheet of paper before you take it to your boss and see what he will choose as the priorities.

The last of each month I plan and lay out my priorities for the next month. I sit down with Barbara, my assistant, and have her place those projects on the calendar. She handles hundreds of things for me on a monthly basis. However, when something is of High Importance/High Urgency, I communicate that to her so it will be placed above other things. All true leaders have learned to say 'No' to the good in order to say 'Yes' to the best.

WHEN LITTLE PRIORITIES DEMAND TOO MUCH OF US, BIG PROBLEMS ARISE.

Robert J. McKain said, "The reason most major goals are not achieved is that we spend our time doing second things first."

Some years ago a headline told of three hundred whales that suddenly died. The whales were pursuing sardines and found themselves marooned in a bay. Frederick Broan Harris commented, "The small fish lured the sea giants to their death. . . . They came to their violent demise by chasing small ends, by prostituting vast powers for insignificant goals."[2]

Often the little things in life trip us up. A tragic example is an Eastern Airlines jumbo jet that crashed in the Everglades of Florida. The plane was the now-famous Flight 401, bound from New York to Miami with a heavy load of holiday passengers. As the plane approached the Miami airport for its landing, the light that indicates proper deployment of the landing gear failed to light. The plane flew in a large, looping circle over the swamps of the Everglades while the cockpit crew checked to see if the gear actually had not deployed, or if instead the bulb in the signal light was defective.

When the flight engineer tried to remove the light bulb, it wouldn't budge, and the other members of the crew tried to help him. As they struggled with the bulb, no one noticed the aircraft was losing altitude, and the plane simply flew right into the swamp. Dozens of people were killed in the crash. While an experienced crew of high-priced pilots fiddled with a seventy-five cent light bulb, the plane with its passengers flew right into the ground.

TIME DEADLINES AND EMERGENCIES
FORCE US TO PRIORITIZE.

We find this in Parkinson's Law: If you have only one letter to write, it will take all day to do it. If you have twenty letters to write, you'll get them done in one day.

When is our most efficient time in our work? The week before vacation! Why can't we always run our lives the way we the week before we leave the office, making decisions, cleaning off the desk, returning calls? Under normal conditions, we are efficient (doing things right). When time pressure mounts or emergencies arise, we become effective (doing the right things). Efficiency is the foundation for survival. Effectiveness is the foundation of success.

On the night of April 14, 1912, the great ocean liner, the *Titanic*, crashed into an iceberg in the Atlantic and sank, causing great loss of life. One of the most curious stories to come from the disaster was of a woman who had a place in one of the lifeboats.

She asked if she could return to her stateroom for something and was given just three minutes. As she hurried through the corridors, she stepped over money and precious gems littering the floor where they had been dropped in haste. In her own stateroom she ignored her own jewelry, and instead grabbed three oranges. Then she quickly returned to her place in the boat.

Just hours earlier it would have been ludicrous to think she would have accepted a crate of oranges in exchange for even one small diamond, but circumstances had suddenly transformed all the values aboard the ship. The emergency had clarified her priorities.

TOO OFTEN WE LEARN TOO LATE WHAT IS REALLY IMPORTANT.

We are like the family that had become fed up with the noise and traffic of the city and decided to move to the country and try life in the wide open spaces. Intending to raise cattle, they bought a western ranch. Some friends came to visit a month later and asked them what they had named the ranch. The father said, "Well, I wanted to call it the Flying-W and my wife wanted to call it the Suzy-Q. But one of our sons liked the Bar-J and the other preferred the Lazy-Y. So we compromised and called it the Flying-W, Suzy-Q, Bar-J, Lazy-Y Ranch." Their friend asked, "Well, where are your cattle?" The man replied, "We don't have any. None of them survived the branding!"

The author is unknown who said, "An infant is born with a clenched fist; a man dies with an open hand. Life has a way of prying free the things we think are so important."

Gary Redding tells this story about Senator Paul Tsongas of Massachusetts. In January, 1984, he announced that he would retire from the U.S. Senate and not seek reelection. Tsongas was a rising political star. He was a strong favorite to be reelected, and had even been mentioned as a potential future candidate for the Presidency or Vice Presidency of the United States.

A few weeks before his announcement, Tsongas had learned he had a form of lymphatic cancer which could not be cured but could be treated. In all likelihood, it would not greatly affect his physical abilities or life expectancy. The illness did not force Tsongas out of the Senate, but it did force him to face the reality of his own mortality. He would not be able to do everything he might want to do. So what were the things he really wanted to do in the time he had?

He decided that what he wanted most of his life, what he would not give up if he could not have everything, was being with his family and watching his children grow up. He would rather do that than shape the nation's laws or get his name in the history books.

Shortly after his decision was announced, a friend wrote a note to congratulate Tsongas on having his priorities straight. The note read: "Nobody on his death bed ever said, 'I wish I had spent more time on my business.'"

THREE

THE MOST IMPORTANT INGREDIENT OF LEADERSHIP:

INTEGRITY

The dictionary defines *integrity* as "the state of being complete, unified." When I have integrity, my words and my deeds match up. I am who I am, no matter where I am or who I am with.

Sadly, integrity is a vanishing commodity today. Personal standards are crumbling in a world that has taken to hot pursuit of personal pleasure and shortcuts to success.

On a job application one question read, "Have you ever been arrested?" The applicant printed the word *No* in the space. The next question was a follow-up to the first. It asked, "Why?" Not realizing he did not have to answer this part, the "honest" and rather naïve applicant wrote, "I guess it's because I never got caught."

A Jeff Danziger cartoon shows a company president announcing to his staff, "Gentlemen, this year the trick is honesty." From one side of the conference table, a vice president gasps, "Brilliant." Across the table, another VP mutters, "But so risky."

In a cartoon in the *New Yorker*, two clean-shaven middle-aged men are sitting together in a jail cell. One inmate turns to the other and says: "All along, I thought our level of corruption fell well within community standards."

The White House, the Pentagon, Capitol Hill, the church, the sports arena, the academy, even the day care center have all been hit hard by scandal. In every case, the lack of credibility can be traced back to the level of integrity of the individuals within those organizations and institutions.

A person with integrity does not have divided loyalties (that's duplicity), nor is he or she merely pretending (that's hypocrisy). People with integrity are "whole" people; they can be identified by their single-mindedness. People with integrity have nothing to hide and nothing to fear. Their lives are open books. V. Gilbert Beers says, "A person of integrity is one who has established a system of values against which all of life is judged."

Integrity is not what we do so much as who we are. And who we are, in turn, determines what we do. Our system of values is so much a part of us we cannot separate it from ourselves. It becomes the navigating system that guides us. It establishes priorities in our lives and judges what we will accept or reject.

We are all faced with conflicting desires. No one, no matter how "spiritual," can avoid this battle. Integrity is the factor that determines which one will prevail. We struggle daily with situations that demand decisions between what we want to do and what we ought to do. Integrity establishes the ground rules for resolving these tensions. It determines who we are and how we will respond before the conflict even appears. Integrity welds what we say, think, and do into a whole person so that permission is never granted for one of those to be out of sync.

Integrity binds our person together and fosters a spirit of contentment within us. It will not allow our lips to violate our hearts. When integrity is the referee, we will be consistent; our beliefs will be mirrored by our conduct. There will be no discrepancy between what we appear to be and what our family knows we are, whether in times of prosperity or adversity. Integrity allows us to predetermine what we will be regardless of circumstances, persons involved, or the places of our testing.

Integrity is not only the referee between two desires. It is the pivotal point between a happy person and a divided spirit. It frees us to be whole persons no matter what comes our way.

"The first key to greatness," Socrates reminds us, "is to be in reality what we appear to be." Too often we try to be a "human doing" before we have become a "human being." To earn trust a leader has to be authentic. For that to happen, one must come across as a good musical composition does—the words and the music must match.

If what I say and what I do are the same, the results are consistent. For example:

I say to the employees: "Be at work on time."	I arrive at work on time.	They will be on time.
I say to the employees: "Be positive."	I exhibit a positive attitude.	They will be positive.
I say to the employees: "Put the customer first."	I put the customer first.	They will put the customer first.

If what I say and do are not the same, the results are inconsistent. For example:

I say to the employees: "Be at work on time."	I arrive at work late.	Some will be on time, some won't.
I say to the employees: "Be positive."	I exhibit a negative attitude.	Some will be positive, some won't.
I say to the employees: "Put the customer first."	I put myself first.	Some will put customers first, some won't.

Eighty-nine percent of what people learn comes through visual stimulation, 10 percent through audible stimulation, and 1 percent through

other senses. So it makes sense that the more
followers see and hear their leader being consistent in action and word, the greater their
consistency and loyalty. *What they hear, they understand. What they see, they believe!*

Integrity is not what
we do as much as
who we are.

Too often we attempt to motivate our followers with gimmicks that are short-lived and shallow. What people need is not a motto to say, but a model to see.

THE CREDIBILITY ACID TEST

The more credible you are the more confidence people place in you, thereby allowing you the privilege of influencing their lives. The less
credible you are, the less confidence people place in you and the more quickly you lose your position of influence.

Image is what people
think we are. Integrity
is what we really are.

Many leaders who have attended my conferences have said to me, "I hope you can give me some insights into how I can change my company." My response is always the same: "My goal is to inspire you to change; if that happens, the organization will also be changed." As I have said time and time again, everything rises and falls on leadership. The secret to rising and not falling is integrity. Let's look at some reasons why integrity is so important.

1. INTEGRITY BUILDS TRUST.

Dwight Eisenhower said: "In order to be a leader a man must have followers. And to have followers, a man must have their confidence. Hence, the supreme quality for a leader is unquestionably integrity. Without it, no real success is possible, no matter whether it is on a section gang, a football field, in an army, or in an office. If a man's associates find him guilty of being phony, if they find that he lacks forthright integrity, he will fail. His teachings and actions must square with each other. The first great need, therefore, is integrity and high purpose."[1]

Pieter Bruyn, a Dutch specialist in administration, holds that authority is not the power a boss has over subordinates, but rather the boss's ability to influence subordinates to recognize and accept that power. He calls it a "bargain": Subordinates tacitly agree to accept the boss as boss in return for being offered the kind of leadership *they* can accept. What does Bruyn's theory boil down to? Quite simply the manager must build—and maintain—credibility. Subordinates must be able to trust that their boss will act in good faith toward them.

Too often people who are responsible for leading look to the organization to make people responsible to follow. They ask for a new title, another position, an organization chart, and a new policy to curtail insubordination. Sadly they never get enough authority to become effective. Why? They are looking to the outside when their problem is on the inside. They lack authority because they lack integrity.

Only 45 percent of four hundred managers in a Carnegie-Mellon survey believed their top management; a third distrusted their immediate bosses. With so much depending on credibility and trust, someone in every organization must provide the leadership to improve these numbers.[2]

Cavett Roberts said: "If my people understand me, I'll get their attention. If my people trust me, I'll get their action." For a leader to have the authority to lead, he needs more than the title on his door. He has to have the trust of those who are following him.

2. INTEGRITY HAS HIGH INFLUENCE VALUE.

Emerson said, "Every great institution is the lengthened shadow of a single man. His character determines the character of the organization." That statement "lines up" with the words of Will Rogers who said, "People's minds are changed through observation and not argument." People do what people see.

According to 1,300 senior executives who responded to a recent survey, integrity is the human quality most necessary to business success. Seventy-one percent put it at the top of a list of sixteen traits responsible for enhancing an executive's effectiveness.[3]

Regrettably we tend to forget the high influence value of integrity in the home. R.C. Sproul, in his book *Objections Answered*, tells about a young Jewish boy who grew up in Germany many years ago. The lad had a profound sense of admiration for his father, who saw to it that the life of the family revolved around the religious practices of their faith. The father led them to the synagogue faithfully.

In his teen years, however, the boy's family was forced to move to another town in Germany. This town had no synagogue, only a Lutheran church. The life of the community revolved around the Lutheran church; all the best people belonged to it. Suddenly, the father announced to the family that they were all going to abandon their Jewish traditions and join the Lutheran church. When the stunned family asked why, the father explained that it would be good for his business. The youngster was bewildered and confused. His deep disappointment soon gave way to anger and a kind of intense bitterness that plagued him throughout his life.

Later he left Germany and went to England to study. Each day found him at the British Museum formulating his ideas and composing a book. In that book he introduced a whole new worldview and conceived a movement that was designed to change the world. He described religion as the "opiate for the masses." He committed the people who followed him to life without God. His ideas became the norm for the governments for almost half the world's people. His name? Karl Marx, founder of the Communist movement. The history of the twentieth century, and perhaps beyond, was significantly affected because one father let his values become distorted.

3. Integrity facilitates high standards.

Leaders must live by higher standards than their followers. This insight is exactly opposite of most people's thoughts concerning leadership. In a world of perks and privileges that accompany the climb to success, little thought is given to the responsibilities of the upward journey. Leaders can give up anything except responsibility, either for themselves or their organizations. John D. Rockefeller, Jr., said, "I believe that every right implies a responsibility; every opportunity, an obligations; every possession, a duty." The diagram on the opposite page illustrates this principle.

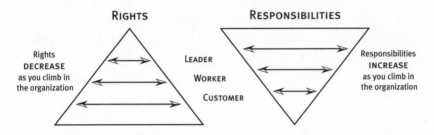

Too many people are ready to assert their rights, but not to assume their responsibilities. Richard L. Evans, in his book *An Open Road*, said: "It is priceless to find a person who will take responsibility, who will finish and follow through to the final detail—to know when someone has accepted an assignment that it will be effectively, conscientiously completed. But when half-finished assignments keep coming back—to check on, to verify, to edit, to interrupt thought, and to take repeated attention—obviously someone has failed to follow the doctrine of completed work."

Tom Robbins said, "Don't let yourself be victimized by the age you live in. It's not the time that will bring us down, any more than it's society. There's a tendency today to absolve individuals of moral responsibility and treat them as victims of social circumstance. You buy that and you pay with your soul. What limits people is lack of character." When the character of leaders is low, so are their standards.

4. INTEGRITY RESULTS IN A SOLID REPUTATION, NOT JUST IMAGE.

Image is what people think we are. Integrity is what we really are. Two old ladies were walking around a somewhat overcrowded English country churchyard and came upon a tombstone. The inscription said: "Here lies John Smith, a politician and an honest man."

"Good heavens!" said one lady to the other. "Isn't it awful that they had to put two people in the same grave!"

All of us have known those who were not the same on the outside as they were inside. Sadly, many who have worked harder on their images than on their integrity don't understand when they suddenly "fall." Even friends who thought they knew them are surprised.

In ancient China the people wanted security against the barbaric hordes to the north, so they built the great wall. It was so high they believed no one could climb over it and so thick nothing could break it down. They settled back to enjoy their security. During the first hundred years of the wall's existence, China was invaded three times. Not once did the barbaric hordes break down the wall or climb over it. Each time they bribed a gatekeeper and then marched right through the gates. The Chinese were so busy relying on the walls of stone they forgot to teach integrity to their children.

Your answers to the following questions will determine if you are into image-building instead of integrity-building:

Consistency:	Are you the same person no matter who you are with? Yes or no.
Choices:	Do you make decisions that are best for others when another choice would benefit you? Yes or no.
Credit:	Are you quick to recognize others for their efforts and contributions to your success? Yes or no.

Thomas Macauley said, "The measure of a man's real character is what he would do if he would never be found out." Life is like a vise; at times it will squeeze us. At those moments of pressure, whatever is inside will be found out. We cannot give what we do not have. Image promises much but produces little. Integrity never disappoints.

5. INTEGRITY MEANS LIVING IT
MYSELF *BEFORE* LEADING OTHERS.

We cannot lead anyone else further than we have been ourselves. Too many times we are so concerned about the product we try to shortcut the process. There are no shortcuts when integrity is involved. Eventually truth will always be exposed.

Recently I heard of a man who interviewed a consultant to some of the largest U.S. companies about their quality control. The consultant said, "In quality control, we are not concerned about the product. We are concerned about the process. If the process is right, the product is guaranteed." The same holds true for integrity; it guarantees credibility.

When the Challenger exploded, America was stunned to discover Quality Control had warned NASA that the space shuttle was not fully prepared to go. But production said, "The show must go on!" *Crash*, just like many leaders.

I remember hearing my basketball coach, Don Neff, repeatedly emphasize to our team, "You play like you practice; you play like you practice." When we fail to follow this principle, we fail to reach our personal potentials. When leaders fail to follow this principle, eventually they lose their credibility.

HOLD IT! I CAN'T SWIM!

6. INTEGRITY HELPS A LEADER BE CREDIBLE, NOT JUST CLEVER.

I once had dinner with Fred Smith. This wise businessman shared with me the difference between being clever and being credible. He said that clever leaders never last. That statement reminded me of the words of Peter Drucker, given to pastors gathered to discuss important issues in the church: "The final requirement of effective leadership is to earn trust. Otherwise there won't be any followers. . . . A leader is someone who has followers. To trust a leader, it is not necessary to agree with him. Trust is the conviction that the leader means what he says. It is a belief in something very old-fashioned called 'integrity.' A leader's actions and a leader's professed beliefs must be congruent or at least compatible. Effective leadership—and again this is very old wisdom—is not based on being clever; it is primarily on being consistent."[3]

Leaders who are sincere don't have to advertise the fact. It's visible in everything they do and soon becomes common knowledge to everyone. Likewise, insincerity cannot be hidden, disguised, or covered up, no matter how competent a manager may otherwise be.

The only way to keep the goodwill and high esteem of the people you work with is to deserve it. No one can fool all of the people all of the time. Each of us, eventually, is recognized for exactly what we are—not what we try to appear to be.

Ann Landers said, "People of integrity expect to be believed. They also know time will prove them right and are willing to wait."

7. INTEGRITY IS A HARD-WON ACHIEVEMENT.

Integrity is not a given factor in everyone's life. It is a result of self-discipline, inner trust, and a decision to be relentlessly honest in all situations in our lives. Unfortunately in today's world, strength of character is a rare commodity. As a result, we have few contemporary models of integrity. Our culture has produced few enduring heroes, few models of virtue. We have become a nation of imitators, but there are few leaders worth imitating.

The meaning of integrity has been eroded. Drop the word into conversations in Hollywood, on Wall Street, even on Main Street, and you'll get blank stares in return. For most Americans, the word conjures up ideas of prudishness or narrow-mindedness. In an age when the meanings of words are manipulated, foundational values such as integrity can be pulverized overnight.

Integrity is antithetical to the spirit of our age. The overarching philosophy of life that guides our culture revolves around a materialistic, consumer mentality. The craving need of the moment supersedes consideration of values that have eternal significance.

When we sell out to someone else we also sell out ourselves. Hester H. Chomondelay underscores this truth in his short poem, "Judas":

> Still as of old
> Men by themselves are priced—
> For thirty pieces Judas sold
> Himself, not Christ.

Billy Graham said, "Integrity is the glue that holds our way of life together. We must constantly strive to keep our integrity intact.

"When wealth is lost, nothing is lost; when health is lost, something is lost; when character is lost, all is lost."[4]

To build your life on the foundation of integrity, use the following poem ("Am I True to Myself?" by Edgar Guest) as a "Mirror Test" to evaluate how you're doing.

> I have to live with myself, and so
> I want to be fit for myself to know,
> I want to be able, as days go by,
> Always to look myself straight in the eye;
> I don't want to stand, with the setting sun,
> And hate myself for things I have done.
> I don't want to keep on a closet shelf
> A lot of secrets about myself,

And fool myself, as I come and go,
Into thinking that nobody else will know
The kind of man I really am;
I don't want to dress up myself in sham.
I want to go out with my head erect,
I want to deserve all men's respect;
But here in the struggle for fame and pelf
I want to be able to like myself.
I don't want to look at myself and know
That I'm bluster and bluff and empty show.
I can never hide myself from me;
I see what others may never see;
I know what others may never know,
I never can fool myself, and so,
Whatever happens, I want to be
Self-respecting and conscience free.

Next, take the "Mentor Rest." It asks, "Am I a true to my leader?" Joseph Bailey interviewed more than thirty top executives. He found that all learned firsthand from a mentor.[5] Ralph Waldo Emerson said, "Our chief want in life is somebody who shall make us what we can be." When we find that person, we need to check our growth on a regular basis, asking, "Am I totally availing myself of the teaching I am receiving?" Taking shortcuts in this process will hurt both your mentor and you.

Finally, take the "Masses Test." It asks, "Am I true to my followers?" As leaders, we quickly understand that wrong decisions not only adversely affect us, but they affect those who follow us. However, making a bad decision because of wrong motives is totally different. Before reaching for the reins of leadership we must realize that we teach what we know and reproduce what we are. Integrity is an inside job.

Advocates of modeling dependability before followers, James P. Cozies and Barry Poser report in their book, *The Leadership Challenger*, that followers expect four things from their leaders: honesty, competence, vision, and inspiration.[6]

Write out what you value in life. A conviction is a belief or principle that you regularly model, one for which you would be willing to die. What are your convictions?

Ask someone who knows you well what areas of your life they see as consistent (you do what you say) and what areas they see as inconsistent (you say but don't always live).

YOU WILL ONLY BECOME WHAT YOU ARE BECOMING RIGHT NOW

Though you cannot go back
and make a brand new start, my friend.
Anyone can start from now
and make a brand new end.

FOUR

THE ULTIMATE TEST OF LEADERSHIP:
CREATING POSITIVE CHANGE

Change the leader, change the organization. Everything rises and falls on leadership! However, I have found that it's not easy to change leaders. In fact, I've discovered that leaders resist change as much as followers do. The result? Unchanged leaders equals unchanged organizations. People do what people see.

PROFILE OF A LEADER IN TROUBLE

Notice that of the twelve trouble spots for a leader listed below, five deal with an unwillingness to change. That spells trouble for the organization.

- Has a poor understanding of people.

- Lacks imagination.

- Has personal problems.

- Passes the buck.

- Feels secure and satisfied.

- Is not organized.

- Flies into rages.

- Will not take a risk.

- Is insecure and defensive.

- Stays inflexible.

- Has no team spirit.

- Fights change.

Nicolo Machiavelli said, "There is nothing more difficult to take in hand, more perilous to conduct or more uncertain in its success, than to take the lead in the introduction of a new order of things."

The first order of things to be changed is me, the leader. After I consider how hard it is to change myself, then I will understand the challenge of trying to change others. This is the ultimate test of leadership.

A Middle-Eastern mystic said, "I was a revolutionary when I was young and all my prayer to God was: 'Lord, give me the energy to change the world.' As I approached middle age and realized that my life was half gone without my changing a single soul, I changed my prayer to: 'Lord, give me the grace to change all those who come into contact with me, just my family and friends, and I shall be satisfied.' Now that I am an old man and my days are numbered, I have begun to see how foolish I have been. My one prayer now is: 'Lord, give me the grace to change myself.' If I had prayed for this right from the start, I would not have wasted my life."[1]

Howard Hendricks, in his book *Teaching to Change Lives*, throws a challenge out to every potential leader: "Write down somewhere in the margins on this page your answer to this question: How have you changed . . . lately? In the last week, let's say? Or in the last month? The last year? Can you be very specific? Or must your answer be incredibly vague? You say you're growing. Okay . . . how? 'Well,' you say, 'In all kinds of ways.' Great! Name one. You see, effective teaching comes only through a changed person. The more you change, the more you become an instrument of change in the lives of others. If you want to become a change agent, you also must change."[2]

Hendricks could have also said: If you want to continue leading, you must continue changing. Many leaders are no longer leading. They have become like Henry Ford who is described in Robert Lacy's best-selling biography, *Ford: the Man and the Machine*.[3] Lacy says Ford was a man who loved his Model T so much he didn't want to change a bolt on it. He even kicked out William Knudsen, his ace production man, because Knudsen thought he saw the sun setting on the Model T. That occurred in 1912, when the Model T was only four years old and at the crest of its popularity. Ford had just returned from a European jaunt, and he went to a Highland Park, Michigan, garage and saw the new design created by Knudsen.

On-the-scene mechanics recorded how Ford momentarily went berserk. He spied the gleaming red lacquer sheen on a new, low-slung version of the Model T that he considered a monstrous perversion of his beloved Model T design. "Ford had his hands in his pockets, and he walked around that car three or four times," recounted an eyewitness. "It was four-door job, and the top was down. Finally, he got to the left-hand side of the car, and he takes his hands out, gets hold of the door, and bang! He ripped the door right off! . . . How the man done it, I don't know! He jumped in there, and bang goes the other door. Bang goes the wind-shield. He jumps over the back seat and starts pounding on the top. He rips the top with the heel of his shoe. He wrecked the car as much as he could."

> Change the leader—change the organization.

Knudsen left for General Motors. Henry Ford nursed along the Model T, but design changes in competitors' models made it more old-fashioned than he would admit. Competitive necessity finally backed him into making the Model A, though his heart was never in it. Even though General Motors was nipping at Ford's heels, the inventor wanted life to freeze where it was.

Underpinning this theme, William A. Hewitt, Chairman of Deere and Co., says, "To be a leader you must preserve all through your life the attitude of being receptive to new ideas. The quality of leadership you will give will depend upon your ability to evaluate new ideas, to separate change for the sake of change from change for the sake of me."

THE LEADER AS CHANGE AGENT

Once the leader has personally changed and discerned the difference between novel change and needed change, then that leader must become a change agent. In this world of rapid change and discontinuities, the leader must be out in front to encourage change and growth and to show the way to bring it about. He must first understand the two important requisites to bringing about change: knowing the technical requirements of the change, and understanding the attitude and motivational demands for bringing it about.

Both requisites are critically necessary. More often than not, though, when failure to change results, it is because of inadequate or inappropriate motivation, not from lack of technical smarts.

> When you're through changing, you're through.

A manager usually will be more skilled in the technical requirements of change, whereas the leader will have a better understanding of the attitudinal and motivational demands that the followers need. Note the difference: in the beginning the skills of a leader are essential. No change will ever occur if the psychological needs are unmet. Once change has begun, the skills of a manager are needed to maintain needed change.

Bobb Biehl, in his book *Increasing Your Leadership Confidence*, states it this way: "A change can make sense logically, but still lead to anxiety in the psychological dimension. Everyone needs a niche, and when the niche starts to change after we've become comfortable in it, it causes stress and insecurities. So before introducing change, we have to consider the psychological dimension."[4]

A good exercise when you face change is to make a list of the logical advantages and disadvantages that should result from the change, and then make another list indicating the psychological impact. Just seeing this on a sheet of paper can be clarifying. You may find yourself saying, "I don't like to admit it, but I'm insecure at this point, even though the change makes sense logically."

Another possibility is that a change you're considering may not affect your psychological security, but it doesn't make sense logically when you examine the advantages and disadvantages. The key is to distinguish between the logical and the psychological aspects of any change.

A HISTORICAL ACCOUNT OF RESISTANCE TO CHANGE

There is nothing more difficult to undertake, more perilous to conduct, or more uncertain in its success than introducing change. Why? The leader has for enemies all those who have done well under the old conditions and only lukewarm defenders in those who may do well with the change.

Resistance to change is universal. It invades all classes and cultures. It seizes every generation by the throat and attempts to stop all forward movement toward progress. Many well-educated people, after being confronted with truth, have been unwilling to change their minds.

Growth equals change.

For example, for centuries people believed that Aristotle was right when he said that the heavier an object, the faster it would fall to earth. Aristotle was regarded as the greatest thinker of all time, and surely he could not be wrong. All it would have taken was for one brave person to take two objects, one heavy and one light, and drop them from a great height to see whether or not the heavier object landed first. But no one stepped forward until nearly 2000 years after Aristotle's death. In 1589, Galileo summoned learned professors to the base of the Leaning Tower of Pisa. Then he went to the top and pushed off two weights, one weighing ten pounds and the other weighing one pound. Both landed at the same time. But the power of belief in the conventional wisdom was so strong the professors denied what they had seen. They continued to say Aristotle was right.

With his telescope, Galileo proved the theory of Copernicus, that the earth was not the center of the universe; the earth and the planets revolve around the sun. Yet, when he tried to change people's beliefs, he was thrown into prison and spent the rest of his life under house arrest.

Resisting change can unwittingly affect one's health and life, as the following account portrays. Hippocrates described scurvy in ancient times. The disease seemed to especially plague armies in the field and cities that were under siege for long periods of time. Later, following the discovery of America, when long sea voyages became common, scurvy became rampant among sailors. Little was known about what caused scurvy and less about its cure, although elaborate theories and remedies were prescribed. None of them was completely effective and most were worthless.

In 1553, Cartier made his second voyage to Newfoundland. Of his 103-man crew, 100 developed agonizing scurvy and were in great anguish when the Iroquois Indians of Quebec came to their rescue with what was described as a "miraculous cure." The Iroquois Indians gave the sick sailors an infusion of bark and leaves of the pine tree.

In 1553, Admiral Sir Richard Hawkins noted that during his career on the high seas, ten thousand seamen under his command had died of scurvy. He also recorded that in his experience sour oranges and lemons had been most effective in curing the disease. Yet these observations had no sweeping effect in bringing about an awareness of what could prevent scurvy, and the observations of this admiral went unheeded.

James Lind, a British naval surgeon, who later became the chief physician of the Naval Hospital at Portsmouth, England, published a book in 1753 in which he stated explicitly that scurvy could be eliminated simply by supplying sailors with lemon juice. He cited many case histories from his experience as a naval surgeon at sea; he proved that such things as mustard cress, tamarinds, oranges, and lemons would prevent scurvy. In fact anything that contains enough vitamin C, which is most abundant in citrus fruit, tomatoes, and to a lesser degree in most green vegetables and other fruits, will prevent scurvy.

You might rightfully expect that Dr. Lind would have been highly honored and praised for this great contribution, but the reverse is true.

He was ridiculed. He became frustrated and remarked bitterly: "Some persons cannot be brought to believe that a disease so fatal and so dreaded can be cured or prevented by such easy means." They would have more faith in an elaborate composition dignified with the title of "an antiscorbutic golden elixir" or the like. The "some persons" to whom Dr. Lind referred were My Lords of the Admiralty and other physicians. In fact they ignored Dr. Lind's advice for forty years. One sea captain did take his advice—the now famous Captain James Cook, who stocked his ships with an ample supply of fresh fruits.

The Royal Society honored Captain Cook in 1776 for his success, but the officials of the navy ignored his report. Not until 1794, the year of Dr. Lind's death, was a British navy squadron supplied with lemon juice before a voyage. On that voyage, which lasted twenty-three weeks, there was not one case of scurvy, yet another decade passed before regulations were enacted requiring sailors to drink a daily ration of lemon juice to prevent scurvy. With this enactment, scurvy disappeared from the British Navy.[5]

The needless loss of life simply because masses of people were resistant to change was more than unfortunate. It was outrageous. Don't let your attitude toward change or your own predisposition to avoid it create detrimental hindrances to your own personal success as a leader.

How Do You Write the Word "Attitude"?

Directions:
1. Write the word *attitude* on the left line with your "writing" hand.
2. Write the word *attitude* on the right line with your other hand.

_____   _____

The word *attitude* written   The word *attitude* written
with your writing hand.   with your other hand.

Application:
When you look at the word *attitude* written by the hand you do not

write with, you see a picture of the kind of attitude we usually have when we are trying to do something new. As one person said, "Nothing should ever be done for the first time."

WHY PEOPLE RESIST CHANGE

In a "Peanuts" cartoon, Charlie Brown says to Linus: "Perhaps you can give me an answer, Linus. What would you do if you felt that no one liked you?" Linus replies, "I'd try to look at myself objectively, and see what I could do to *improve*. That's *my* answer, Charlie Brown." To which Charlie replies, "I *hate* that answer!"

There are a number of reasons why many of us, like Charlie Brown, resist change.

THE CHANGE ISN'T SELF-INITIATED.

When people lack ownership of an idea, they usually resist it, even when it is in their best interest! They simply don't like the idea of being manipulated or feeling like pawns of the system. Wise leaders allow followers to give input and be a part of the process of change. Most of the time the key to my attitude about change is whether I am initiating it (in which case I am all for it) or someone else is imposing the change on me (which tends to make me more resistant).

ROUTINE IS DISRUPTED.

Habits allow us to do things without much thought, which is why most of us have so many of them. Habits are not instincts. They are acquired reactions. They don't just happen; they are caused. First we form habits, but then our habits form us. Change threatens our habit patterns and forces us to think, reevaluate, and sometimes unlearn past behavior.

When I was a teenager I became interested in golf. Regrettably, I taught myself instead of taking lessons. After a few years and the innocent acquisition of many bad habits, I played a game of golf with an excellent player. At the close of the round he kiddingly said my main problem seemed to be that I was too close to the ball after I hit it! Then he seriously offered to help me. He shared honestly how I would need to make some changes if my golf game was to improve. When I asked him to specify what changes I needed to make, he said, "Everything!" For the next year I had to unlearn old habits. It was one of the most difficult experiences of my life. Many times I was tempted to return to my old habits for temporary relief from working so hard and still playing so badly.

CHANGE CREATES FEAR OF THE UNKNOWN.

Change means traveling in uncharted waters, and this causes our insecurities to rise. Therefore, many people are more comfortable with old problems than with new solutions. They are like the congregation that desperately needed a new building but were afraid to venture out. During a service some plaster fell from the ceiling and hit the chairman of the board. Immediately a meeting was called and the following decisions were made:

One: We will build a new church.
Two: We will build a new church on the same site
            as the old one.
Three: We will use the materials of the old church
            to build the new one.
Four   We will worship in the old church until
            the new church is built.

Some people are open to change as long as it doesn't inconvenience them or cost anything.

THE PURPOSE OF THE CHANGE IS UNCLEAR.

Employees resist change when they hear about it from a second-hand source. When a decision has been made, the longer it takes for employees to hear and the further the desired change is from the decision-maker, the more resistance it will receive. That's why decisions should be made at the lowest level possible. The decision-maker, because of close proximity to the issue, will make a better decision, and those most affected by the decision will know it quickly by hearing it form a source close to them and to the problem.

CHANGE CREATES FEAR OF FAILURE.

Elbert Hubbard said that the greatest mistake a person can make is to be afraid of making one. It is tragic when success has "gone to my head." It is even more tragic if failure goes to my head. When this happens I begin to agree with Larry Anderson, the pitcher for the San Diego Padres. He said, "If at first you don't succeed, failure may be your thing." Too many people, fearing that failure is their thing, hold tenaciously to whatever they feel comfortable with and continually resist change.

THE REWARDS FOR CHANGE DON'T MATCH THE EFFORT CHANGE REQUIRES.

People will not change until they perceive that the advantages of changing outweigh the disadvantages of continuing with the way things are. What leaders sometimes fail to recognize is that the followers will always weigh the advantage/disadvantage issue in light of personal gain/loss, not organization gain/loss.

PEOPLE ARE TOO SATISFIED WITH THE WAY THINGS ARE.

As the following story from *Parables* reveals, many organizations and people will choose to die before they will choose to change.

In the 1940s, the Swiss watch was the most prestigious and best quality watch in the world. Consequently 80 percent of the watches sold in the world were made in Switzerland. In the late '50s, the digital watch was presented to the leaders of the Swiss watch company. They rejected this new idea because they knew they already had the best watch and the best watchmakers. The man who developed the digital watch subsequently sold the idea to Seiko.

In 1940, Swiss watch-making companies employed eighty thousand people. Today they employ eighteen thousand. In 1940, 80 percent of the watches sold in the world were made in Switzerland. Today 80 percent of the watches are digital. This story represents what happens to many organizations and people: We choose to die rather than choose to change.

CHANGE WON'T HAPPEN WHEN PEOPLE ENGAGE IN NEGATIVE THINKING.

Regardless of his state in the present, the negative thinker finds disappointment in the future. The epitaph on a negative person's headstone should read, "I expected this." This type of thinking can best be described by a sign I read several years ago in an office building:

Don't look—you might see.
Don't listen—you might hear.
Don't think—you might learn.
Don't make a decision—you might be wrong.
Don't walk—you might stumble.
Don't run—you might fall.
Don't live—you might die.

I would like to add one more thought to this depressing list:

Don't change—you might grow.

THE FOLLOWERS LACK RESPECT FOR THE LEADER.

When followers don't like the leader who oversees the change, their feelings won't allow them to look at the change objectively. In other words, people view the change according to the way they view the change-agent.

One of the principles I share in leadership conferences is, "You've got to love 'em before you can lead 'em." When you love your followers genuinely and correctly, they'll respect and follow you through many changes.

THE LEADER IS SUSCEPTIBLE TO FEELINGS OF PERSONAL CRITICISM.

Sometimes leaders resist change. For example, if a leader has developed a program that is now being phased out for something better, he or she may feel the change is a personal attack and will react defensively.

For growth and continual effectiveness, every organization must go through a continuous four-stage cycle of create, conserve, criticize, and change. The figure below illustrates the cycle.

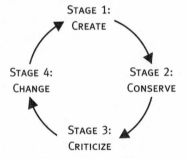

Stages 1 and 4 are the offensive functions of an organization. States 2 and 3 are the defensive functions. Either the creators handle criticism positively and begin to make changes or they will be replaced by those who will embrace change and, therefore, create.

CHANGE MAY MEAN PERSONAL LOSS.

Whenever change is imminent, the question on everyone's mind is, "How will this affect me?" Usually there are three groups of people within the organization: (1) those who will lose; (2) those who are neutral; and (3) those who will benefit. Each group is different and must be handled with sensitivity, but also with straightforwardness.

CHANGE REQUIRES ADDITIONAL COMMITMENT.

Time is the most precious commodity for many people. Whenever change is about to happen, we all look to see how it will affect our time. Usually we conclude that increased change will be fine *if* it does not increase our time commitment. Sidney Howard said that one half of knowing what you want is knowing what you must give up before you get it. When the cost of change is time, many will resist the change.

When it comes to the commitment of time, the leader must determine if the person is *unwilling* or *unable* to change. Willingness deals with attitude, and there is little you can do if your followers resist change because of attitude. But ability to change deals with perspective. Many people are willing to change but, because of the way they perceive their present circumstances and responsibilities, they are unable to change. At this point, the leader can help by prioritizing tasks, eliminating nonessentials, and focusing on the consequential value of changing.

NARROW-MINDEDNESS THWARTS
ACCEPTANCE OF NEW IDEAS.

In 1993, approximately sixteen hundred people belonged to the International Flat Earth Research Society of America. Their president, Charles K. Johnson, said he's been a flat-earther all his life. "When I saw the globe in grade school I didn't accept it then and I don't accept it now."

That reminds me of the man who lived in Maine and turned one hundred years of age. A reporter drove up from New York City to interview the old man. Sitting on the front porch, the reporter said, "I'll bet you've seen a lot of changes in your lifetime." The old man replied, "Yes, and I've been agin' every one of them."

TRADITION RESISTS CHANGE.

I love this joke: "How many people does it take to change a light bulb?" Answer: "Four. One to change the bulb and three to reminisce about how good the old light bulb was."

People like that remind me of the old army sergeant who was put in charge of a plot of grass in front of administrative headquarters in a camp in Michigan. The sergeant promptly delegated the job to a buck private and told him to water the grass every day at five o'clock. The private did this conscientiously. One day there was a terrific thunderstorm, and the sergeant walked into the barracks and saw the private doing bunk fatigue.

"What's the matter with you?" the sergeant bellowed. "It's five o'clock and you're supposed to be out watering the grass!"

"But, Sergeant," the private said, looking confused, "it's raining; look at the thunderstorm."

"So what!" yelled the sergeant, "You've got a raincoat haven't you?"

Cornfield's Law says that nothing is ever done until everyone is convinced that it ought to be done, and has been convinced for so long that it is now time to do something else.

A CHECKLIST FOR CHANGE

Below are the questions you should review *before* attempting changes within an organization. When the questions can be answered with a yes, change tends to be easier. Questions that can only be answered with no (or maybe) usually indicate that change will be difficult.

YES   NO

____   ____   Will this change benefit the followers?

____   ____   Is this change compatible with the purpose of the organization?

____   ____   Is this change specific and clear?

_____ _____ Are the top 20 percent (the influencers) in favor of this change?

_____ _____ Is it possible to test this change before making a total commitment to it?

_____ _____ Are physical, financial, and human resources available to make this change?

_____ _____ Is this change reversible?

_____ _____ Is this change the next obvious step?

_____ _____ Does this change have both short- and long- range benefits?

_____ _____ Is the leadership capable of bringing about this change?

_____ _____ Is the timing right?

At times every leader feels like Lucy when she was leaning against a fence with Charlie Brown. "I would like to change the world," she said. Charlie Brown asked, "Where would you start?" She replied, "I would start with you!"

The last question, "Is the timing right?" is the ultimate consideration for implementing change. A leader's success in bringing about change in others will happen only if the timing is right. In my book, _The Winning Attitude_, this subject is discussed in short order:

> The wrong decision at the wrong time = disaster.
> The wrong decision at the right time = mistake.
> The right decision at the wrong time = unacceptance.
> The right decision at the right time = success.

People change when they _hurt_ enough they _have_ to change; _learn_ enough they _want_ to change; _receive_ enough they are _able_ to change. The leader must recognize when people are in one of these three stages. In fact, top leaders create an atmosphere that causes one of these three things to occur.[6]

THE EVOLUTIONARY PROCESS OF CHANGE

It is helpful to remember that change can be seen as either *revolutionary* (something totally different from what has been) or *evolutionary* (a refinement of what has been). It is usually easier to present change as a simple refinement of "the way we've been doing it" rather than something big, new, and completely different. When a proposal for change is introduced in the organization, people fall into five categories in terms of their response.

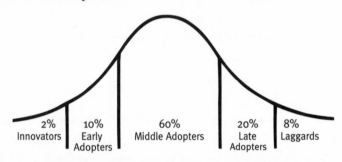

| 2% Innovators | 10% Early Adopters | 60% Middle Adopters | 20% Late Adopters | 8% Laggards |

INNOVATORS ARE THE DREAMERS.

They are the originators of new ideas and generally are not acknowledged as leaders or policy makers.

EARLY ADOPTERS ARE THOSE WHO KNOW A GOOD IDEA WHEN THEY SEE IT.

Their opinions are respected in the organization. Although they did not create the idea, they will try to convince others to accept it.

MIDDLE ADOPTERS ARE THE MAJORITY.

They will respond to the opinions of others. Generally they are reasonable in their analysis of a new idea, but inclined to maintain the status quo. They can be influenced by the positive or negative influencers of the organization.

LATE ADOPTERS ARE THE LAST GROUP TO ENDORSE AN IDEA.

They often speak against proposed changes and may never verbally acknowledge acceptance. Generally they will adopt it if the majority demonstrates support.

LAGGARDS ARE ALWAYS AGAINST CHANGE.

Their commitment is to the status quo and the past. Often they try to create division within the organization.[7]

The evolutionary process of successful change within an organization can be summed up in the eight steps that must occur as the organization moves from ignorance about the desired change and the effects it will have to a mind-set of willingness and innovation.

Step 1: **Ignorance.** No unified direction or sense of priorities is felt among the followers. They are "in the dark."

Step 2: **Information.** General information is given to the people. Initially the ideas for change are not embraced.

Step 3: **Infusion.** The penetration of new ideas into the status quo may cause confrontations with apathy, prejudice, and tradition. The general tendency is to focus on problems.

Step 4: **Individual Change.** The "early adopters" begin to see the benefits of the proposed change and embrace them. Personal convictions replace complacency.

Step 5: **Organizational Change.** Two sides of the issue are being discussed. Less defensiveness and more openness concerning proposed changes can be observed. The momentum shifts from anti-change to pro-change.

Step 6: **Awkward Application.** Some failures and some successes are experienced as the change is implemented. The learning process is rapid.

Step 7: **Integration.** Awkwardness begins to decrease and

the acceptance level increases. A growing sense
of accomplishments and a secondary wave of results
and successes occur.

Step 8: **Innovation.** Significant results create confidence and
a willingness to take risks. The result is a willingness
to change more rapidly and boldly.

As Step 8 is taken, the organization as a whole is more willing to go
through the process again. The major effect of the process develops as
the majority of the organization is exposed repeatedly to the new idea.

1st Exposure:	"I reject that thought because it conflicts with my preconceived ideas."
2nd Exposure:	"Well, I understand it, but I can't accept it."
3rd Exposure:	"I agree with the idea but have reservations as to its use."
4th Exposure:	"You know, that idea pretty well expresses the way I feel about the subject."
5th Exposure:	"I used that idea today. It's terrific!"
6th Exposure:	"I gave that idea to someone yesterday. In the truest sense of the word, that idea now belongs to me."

CREATING A CLIMATE FOR CHANGE

Human behavior studies show that people do not basically resist
change; they resist "being changed."[8] This section will emphasize how to
create an atmosphere that will encourage others to be changed. Unless
people are changed, change will not happen. The first statement of this
chapter read, "Change the leader, change the organization." Now we
will start with the leader and develop a strategy for the organization.

THE LEADER MUST DEVELOP A TRUST WITH PEOPLE.

It is wonderful when the people believe in the leader. It is more wonderful when the leader believes in the people. When both are a reality,

trust is the result. The more people trust the leader, the more willing they will be to accept the leader's proposed changes. Warren Bennis and Bert Nanus say that "trust is the emotional glue that binds followers and leaders together."[9] Abraham Lincoln said, "If you would win a man to your cause, first convince him that you are his true friend. Next, probe to discover what he wants to accomplish."

My first question to a leader who wants to make changes within an organization is always, "What is your relationship with your people?" If the relationship is positive, then the leader is ready to take the next step.

THE LEADER MUST MAKE PERSONAL CHANGES BEFORE ASKING OTHERS TO CHANGE.

Sadly, too many leaders are like my friend who made a list of New Year's resolutions: be nicer to people; eat nutritious food; be more giving to my friends; cut down on sweets and fats; be less critical of others.

My friend showed me the list, and I was quite impressed. They were great goals. "But," I asked her, "do you think you'll be able to meet all of them?"

"Why should I?" she answered "This list is for you!"

Andrew Carnegie said, "As I grow older, I pay less attention to what men say. I just watch what they do." Great leaders not only say what should be done, they show it!

GOOD LEADERS UNDERSTAND THE HISTORY OF THE ORGANIZATION.

The longer an organization has gone without change, the more effort introducing it will require. Also, when change is implemented and the result is negative, people within the organization will be leery of embracing future changes. The opposite is also true. Successful changes in the past prepare people to readily accept more changes.

G.K. Chesterton suggests, "Don't take the fence down until you know the reason it was put up." It is important to know what happened in the past before making changes for the future.

PLACE INFLUENCERS IN LEADERSHIP POSITIONS.

Leaders have two characteristics. First, they are going somewhere; and second, they are able to persuade other people to go with them. They are like the chairman of a large corporation who was late for a meeting. Bolting into the room, he took the nearest available seat rather than moving to his accustomed spot. One of his young aides protested, "Please, sir, you should be at the head of the table." The executive, who had a healthy understanding of his place in the company, answered, "Son, wherever I sit is the head of the table."

CHECK THE "CHANGE IN YOUR POCKET."

Every leader is given a certain amount of "change" (emotional support in the form of bargaining chips) at the beginning of a relationship. If the relationship weakens, the leader gives up "change" until it is possible for him to become bankrupt with the organization. If the relationship strengthens, the leader receives "change" until it is possible for him to become rich with the organization. Always remember: *It takes "change" to make change.* The more "change" in the pocket of the leader, the more changes that can be made in the lives of the people. Sadly, the opposite is also true.

GOOD LEADERS SOLICIT THE SUPPORT OF INFLUENCERS *BEFORE* THE CHANGE IS MADE PUBLIC.

This ten-item checklist includes all the steps a good leader will go through in soliciting support for a change from the major influencers in his organization.

1. List the major influencer(s) of the major groups within your organization.

2. How many will be affected *directly* by this change? (These people are the most important group.)

3. How many will be affected *indirectly* by this change?

4. How many will probably be positive?

5. How many will probably be negative?

6. Which group is the majority?

7. Which group is the most influential?

8. If the positive group is stronger, bring the influencers together for discussion.

9. If the negative group is stronger, meet with the influencers individually.

10. Know the "key" to each influencer.

DEVELOP A MEETING AGENDA THAT WILL ASSIST CHANGE.

Every new idea goes through three phases: It will not work; it will cost too much; and, I thought it was a good idea all along.

A wise leader, understanding that people change through a process, will develop a meeting agenda to enhance this process. One that I have used for fifteen years has proved quite effective.

Information Items:	Items of interest to those attending the meeting; positive items that boost morale. (This starts the meeting off on a high level.)
Study Items:	Issues to be discussed but not voted on. (This allows the sharing of ideas without the pressure to represent a particular point of view.
Action Items:	Issues to be voted on that have previously been study items. (This allows discussion to be made that has already been processed. If major change is required, keep the issue in the study category until it has been allowed time for acceptance.)

ENCOURAGE THE INFLUENCERS TO INFLUENCE OTHERS INFORMALLY.

Major changes should not surprise people. A "leadership leak" done properly will prepare the people for the formal meeting.

Each year I explain to my key leaders that they carry two buckets around with them. One bucket is filled with gasoline and the other with water. Whenever there is a "little fire" of contention within the organization because the people fear a possible change, the influencers are the first to hear about it. When they arrive on the scene they will either throw the bucket of gasoline on the situation and really cause a problem, or they will throw the bucket of water on the little fire and extinguish the problem. In other words, key influences are either the leader's greatest asset or his greatest liability.

Leadership leaks should be planned and positive, preparing the people for the meeting where the change will be formally presented.

SHOW THE PEOPLE HOW THE CHANGE WILL BENEFIT THEM.

Assumption: The proposed change is what is best for the people, not the leader. The people must be first.

A sign on the door in a bus station read: "For the convenience of others, please close the door." Too often the door remained open until the sign was changed to read: "For your *own* personal comfort, please close the door." The door was always shut. Too often leaders of an organization tend to think and lead from the company's perspective, not the people's.

GIVE THE PEOPLE OWNERSHIP OF THE CHANGE.

Openness by the leader paves the way for ownership by the people. Without ownership, changes will be short-term. Changing people's habits and ways of thinking is like writing instructions in the snow during a snowstorm. Every twenty minutes the instructions must be rewritten, unless ownership is given along with the instructions.

How to Offer Ownership of Change to Others

1. Inform people in advance so they'll have time to think about the implications of the change and how it will affect them.

2. Explain the overall objectives of the change—the reasons for it and how and when it will occur.

3. Show people how the change will benefit them. Be honest with the employees who may lose out as a result of the change. Alert them early and provide assistance to help them find another job if necessary.

4. Ask those who will be affected by the change to participate in all stages of the change process.

5. Keep communication channels open. Provide opportunities for employees to discuss the change. Encourage questions, comments, and other feedback.

6. Be flexible and adaptable throughout the change process. Admit mistakes and make changes where appropriate.

7. Constantly demonstrate your belief in and commitment to the change. Indicate your confidence in their ability to implement the change.

8. Provide enthusiasm, assistance, appreciation, and recognition to those implementing the change.[10]

CHANGE WILL HAPPEN

The question should not be "Will we ever change?" but "When and how much will we change?" Nothing stays the same except the fact that change is always present. Even in the beginning, Adam reportedly said to Eve, as they were led out of paradise, "My dear, we live in a time of transition."

Charles Exley, CEO of NCR Corporation, said, "I've been in business thirty-six years. I've learned a lot and most of it doesn't apply anymore."

Writer Lincoln Barnett once described the excitement he shared with a group of students emerging from a physics lecture at the Institute for Advanced Study at Princeton. "How did it go?" someone asked.

"Wonderful!" Mr. Barnett replied. "Everything we knew last week isn't true."

Keeping current with the changes and relating them to the organization is a constant challenge for the leader. Leaders should be aware, for example, of information such as the following, which was outlined in an article written by Dr. Richard Caldwell.[11] He contrasts some of the values of the 1950s and those of the 1990s.

1950s	1990s
Saving	Spending
Delayed gratification	Instant gratification
Ozzie and Harriet	Latchkey kids
Certainty	Ambivalence
Orthodoxy	Skepticism
Investing	Leveraging
Neighborhood	Life-style
Middle class	Under class
Export	Import
Public virtue	Personal well-being
Mom and Dad	Nanny and day care
Press conference	Photo opportunity
Achievement	Fame
Knowledge	Credential
Manufacturing	Service
Duty	Divorce
"We"	"Me"

NOT ALL CHANGE IS IMPROVEMENT, BUT WITHOUT CHANGE THERE CAN BE NO IMPROVEMENT.

Change = Growth

or

Change = Grief

Change represents both possible opportunity and potential loss. My observation is that change becomes grief when:

- The change proposed is a bad idea.

- The change proposed is not accepted by the influencers.

- The change proposed is not presented effectively.

- The change proposed is self-serving to the leaders.

- The change proposed is based solely on the past.

- The changes proposed are too many, happening too quickly.

In 1950, *Fortune* magazine asked eleven distinguished Americans to predict what life would be like in 1980. In those days, the United States enjoyed a trade surplus of $3 billion, so no one predicted a trade deficit thirty years later. David Sarnoff, chairman of RCA, was sure that by 1980, ships, airplanes, locomotives, and even individual automobiles would be atomically fueled. He said that homes would have atomic generators and that guided missiles would transport mail and other freight over great distances. Henry R. Luce, editor-in-chief of *Time* magazine, predicted the end of poverty by 1980. Mathematician John von Neumann expected energy to be free thirty years later.

IT'S NEVER TOO LATE TO CHANGE.

Max Depree said, "In the end, it is important to remember that we cannot become what we need to be by remaining what you are."[12] It's a fact that when you're through changing, you're through.

When you hear the name Alfred Nobel, what do you think of? The Nobel Peace Prize might come to mind. However, that's only chapter two of his story. Alfred Nobel was the Swedish chemist who made his fortune by inventing dynamite and the other powerful explosives used for weapons. When his brother died, one newspaper accidentally printed Alfred's obituary instead. It described the dead man as one who became rich by enabling people to kill each other in unprecedented numbers. Shaken by this assessment, Nobel resolved to use his fortune from then on to award accomplishments that benefited humanity. Nobel had the rare opportunity to evaluate his life at its end and yet live long enough to change that assessment.[13]

Comedian Jerry Lewis says that the best wedding gift he received was a film of the entire wedding ceremony. He says that when things got really bad in his marriage, he would go into a room, close the door, run the film backward, and walk out a free man.

I doubt you will be able to run the film backward or read your obituary in the newspaper. You can, however, make a choice today to change. And when change is successful, you will look back at it and call it growth.

FIVE

THE QUICKEST WAY TO GAIN LEADERSHIP:
PROBLEM-SOLVING

According to F. F. Fournies, writing in *Coaching for Improved Work Performance*,[1] there are four common reasons why people do not perform the way they should:

1. They do not know *what* they are supposed to do.

2. They do not know *how* to do it.

3. They do not know *why* they should.

4. There are obstacles beyond their control.

These four reasons why people fail to perform at their potential are all responsibilities of leadership. The first three reasons deal with starting a job correctly. A training program, job description, proper tools, and vision, along with good communication skills, will go a long way in effectively meeting the first three issues.

This chapter will deal with the fourth reason that causes many people to fail to reach their performance potential. Problems continually occur at work, at home, and in life in general. My observation is that people don't like problems, weary of them quickly, and will do almost anything to get away from them. This climate makes others place the reins of leadership into your hands—*if* you are willing able to either tackle their problems or train them to solve them. Your problem-solving skills will always be needed because people always have problems. And, when problems occur, notice where people go to solve them (see chart below).

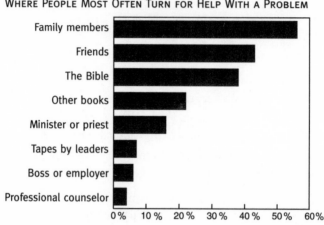

WHERE PEOPLE MOST OFTEN TURN FOR HELP WITH A PROBLEM

This chapter will deal with the two things needed to effectively solve problems: the right attitude and the right action plan.

Before these two areas are explored, I want to share with you some observations I have made about people and their problems.

WE ALL HAVE PROBLEMS.

Sometimes our problems overwhelm us like they did my friend Joe. Before Joe could get out of his house and head for work, he had four long distance calls. Everyone seemed to have a problem. And they all wanted Joe to get on a plane that day and come help out. He finally told his wife to forget about his breakfast. He rushed out of the house as fast as he could. Then, when he stepped into the garage he discovered his car would not start. So he called a taxi. While he was waiting for the taxi, he got another call about another problem. Finally, the taxi came and Joe rushed out, piled in the back seat, and yelled, "All right, let's get going."

"Where do you want me to take you?" the taxi driver asked.

"I don't care where we go," Joe shouted. "I've got problems everywhere."

Sometimes we think our generation has more problems than the last. I laughed at this idea after I reflected on the words of Dwight Bohmbach in *What's Right with America.*

> **The size of the person is more important than the size of the problem.**

"America's elders lived through the great 1929 stock market crash that ruined many of their families; the Depression years; the Bonus March on Washington, when veterans were dispersed by Army troops; the New Deal years; Pearl Harbor; the loss of the Philippines; years of long days and nights in defense plants in the 1940s; fighting in Europe and the Pacific; D-Day; the Battle of the Bulge; V-E Day; the hope-filled beginning of the United Nations in America; the A-bomb; V-J Day; the Marshall Plan in Europe; the Berlin airlift; war in Korea; the U-2 incident; the Bay of Pigs invasion; the Cuban missile crisis; the killings of President Kennedy, Bobby Kennedy, and Martin Luther King, Jr.; the civil rights struggle; the Vietnam War; Americans on the moon; Watergate and the resignation of a president and vice president; the energy crisis; Three-Mile Island; Iranian hostages; a new president shot in 1981; the bombing of our embassy and hundreds of Marines in Lebanon; becoming a debtor nation, with the highest budget deficit in history. What a lifetime!"

We should remember the words of Paul Harvey who said that in times like these it is always helpful to remember that there have always been times like these.

PROBLEMS GIVE MEANING TO LIFE.

A wise philosopher once commented that an eagle's only obstacle to overcome for flying with greater speed and ease is the air. Yet, if the air were withdrawn, and the proud bird were to fly in a vacuum, it would fall instantly to the ground, unable to fly at all. The very element that offers resistance to flying is at the same time the condition for flight.

The main obstacle that a powerboat has to overcome is the water against the propeller, yet, if it were not for this same resistance, the boat would not move at all.

People need to change their perspectives, not their problems.

The same law, that obstacles are conditions of success, holds true in human life. A life free of all obstacles and difficulties would reduce all possibilities and powers to zero. Eliminate problems and life loses its creative tension. The problem of mass ignorance gives meaning to education. The problem of ill health gives meaning to medicine. The problem of social disorder gives meaning to government.

In the South, when cotton was "king," the boll weevil crossed over from Mexico to the United States and destroyed the cotton plants. Farmers were forced to grow a variety of crops, such as soybeans and peanuts. They learned to use their land to raise cattle, hogs, and chickens. As a result, many more farmers became prosperous than in the days when the only crop grown was cotton.

The people of Enterprise, Alabama, were so grateful for what had occurred that in 1910 they erected a monument to the boll weevil. When they turned from the single-crop system to diversified farming, they became wealthier. The inscription on the monument reads: "In profound appreciation of the boll weevil and what it has done to herald prosperity."

We all have a tendency all of our lives to want to get rid of problems and responsibilities. When that temptation arises, remember the youth who was questioning a lonely old man. "What is life's heaviest burden?" he asked. The old fellow answered sadly, "Having nothing to carry."

MANY OUTSTANDING PEOPLE HAVE OVERCOME PROBLEMS IN THEIR LIVES.

Many of the Psalms were born in difficulty. "Most of the Epistles were written in prisons. Most of the greatest thoughts of the greatest thinkers

---

of all time had to pass through the fire. Bunyan wrote *Pilgrim's Progress* from jail. Florence Nightingale, too ill to move from her bed, reorganized the hospitals of England. Semiparalyzed and under constant menace of apoplexy, Pasteur was tireless in his attack on disease. During the greater part of his life, American historian Francis Parkman suffered so acutely that he could not work for more that five minutes at a time. His eyesight was so wretched that he could scrawl only a few gigantic words on a manuscript, but he contrived to write twenty magnificent volumes of history."[2]

> Policies are many; principles are few. Policies will change; principles never do.

Bury a person in the snows of Valley Forge, and you have a George Washington. Raise him in abject poverty, and you have an Abraham Lincoln. Strike him down with infantile paralysis, and he becomes a Franklin D. Roosevelt. Burn him so severely that the doctors say he will never walk again, and you have a Glenn Cunningham, who set the world's one-mile record in 1934. Have him or her born black in a society filled with racial discrimination, and you have a Booker T. Washington, a Marian Anderson, a George Washington Carver, or a Martin Luther King, Jr. Call him a slow learner and retarded—writing him off as uneducable—and you have an Albert Einstein.

Dolly Parton sums it all up with these words, "The way I see it, if you want the rainbow you gotta put up with the rain."

MY PROBLEM IS *NOT* MY PROBLEM.

There is a world of difference between a person who has a big problem and a person who makes a problem big. For several years I would do between twenty and thirty hours of counseling each week. I soon discovered that the people who came to see me were not necessarily the ones who had the most problems. They were the ones who were problem conscious and found their difficulties stressful. Naïve at first, I would try to fix their problems only to discover they would go out and find others. They were like Charlie Brown in a Christmas special—he just couldn't get the Christmas spirit. Linus finally said, "Charlie Brown, you're the only person I know who can take a wonderful season like Christmas and turn it into a problem."

Linus, I have news for you. There are many people like Charlie Brown! Their "problems" are not their real problems. The problem is that they react wrongly to "problems" and therefore make their "problems" real problems. What really counts is not what happens *to me* but what happens *in me*.

A study of three hundred highly successful people, people like Franklin Delano Roosevelt, Helen Keller, Winston Churchill, Albert Schweitzer, Mahatma Gandhi, and Albert Einstein, reveals that one-fourth had handicaps, such as blindness, deafness, or crippled limbs. Three-fourths had either been born in poverty, came from broken homes, or at least came from exceedingly tense or disturbed situations.

Why did the achievers overcome problems while thousands are overwhelmed by theirs? They refused to hold on to the common excuses for failure. They turned their stumbling blocks into stepping stones. They realized they could not determine every circumstance in life but they could determine their choice of attitude toward every circumstance.

> Always take the high road.

I read about a church choir that was raising money to attend a music competition and decided to have a car wash. To their dismay, after a busy morning, rain began to pour in midafternoon, and the customers stopped coming. Finally, one of the women printed this poster: "WE WASH;" (and with an arrow pointed skyward), "HE RINSES!"

The *Los Angeles Times* recently ran this quote: "If you can smile whenever anything goes wrong, you are either a nitwit or a repairman." I would add: or a leader in the making—one who realizes that the only problem you have is the one you allow to be a problem because of your wrong reaction to it. Problems can stop you temporarily. You are the only one who can do it permanently.

A PROBLEM IS SOMETHING I CAN DO SOMETHING ABOUT.

My friend and mentor, Fred Smith, taught me this truth. If I can't do something about a problem, it's not my problem; it's a fact of life.

In 1925, an American company manufacturing and marketing shaving cream was concerned about the effectiveness of its roadside advertising. With the introduction of "high speed" automobiles, they were concerned that nobody had time to read their billboards. So the company, Burma Shave, created a series of small signs spaced at sufficient intervals so they could be read even at high speeds. The unique approach to advertising made Burma Shave a household name for forty-six years.

As a child growing up in Ohio, I loved the Burma Shave advertisements. This was my favorite:

> A peach looks good
> With lots of fuzz . . .
> But man's no peach . . .
> And never was.

The Burma Shave company became creative with a changing society. If there had been no answer to the problem, then there would have been no problem—just a fact of life. Be careful in resigning yourself to the position that there is no answer to a problem. Someone else may come along with a solution.

A TEST OF A LEADER IS THE ABILITY TO RECOGNIZE A PROBLEM BEFORE IT BECOMES AN EMERGENCY.

Under excellent leadership a problem seldom reaches gigantic proportions because it is recognized and fixed in its early stages.

Great leaders usually recognize a problem in the following sequence:

1. They sense it before they see it (intuition).

2. They begin looking for it and ask questions (curiosity).

3. They gather data (processing).

4. They share their feelings and findings to a few trusted colleagues (communicating).

5. They define the problem (writing).

6. They check their resources (evaluating).

7. They make a decision (leading).

Great leaders are seldom blind-sided. They realize that the punch that knocks them out is seldom the hard one—it's the one they didn't see coming. Therefore, they are always looking for signs and indicators that will give them insight into the problem ahead and their odds of fixing it. They treat problems like the potential trespasser of an Indiana farm who read this sign on a fence post, "If you cross this field you better do it in 9.8 seconds. The bull can do it in 10 seconds."

You can judge leaders by the size of the problems they tackle.

In one of the "Peanuts" comic strips, Charlie Brown says, "There's no problem so big that I can't run from it." We all have felt exactly like the lion tamer who put this advertisement in the paper: "Lion tamer wants tamer lion."

Yet, in my observations of people and their problems, I have noticed that the size of the person is more important than the size of the problem. Problems look larger or smaller according to whether the person is large or small.

Recently, I spoke with Marcia, a lady who was diagnosed with cancer two years ago and had a mastectomy. She is doing very well. But she shared with me a concern for others who had the problem and were not doing well. There seemed to be a big difference between Marcia and others who had the same problem. I could have predicted physical recovery for Marcia. She was positive from the beginning of her problem. Our focus as a leader should be to build big people. Big people will handle big issues effectively.

SOLVE TASK-PROBLEMS QUICKLY; PEOPLE-PROBLEMS WILL TAKE LONGER.

Solving problems may be the immediate agenda, but that should never be where we spend most of our time. If all we do is focus on solving the next problem at hand, we will soon feel like the farmer who said, "The hardest thing about milking cows is that they never stay milked." Problems never stop but people can stop problems. My suggestion for producing problem-solvers are:

1. *Make a time commitment to people.* Those who never take time to develop people are forced to take time to solve their problems.

2. *Never solve a problem for a person; solve it with that person.* Take that individual through the sequence that has already been given for recognizing a problem. In fact, spend time with that person and study this entire chapter together.

Problems should be solved at the lowest level possible. President John F. Kennedy said that President Eisenhower gave him this advise the day before his inauguration: "You'll find no easy problems ever come to the President of the United States. If they are easy to solve, somebody else has solved them." That statement should be true of every leader. Climbing the ladder of leadership means that fewer but more important decisions will be made. The problem-solving skills of a leader must be sharpened because every decision becomes a major decision. John E. Hunter said, "A situation only becomes a problem when one does not have sufficient resources to meet it." The rest of the chapter will deal with what is needed to effectively solve problems.

THE RIGHT ATTITUDE.

The subject of our attitude is so important for potential leaders that the next chapter will be given to it totally. Therefore, a few thoughts will be sufficient at this time. Norman Vincent Peale was right when he said that positive thinking is how you *think* about a problem. Enthusiasm is how you *feel* about a problem. The two together determine what you do about a problem. If I could do anything for people, I would help them change their perspectives, not their problems. Positive thinking does not always change our circumstances, but it will always change us. When we are able to think right about tough situations, then our journeys through life become better.

G.W. Target, in his essay " The Window," tells the story of two men confined to hospital beds in the same room. Both men were seriously ill and though they were not allowed much diversion—no television, radio, or books—their friendship developed over months of conversation. They discussed every possible subject in which they both had interest or experience, from family to jobs to vacations, as well as much of their own personal histories.

Neither man left his bed, but one was fortunate enough to be next to the window. As part of his treatment he could sit up in bed for just an hour a day. At this time he would describe the world outside to his roommate. In very descriptive terms he would bring the outside world inside to his friend, describing to him the beautiful park he could see, with its lake, and the many interesting people he saw spending their time there. His friend began to live for those descriptions.

After a particularly fascinating report, the one man began to think it was not fair his friend got to see everything while he could see nothing. He was ashamed of his thoughts, but he had quite a bit if time to think and he couldn't get this out of his mind. Eventually his thoughts began to take their effect on his health, and he became even more ill, with a disposition to match.

One evening his friend, who sometimes had difficulty with congestion and breathing, awoke with a fit of coughing and choking and was unable to push the button for the nurse to come to his aid. The frustrated, sour man lay there looking at the ceiling, listening to this struggle for life next to him, and doing nothing.

The next morning the day nurse came in to find the man by the window dead.

After a proper interval, the man who was so eager to see out that window asked if he could be moved, and it was quickly done. As soon as the room was empty, the man struggled up on his elbow to look out the window and fill his spirit with the sights of the outside world.

It was then he discovered the window faced a blank wall.[3]

THE RIGHT ACTION PLAN.

Is it not true that too many times we have a surplus of simple answers and a shortage of simple problems? Occasionally we all feel like the guy in a cartoon who said, "I try to take just one day at a time but lately several days have attacked me at once." One thing is certain, life is not problem-free!

The story is told that when the Apollo series of space vehicles was being designed, a rift developed between the scientists and the engineers. The scientists insisted that every available ounce of weight be reserved for scientific equipment that could be used to explore and report on outer space. They wanted the engineers to design a space vehicle that would be free from all defects. (That was the era when "zero defects" was a popular expression in industry.) That would mean a large proportion of the space and weight would be available for scientific equipment.

The engineers argued that was an impossible goal. They contended the only safe assumption was that something would go wrong, but they could not predict with certainty where the malfunctions would occur. Therefore, they would need to build in a series of backup systems to compensate for every possible malfunction. That would mean far less weight and cargo space would be available for scientific equipment.

Allegedly this conflict was resolved by asking the astronauts in training which assumption they supported. They all voted in favor of lots of backup systems! This story illustrates the importance of assumptions. Some people assume that a defect-free system can be developed for their lives. Others assume that something will go wrong and they need a backup system. Too many times when a problem arises, we want to blame someone else and take the easy way out. Recently I studied a humorous problem-solving chart (see opposite page) that underscores our desire to duck responsibility.

THE PROBLEM-SOLVING PROCESS

Now, even if we don't wish to duck responsibilities and we have a right attitude and a solid action plan, it is still important to follow a process when we're looking for a solution. I suggest following these steps to problem-solving.

IDENTIFY THE PROBLEM.

Too many times we attack the symptoms, not the cause. Ordering your staff to stay at their desks until quitting time is a Band-Aid solution that does not answer the question, "Why does the staff leave early?" Your job is to identify the real issues that lie beneath the symptoms. Failing to do this places you in the same situation as a young soldier who was learning to parachute. He was given the following instructions:

1. Jump when you are told;

2. Count to ten and pull the ripcord;

3. In the very unlikely event that it doesn't open, pull the second chute open; and

4. When you get down, a truck will take you back to the base.

The plane got up to the proper altitude and the men started peeling out; the soldier jumped when it was his turn. He counted to ten, pulled the cord, but the chute failed to open. He proceeded to the backup plan and pulled the cord of the second chute. It, too, failed to open. "And I suppose," he complained to himself, "the truck won't be there when I get down."

PRIORITIZE THE PROBLEM.

Richard Sloma says never to try to solve all the problems all at once—make them line up for you one-by-one. Whether you face three problems, thirty, or three hundred, "make them stand in single file so you face only one at a time." Approach these problems, not with a view of finding what you hope will be there, but to get the truth and the realities that must be grappled with. You may not like what you find. In that case, you are entitled to try to change it. But do not deceive yourself. What you do find may or may not be the real problem.

DEFINE THE PROBLEM.

In a single sentence, answer the question, "What is the problem?" Bobb Biehl encourages us to keep in mind the difference between solving a problem and making a decision. A "decision is a choice you make between two or more alternatives, such as 'Should I fly to Phoenix or Chicago?' A problem is a situation that's counter to your intentions or expectations: 'I meant to fly to Chicago, but I ended up in Detroit,' or 'I meant to have $50,000 in the bank, but I'm $50,000 in the hole.'"[4]

Defining the problem in a single sentence is a *four-step process.*

1. Ask the Right Questions.

If you have a vague idea, don't ask a general question such as "What is happening here?" and don't speculate. Instead, ask process-related questions.

PROBLEM-SOLVING FLOW CHART

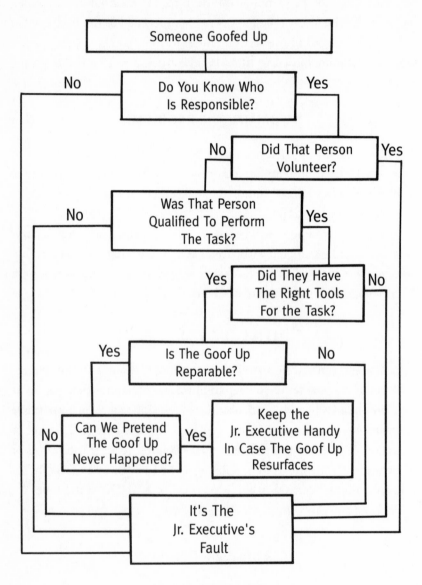

Created by David B. McGinnis

Two words that always govern my questions are *trends* and *timing*. Most problem trails can be sniffed out if specific questions are asked in these two areas.

2. Talk to the Right People.

Beware of authorities with a we-know-better attitude. These people have blind spots and are resistant to change. Creativity is essential for problem-solving. In leadership conferences I often illustrate the principle by using the nine-dot problem.

Connect the nine points below with four straight lines without lifting your pen or pencil from the paper.

If you haven't encountered this problem before, try it. You were stymied if you made certain assumptions about the problem that limited your range of answers. Did you assume the lines could not extend beyond the imaginary square formed by the dots? Break that assumption and you can solve the puzzle more easily.

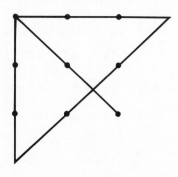

This creative solution is fairly commonplace. Less well-known are alternate solutions that stem from breaking other assumptions, such as these suggested by astronomer Tom Wujec: Assumption: The lines must pass through the center of the dots. If you draw lines that just touch the dots, you can solve the puzzle in just three strokes.

Assumption: The lines must be thin. Connect the lines with one fat line to solve this problem.

Assumption: You may not crease the paper. Fold the paper twice, so the dots all are together on the surface, and you need only one wide line.

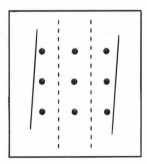

Assumption: The paper must be flat. Roll the paper into a tube. It's possible to connect the dots with a spiral.

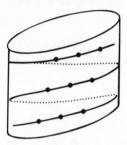

Assumption: You cannot rip the paper. Tear the paper into nine pieces with one dot on each, and connect all the dots by poking a hole through all the dots with your pencil.

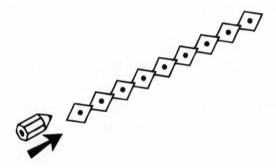

These alternate solutions make the classic nine-dot problem even more effective in conveying the message that we can find more ways to solve more problems if we break stultifying assumptions.[5]

3. Get the Hard Facts

Remember Peter Drucker's words, "Once the facts are clear, the decisions jump out at you." For example, don't let someone say to you, "That person is a good worker." Get concrete examples of that individual's performance. Listen to what is *not* being said and gather the important data.

4. Get Involved in the Process.

Most problems are not what they seem. Don't just ask the right questions and gather hard facts. Get involved in the process by doing the actual jobs of the people concerned and see what problems arise. Problems should be solved at the lowest level possible because that is where they appear. That is also the level where they are most clearly defined.

SELECT PEOPLE TO HELP YOU IN THE PROBLEM-SOLVING PROCESS.

"Socrates developed this method 2,400 years ago: After defining the problem at hand, he would gather others around him and ask for their opinions and logical support to back their opinions up. As self-appointed gadfly, Socrates spent most of his life causing trouble in complacent, conservative Athens. By debating, cajoling, and prodding, he forced Athenians to question beliefs they took for granted.

"This finally got him into trouble. The Athenians charged him with impiety toward the gods and corrupting Athens' youth. He was thrown into prison, tried, and sentenced to death. After a month, during which he refused friends' offers to help him escape, Socrates drank a cup of hemlock and died.

"Nobody expects you to go that far. But practicing the Socratic method will help you to be a better leader."[6]

Before inviting people to attend a problem-solving meeting, ask these questions:

- Is it a real problem?
- Is it urgent?
- Is the true nature of the problem known?
- Is it specific? (If people talk about everything, they will eventually talk about nothing.)
- Has the group most competent to discuss the problem been invited and is each participant concerned about solving this issue?

COLLECT PROBLEM CAUSES.

List all the possible causes of the problem by asking what caused the problem and how the problem can be avoided in the future.

COLLECT PROBLEM-SOLVING SOLUTIONS.

List as many solutions to a problem as possible. The more, the better. Seldom is there just one way to solve a problem. Options are essential because a problem continually shifts and changes. The leader without a backup solution for the primary answer will soon be in trouble.

PRIORITIZE AND SELECT THE "BEST" SOLUTIONS.

Weigh all the possible solutions before deciding. The following questions should always be asked by the leader:

- Which solution has the greatest potential to be right?
- Which solution is in the best interests of the organization?
- Which solution has momentum and timing on its side?
- Which solution has the greatest chance for success?

IMPLEMENT THE BEST SOLUTION.

Norman Bushnell, founder of Atari, said, "Everyone who's ever taken a shower has an idea. It's the person who gets out of the shower, dries off, and does something about it who makes a difference."

EVALUATE THE SOLUTION.

Let others test it out and punch holes in it. If they punch intellectual holes (such as, "I don't think it will continue working because . . ."), ignore them. If they point out real operative problems you can observe, then you must make the adjustment. Ask these questions to evaluate the responses:

- Were we able to identify the real causes of the problem?
- Did we make the right decision?
- Has the problem been resolved?
- Have the key people accepted this solution?
- Did I help people to develop problem-solving skills to manage conflict in the future?

SET UP PRINCIPLES OR POLICIES
TO KEEP PROBLEMS FROM RECURRING.

Whereas policies are set up for a particular function in a specific area, principles are guidelines for everyone and are more general. Policies change when their use is no longer essential. Principles do not change.

> Policies are many,
> Principles are few,
> Policies will change,
> Principles never do.

Policies work well for lower management and operational matters. A policy should never be held on to and defended when it impedes the program and delays the change needed to make progress. A policy's intent is to give clear direction and allow a better flow in the organization. Many operational problems will stay solved with the implementation of solid policy.

A principle within my organization is: "Always take the high road." This principle means that whenever there is debate, questions, tension, or confrontation between staff and people, I always expect my staff to give the benefit of the doubt to others. This principle is for everyone in my organization at all times. It may have nothing to do with an operational procedure with machines and paper, but it has everything to do with people. To teach principles effectively to my staff, I must:

- Model them,

- Relate them by answering the question, "How can I use this in my life?" and

- Applaud when I see the principles being applied in their lives.

Later on in this book I will spend an entire chapter on the importance of having the right people around you. In regard to problem solving, if you are always the problem solver and never teach the people around you to think and decide for themselves, you will have a dependent group of followers. Many years ago I decided to focus on helping people solve problems rather than helping solve people's problems. These suggestions are some approaches you should find effective:

- Never allow others to think you always have the best answers. This will only make them dependent on you.

- Ask questions. Help people to think through the entire process of their problem.

- Become a coach, not a king. A coach brings out the best in others, helping them to reach deep down inside and discover their potential. A king only gives commands.

- List their solutions on paper. Integrate your ideas with theirs until they have ownership of them.

- Ask them to decide on the best solution to their problem.

- Develop a game plan.

- Ask them to take ownership and responsibility for the game plan. Let them set up a time frame and accountability process.

Your goal should be that when the meeting is over the other person has processed the problem, selected a solution, developed a game plan, and taken ownership of it. His or her relationship with you will not be a dependent one, but a deepening one.

SIX

THE EXTRA PLUS IN LEADERSHIP:
ATTITUDE

When I speak at a leadership conference I often ask everyone to do this exercise:

Write the name of a friend whom you greatly admire

_____

Write one thing that you admire most about that friend

_____

I'd like you to take a moment and contemplate this exercise before you continue reading. I think you'll gain an interesting and important insight. The odds are high that the thing you most admire about your friend has to do with attitude. After all the conference participants have completed this exercise, I ask them to tell me their answers. I list the first twenty-five responses on an overhead projector for everyone to see. I put an *A* beside the characteristics that describe attitudes, an *S* beside those describing skills, and an *L* if the words deal with looks. Every time I conduct this exercise, 95 percent of the descriptive words represent attitudes for which the friends are admired.

Charles Swindoll said, "The longer I live, the more I realize the impact of attitude on life. Attitude, to me, is more important than facts. It is more important than the past, than education, than money, than circumstances, than failures, than successes, than what other people think or say or do. It is more important than appearance, giftedness, or skill. It will make or break a company, a church, or a home. The remarkable thing is that we have a choice every day regarding the attitude we will embrace for that day. We cannot change our past. Nor can we change the fact that people will act in a certain way. We also cannot change the inevitable. The only thing that we can do is play on the one string we have, and that is our attitude. I am convinced that life if 10 percent what happens to me and 90 percent how I react to it. And so it is with you—we are in charge of our attitudes."[1]

Just as our attitudes are the extra pluses in life, they also make the difference in leading others. Leadership has less to do with position than it does with disposition. The disposition of a leader is important because it will influence the way the followers think and feel. Great leaders understand that the right attitude will set the right atmosphere, which enables the right responses from others.

OUR ATTITUDES ARE OUR MOST IMPORTANT ASSETS.

Our attitude may not be the asset that makes us great leaders, but without good ones we will never reach our full potential. Our attitudes are the "and then some" that allows us the little extra edge over those whose thinking is wrong. Walt Emerson said, "What lies behind us and what lies before us are tiny matters compared to what lies within us."

The 1983 Cos Report on American Business said that 94 percent of all Fortune 500 executives attributed their success more to attitude than to any other basic ingredient.

Robert Half International, a San Francisco consulting firm, recently asked vice-presidents and personnel directors at one hundred of America's largest companies to name the single greatest reason for firing an employee. The responses are very interesting and underscore the importance of attitude in the business world:

- Incompetence: 30 percent
- Inability to get along with other workers: 17 percent
- Dishonesty or lying: 12 percent
- Negative attitude: 10 percent
- Lack of motivation: 7 percent
- Failure or refusal to follow instructions: 7 percent
- All other reasons: 8 percent

Notice that although incompetence ranked first on the list, the next five were all attitude problems.

The Carnegie Institute not long ago analyzed the records of ten thousand persons and concluded that 15 percent of success is due to technical training. The other 85 percent is due to personality, and the primary personality trait identified by the research is attitude.

Our attitudes determine what we see and how we handle our feelings. These two factors greatly determine our success

What we see: Psychology 101 taught me that we see what we are prepared to see. A suburbanite, unable to find his best saw, suspected that his neighbor's son—who was always tinkering around with woodworking—had stolen it. During the next week everything the teenager did looked suspicious—the way he walked, the tone of his voice, his gestures. But when the older man found the saw behind his own workbench, where he had accidentally knocked it, he could no longer see anything at all suspicious in his neighbor's son.

Nell Mohney, in her book *Beliefs Can Influence Attitudes*, pointedly illustrates this truth. Mohney tells of a double-blind experiment conducted in the San Francisco Bay area. The principal of a school called three professors together and said, "Because you three teachers are the finest in the system and you have the greatest expertise, we're going to give you ninety high-IQ students. We're going to let you move these students through this next year at their own pace and see how much they can learn."

Everyone was delighted—faculty and students alike.

Over the next year the professors and the students thoroughly enjoyed themselves. The professors were teaching the brightest students; the students were benefiting from the close attention and instruction of highly skilled teachers. By the end of the experiment, the students had achieved from 20 to 30 percent more than the other students in the whole area.

> Life is 10 percent what happens to me and 90 percent how I react to it.

The principal called the teachers in and told them, "I have a confession to make. You did not have ninety of the most intellectually prominent students. They were run-of-the-mill students. We took ninety students at random from the system and gave them to you."

The teachers said, "This means that we are exceptional teachers."

The principal continued, "I have another confession. You're not the brightest of the teachers. Your names were the first three names drawn out of a hat."

The teachers asked, "What made the difference? Why did ninety students perform at such an exceptional level for a whole year?"[2]

> Leadership has less to do with position than it does disposition.

The difference, of course, was the teachers' expectations. Our expectations have a great deal to do with our attitudes. And these expectations may be totally false, but they will determine our attitudes.

How we handle our feelings: Notice I did not say our attitudes determine how we feel. There is a great difference between how we feel and how we handle our feelings. Everyone has times when they feel bad. Our attitudes cannot stop our feelings, but they can keep our feelings from stopping us. Unfortunately too many allow their feelings to control them until they end up like poor Ziggy in the comic strip.

He is sitting beneath a tree, gazing at the moon, and says, "I've been here and I've been there. I've been up and I've been down. I've been in and I've been out. I've been around and I've been about. But not once, not even once, have I ever been 'where it's at'!"

> We cannot continue to function in a manner that we do not truly believe about ourselves.

Every day I see people who are feeling controlled. A recent survey indicates that people with emotional problems are 144 percent more likely to have automobile accidents than those who are emotionally stable. An alarming factor revealed by this study is that one out of every five victims of fatal accidents had a quarrel within six hours before his or her accident.

IT IS IMPROBABLE THAT A PERSON WITH A BAD ATTITUDE CAN CONTINUOUSLY BE A SUCCESS.

Norman Vincent Peale relates this story in his book, *Power of the Plus Factor*. "Once walking through the twisted little streets of Kowloon in Hong Kong, I came upon a tattoo studio. In the window were displayed samples of the tattoos available. On the chest or arms you could have tattooed an anchor or flag or mermaid or whatever. But what struck me with force were three words that could be tattooed on one's flesh, *Born to lose*.

> A leader's attitude is caught by his or her followers more quickly than his or her actions.

"I entered the shop in astonishment and, pointing to those words, asked the Chinese tattoo artist, 'Does anyone really have that terrible phrase, *Born to lose*, tattooed on his body?'

"He replied, 'Yes sometimes.' 'But,' I said, 'I just can't believe that anyone in his right mind would do that.'

"The Chinese man simply tapped his forehead and in broken English said, 'Before tattoo on body, tattoo on mind.'"[3]

Once our minds are "tattooed" with negative thinking, our chances for longterm success diminish. We cannot continue to function in a manner that we do not truly believe about ourselves. Often I see people sabotage themselves because of wrong thinking.

The sports world has always appreciated Arnold Palmer. The member's of "Arnie's army" can still be counted among young and old. This great golfer never flaunted his success. Although he has won hundreds of trophies and awards, the only trophy in his office is a battered cup that he got for his first professional win at the Canadian Open in 1955. In addition to the cup, he has a lone framed plaque on the wall. The Plaque tells you why he has been successful on and off the golf course. It reads:

> If you think you are beaten, you are.
> If you think you dare not, you don't.
> If you'd like to win but think you can't,
> It's almost certain you won't.
> Life's battles don't always go
> To the stronger or faster man,
> But sooner or later, the man who wins
> Is the man who thinks he can.

What is the difference between a golfer who wins one golf tournament and an Arnold Palmer? Is it ability? Lucky breaks? Absolutely not! When an average of less than two strokes per tournament separates the top twenty-five golfers in the world, the difference has to be something more than ability.

It's the attitude that makes the difference. People with negative thinking may start well, have a few good days, and win a match. But sooner or later (it's usually sooner), their attitude will pull them down.

WE ARE RESPONSIBLE FOR OUR ATTITUDES.

Our destinies in life will never be determined by our complaining spirits or high expectations. Life is full of surprises and the adjustment of our attitudes is a lifelong project.

The pessimist complains about the wind.

> The optimist expects it to change.
> The leader adjusts the sails.

My father, Melvin Maxwell, has always been my hero. He is a leader's leader. One of his strengths is his positive attitude. Recently Dad and Mom spent some time with my family. As he opened his briefcase, I noticed a couple of motivational attitude books.

I said, "Dad, you're seventy years old. You've always had a great attitude. Are you still reading that stuff?"

He looked me in the eye and said, "Son, I have to keep working on my thought life. I am responsible to have a great attitude and to maintain it. My attitude does not run on automatic."

Wow! That's a lesson for all of us. We choose what attitudes we have right now. And it's a continuing choice. I am amazed at the large number of adults who fail to take responsibility for their attitudes. If they're grumpy and someone asks why, they'll say, "I got up on the wrong side of the bed." When failure begins to plague their lives, they'll say, "I was born on the wrong side of the tracks." When life begins to flatten out and others in the family are still climbing, they'll say, "Well, I was in the wrong birth order in my family." When their marriages fail, they believe they married the wrong person. When someone else gets a promotion they wanted, it's because they were in the wrong place at the wrong time.

Do you notice something? They are blaming everyone else for their problems.

The greatest day in your life and mine is when we take total responsibility for our attitudes. That's the day we truly grow up.

An advisor to President Lincoln suggested a certain candidate for the Lincoln cabinet. But Lincoln refused, saying, "I don't like the man's face."

"But, sir, he can't be responsible for his face," insisted the advisor.

"Every man over forty is responsible for his face," replied Lincoln, and the subject was dropped. No matter what you think about your attitude, it shows on your face!

The other day I saw a bumper sticker that read, "Misery is an option." I believe it! So does the daughter of a woman I heard about. The woman and her daughter went Christmas shopping together. The crowds were awful. The woman had to skip lunch because she was on a tight schedule. She became tired and hungry, and her feet were hurting. She was more than a little irritable.

As they left the last store, she asked her daughter, "Did you see the nasty look that salesman gave me?

The daughter answered, "He didn't give it to you, Mom. You had it when you went in."

> We cannot choose how many years we will live, but we can choose how much life those years will have.
>
> We cannot control the beauty of our face, but we can control the expression on it.
>
> We cannot control life's difficult moments, but we can choose to make life less difficult.
>
> We cannot control the negative atmosphere of the world, but we can control the atmosphere of our minds.
>
> Too often, we try to choose to control things we cannot.
>
> Too seldom, we choose to control what we can . . . our attitude.[4]

IT'S NOT WHAT HAPPENS *TO* ME THAT MATTERS BUT WHAT HAPPENS *IN* ME.

Hugh Downs says that a happy person is not a person with a certain set of circumstances, but rather a person with a certain set of attitudes. Too many people believe that happiness is a condition. When things are going great, they're happy. When things are going bad, they're sad. Some people have what I call "destination disease." They think that happiness can be found in a position or a place. Others have what I call "someone sickness." They think happiness results from knowing or being with a particular person.

I am impressed with the philosophy of the following statement: "God chooses what we go through. We choose how we go through it." It describes Viktor Frankl's attitude as he was terribly mistreated in a Nazi concentration camp. His words to his persecutors have been an inspiration to millions of people. He said, "The one thing you cannot take away from me is the way I choose to respond to what you do to me. The last of one's freedoms is to choose one's attitude in any given circumstance."[5]

Clara Barton, the founder of the American Red Cross, understood the importance of choosing a right attitude even in wrong situations. She was never known to hold a grudge against anyone. One time a friend recalled to her a cruel thing that had happened to her some years previously, but Clara seemed not to remember the incident.

"Don't you remember the wrong that was done to you?" the friend asked.

"No," Clara answered calmly. "I distinctly remember forgetting that."

Many times people who have suffered adverse situations in their lives become bitter and angry. Over time, their lives will be negative and hardened toward others. The tendency for them is to point back to a difficult time and say, "That incident ruined my life." What they do not realize is that the incident called for an attitude decision—a response. Their wrong attitude choice, not the condition, ruined their lives.

C.S. Lewis said, "Everytime you make a choice you are turning the control part of you, the part that chooses, into something a little different from what is was before. And taking your life as a whole, with all your innumerable choices, you are slowly turning this control thing either into a heavenly creature or into a hellish one."[6]

THE LEADER'S ATTITUDE HELPS DETERMINE THE ATTITUDES OF THE FOLLOWERS.

Leadership is influence. People catch our attitudes just like they catch our colds—by getting close to us. One of the most gripping thoughts to ever enter my mind centers on my influence as a leader. It is important that I possess a great attitude, not only for my own success, but also for the benefit of others. My responsibilities as a leader must always be viewed in light of the many, not just myself.

Dr. Frank Crane reminds us that a ball rebounds from the wall with precisely the force with which it was thrown against the wall. There is a law in physics to the effect that action is equal to reaction. The law is also true in the realm of influence. In fact, its effects multiply with a leader's influence. The action of a leader multiplies in reaction because there are several followers. To a smile given, many smiles return. Anger unleashed toward others results in much anger returned from many. There are few actual victims of fate. The generous are helped and the stingy are shunned.

Remember the four-minute mile? People had been trying to achieve it since the days of the ancient Greeks. In fact, folklore has it that the Greeks had lions chase the runners, thinking that would make them run faster. They also tried drinking tiger's milk—not the stuff you get down at the health food store, but the real thing. Nothing they tried worked. So they decided it was impossible for a person to run a mile in four minutes or less. And for over a thousand years everyone believed it. Our bone structure is all wrong. Wind resistance is too great. We have inadequate lung power. There were a million reasons.

Then one man, one single human being, proved that the doctors, the trainers, the athletes, and the millions of runners before him, who tried and failed, were all wrong. And, miracle of miracles, the year after Roger Bannister broke the four-minute mile, thirty-seven other runners broke the four-minute mile. The year after that three hundred runners broke the four-minute mile. And a few years ago in a single race in New York, thirteen out of thirteen runners broke the four-minute mile. In other words, a few decades ago the runner who finished dead last in the New York race would have been regarded as having accomplished the impossible.

What happened? There were no great breakthroughs in training. No one discovered how to control wind resistance. Human bone structure and physiology didn't suddenly improve. But human attitudes did.

You can accomplish your goals, if you set them. Who says you're not tougher, smarter, better, harder-working, more able than your competition? It does not matter if they say you can't do it. What matters, the *only* thing that matters, is if *you* say it.

Until Roger Bannister came along, we all believed the experts. And "the experts" continue to keep others from reaching their potential. Why? Because experts have influence. I believe that a leader's attitude is caught by his followers more quickly than his actions. An attitude is reflected by others even when they don't follow the action. An attitude can be expressed without a word being spoken.

The effect of a leader's attitude on others is the main reason for the importance of considering a candidate's attitude when hiring executives. Practicing psychologists list areas needing significant appraisal when employees are being considered for executive promotion: ambition; attitudes toward policy; attitudes toward colleagues; supervisory skills; and attitudes toward excessive demands on time and energy. A candidate who is out of balance in one or more of these areas would be likely to project a negative attitude and, therefore, prove to be a poor leader.

Take a moment and list the negative attitudes you possess that are influencing others right now.

1.

2.

3.

4.

HOW TO CHANGE YOUR ATTITUDE

Many people seem to suffer from what Ashley Montagu, the great Rutgers anthropologist, called *psychosclerosis*. Psychosclerosis is like arteriosclerosis, which is hardening of the arteries. Psychosclerosis is *hardening of the attitude*.

David Neiswanger of the Menninger Foundation says that if each of us can be helped by science to live a hundred years, "what will it profit us if our hates and fears, our loneliness and our remorse, will not permit us to enjoy them?"

The following sections will help you to help yourself in changing your attitude.

REVIEW.

Many years ago my wife, Margaret, and I bought our first house. Our limited finances forced us to find some ways of getting what we wanted without spending a great deal of money. We agreed we would work on the front yard ourselves to save labor expenses and still create a proper setting for our home. It looked great.

One day, while I was standing in our backyard, I began to realize that we had spent no time or money making the back look good. Why? Because it couldn't be seen by others as they passed our house. We were careless about the area that was hidden.

That is exactly what people do in their personal lives. Their appearances, which can be seen outwardly, are spared no expense or energy. Yet their attitudes are neglected and underdeveloped. Remember the opening part of this chapter? Go back and read it again, and then put the necessary energy and effort into changing the inner areas of your life.

THE SIX STAGES OF ATTITUDE CHANGE

1. Identify Problem Feelings.

This is the earliest stage of awareness and the easiest to declare.

2. Identify Problem Behavior.

Now we go beneath the surface. What triggers wrong feelings? Write down actions that result in negative feelings.

3. Identify Problem Thinking.

William James said, "That which holds our attention determines our action."

4. Identify Right Thinking.

Write on paper the thinking that is right and what you desire. Because your feelings come from your thoughts, you can control your feelings by changing one thing—your thoughts!

5. Make a Public Commitment to Right Thinking.

Public commitment becomes powerful commitment.

6. Develop a Plan for Right Thinking.

This plan should include:

- A written definition of desired right thinking
- A way to measure progress
- A daily measuring of progress
- A person to whom you are accountable
- A daily diet of self-help materials
- Associating with right thinking people

This is a general plan for attitude self-improvement. The following steps will increase the probability of your success.

RESOLVE.

Whenever a leader needs to ask others to make a commitment of time, two questions must always be answered: "Can they?" (this deals with ability) and "Will they?" (this deals with attitude). The more important question of the two is "Will they?" Two other questions usually answer the "Will they?" issue. The first is, "Is the timing right?" In other words, are the conditions right to enable positive change? The second question is, "Is their temperature hot?" Are right conditions accompanied with a red-hot desire to pay the price necessary for needed change? When both questions can be answered with a resounding Yes!, then the resolve is strong and success is possible.

REFRAME.

Dennis Waitley says that the winners in life think constantly in terms of I can, I will, and I am. Losers, on the other hand, concentrate their waking thoughts on what they should have done or what they didn't do. If we don't like our performances, then we must first change the picture.

Cancer researchers at King's College in London did a long-term study of fifty-seven breast cancer victims who'd had mastectomies. They found that seven out of ten women "with a fighting spirit" were alive ten years later, while four out of five women "who felt hopeless" at the diagnosis had died.

The study of hope as it affects health even has a fancy name—*psychoneuroimmunology*. Harborview Medical Center in Seattle is researching in this field, and their findings support the conclusions of the King's College researchers. In a two-year study of burn victims, the Harborview research team discovered that patients with positive attitudes recovered more quickly than those with negative ones.[7]

Reframing your attitude means:

I may not be able to change the world I see around me,
but I can change the way I see the world within me.

REENTER.

As you begin changing your thinking, start immediately to change your behavior. Begin to act the part of the person you would like to become. Take action on the behavior you admire by making it your behavior. Too many people want to feel, then take action. This never works.

One day while visiting a doctor's office, I read this in a medical magazine: "We hear it almost every day . . . sigh . . . sigh . . . sigh. 'I just can't get myself motivated to lose weight, test my blood sugar, etc.' And we hear an equal number of sighs from diabetes educators who can't get their patients motivated to do the right things for their diabetes and health.

"We have news for you. Motivation is not going to strike you like lightning. And motivation is not something that someone else—nurse, doctor, family member—can bestow or force on you. The whole idea of motivation is a trap. Forget motivation. Just do it. Exercise, lose weight, test your blood sugar, or whatever. Do it without motivation. And then, guess what? After you start doing the thing, that's when the motivation comes and makes it easy for you to keep on doing it."

"Motivation," says John Bruner, "is like love and happiness. It's a by-product. When you're actively engaged in doing something, the motivation to keep on doing it sneaks up and zaps you when you least expect it."

As Harvard psychologist Jerome Bruner says, you're more likely to act yourself into feeling than feel yourself into action. So act! Whatever it is you know you should do, do it.

The attitude development of our children, Elizabeth and Joel Porter, is very important to my wife Margaret and me. We learned a long time ago that the most effective way to change our children's attitudes is to work on their behaviors. But when we tell one of our children, "Change your attitude," the message is too general and the change we want is unclear. A more effective approach is explaining behaviors that signify bad attitudes. If we help them change their behaviors, the attitudes will change on their own. Instead of saying to our kid's, "Get a grateful attitude," we ask them to give one compliment to every member of the family each day. As this becomes a habit in their lives, the attitude of gratitude follows.

REPEAT.

Paul Meier said, "Attitudes are nothing more than habits of thought, and can be acquired. An action repeated becomes an attitude realized." Once, while leading a conference, I was asked for a simple plan to help a person change some wrong attitudes. I recommended two things to help her change her attitude. First:

> Say the right words,
> Read the right books,
> Listen to the right tapes,
> Be with the right people,
> Do the right things,
> Pray the right prayer.

The second was to do number one every day, not just once or only when you feel like it, and watch your life change for the better.

RENEWAL.

Fortunately, over a period of time a positive attitude can replace a negative one. Again, let me emphasize that the battle is never over, but it is well worth our efforts. The more that negative thoughts are weeded out and replaced by positive ones, the more personal renewal will be experienced. My friend Lena Walker wrote a tribute about her grandfather and a practice in his life that he passed on to her. These words effectively describe the ongoing process of attitude development and the worthiness of overcoming negative thinking.

Each year as spring approaches, my thoughts turn to a white-haired old man who went forth at this time of year to do battle. The enemy was not flesh and blood, but a small yellow flower called "mustard." As one gazes out over the fields and meadows, this yellow touch seems harmless enough, but year-by-year it continues its march, and can eventually take over entire fields. Each spring my grandfather would walk through his fields pulling these yellow flowers out by the roots.

Eventually I was married and lived on a farm in Ohio. Each spring I, too, would look out and see these same yellow flowers. The first few years on the farm I did nothing about them, but as maturity came upon me, I could see the wisdom of my grandfather's efforts. I, too, decided to go forth as he had done and do battle with the enemy.

Now, each year I walk through the fields pulling an occasional mustard plant, I feel I am doing it in tribute to my grandfather.

To me this weed represents our bad habits and negative thoughts. We need to constantly prune out these things so our lives can be lush and green in our quest for a happy and productive life.

SEVEN

DEVELOPING YOUR MOST APPRECIABLE ASSET:
PEOPLE

The one who influences others to follow only is a leader with certain limitations. The one who influences others to lead others is a leader without limitations. As Andrew Carnegie said, no man will make a great leader who wants to do it all himself or to get all the credit for doing it.

Guy Ferguson puts it this way:

> To know how to do a job is the accomplishment of labor;
> To be available to tell others is the accomplishment of the teacher;
> To inspire others to do better work is the accomplishment of management;
> To be able to do all three is the accomplishment of true leaders.

This chapter will focus on the importance of developing people to share in and assist you with the implementation of your dreams as a leader. The thesis is: *The more people you develop, the greater the extent of your dreams.*

People who are placed in leadership positions, but attempt to do it all alone, will someday come to the same conclusion as the brick layer who tried to move five hundred pounds of bricks from the top of a four-story building to the sidewalk below. His problem was that he tried to do it alone. On an insurance claim form, he explained what happened: "It would have taken too long to carry the bricks down by hand, so I decided to put them in a barrel and lower them by a pulley which I had fastened to the top of the building. After tying the rope securely at the ground level, I then went up to the top of the building. I fastened the rope around the barrel, loaded it with bricks, and swung it out over the sidewalk for the descent

"Then I went down to the sidewalk and untied the rope, holding it securely to guide the barrel down slowly. But, since I weigh only one hundred and forty pounds, the five-hundred pound load jerked me form the ground so fast I didn't have time to think of letting go of the rope. And as I passed between the second and third floors, I met the barrel coming down. This accounts for the bruises and lacerations on my upper body.

"I held tightly to the rope until I reached the top, where my hand became jammed in the pulley. This accounts for my broken thumb. At the same time, however, the barrel hit the sidewalk with a bang and the bottom fell out. With the weight of the bricks gone, the barrel weighed only about forty pounds. Thus, my one-hundred-forty-pound body began a swift descent, and I met the empty barrel coming up. This accounts for my broken ankle.

"Slowed only slightly, I continued the descent and landed on the pile of bricks. This accounts for my sprained back and broken collar bone.

"At this point, I lost my presence of mind completely and let go of the rope. And the empty barrel came crashing down on me. This accounts for my head injuries.

"As for the last question on the form, 'What would you do if the same situation arose again?' please be advised that I am finished trying to do the job alone."

I have observed that there are three levels of people/work skills:

Level 1: The person who works better with people is a follower.
Level 2: The person who helps people work better is a manager.
Level 3: The person who develops better people to work is a leader.

PRINCIPLES FOR PEOPLE DEVELOPMENT

My success in developing others will depend on how well I accomplish each of the following:

- **Value of people.** This is an issue of my attitude.
- **Commitment to people.** This is an issue of my time.
- **Integrity with people.** This is an issue of my character.
- **Standard for people.** This is an issue of my vision.
- **Influence over people.** This is an issue of my leadership.

From my own experience and through observation of other leaders who excel in this vital area, I have discovered that there are three areas in which successful people-developers are different from those who are not successful in developing others. Successful people-developers:

1. Make the right assumptions about people:

2. Ask the right questions about people; and

3. Give the right assistance to people.

SUCCESSFUL PEOPLE DEVELOPERS . . . MAKE THE RIGHT ASSUMPTIONS ABOUT PEOPLE

Motivating others has always been relatively easy for me. For years I was asked, "John, how to you motivate people?" My pat answers were things like, "Stay enthusiastic"; "encourage others"; "lead the way"; "believe in people." I would watch others follow my advice and be successful for a short time, only to fall back into the old habit patterns and the resulting low morale.

Observing this downward cycle, I would ask myself why the people who took my advice couldn't continually motivate others. Then one day it hit me! I was giving them the *fruit* of my motivational gifts, but not the *root*. They were writing down my outward answers without the benefit of my inward assumptions about people. My assumptions about

others are what allow me to continually moti-vate and develop them. In fact a leader hav-ing the right assumptions about people is the key factor in their continual development.

> The one who influences others to lead is a leader without limitations.

An assumption is an opinion that some-thing is true. My assumptions about people largely determine how I treat them. Why? What I assume about people is what I look for. What I look for is what I find. What I find influences my response. Therefore, negative assumptions about others will stimu-late negative leadership of them. Positive assumptions about others will stimulate positive leadership of them. Here are several such assump-tions about people that I have found to be extremely valuable.

ASSUMPTIONS: EVERYONE WANTS TO FEEL WORTHWHILE.

The most successful teacher, writers, managers, politicians, philoso-phers, and leaders who deal with people instinctively know this simple fact: Every person in the world is hungry. Yes, every person in this world is hungry for something, be it recognition, companionship, understand-ing, love—the list is endless. One thing I always find on a list of people's needs is the desire to feel worthwhile. People want to feel important! Donald Laird says to always help people increase their own self-esteem. Develop your skills in making other people feel important. There is hardly a higher compliment you can pay an individual than to help that person be useful and find satisfaction and significance. I believe that!

My travel schedule is heavy, and often I stop in the terminal in San Diego to get my shoes shined. Melvin, the man who shines my shoes, has become a friend. As we talk I always try to bring two things into the conversation. I inquire about the Little League team he coaches, because that is the love of his life. And then I tell him, and anyone else who might be listening, that Melvin can polish shoes better than anyone I've ever known.

Napoleon Bonaparte, a leader's leader, knew every officer of his army by name. He liked to wander through his camp, meet an officer, greet him by name, and talk about a battle or maneuver he knew this officer had been involved in. He never missed an opportunity to inquire about a soldier's hometown, wife, and family; the men were always amazed to see how much detailed personal information about each one the emperor was able to store in his memory.

Since every officer felt Napoleon's personal interest in him—proved by his statements and questions—it is easy to understand the devotion they all felt for him.

ASSUMPTION: EVERYONE NEEDS AND RESPONDS TO ENCOURAGEMENT.

For twenty-three years I have been responsible for developing people. I have yet to find a person who did not do better work and put forth greater effort under a spirit of approval than under a spirit of criticism. Encouragement is oxygen to the soul.

Researchers are turning up new evidence to support the old truth that encouragement brings out the best in people. In one experiment, adults were given ten puzzles to solve. All ten were exactly the same for all the adults. They worked on them and turned them in and were given results at the end. However, the results were fictitious. Half of the exam takers were told they had done well, getting seven of ten correct. The other half were told they had done poorly, getting seven of ten wrong. Then all were given another ten puzzles. Again, the puzzles were the same for each person. The half who had been told they had done well with the first puzzles did better with the second set. The other half did worse.[1] Criticism, even though it was given falsely, ruined them.

Viktor Frankl said, "If you treat people to a vision of themselves, if you apparently overrate them, you make them become what they are capable of becoming. You know, if we take people as they are, we make them worse. If we take them as they should be, we help them become what they can be. . . . If you say this is idealism—overrating man—then I must answer, 'Idealism is the real realism, because you help people actualize themselves.'"[2]

Take a moment and link the definition of leadership (influence) with the responsibility of leadership (people development). How do we who influence others truly motivate and develop them? We do it through encouragement and belief in them. People tend to become what the most important people in their lives think they will become. I try to model and then encourage my staff to say something uplifting to others in the first sixty seconds of a conversation. That sets a positive tone for everything else.

> People tend to become what the most important people in their lives think they will become.

In describing what makes a great baseball manager, Reggie Jackson said that a great manager had a knack for making ball players think they are better than they are. He forces you to have a good opinion of yourself. He lets you know he believes in you. He makes you get more out of yourself. And once you learn how good you really are, you never settle for playing anything less than your best.

Henry Ford said, "My best friend is the one who brings out the best in me." How true. Every leader wants to bring out the best that is in people. And every successful leader knows that encouragement is the way to do it.

ASSUMPTION: PEOPLE " BUY INTO" THE LEADER BEFORE THEY "BUY INTO" HIS OR HER LEADERSHIP.

Too often we expect people to be loyal to the position of a leader instead of the person who occupies that position. But people are not motivated by organizational charts, they respond to people. The first thing a leader must declare is not authority because of rights, but authority because of relationships. People do not care how much you know until they know how much you care. You've got to give loyalty down before you receive loyalty up. If people do not believe in their leader, anything will hinder them from following. If people believe in their leader, nothing will stop them.

Most of us think of Christopher Columbus as a great discoverer, but he was also a great leader and salesman. Before he could begin his voyage of discovery that changed the world, he had to see what, to his contemporaries, was an utterly ridiculous idea! And that was no "one call" sale! Consider the circumstances and conditions that were stacked against him.

> People do not care how much you know until they know how much you care.

First, there was absolutely no market for a transatlantic voyage. And hundreds of years of tradition and superstition practically guaranteed there never would be.

Second, although Columbus had made sea voyage as a passenger, he had never been the captain of a ship.

Third, Columbus was a foreigner (an Italian) living in Portugal and then in Spain.

Fourth, Columbus did not have sufficient money to fund such an adventure. In fact, the only one who could legally fund a voyage of discovery was a head of state—a king or a queen. So his prospect list of benefactors was rather short.

Fifth, his price was not cheap. In addition to needing ships and support, Columbus had a long list of personal demands, including: (a) a 10 percent commission on all commerce between his discoveries and the mother country; (b) a title—Admiral of the Ocean Sea; (c) the permanent position of governor of all new territories; and (d) all if his honors and rights passed on to his heirs.

Remarkably, Columbus made the sale and did it on his own terms! Modern salespeople could learn a lot from Columbus's sales techniques. He was propelled by a single-minded passion. He wholeheartedly believed he could reach Asia by crossing the Atlantic. Even though his belief was wrong, it gave him the stamina, conviction, and confidence to convince others. And he never stopped selling.

He didn't mind asking for the order again and again and again! He spent seven years asking King John of Portugal to fund the voyage.

Then he went to Spain and worked on Ferdinand and Isabella for seven years before he finally got his Yes.

Columbus had to see before he could sail. Any successful leader knows this truth. People must buy into you before they buy into your dreams. High morale in an organization comes from having faith in the person at the top.

ASSUMPTION: MOST PEOPLE DO NOT KNOW HOW TO BE SUCCESSFUL.

Most people think success is luck, and they keep trying to win the lottery of life. But success is really the result of planning. It happens where preparation and opportunity meet.

Most people think success is instantaneous. They look at it as a moment, an event, or a place in time. It's not. Success is really a process. It is growth and development. It is achieving one thing and using that as a stepping-stone to achieve something else. It is a journey.

> People do what people see.

Most people think that success is learning how to never fail. But that's not true. Success is learning from failure. Failure is the opportunity to begin again more intelligently. Failure only truly becomes failure when we do not learn from it.

Once people realize that you, as a leader, can help them become successful, they're yours! Someone said, "Success is relative. Once you have it, all the relatives come." This is also true in an organization. Once the leader has proven to be successful and shown an interest in help-

> Failure is the opportunity to begin again more intelligently.

ing others achieve success through the company, that leader will have loyal followers who are willing to develop and grow.

ASSUMPTION: MOST PEOPLE ARE NATURALLY MOTIVATED.

Just watch a one-year old try to explore and find out what is in a house. That is natural motivation. My observation is that people begin an endeavor with a desire to participate, but are often de-motivated and then must be re-motivated to participate.

Little children want to go to school. Three- and four-year-old children "play" school. They can't wait to begin. They start off in first grade with shiny new lunch boxes and a high degree of motivation. However, by the time they are in school for two or three years, some kids hate it. They make excuses not to go, complaining, "I have a sore tummy." What happened? The schools effectively de-motivated the original high degree of enthusiasm and excitement.

The true secret of motivation is creating an environment in which people are free from the influences that de-motivate.

What Motivates People?

Significant contributions. People want to join in a group or pursue a cause that will have lasting impact. They need to see that what they are doing is not wasted effort, but is making a contribution. People must see value in what they are doing. Motivation comes not by activity alone, but by the desire to reach the end result.

Goal participation. People support what they create. Being part of the goal-setting process is motivating and it allows people to feel needed. They like to feel they are making a difference. When people have given input, they have a stake in the issue. They own it and support it. Seeing goals become reality and helping to shape the future is fulfilling. Goal participation builds team spirit, enhances morale, and helps everyone feel important.

Positive dissatisfaction. Someone said that *dissatisfaction* is the one-word definition for *motivation*. Dissatisfied people are highly motivated people, for they see the need for immediate change. They know something is wrong and often know what needs to be done. Dissatisfaction can inspire change or it can lead to a critical spirit. It can lead to apathy or stir one to action. The key is harnessing this energy toward effective change.

Recognition. People want to be noticed. They want credit for personal achievements and appreciation for their contributions. Often, giving recognition is another way of saying thanks. Personal accomplishment is motivating, but it is much more so when someone notices the accomplishment and gives worth to it. Recognition is one way to give meaning to a person's existence.

Clear expectations. People are motivated when they know exactly what they are to do and have the confidence that they can do it successfully. No one wants to jump into a task that is vague or a job whose description is uncertain. Motivation rises in a job when the goals, expectations, and responsibilities are clearly understood. When delegating responsibility, be sure to give the necessary authority to carry out the task. People perform better when they have some control over their work and their time.

What De-Motivates People?

Certain behavior patterns can be de-motivating. We sometimes behave in these ways without realizing the negative influences they have on others. Here's how we can avoid de-motivating behavior.

Don't belittle anyone. Public criticism and cutting conversations, even in jest, can hurt. We must be alert and sensitive. Taken to the extreme, belittling can destroy a person's self-esteem and self-confidence. If you have to give criticism, remember that it takes nine positive comments to balance one negative correction.

Don't manipulate anyone. No one likes to feel maneuvered or used. Manipulation, no matter how slight, tears down the walls of trust in a relationship. We gain more by being honest and transparent than we do by being cunning and crafty. Build people up through affirmation and praise, and they'll be motivated and loyal. Remember, give and it shall be given to you.

Don't be insensitive. Make people your priority. People are our greatest resources; therefore, take time to know and care about them. This means being responsive in conversation, never appearing preoccupied with self or in a hurry. Stop talking and develop the art of really listening. Quit thinking of what you will say next, and begin to hear, not only what they say, but how they feel. Your interest in even insignificant matters will demonstrate your sensitivity.

Don't discourage personal growth. Growth is motivating, so encourage your staff to stretch. Give them opportunities to try new things and acquire new skills. We should not feel threatened by the achievements of others, but should be very supportive of their successes. Allow your staff to succeed and fail. Build the team spirit approach that says, "If you grow, we all benefit."

SUCCESSFUL PEOPLE DEVELOPERS . . . ASK THE RIGHT QUESTIONS ABOUT PEOPLE

Now, we have completed the discussion of how making the right assumptions about people must be our first principle to follow as a successful people developer. Next, we need to become familiar with the right questions to ask people. There are six.

Am I Building People or am I Building My Dream and Using People to Do It?

People must come first. Fred Smith says that Federal Express, from its inception, has put its people first because it is right to do so and because it is good business as well. "Our corporate philosophy is succinctly stated: People-Service-Profits."

This question deals with the leader's motives. There is a slight but significant difference between manipulation and motivation.

Manipulation is moving together for *my* advantage.

Motivation is moving together for *mutual* advantage.

Do I Care Enough to Confront People When It Will Make a Difference?

Confrontation is very difficult for most people. If you feel uneasy just reading the word *confront*, I'd like to suggest that you substitute the word *clarify*. Clarify the issue instead of confronting the person. Then follow these ten commandments.

The Ten Commandments of Confrontation

1. Do it privately, not publicly.

2. Do it as soon as possible. That is more natural than waiting a long time.

3. Speak to one issue at a time. Don't overload the person with a long list of issues.

4.   Once you've made a point don't keep repeating it.

5. Deal only with actions the person can change. If you ask the person to do something he or she is unable to do, frustration builds in your relationship.

6. Avoid sarcasm. Sarcasm signals that you are angry at people, not at their actions, and may cause them to resent you.

7. Avoid words like *always* and *never*. They usually detract from accuracy and make people defensive.

8. Present criticisms as suggestions or questions if possible.

9. Don't apologize for the confrontational meeting. Doing so detracts from it and may indicate you are not sure you had the right to say what you did.

10. Don't forget the compliments. Use what I call the "sandwich" in these types of meetings: Compliment—Confront—Compliment.

Am I Listening to People with More Than My Ears; Am I Hearing More Than Words?

The following test is one I have found useful and have given to my own staff.

Am I a Good Listener?

Give yourself four points if the answer to the following questions is *Always*: three points for *Usually*; two points for *Rarely*; and one point for *Never*.

_____ Do I allow the speaker to finish without interrupting?

_____ Do I listen "between the lines"; that is, for the subtext?

_____ When writing a message, do I listen for and write down the key facts and phrases?

_____ Do I repeat what the person just said to clarify the meaning?

_____ Do I avoid getting hostile and/or agitated when I disagree with the speaker?

_____ Do I tune out distractions when listening?

_____ Do I make an effort to seem interested in what the other person is saying?

Scoring:
26 or higher: You are an excellent listener.
22–25: Better than average score.
18–21: Room for improvement.
17 or lower: Get out there right away and practice your listening.[3]

David Burns, a medical doctor and professor of psychiatry at the University of Pennsylvania, says: "The biggest mistake you can make in trying to talk convincingly is to put your highest priority on expressing your ideas and feelings. What most people really want is to be listened to, respected, and understood. The moment people see that they are being understood, they become more motivated to understand your point of view."

What Are the Major Strengths of This Individual?

Anyone who continually has to work in areas of personal weakness instead of personal strengths will not stay motivated. If individuals have been grinding away at tasks assigned in their weak areas and you reassign them to work in areas of strength, you'll see a dramatic increase in natural motivation.

Have I Placed a High Priority on the Job?

People tend to stay motivated when they see the importance of the things they are asked to do. The five most encouraging words in an organization are: "It will make a difference." The five most discouraging words in an organization are: "It won't make any difference."

I can still remember the day Linda was hired to oversee the computer system in our offices. She came into my office for an initial meeting. My goal was to give her the big picture to help her see that her work was more than computers. I conveyed that doing her job with excellence would encourage every worker to do a better job. I can still see her eyes moisten as she realized that her work would positively contribute to everyone's success.

Have I Shown the Value the Person will Receive from This Relationship?

People tend to stay motivated when they see the value to them of the things they are asked to do. The simple fact is when we hear an announcement, see a commercial, or are asked to make a commitment, a small voice in the back of our minds asks, "What's in it for me?" The reason people skip the meeting you worked so hard to plan is simple: they haven't seen the value (benefits and rewards) they will receive by being there.

Think about an important relationship you have with a subordinate or perhaps with your boss. On the left-hand side of a page, draw up a list of all the contributions you are making to this relationship, that is, what you are giving. With a subordinate, your list might include pay, job security, time, and professional development. Title this list "What I Give."

On the right-hand side of the page, make a second list, entitled "What I Get." Write all the benefits you are receiving. Then sit back and compare your two lists. Don't count the number of items on each one. (Some things are more important than others, and you probably left some items off both lists.) Instead, answer this simple question: *Considering all that you give to your relationship versus all that you're getting from it, who is getting the better deal?* Choose your answer from the following options:

1. *I am getting a better deal.* This can produce complacency and ingratitude.

2. *The other person is getting a better deal.* This can produce resentment.

3. *We are getting an equally good deal.* This usually produces mutual respect and motivation.

Analyze your answer by looking at the three axioms of the Equity Factor (found in Huseman and Hatfield's *Managing the Equity Factor*):
1. People evaluate relationships by comparing what they give to a relationship with what they get from it.

2. When what people give does not equal what they get, they feel distress.

3. People who feel distress because they give more than they get will restore equity. This becomes a negative. Do you commit here?[4]

SUCCESSFUL PEOPLE DEVELOPERS . . . GIVE THE RIGHT TO ASSISTANCE TO PEOPLE

I need to work out their strengths and work on their weaknesses. The question that as a leader I must continually ask is not, "How hard does this person work?" (Is he or she faithful?) but "How much does this person accomplish?" (Is he or she fruitful?).

Some of the most capable people in an organization never utilize their greatest strengths. They may be locked into what management considers important jobs, and they may do them well. But they may never get an opportunity to do what they can do best. When this happens, everybody loses. The person loses because of lack of opportunity and lack of job satisfaction; the organization loses because it wastes some of its most valuable assets. The whole venture operates at less than capacity.

I must give them myself. You can *impress* people at a distance but you can *impact* them only up close.

- List all the people you spent thirty minutes with this week.

- Did you initiate the time or did they?

- Did you have an agenda before the meeting?

- Was the meeting for the purpose of relationships, counseling, communication, or development?

- Was it a win-win meeting?

- Was it with the influential top 20 or the lower 80 percent?

Love everyone, but give yourself to the top 20 percent in your organization. Encourage the many; mentor the few. Be transparent with them. Develop a plan for their growth. Become a team.

I must give them ownership. As Sidney J. Harris believes:

People want to be appreciated, not impressed.
They want to be regarded as human beings,
Not as sounding boards for other people's egos.
They want to be treated as an end in themselves,
Not as a means toward the gratification of another's vanity.

I must give them every chance for success. My responsibility as a leader is to provide assistance for those who work with me by giving them:

- An excellent atmosphere to work in. It should be positive, warm, open, creative, and encouraging.

- The right tools to work with. Do not hire excellent people to do excellent work with average tools.

- A continual training program to work under. Growing employees make growing companies.

- Excellent people to work for. Develop a team. Coming together is the beginning. Working together is success.

- A compelling vision to work toward. Allow your people to work for something larger than themselves.

Great leaders always give their people a head start over those who work under an average leader. Excellent leaders add value to their people and help them become better than they would be if they worked alone. The first question a leader should ask is: "How can I help make those around me more successful?" When that answer is found and implemented, everyone wins!

PEOPLE DEVELOPMENT PRINCIPLES

PEOPLE DEVELOPMENT TAKES TIME.

At one time Andrew Carnegie was the wealthiest man in America. He came to America from his native Scotland when he was a small boy, did a variety of odd jobs, and eventually ended up as the largest steel manufacturer in the United States. At one time he had forty-three millionaires working for him. In those days, a millionaire was a rare person; conservatively speaking, a million dollars in his day would be equivalent to at least twenty million dollars today.

A reporter asked Carnegie how he hired forty-three millionaires. Carnegie responded that those men were not millionaires when they started working for him but had become millionaires as a result.

The reporter then asked how he had developed these men to become so valuable that he would pay them so much money.

Carnegie replied that men are developed the same way gold is mined. When gold is mined, several tons of dirt must be moved to get an ounce of gold, but one doesn't go into the mine looking for dirt. One goes in looking for gold.

Robert Half said, "There is something that is much more scarce, something rarer than ability. It is the ability to recognize ability." There is still another step that must be taken beyond the ability to discover the gold that is in the leader's mine. It must also be developed. It is better to train ten people to work than to do the work of ten people, but it is harder. "The man who goes alone can start the day. But he who travels with another must wait until the other is ready."[5]

PEOPLE SKILLS ARE ESSENTIAL FOR SUCCESS.

Companies that go along successfully have leaders who get along with people. Dave E. Smalley records in his book, *Floorcraft*, that Andrew Carnegie once paid Charles Schwab a salary of one million dollars a year simply because Schwab got along with the people. Carnegie had men who understood the job better and who were better fitted by experience and training to execute it, but they lacked the essential human quality of being able to get others to help them—to get the best out of the workers.

Most chief executives of major companies, when asked what one single characteristic is most needed by those in leadership positions, replied, "The ability to work with people."

Teddy Roosevelt said, "The most important single ingredient to the formula of success is knowing how to get along with people."

John Rockefeller, who built giant corporations, stated that he would pay more for the ability to deal with people than any other ability under the sun.

The Center for Creative Leadership in Greensboro, North Carolina, studied 105 successful executives and discovered the following:

- They admitted their mistakes and accepted the consequences, rather than trying to blame others.

- They were able to get along with a wide variety of people.

- They had strong interpersonal skills, sensitivity to others, and tact.

- They were calm and confident, rather than moody and volatile.

Unsuccessful executives tended to be too tough, abusive, sarcastic, aloof, or unpredictable. Their worst fault was being insensitive to others.

Lack of people skills can result in the kind of situation former Denver Bronco coach, John Ralston, experienced when he left the team. "I left because of illness and fatigue—the fans were sick and tired of me."

BE A MODEL THAT OTHERS CAN FOLLOW.

The number one motivational principle in the world is: *People do what people see.* The speed of the leader determines the speed of the followers. And followers will never go any further than their leader. For years I have followed and taught this process for developing others:

ACTION	RESULT
I do it:	I model.
I do it and you are with me:	I mentor.
You do it and I am with you:	I monitor.
You do it:	You move forward.
You do it and someone is with you:	We multiply.

People's minds are changed more through observation than through arguments.

Benjamin Franklin learned that plaster scattered in the fields would make things grow. He told his neighbors, but they did not believe him. They argued with him, trying to prove that plaster could be of no use at all to grass or grain. After a little while he allowed the matter to drop and said no more about it.

Early the next spring Franklin went into the field and sowed some grain. Close by the path, where men would walk, he traced some letters with his finger, put plaster into them, and then sowed seed in the plaster. After a week or two the seed sprang up.

As they passed that way, the neighbors were very surprised to see, in brighter green than all the rest of the field, large letters saying, "This has been plastered." Benjamin Franklin did not need to argue with his neighbors anymore about the benefits of plaster for the field.

LEAD OTHERS BY LOOKING THROUGH THEIR EYES.

Henry Wadsworth Longfellow said, "We judge ourselves by what we feel capable of doing; while others judge us by what we have already done."

Any leader who successfully deals with a group of people realizes that they each have their own agenda and perception of how things are. Long ago I learned that people think their:

> Problems are the biggest,
> Children are the smartest,

Jokes are the funniest, and
Faults ought to be overlooked.

An amusing story beautifully illustrates how each of us views life.

After World War II, a general and his young lieutenant boarded a train in England. The only seats left were across from a beautiful young lady and her grandmother. The general and the lieutenant sat facing the women. As the train pulled out, it went through a long tunnel. For about ten seconds there was total darkness. In the silence of the moment those on the train heard two things—a kiss and a slap. Everyone on the train had his or her own perception of what happened.

The young lady thought to herself, "I'm flattered that the lieutenant kissed me, but I'm terribly embarrassed that Grandmother hit him!"

The Grandmother thought, "I'm aggravated that the young man kissed my granddaughter, but I'm proud she had the courage to retaliate!"

The general sat there, thinking to himself, "My lieutenant showed a lot of guts in kissing that girl, but why did she slap me by mistake!"

The lieutenant was the only one on the train who really knew what happened. In that brief moment of darkness he had the opportunity to kiss a pretty girl *and* slap his general.[6]

These questions will help you discover another person's agenda in a variety of situations:

- Background question: What is this person's history with this organization or another?

- Temperament question: What is this person's primary and secondary temperament?

- Security question: Is this, in any way, affecting the individual's job?

- Relationship question: How is he or she related to me, or someone else, organizationally?

- Motive question: What is the real reason this is on his or her agenda?

- Potential question: Does this person or issue merit the leader's time and energy?

I have discovered that the development of people is more successful when I:

> Listen well enough to lead through their eyes;
> Relate well enough to communicate with their hearts;
> Work well enough to place tools in their hands;
> Think well enough to challenge and expand their minds.

LEADERS MUST CARE FOR PEOPLE BEFORE THEY CAN DEVELOP THEM.

Too often I see leaders who request commitment from people without showing them proper care. They are like Narvaez, the Spanish patriot, who, while dying, was asked by his father-confessor whether he had forgiven all his enemies. Narvaez looked astonished and said, "Father, I have no enemies. I shot them all."

Narvaez didn't know that "nice guys" get the best results from subordinates. Teleometrics International studied the perception high achieving executives have of the people in their organizations compared to low achieving executives. Their results were reported in the *Wall Street Journal.*

Of the 16,000 executives studied, the 13 percent identified as "high achievers" tended to care about people as well as profits. Average achievers concentrated on production, while low achievers were preoccupied with their own security. High achievers viewed subordinates optimistically, while low achievers showed a basic distrust of subordinates' abilities. High achievers sought advice from their subordinates: low achievers didn't. High achievers were listeners; moderate achievers listened only to superiors; low achievers avoided communication and relied on policy manuals.

PEOPLE DEVELOPERS LOOK FOR OPPORTUNITIES TO BUILD UP PEOPLE.

Most people in leadership positions daily steal someone's ego food—the satisfaction of their needs for esteem. In fact, they steal it and don't even know it. For example, someone says, "I've really had a busy day," and the leader replies, "You've been busy! You should see all the work piled on my desk and I can't even get to it." Or someone says, "I finally finished that project I've been working on for eight months," and the leader replies, "Yeah, Jim finally finished that big project he's been working on too."

What is the leader doing? Well, he's taking away the food that people need for their ego. In effect, he's saying, "You may think you're pretty good, but let me tell you about someone else who is probably better."

Just for fun, check yourself tomorrow and see how many times you catch yourself satisfying your own esteem needs by stealing away someone else's ego food.

J.C. Staehle, after analyzing many surveys, found that the principal causes of unrest among workers are actions good leaders can avoid. They are listed in the order of their importance.

1. Failure to give credit for suggestions.

2. Failure to correct grievances.

3. Failure to encourage.

4. Criticizing employees in front of other people.

5. Failure to ask employees their opinions.

6. Failure to inform employees of their progress.

7. Favoritism.

Note: Every issue is an example of the leader stealing or keeping ego food from the workers.

THE GREATEST POTENTIAL FOR GROWTH
OF A COMPANY IS GROWTH OF ITS PEOPLE.

In a survey of workers across the United States, nearly 85 percent said they could work harder on the job. More than half claimed they could double their effectiveness "if [they] wanted to."[7]

People are the principal asset of any company, whether it makes things to sell, sells things made by other people, or supplies intangible services. Nothing moves until your people can make it move. In actual studies of leadership in American business, the average executive spends three-fourths of his working time dealing with *people*. The largest single cost in most business is *people*. The largest, most valuable asset any company has is its *people*. All executive plans are carried out, or fail to be carried out, by *people*.

According to William J. H. Boetcker, people divide themselves into four classes:

1. Those who always do less than they are told.

2. Those who will do what they are told, but no more.

3. Those who will do things without being told.

4. Those who will inspire others to do things.

It's up to you.

As Ralph Waldo Emerson said, "Trust men and they will be true to you: treat them greatly and they will show themselves great."

Some of the best advice you can find about being a good leader is found in the old Chinese poem.

Go to the people,
Live among them.
Learn from them.
Love them.
Start with what they know,
Build on what they have.
But of the best leaders,
When their task is accomplished,
Their work is done,
The people will remark,
"We have done it ourselves."

EIGHT

THE INDISPENSABLE QUALITY OF LEADERSHIP:
VISION

Robert K. Greenleaf, in his book, *The Servant as Leader*, says, "Foresight is the 'lead' that the leader has. Once he loses this lead and events start to force his hand, he is leader in name only. He is not leading; he is reacting to immediate event and he probably will not long be a leader. There are abundant current examples of loss of leadership which stem from a failure to foresee what reasonably could have been foreseen, and from failure to act on that knowledge while the leader has freedom to act."[1]

My observation over the last twenty years has been that all effective leaders have a vision of what they must accomplish. That vision becomes the energy behind every effort and the force that pushes through all the problems. With vision, the leader is on a mission and a contagious spirit is felt among the crowd until others begin to rise alongside the leader. Unity is essential for the dream to be realized. Long hours of labor are given gladly to accomplish the goal. Individual rights are set aside because the whole is much more important than the part. Time flies, morale soars upward, heroic stories are told, and commitment is the watchword. Why? Because the leader has a vision!

All that is necessary to remove the excitement form the preceding paragraph is one word—*vision*. Without it, energy ebbs low, deadlines are missed, personal agendas begin to surface, production falls, and people scatter.

Helen Keller was asked, "What would be worse than being born blind?" She replied, "To have sight without vision." Sadly too many people are placed into leadership positions without a vision for the organization that they will lead. All great leaders possess two things: They know where they are going, and they are able to persuade others to follow. They are like the sign in an optometrist's office: "If you don't see what you want, you've come to the right place." This chapter will deal with the leader's foresight and the ability to gather people around it.

The word *vision* has perhaps been overused in the last few years. The first goal of many a management workshop is to develop a statement of purpose for the organization. Other will look at you oddly if you cannot recite your organization's purpose by memory and produce a card with the statement of purpose printed on it.

Why all the pressure to develop a purpose for your organization? There are two reasons. First, vision becomes the distinctive, rallying cry of the organization. It is a clear statement in a competitive market that you have an important niche among all the voices clamoring for customers. It is your real reason for existence. Second, vision becomes the new control tool, replacing the 1,000 page manual that is boxy and constrains initiative. In an age when decentralization all the way to the front line is required to survive, the vision is the key that keeps everyone focused.

VISION STATEMENTS

What you see is what you can be. This deals with your potential. I have often asked myself: Does the vision make the leader? Or, does the leader make the vision?

I believe the vision comes first. I have known many leaders who lost the vision and, therefore, lost their power to lead. People do what people see. That is the greatest motivational principle in the world. Stanford Research says that 89 percent of what we learn is visual, 10 percent of what we learn is auditory, and 1 percent of what we learn is through other senses.

In other words, people depend on visual stimulation for growth.

Couple a vision with a leader willing to implement that dream and a movement begins. People do not follow a dream in itself. They follow the leader who has that dream and the ability to communicate it effectively. Therefore, vision in the beginning will make a leader, but for that vision to grow and demand a following, the leader must take responsibility for it.

FOUR VISION-LEVELS OF PEOPLE

1. Some people never see it. (They are wanderers.)

2. Some people see it but never pursue it on their own. (They are followers.)

3. Some people see it and pursue it. (They are achievers.)

4. Some people see it and pursue it and help others see it. (They are leaders.)

Hubert H. Humphrey is an example of "what you see is what you can be." During a trip to Washington, D. C., in 1935, he wrote this in a letter to his wife: "Honey, I see how someday, if you and I just apply ourselves and make up our minds to work for bigger and better things, we can someday live here in Washington and probably be in government, politics, or service. . . . Oh, gosh, I hope my dream comes true—I'm going to try anyhow."

> All great leaders possess two things: one, they know where they are going and two, they are able to persuade others to follow.

YOU SEE WHAT YOU ARE PREPARED TO SEE.

This deals with perception. Konrad Adenauer was correct when he said, "We all live under the same sky, but we don't all have the same horizon."

Automobile genius Henry Ford once came up with a revolutionary plan for a new kind of engine. We know it today as the V-8. Ford was eager to get his great new idea into production. He had some men draw up the plans and presented them to the engineers.

As the engineers studied the drawings, one by one they came to the same conclusion. Their visionary boss just didn't know much about the fundamental principles of engineering. He'd have to be told gently—his dream was impossible.

Leaders can never take their people farther than they have traveled. Like leader, like people.

Ford said, "Produce it anyway."

They replied, "But it's impossible."

"Go ahead," Ford commanded, "and stay on the job until you succeed, no matter how much time is required."

For six months they struggled with drawing after drawing, design after design. Nothing. Another six months. Nothing. At the end of the year Ford checked with his engineers, and once again they told him that what he wanted was impossible. Ford told them to keep going. They did. And they discovered how to build a V-8 engine

Henry Ford and his engineers both lived under the same sky, but they didn't all have the same horizon.

In _A Savior for All Seasons_, William Barker related the story of a bishop from the East Coast who many years ago paid a visit to a small, Midwestern religious college. He stayed at the home of the college president, who also served as professor of physics and chemistry. After dinner the bishop declared that the millennium couldn't be far off, because just about everything about nature had been discovered and all inventions conceived.

The young college president politely disagreed and said he felt there would be many more discoveries. When the angered bishop challenged the president to name just one such invention, the president replied he was certain that within fifty years men would be able to fly.

"Nonsense!" sputtered the outraged bishop. "Only angels are intended to fly."

The bishop's name was Wright, and he had two boys at home who would prove to have greater vision than their father. Their names were Orville and Wilbur. The father and his sons both lived under the same sky, but they didn't all have the same horizon.

How can this be? Why is it that two people can be in the same place at the same time and both see entirely different things? It's simple. We see what we are prepared to see, not what is. Every successful leader understands this about people and asks three questions: What do others see; why do they see it that way; and how can I change their perception?

WHAT YOU SEE IS WHAT YOU GET.

The following illustration originated in Luis Palau's book *Dream Great Dreams* (1984, Multnomah Press).

Think about how nice and refreshing it is to taste a cold Coke. Hundreds of millions of people around the world have enjoyed this experience, thanks to the vision of Robert Woodruff. During his tenure as president of Coca-Cola (1923–1955), Woodruff boldly declared, "We will see that every man in uniform gets a bottle of Coca-Cola for five cents wherever he is and whatever the costs." When World War II had ended, Woodruff stated that before he died he wanted every person in the world to have tasted Coca-Cola. Robert Woodruff was a man of vision!

> God's gift to me is my potential. My gift back to God is what I do with that potential.

With careful planning and a lot of persistence, Woodruff and his colleagues reached their generation around the globe for Coke.

When Disney World first opened, Mrs. Walt Disney was asked to speak at the Grand Opening, since Walt had died. She was introduced by a man who said, "Mrs. Disney, I just wish Walt could have seen this." She stood up and said, "He did," and sat down. Walt Disney knew it. Robert Woodruff knew it. Even Flip Wilson knew it! What you see is what you get.

At this point, I feel compelled to ask a question before we go on to the subject of personal ownership of a vision: "Is my dream going to make a difference in the world in which I live?"

Bobb Biehl, in his book *Increasing Your Leadership Confidence*, says, "Keep in mind the difference between a winner's and a loser's mentality. Winners focus on winning big—not just how to win, but how to win big. Losers, however, don't focus on losing; they just focus on getting by!"[2]

Keep asking yourself, "Survival, success, or significance?" Are you striving to simply survive, are you dreaming about success, or are you really out to make a truly significant difference?

Moishe Rosen teaches a one-sentence mental exercise that's an effective tool in dreaming. It is simply this:

If I had _____,

I would _____.

If you had anything you wanted—unlimited time, unlimited money, unlimited information, unlimited staff—all the resources you could ask for, what would you do? Your answer to that question is your dream. Make it worthwhile.

One day Lucy and Linus had a chicken wishbone and were going to pull it to make a wish. Lucy explained to Linus that if he got the bigger half of the wishbone his wish would come true. Linus said, "Do I have to say the wish out loud?" Lucy said, "Of course. If you don't say it out loud it won't come true." So Lucy went ahead and made her wish first. She said, "I wish for four new sweaters, a new bike, a new pair of skates, a new dress, and one hundred dollars." Then it was time for Linus to make his wish. He said, "I wish for a long life for all my friends, I wish for world peace, I wish for great advancements in medical research." About that time, Lucy took the wishbone and threw it away. She said, "Linus, that's the trouble with you. You're always spoiling everything."

PERSONAL OWNERSHIP OF A VISION

My friend Rick Warren says, "If you want to know the temperature of your organization, put a thermometer in the leader's mouth." Leaders can never take their people farther than they have traveled. Therefore, the focus of vision must be on the leader—like leader, like people. Followers find the leader and then the vision. Leaders find the vision and then the people.

I am asked many questions when I speak at leadership conferences throughout the country. One of the most common questions asked by those in leadership positions is: "How do I get a vision for my organization?" This question is crucial. Until it is answered, a person will be a leader in name only. Although I cannot give you a vision, I can share the process of receiving one for you and those around you.

Look Within You: What Do You Feel?

Theodore Hesburgh said, "The very essence of leadership is that you have a vision. It's got to be a vision you can articulate clearly and forcefully on every occasion. You can't blow an uncertain trumpet." An "uncertain trumpet" is usually the result of an individual who either lacks a vision or is trying to lead with someone else's dream. Certain trumpet sounds come forth from a leader who has birthed a vision from within. There is a vast difference between a person with a vision and a visionary person.

- A person with a vision talks little but does much.

- A visionary person does little but talks much.

- A person with a vision finds strength from inner convictions.

- A visionary person finds strength from outward conditions.

- A person with vision continues when problems arise.

- A visionary person quits when the road becomes difficult.

Many great people began life in the poorest and most humble of homes, with little education and no advantages. Thomas Edison was a newsboy on trains. Andrew Carnegie started work at $4 a month, John D. Rockefeller at $6 a week. The remarkable thing about Abraham Lincoln was not that he was born in a log cabin, but that he got out of the log cabin.

Demosthenes, the greatest orator of the ancient world, stuttered! The first time he tried to make a public speech, he was laughed off the rostrum. Julius Caesar was an epileptic. Napoleon was of humble parentage and far from being a born genius (he stood forty-sixth in his class at the Military Academy in a class of sixty-five). Beethoven was deaf, as was Thomas Edison. Charles Dickens was lame; so was Handel. Homer was blind; Plato was a hunchback; Sir Walter Scott was paralyzed.

What gave these great individuals the stamina to overcome severe setbacks and become successful? Each person had an inner dream that lit a fire which could not be extinguished. Great visions begin as an "inside job." Napoleon Hill said, "Cherish your visions and dreams as they are the children of your soul: the blueprints of your ultimate achievements."

LOOK BEHIND YOU: WHAT HAVE YOU LEARNED?

A person without experience sees a vision idealistically. To this individual the vision alone is enough. Naively this person casts the vision to others, expecting the dream to do the work and failing to realize that a vision needs support. A person with experience learns that people buy into the leader *before* they buy into the vision. Experienced leaders realize that people are fickle and dreams are fragile. Experience had taught me these principles about vision:

- The credibility of a vision is determined by the leader.
- The acceptance of a vision is determined by the timing of its presentation.
- The value of a vision is determined by the energy and direction it gives.
- The evaluation of a vision is determined by the commitment level of people.

- The success of a vision is determined by its ownership by both the leader and the people.

Leonard Lauder, president of Estee Lauder, said, "When a person with experience meets a person with money, the person with experience will get the money. And the person with the money will get the experience."

Look Around you: What Is Happening to Others?

A little boy attended his first symphonic concert. He was excited by the splendid hall, the beautiful people in their formal finery, and the sound of the large, enthusiastic orchestra. Of all the instruments in the orchestra, however, his favorite was the cymbals. The first loud, dramatic crash of those brass disks won him over without reservation. He noticed, though, that most of the evening the cymbal player stood motionless while the other musicians played. Only occasionally was the cymbal player called upon to make his contribution, and even then his time of glory was quite brief.

After the concert, the little boy's parents took him backstage to meet some of the musicians. The little fellow immediately sought out the cymbalist. "Say, mister," he said sincerely, "how much do you need to know to play the cymbals?" The musician laughed and answered, "You don't have to know much at all. You only have to know when."

A good idea becomes great when the people are ready. The individual who is impatient with people will be defective in leadership. The evidence of strength lies not in streaking ahead, but in adapting your stride to the slower pace of others while not forfeiting your lead. If we run too far ahead, we lose our power to influence.

Look Ahead of You: What Is the Big Picture?

This question often separates leaders from managers. Leaders are concerned with the organization's basic purpose—why it exists and what it should achieve. They are not preoccupied with the "how to" or nuts and bolts aspect of the operation.

LOOK ABOVE YOU: WHAT DOES GOD EXPECT OF YOU?

Richard E. Day said, "Every golden era in human history proceeds from the devotion and righteous passion of some single individual. There are no bona fide mass movements; it just looks that way. There is always one man who knows his God and knows where he is going."

God's gift to me is my potential. My gift back to God is what I do with that potential. I believe great leaders sense a "higher calling"—one that lifts them above themselves. What a terrible waste of life to be climbing the ladder of success only to find when you reach the top that you were leaning against the wrong building. Great visions are bigger than the person. My definition of success is:

Knowing God and His desires for me;
Growing to my maximum potential; and
Sowing seeds that benefit others.

LOOK BESIDE YOU: WHAT RESOURCES ARE AVAILABLE TO YOU?

A vision should be greater that the person who has it. Its accomplishment must be the result of many people bringing many resources to the job. Many times I have read the speech of President John F. Kennedy that cast the vision of America landing on the moon during the decade of the '60s. That dream captured the people and resources of our country and became a reality.

The experienced leader is always looking for others to make the dream come true. My top priority in the vision for the twenty-five million dollar relocation of the congregation I pastor is to develop and find winners to help make the vision a reality. I continually evaluate the progress of this relocation project by the commitment of the people.

Too often leaders hesitate to test the commitment levels of those around them. What is the result? They are never sure where the project stands, or where their people stand. I remember well the conclusions I felt when we finished our first four million dollar fund-raising effort. We worked hard, and I knew where the people stood.

The leader continually passes on the vision to those who come around, knowing that dreams, if presented right, are contagious.

In the movie *Tucker: The Man and His Dream*, Abe, the bottom-line businessman and beleaguered bookkeeper for Preston Tucker, who conceived a radical new automobile—a low-cost car with fuel injector, rear-mounted engine, disc brakes, pop-out windows, seat belts, and aerodynamic design—caught Tucker's dream.

Despite a misremembered warning from his mother, he bought a share of Tucker's idealism.

Abe thought his mother said, "Don't get too close to people, you'll catch their dreams."

Years later he realized she had said, *germs*, not *dreams*.[3]

CORPORATE OWNERSHIP OF A VISION

A vision is a clear picture of what the leader sees his or her group being or doing. According to a survey reported by *Leadership* magazine, communicating a vision is one of the most frustrating areas of leading an organization.

Recently I was a guest on a radio talk show. The host poured out his frustration to me during the break concerning this very issue. He said, "I have a vision for my people but find it difficult to transfer that vision to others." One fact is true: leaders who effectively communicate goals to their followers achieve far more than those who don't.

Successful leaders see on three levels:

Level 1. Perception: Seeing what is now with the eyes of reality.
Level 2. Probability: Seeing what will be with the eyes of discernment.
Level 3. Possibility: Seeing what can be with the eyes of vision.

A *futurist* lives only on Level 3. A *forecaster* lives only on Level 2. A *follower* lives only on Level 1. A *leader* lives on Level 3, leads on Level 2, and listens on Level 1.

For example, an organization sets changing its name as a goal. The great leader, through eyes of vision, already sees a new name for the company (Level 3). That leader, through the eyes of discernment, sees the trend of the organization (Level 2). The leader knows the direction of the company by looking through the eyes of reality (Level1).

Surprisingly, vision-casting does not begin with Level 3 (the big picture). It begins with Level 1 (the small picture) and will only be successful if the leader can influence Level 2 (the next picture).

Understanding What Hinders a Vision—Level 1

We see things, not as they are, but as we are. Therefore, when a vision is hindered, it is usually a people problem. There are ten types of people who usually hinder the vision of the organization.

1. Limited Leaders.

Everything rises and falls on leadership. That statement is certainly true with vision-casting. A limited leader will either lack the vision or the ability to successfully pass it on.

The Prime Minister of France once said, "If you are doing big things, you attract big men. If you are doing little things, you attract little men. Little men usually cause trouble." Then he paused, shook his head sadly, and added, "We are having an awful lot of trouble.

2. Concrete thinkers.

George Bernard Shaw said, "Some men see things as they are and say, 'Why?' [concrete thinker]. I dream of things that never were and say 'Why not?' [creative thinker]."

Charlie Brown holds up his hands before his friend Lucy and says,

"These are hands which may some day accomplish great things. These are hands which may some day do marvelous works! They may build mighty bridges, or heal the sick, or hit home runs, or write soul-stirring novels! These are hands which may someday change the course of destiny!"

Lucy, who always sees things as they are, replies, "They've got jelly on them."

3. Dogmatic Talkers.

Many visions aren't realized because of strong, dogmatic people. To be absolutely certain about something, one must either know everything or nothing about it. Most of the time, the dogmatist knows nothing but conventionally says something. For example, "Everything that can be invented has been invented." That was Charles H. Duell, director of the U.S. Patent Office, speaking in 1899! Of course, Duell was not alone. President Grover Cleveland once commented (in 1905) that "sensible and responsible women do not want to vote." Then there was Robert Miliken, Nobel Prize winner in physics, who said in 1923, "There is no likelihood man can ever tap the power of the atom." Lord Kelvin, president of England's Royal Society (a scientific organization), noted in 1885, "Heavier-than-air flying machines are impossible."

My favorite is a statement of baseball great Tris Speaker. He was quoted in 1921 as saying, "[Babe] Ruth make a big mistake when he gave up pitching."

4. Continual Losers.

Many people look at their past failures and fear the risk of pursuing a vision. Their motto is, "If at first you don't succeed, destroy all evidence that you've tried." They also destroy everyone's attempt to ever try again.

5. Satisfied Sitters.

People strive for comfort, predictability, and security in life. On the heels of comfort comes complacency; of predictability, boredom; and of security, no vision. A nest is good for a robin while it is an egg. But it is bad for a robin when it has wings. It's a good place to be hatched in, but it's a poor place to fly in. It's always sad when people don't want to leave the nests of their lives.

In a *Leadership* magazine article, Lynn Anderson described what happens when people lose their vision. A group of pilgrims landed on the shores of America about 370 years ago. With great vision and courage they had come to settle in the new land. In the first year, they established a town. In the second, they elected town council. In the third, the government proposed building a road five miles westward into the wilderness. But in the fourth year, the people tried to impeach the town council because the people thought such a road into the forest was a waste of public funds. Somehow these forward-looking people had lost their vision. Once able to see across oceans, they now could not look five miles into the wilderness.

6. Tradition Lovers.

The British have always been good with the patronage system. John F. Barker in *Roll Call* tells the story that for more than twenty years, for no apparent reason, an attendant stood the foot of the stairway leading to the House of Commons. At last someone checked and discovered that the job had been held in the attendant's family for three generations. It seems it originated when the stairs were painted and the current attendant's grandfather was assigned the task of warning people not to step on the wet paint.

One British newsman, told of the situation, commented, "The paint dried up but not the job."

7. Census Takers.

Some people never feel comfortable stepping out of the crowd. They desire to be a part of, not apart from, the group. These people will only embrace the vision when the majority does. They are never in front.

True leaders are always in the minority because they are thinking ahead of the present majority. Even when the majority catches up, these leaders will have moved ahead and so, again, will be in the minority.[4]

8. Problem Perceivers.

Some people can see a problem in every solution. Usually obstacles are the things you see when you take your eyes off the goal. Interestingly, some people think the ability to see problems is a mark of maturity. Not so. It's the mark of a person without a vision. These people abort great visions by presenting problems without any solutions.

Cardinal John Henry Newman said that nothing would get done at all if a man waited until he could do something so well that no one could find fault with it.

9. Self-Seekers.

People who live for themselves are in a mighty small business. They also never accomplish much. Great goals are only reached by the united effort of many. Selfish people are vision-busters.

10. Failure Forecasters.

Some people have a faculty for touching the wrong keys. From the finest instrument, they extract only discord. All their songs are in a minor key. They send the note of pessimism everywhere. The shadows dominate all their pictures. Their outlook is always gloomy, times are always bad, and money is tight. Everything in them seems to be contracting; nothing in their lives expands or grows.

These people are like the man who gathered with many others at the Hudson River to see the first steamship launched. He kept saying, "They'll never get her going. They'll never get her going." But they did. The steamship belched and moved out fast. Immediately the same man said, "They'll never get her stopped. They'll never get her stopped."

I love the Chinese proverb that states, "Man who says, 'it cannot be done' should not interrupt man who is doing it."

SETTING THE PROPER ENVIRONMENT—LEVEL 2

Knowing people and the keys to their lives will allow the leader to go to the "next picture" in Level 2. It is essential that the leader begin to influence what will be seen by the people. Remember, if the leader and a few others see Level 3, then only they will know if Level 2 is set correctly to take others into the vision area. The following steps will set Level 2 correctly.

Come Alongside of Them.

Let them see your heart before they see your hope. People don't care how much you see until they see how much you care. I emphasize again: People buy into the leader before they buy into that leader's vision. Cultivate trust. Be transparent and patient. Start where they are by seeing through their eyes. Seek to find their hopes and dreams. Begin building a bridge between the vision of the organization and their personal goals. Done correctly, both can be accomplished. Go for the win-win. Remember, when you help people get what they want, they will help you get what you want. This can only be accomplished by building strong relationships with people.

Paint the Picture for Them.

One time I read that a great teacher never strives to explain his vision; he simply invites you to stand beside him and see for yourself. I agree with the relationship part of this statement, but I believe great leaders explain their vision by painting a picture for the people. John W. Patterson, founder of National Cash Register, said, "I have been trying all my life, first to see for myself, and then to get other people to see with me. To succeed in business it is necessary to make the other man see things as you see them. Seeing . . . was the objective. In the broadest sense, I am a visualizer."

Every great vision has certain ingredients, and the great leader makes the people understand, appreciate, and "see" them:

Horizon: A leader's vision of the horizon allows people to see the heights of their possibilities. Each individual will determine how high he or she wants to go. Your responsibility is to put plenty of sky into the picture. Paul Harvey said that a blind man's world is bounded by the limits of his touch; an ignorant man's world by the limits of his knowledge; a great man's world by the limits of his vision.

Sun: This element represents warmth and hope. Light brings out the optimism in people. A prime function of a leader is to keep hope alive. Napoleon said, "Leaders are dealers in hope."

Mountains: Every vision had its challenges. Edwin Land, founder of Polaroid, said, "The first thing you do is teach the person to feel that the vision is very important and nearly impossible. That draws out the drive in the winner."

Birds: This element represents freedom and the spirit of man. Watching an eagle rise causes you to feel your own spirit soar. "Wars may be fought with weapons, but it is the spirit of the men who fight and of the man who leads that gains victory."[5]

Flowers: The journey toward the realization of any great vision takes time. Make sure the scenery includes rest stops—places to smell flowers and become refreshed mentally and physically. Success is the progressive realization of a predetermined, worthwhile goal.

Path: People need direction, a place to begin, and a path to follow. A traveler through a rugged country asked his Indian guide, "How are you able to pick your way over these jagged peaks, by treacherous trails, without ever losing your direction?"

The guide answered, "I have the near look and the far vision. With the one I see what is directly ahead of me; with the other I guide my course by the stars."[6]

Yourself: Never paint the vision without placing yourself in the picture. This will show your commitment to the vision and your desire to walk with the people through the process. They need a model to follow. As Warren R. Austin said in UN *World*, "If you would lift me, you must be on higher ground."

Why should a leader paint the picture and place these essentials in it? Roger von Oech, in his book, *A Kick in the Seat of the Pants*, gives an excellent answer. "Take a look around where you're sitting and find five things that have blue in them. Go ahead and do it.

"With a 'blue' mind-set, you'll find that blue jumps out at you: a blue book on the table, a blue pillow on the couch, blue in the painting on the wall, and so on.

"In like fashion, you've probably noticed that after you buy a new car, you promptly see that make of car everywhere. That's because people find what they are looking for."[7]

The leader helps the people develop this sensitivity and an eye for knowing what to look for. If the picture is painted clearly and shown continually, soon others will begin to see how to see how it fits into everything they do. They will have a vision mind-set. Then there will be only one thing left to bring the vision into the ownership of others.

Put the Things They Love in the Picture.

People carry pictures of other people and things they love. Put what is important to the people within the frame of the vision and you will have transferred the vision to the people.

During World War II, parachutes were being constructed by the thousands. From the workers' point of view, the job was tedious. It involved crouching over a sewing machine eight to ten hours a day and stitching endless lengths of colorless fabric. The result was a formless heap of cloth.

But every morning the workers were told that each stitch was part of a life-saving operation. They were asked to think as they sewed that each parachute might be the one worn by their husbands, their brothers, their sons.

Although the work was hard and the hours long, the women and the men on the home front understood their contribution to the larger picture.[8]

OPENING EYES TO POSSIBILITIES—LEVEL 3

On this level we need to ask ourselves how to grow people to the size of the vision. This represents the one thing the leader must continually do . . . grow people to the vision once they see it.

There are several steps a Level 3 leader must take. First, the leader must seek and find winners to add to the team. These qualitites of winners will guide the search:

- Winners are less sensitive to disapproval and rejection—they brush it off.

- Winners think "bottom line."

- Winners focus on the task at hand.

- Winners are not superstitious—they say, "that's life."

- Winners refuse to equate failure with self-worth.

- Winners don't restrict thinking to established, rigid patterns.

- Winners see the big picture.

- Winners welcome challenge with optimism.

- Winners don't waste time in unproductive thought.

Once the winners are added to the team, they join others as the major influencers in the organization. At this point, it is extremely important for the leader to spend time with the influencers to discover the "keys" to their lives. What is most valued by these influencers should help them through tough personal issues; provide a time and place for them to grow; add value to their family and job; assist them in finding their strengths; and plug them into the organziation.

Also, it is very important for the leader to mentor these winners. They should be exposed to great books (past and present), great places, great events, and great people. They should find great ideas in you, the leader, and they should develop a desire to pursue your interests and vision in an attempt to build a mutually beneficial relationship. When this occurs, you will find that the winners naturally pass on the vision that you hold dear for your organization and for them.

The successful Level 3 leader will see on three levels:

1. **The Perceptible Level:** What is now seen—the eyes of reality. A leader listens on this level.

2. **The Probable Level:** What will be seen—the eyes of discernment. A leader leads on this level.

3. **The Possible Level:** What can be seen—the eyes of vision. A leader lives on this level.

Vision is empowering to the leader who has it. The leader with vision believes not only that what he envisions can be done, but that it must be done. There was a study done of concentration camp survivors regarding the common characteristics of those who did not succumb . . . in the concentration camps. Viktor Frankl was a living answer to that question. He was a successful Viennese psychiatrist before the Nazis threw him into such a camp. Years later when giving lectures he would say: "There is only one reason why I am here today. What kept me alive was you. Others gave up hope. I dreamed that some day I would be here telling you how I, Viktor Frankl, had survived Nazi concentration camps. I've never been here before, I've never seen any of you before, I've never given this speech before. But in my dreams I have stood before you and said these words a thousand times." It was the vision that made the difference.

As a young man I learned this poem. It is an appropriate way to end this chapter.

> Ah, great it is believe the dream,
> As we stand in youth by the starry stream.
> But a greater thing is to live life through,
> And say at the end, the dream came true.

Leaders do that for themselves, and others.

NINE

THE PRICE TAG OF LEADERSHIP:
SELF-DISCIPLINE

I n reading the lives of great men, I found that the first victory they won was over themselves. . . . Self-discipline with all of them came first."[1]

The Greek word for *self-control* comes from a root word meaning "to grip" or "take hold of." This word describes people who are willing to get a grip on their lives and take control of areas that will bring them success or failure.

Aristotle used this same word to describe "the ability to test desire by reason . . . to be resolute and ever in readiness to end natural vent and pain." He explained that people who are not controlled have strong desires which try to seduce them from the way of reason; but to succeed they must keep those desires under control.

Once, while conducting a leadership seminar, I defined discipline in the beginning of life as the choice of achieving what you really want by doing things you don't really want to do. After successfully doing this for some time, discipline becomes the choice of achieving what you really want by doing things you now want to do! I truly believe we can become disciplined and enjoy it—after years of practicing it.

All great leaders have understood that their number one responsibility was for their own discipline and personal growth. If they could not

DEVELOPING THE LEADER WITHIN YOU

lead themselves, they could not lead others. Leaders can never take others farther than they have gone themselves, for no one can travel without until he or she has first traveled within. A great person will lead a great organization, but growth is only possible when the leader is willing to "pay the price" for it. Many potentially gifted leaders have stopped short of the payment line and found out that shortcuts don't pay off in the long run.

This us what Edwin Markham has to say about human worth:

> We are blind until we see
> That in the human plan
> Nothing is worth the making
> If it does not make the man.
> Why build these cities glorious
> If man unbuilded goes?
> In vain we build the world
> Unless the builder also grows.[2]

THE PROCESS FOR DEVELOPING PERSONAL DISCIPLINE

Frederick the Great of Prussia was walking on the outskirts of Berlin when he encountered a very old man proceeding in the opposite direction.

"Who are you?" asked Frederick.

"I am a king," replied the old man.

"A king!" laughed Frederick. "Over what kingdom do you reign?"

"Over myself," was the proud reply.

"Reigning" over yourself required personal discipline.

START WITH YOURSELF.

A reporter once asked the great evangelist D. L. Moody which people gave him the most trouble. He answered immediately, "I've had more trouble with D.L. Moody than any man alive." The late Sammuel

Hoffenstein said, "Wherever I go, I go too, and spoil everything." And there is the classic Jack Paar line, "Looking back, my life seems to be one long obstacle course, with me as the chief obstacle."

> We cannot travel without until we first travel within.

My observation is that more potential leaders fail because of inner issues than outer ones.

Each month I teach a leadership lesson to my staff, which is recorded live and sent to other leaders across the United States. Recently I spoke on the subject, "How to get Out of Your Own Way." A tremendous response was received from many listeners who said, "The lesson was needed in my life. I am my worst problem!" Most of us can relate to the sign I

> When we are foolish we want to conquer the world. When we are wise we want to conquer ourselves.

saw in an office: "If you could kick the person responsible for most of your troubles, you wouldn't be able to sit down for weeks."

Your Competitor

An enemy I had, whose face I stoutly strove to know,
For hard he dogged my steps unseen, wherever did go.
My plans he balked, my aims he foiled, he blocked my
onward way.
When for some lofty goal I toiled, he grimly said to me, Nay.
One night I seized him and held him fast, from him the
veil did draw,
I looked upon his face at last and lo . . . myself I saw.

When we are foolish, we want to conquer the world. When we are wise, we want to conquer ourselves.

START EARLY.

Perhaps the most valuable result of all education is the ability to make yourself do the thing you have to do, when it ought to be done, whether you like it or not; it is the first lesson that ought to be learned and, however early a man's training begins, it is probably the last lesson that he learns thoroughly.

> Hard work is the accumulation of easy things you didn't do when you should have.

I'm not sure that my parents ever read these preceding words of Thomas Huxley, but they certainly practiced them! They modeled discipline and insisted that their three children develop that life-style. Time management, hard work, persistence, honesty, responsibility, and a positive attitude, regardless of the situation, were always expected of us. However, I didn't appreciate this training until I went to college. There I saw many students who couldn't get a grip on their lives or their studies. I began to realize that I had a decided advantage over others because of the disciplines already "under my belt." It is true—when you do the things you ought to do when you ought to do them, the day will come when you will do the

> What you are going to be tomorrow, you are becoming today.

things you want to do when you want to do them. Hard work is the accumulation of the easy things you didn't do when you should have.

START SMALL.

What you are going to be tomorrow, you are becoming today. It is essential to begin developing self-discipline in a small way today in order to be disciplined in a big way tomorrow.

A Small Plan that Will Make A Big Difference

1. List five areas in your life that lack discipline.

2. Place them in order of your priority for conquering them.

3. Take them on, one at a time.

4. Secure resources, such as books and tapes, that will give you instruction and motivation to conquer each area.

5. Ask a person who models the trait you want to possess to hold you accountable for it.

6. Spend fifteen minutes each morning getting focused in order to get control of this weak area in your life.

7. Do a five-minute checkup on yourself at midday.

8. Take five minutes in the evening to evaluate your progress.

9. Allow sixty days to work on one area before you go to the next.

10. Celebrate with the one who holds you accountable as you show continued success.

Remember, having it all doesn't mean having it all at once. If takes time. Start small and concentrate on today. The slow accumulation of disciplines will one day make a big difference. Ben Franklin said, "It is easier to suppress the first desire than to satisfy all that follow it."

START NOW.

As John Hancock Field says, "All worthwhile men have good thoughts, good ideas, and good intentions, but precious few of them ever translate those into action."

In 1976, Indiana University's basketball team was undefeated throughout the regular season and captured the NCAA National Championship. Controversial and colorful coach Bobby Knight led them to that championship. Shortly afterward, Coach Knight was interviewed on the

> Great leaders never set themselves above their followers except in carrying out responsibilities.

413

television show *60 Minutes*. The commentators asked him, "Why is it, Bobby, that your basketball teams at Indiana are always so successful? Is it the will to succeed?"

"The will to succeed is important," Knight replied, "but I'll tell you what's more important: It's the will to prepare. it's the will to go out there every day training and building those muscles and sharpening those skills!"

> Success depends not merely on how well you do the things you enjoy, but how conscientiously you perform those duties you don't.

Abraham Lincoln said, "I will get ready and then perhaps my chance will come." Too often the disciplines have not been developed and an opportunity is missed. Charlie Brown of the "Peanuts" comic strip once said that his life was mixed up because he missed all of the rehearsals. Before you can become a "star" you have to start. Now is the best time.

ORGANIZE YOUR LIFE.

"One of the advantages of being disorderly is that one is constantly making exciting discoveries." That statement by A.A Milne is true, but the discoveries are usually too late and consequently an opportunity is missed. Then you as a leader are perceived as being "out of control." This leads to uncertainty and insecurity among followers.

When you are organized, you have a special power. You walk with a sure sense of purpose. Your priorities are clear in your mind. You orchestrate complex events with a masterful touch. Things fall into place when you reveal your plans. You move smoothly from one project to the next with no wasted motion. Throughout the day you gain stamina and momentum as your successes build. People believe your promises because you always follow through. When you enter a meeting, you are prepared for whatever they throw at you. When at last you show your hand, you're a winner.

Christopher Robin, in *Winnie the Pooh*, gives my favorite definition of organization: "Organizing is what you do before you do something, so that when you do it, it's not all mixed up."

Here is my top ten list for personal organization:

1. Set Your Priorities.

Two things are difficult to get people to do. The first is to do things in order of importance, and the second is to *continue* doing things in order of importance. William Gladstone said, "He is a wise man who wastes no energy on pursuits for which he is not fitted; and he is wiser still who from among the things he can do well, chooses and resolutely follows the best."

Major events, such as my speaking at conferences, are scheduled a year or two in advance. The last week of each month I spend two hours planning my schedule for the next thirty days. On paper I list all my major responsibilities according to importance and time needed to accomplish those tasks. This becomes the gauge to help me "keep on track" and keep moving. As each assignment is completed in its allotted time, I check it off my monthly list.

2. Place Your Priorities in Your Calendar.

Once this list is written out on paper, I give it to my personal assistant who writes it on my calendar. This protects me from outside pressures that clamor daily for my time. This also makes me accountable to someone else who help me stay on track.

3. Allow a Little Time for the Unexpected.

The kinds of work you do will determine the amount of time you set aside for interruptions. For example, the more you interact with people, the more time you must set aside. I set aside one-half day each week in my calendar for the unexpected.

4. Do Projects One at a Time.

A good general fights only on one front at a time. That is also true of a good leader. A feeling of being overwhelmed is the result of too many projects clamoring for your attention. For years I have followed this simple process:

> Itemize all that needs to be done.
> Prioritize things in order of importance.
> Organize each project.
> Emphasize only one project at a time.

5. Organize Your Work Space.

My work space is organized in two places: administrative and creative. My administrative office includes a room for small group meetings, my work desk, and a desk for my personal assistant. This allows me to constantly communicate any details immediately to my key people. This office contains my calendar, computers, and files, and allows me easy access to administrative help. My creative office is separated from everyone. It contains my books, a copy machine, and my writing files. This secluded place is off-limits to my staff and allows me a proper environment for thinking, reading, and writing.

6. Work According to Your Temperament.

If you are a morning person, organize your most important work for the morning hours. Obviously, if you are a late starter do the opposite. However, be sure not to allow the weaknesses of your temperament to excuse you from what you know you need to do to work most effectively.

7. Use Your Driving Time for Light Work and Growth.

My father gave me some great advice the day I became sixteen and received my driver's license. Climbing into the passenger side of the car, he placed a book in my glove compartment and said "Son, never be in a car without a book. Whenever you are delayed in traffic you can pull out this book and read." My car also contains many tapes for me to listen to and a note pad to jot down thoughts. My hands-free car phone also allows me to make calls to people on the way home from work. Recently while driving I made twenty-one calls and saved hours of office time. Many times I take a staff person with me so we can discuss business and develop a closer relationship. I estimate that the average person could achieve eight additional hours of personal growth and work in each week by using driving time wisely.

8. Develop Systems That Work for You.

Bobb Biehl says, "Systems—from to-do lists and calendars to libraries and computers—are your servants. They help you do things better and quicker, and by improving them, you decrease your time expenses and increase your results." Don't fight systems. Improve them.

9. Always Have a Plan for Those Minutes Between Meetings.

Hours can be saved by making the best use of minutes. I keep a list of things to do that can be done anywhere in very short amounts of time. There are calls to make, memos to reply to or send, reports to scan, thank-you notes to write, and communication to share. Keep handy a list of things you can do in a short time.

10. Focus on Results, Not the Activity.

Remember Peter Drucker's definition of efficiency (doing things right) versus effectiveness (doing the right things)? As you spend time on personal organization, be sure to keep your focus on doing the right things, that is, doing what is truly important. Then use this rule of thumb for organizing your overall work strategy:

Work where you are the strongest 80 percent of the time.
Work where you are leaning 15 percent of the time.
Work where you are weak 5 percent of the time.

WELCOME RESPONSIBILITY.

Winston Churchill said, "The price of greatness is responsibility." To increase your ability to take responsibility, do the following:

Be responsible for who you are. I believe that statement. In fact, I'd like you to consider how it relates to research done by a psychologist who studied some people on the bottom.

The psychologist visited a prison and asked various inmates, "Why are you here?" The answers were very revealing, even though expected. There were many of them: "I was framed"; "They ganged up on me"; "It was a case of mistaken identity"; "It was not me—it was somebody else." The psychologist wondered if one could possibly find a larger group of "innocent" people anywhere else but in prison!

That reminds me of one of Abraham Lincoln's favorite stories about the man who murdered both his parents and then when his sentence was about to be pronounced, pleaded for mercy on the grounds that he was an orphan! As the politician said to the judge, "It's not my fault, your honor, I never could have done all that stuff if the people hadn't elected me!"

Be responsible for what you do. It is rare to find a person who will be responsible, who will follow through correctly and finish the job. But when half-finished assignments keep returning to your desk to check up on, verify, edit, and upgrade, obviously someone is failing to take hold of the reins of responsibility.

> I am only one,
> But still I am one.
> I cannot do everything,
> But still I can do something;
> And because I cannot do everything
> I will not refuse to do the
> something that I can do.[3]

Be responsible for what you have received. John D. Rockefeller, Jr., said "I believe that every right implies a responsibility; every opportunity, an an obligation; every possession, a duty." Winston Churchill said, "It is not enough that we do our best; sometimes we have to do what's required." And Jesus said, "Everyone to whom much is given, from him much will be required." (Luke 12:48).

Be responsible to those you lead. Great leaders never set themselves above their followers, except in carrying out responsibilities.

Coach Bo Schembechler tells about the third game of the 1970 season. His University of Michigan Wolverines were playing Texas A&M and they could not move the ball. All of a sudden, Dan Dierdorf, their offensive lineman—who was probably the best in the country at that time—came rushing over to the sidelines. Fed up with the team's performance, he yelled at Schembechler in front of everybody on the sidelines.

"Listen, coach! Run every play over me! Over me! Every play!" And they did. Michigan ran off-tackle six times in a row and marched right down the field. Michigan won the game.

When the game is on the line, great leaders always take responsibility for leading their teams to victory. This is my favorite "take responsibility" story.

The sales manager of a dog food company asked his salespeople how they liked the company's new advertising program. "Great! Best in the business!" the salespeople responded.

"How do you like our new label and package?"

"Great! Best in the business!" the salespeople responded.

"How do like our sales force?"

They were the sales force. They had to admit they were good. "Okay, then," said the manager. "So we've got the best label, the best package, and the best advertising program being sold by the best sales force in the business. Tell me why we are in seventeenth place in the dog food business?"

There was silence. Finally someone said, "It's those lousy dogs. They won't eat the stuff!"

ACCEPT ACCOUNTABILITY.

Plato said, "The unexamined life is not worth living." Success and power have often crowded out of the leader's life a willingness to become accountable to others. Leaders in all areas of life are increasingly falling before the public because of this problem. Why does this happen?

Human Nature Cannot Handle Unchecked Power.

Abraham Lincoln said, "Nearly all men can stand adversity, but if you want to test a man's character, give him power." Power can be compared to a great river; while within bounds it is both beautiful and useful. But when it overflows its bounds, it destroys. The danger of power lies in the fact that those who are vested with it tend to make its preservation their first concern. Therefore, they will naturally oppose any changes in the forces that have given them this power. History tells us that power leads to the abuse of power, and abuse of power leads to loss of power.

George Bush prayed in his Inaugural Address of 1989, "For we are given power not to advance our own purposes nor to make a great show in the world, nor a name. There is but one use of power and it is to serve people."

Leaders Can Easily Be Separated from Their People.

When Harry Truman was thrust into the presidency at the death of FDR, Sam Rayburn gave him some fatherly advice: "From here on out you're going to have lots of people around you. They'll try to put a wall around you and cut you off from any ideas but theirs. They'll tell you what a great man you are, Harry. But you and I both know you ain't."

Hubert H. Humphrey said, "There is no party, no Chief Executive, no Cabinet, no legislature in this or any other nation, wise enough to govern without constant exposure to informed criticism." That is true for any person who occupies a leadership position.

Develop Integrity.

The book *Profiles of Leadership* reveals the answers America's top business and government leaders gave when asked what quality they thought was most important to their success as leaders. Their unanimous answer: *integrity*.

Integrity is the human quality most necessary to business success according to the 1,300 senior executives who responded to a recent survey. Seventy-one percent put it at the top of a list of sixteen traits responsible for enhancing an executive's effectiveness. The dictionary defines integrity as "the state of being complete, unified." When people have integrity, their words and deeds match up. They are who they are, no matter where they are or who they're with. People with integrity are not divided (that's duplicity) or merely pretending (that's hypocrisy). They are "whole" and their lives are "put together." People with integrity have nothing to hide and nothing to fear. Their lives are open books.

Integrity in a leader must be demonstrated daily in a number of tangible ways. These are five that I strive to demonstrate to those I lead.

1. I will live what I teach. Deciding what to be is more important than deciding what to do. Often we ask young people "What are you going to do when you grow up?" But the more important question is, "What are going to *be?*" The character decision must be made before a career is chosen.

Early in my years of leadership, I read this poem by Howard A. Walter and adopted its principles:

Character

I would be true, for there are those who trust me;
I would be pure, for there are those who care;
I would be strong, for there are those who suffer;
I would be brave, for there is much to dare.
I would be friend of all—the foe, the friendless;
I would be giving, and forget the gift;
I would be humble, for I know my weakness;
I would look up, and laugh, and love, and lift.

2. I will do what I say. If I promise something to a subordinate, colleague, or superior, I want to keep my word. The Center for Creative Leadership in Greensboro, North Carolina, released a study of twenty-one high potential executives who were terminated from their companies or forced to retire early. The one universal character flaw or unforgivable sin which always led to downfall was betraying a trust; that is, not doing something that was promised.

3. I will be honest with others. If those who work with me ever catch me misrepresenting the facts or covering up a problem, I will instantly lose credibility. And it will not be easy to repair.

Dr. William Schultz, a noted psychologist who developed truth-in-management strategies at Proctor and Gamble and NASA, believes the key to productivity is "how well people work together," and he believes that nothing "increases compatibility like mutual trust and honesty." Dr. Schultz says, "If people in business just told the truth, 80 percent to 90 percent of their problems would disappear." Trust and honesty are the means that allow individuals to cooperate so that they can all prosper.

4. I will put what is best for others ahead of what is best for me. The organization I lead and those I work with must come first. When I put the organization's best interests ahead of mine, I keep integrity with those who hired me. When I put the interest of those I work with ahead of mine, I develop friendships and loyalty. Below is the leadership pyramid that I have always tried to follow.

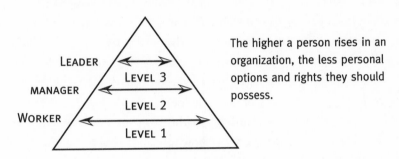

The higher a person rises in an organization, the less personal options and rights they should possess.

5. I will be transparent and vulnerable. Long ago I realized that in working with people I have two choices. I can close my arms or I can open them. Both choices have strengths and weaknesses. If I close my arms, I won't get hurt, but I will not get much help either. If I open my arms I likely will get hurt, but I will also receive help. What has been my decision? I've opened my arms and allowed others to enjoy the journey with me. My greatest gift to others is not a job, but myself. That is true of any leader.

PAY NOW, PLAY LATER.

There are two paths that people can take. They can either play now and pay later or pay now and play later. Regardless of the choices, one thing is certain. Life will demand a payment.

My father taught me this important discipline. Each week he would lay out the chores for the next seven days. Many of them could be done any time during the week. Our goal was to complete them by Saturday noon. If completed, we could do something fun with the family. If not completed, fun was forfeited and that individual stayed home to complete the chore. I needed to miss my deadline only a couple of times to realize that I needed to "pay up front" and finish my work on time.

This lesson has been valuable to me, and I'm teaching it to my children, Elizabeth and Joel Porter. I want them to realize that there is no such thing as a "free lunch," that life is not a gift—it is an investment. The sooner they can take control of their desires and submit them to life's demands, the more successful they will become. John Foster said, "A man without decision of character can never be said to belong to himself. He belongs to whatever can make captive of him." My friend Bill Klassen often reminds me that "when we pay later the price is greater!"

"I've never known a man worth his salt who in the long run, deep down in his heart, didn't appreciate the grind, the discipline," said Vince Lombardi. "I firmly believe that any man's finest hour—this greatest fulfillment to all he holds dear—is that moment when he has worked his heart out in a good cause and lies exhausted on the field of battle—victorious."

BECOME CHARACTER DRIVEN INSTEAD OF EMOTION DRIVEN.

Most of the significant things done in the world were done by persons who were either too busy or too sick! "There are few ideal and leisurely settings for the disciplines of growth," Robert Thornton Henderson said. "Ninety percent of the work is done in this country by people who don't feel well."

It is not doing the things we like to do, but doing the things we have to do that causes growth and makes us successful. John Luther said: "There's no such thing as a perfect job. In any position you'll find some duties which, if they aren't onerous immediately, eventually will be." Success depends not merely on how well you do the things you enjoy, but how conscientiously you perform those duties you don't.

Tenor Luciano Pavarotti is such a winner. He is often described by his admirers as "the new Caruso." In a newspaper interview, the six-foot, three hundred-pound tenor asked: "Do you want to know the hardest thing about being a singer? It is to sacrifice yourself every moment of your life, with not one exclusion. For example, if it is raining, don't go out; eat this, do this, sleep ten hours a day. It is not a very free life. You cannot jump on a horse. You cannot go to swim."

Successful people are willing to do things unsuccessful people will not do. My observation is that one of those things that makes a difference is this issue of being character driven instead of emotion driven. This is the difference:

CHARACTER-DRIVEN PEOPLE	EMOTION-DRIVEN PEOPLE
Do right, then feel good	Feel good, then do right
Are commitment driven	Are convenience driven
Make principle based decisions	Make popular based decisions
Action controls attitude	Attitude controls action
Believe it, then see it	See it, then believe it
Create momentum	Wait for momentum
Ask: "What are my Responsibilities?"	Ask: "What are my rights?"
Continue when problems arise	Quit when problems arise
Are steady	Are moody
Are leaders	Are followers

The late Louis L'Amour is one of the best-selling authors of all time. Nearly 230 million copies of his books are in print worldwide, and every one of his more than one hundred books is still in print. When asked the key to his writing style, he responded, "Start writing, no matter what. The water does not flow until the faucet is turned on."

That's a good word for life. Sometimes, what we need to do is just to do something. Help someone. Sometimes, just getting into action will release power in our lives. We ought to adopt this as our motto for life: "The water does not flow until the faucet is turned on."

Good character is more to be praised than outstanding talent. Most talents are, to some extent, gifts. By contrast, good character is not given to us. We have to build it piece by piece—by thought, choice, courage, and determination. This will only be accomplished with a disciplined life-style.

Stephen Covey said, "If I try to use human influence strategies and tactics of how to get other people to do what I want, to work better, to be more motivated, to like me and each other—while my character is fundamentally flawed, marked by duplicity or insincerity—then, in the long run, I cannot be successful. My duplicity will breed distrust and everything I do even using so-called good human relations techniques-will be perceived as manipulative.

"It simply makes no difference how good the rhetoric is or even how good the intentions are: if there is little or no trust there is no foundation for permanent success. Only basic goodness gives life to technique."[4]

THE MOST IMPORTANT LESSON OF LEADERSHIP:
STAFF DEVELOPMENT

The growth and development of people is the highest calling of leadership. Chapter 7 emphasized the general development of people. This chapter will center on the development of a staff, but it is impossible to go into depth on this important subject in one chapter. The intent of this book is to help establish a leadership foundation. Therefore, I have dealt only with basics in the hope that I can help you develop the leader in you. I will write another book that will enable you to develop the leaders around you.

When I turned forty, I began to review my life. I made a list of all the things I was doing at that time. My list included:

Senior pastor of a congregation of 3,500 attenders;

Oversight and development of thirteen pastors;

President of Injoy, Inc., a company that develops resource materials for thousands of people;

A national and international speaking schedule with over four hundred engagements annually;

Producing a monthly leadership tape for Injoy Life Club subscribers;

Writing a book every eighteen months;

Working on another education degree;

And most important—taking enough time for my wife, Margaret, and our two children, Elizabeth and Joel Porter.

After writing out my list my conclusion was twofold: I didn't have any more hours and therefore I couldn't work and harder: and my future growth in production would be determined by my ability to work through other people.

These two realities enabled me to search for and find the most important leadership lesson I've ever learned:

THOSE CLOSEST TO THE LEADER WILL DETERMINE THE LEVEL OF SUCCESS FOR THAT LEADER.

Niccolo Machiavelli said, "The first method for estimating the intelligence of a ruler is to look at the men he has around him." I'm not certain this subject is an issue of I.Q., but I am sure that it is a test of leadership. Leaders who continue to grow personally and bring growth to their organizations will influence many and develop a successful team around them. The better the players, the better the leader. Few people are successful unless a lot of people want them to be. Andrew Carnegie said, "It marks a big step in your development when you come to realize that other people can help you do a better job than you could do alone."

Below is and illustration of what can happen to an organization when the key players slightly increase their potential while they work for the same team.

$$3 \times 3 \times 3 \times 3 \times 3 = \underline{243} + 25\% \text{ increase individually}$$
$$4 \times 4 \times 4 \times 4 \times 4 = \underline{1024} + 400\% \text{ increase together}$$

A great leader develops a team of people who increase production. The result? The leader's influence and effectiveness begin to multiply (working through others) instead of adding (working by oneself). That no man can sincerely try to help another without helping himself is, according to Ralph Waldo Emerson, one of the most beautiful compensations of this life.

David Jackson, founder and chief executive officer of Altos Computer Systems, said, "In my experience, the real turning point in a company is when you go from one to two people. Then, at least, there's someone to answer the phone wile you eat your lunch."

All leaders have "war stories" of bad experiences in leading and developing staff. Perhaps this humorous illustration will help us laugh about our past experiences and allow us to get a second wind to begin building a winning team around us.

As nearly everyone knows, a leader has practically nothing to do except to decide what is to be done; tell somebody to do it; listen to reasons why it should not be done or why it should be done in a different way; follow up to see if the thing has been done; discover that it has not; inquire why; listen to excuses from the person who should have done it; follow up again to see if the thing has been done only to discover that is had been done incorrectly; point out how it should have been done; conclude that as long as it has been done, it may as well be left where it is; wonder if it is not time to get rid of a person who cannot do a thing right; reflect that the person probably has a spouse and a large family and any successor would be just as bad and maybe worse; consider how much simpler and better matters would be now if he had done it himself in the first place; reflect sadly that he could have done it right in twenty minutes and, as things turned out, he has had to spend two days to find out why it has taken three weeks for somebody else to do it wrong.

In spite of all the problems that arise in the development of staff, two facts are certain. First, only as we develop a team do we continually succeed. A Chinese proverb says, "If you are planning for one year, grow rice. If you are planning for twenty years, grow trees. If you are planning for centuries, grow men." Second, only as we develop a team do we continually multiply.

A PICTURE OF A WINNING TEAM

Winning teams. . . .

- Have great leaders
- Pick good people
- Play to win
- Make other team members more successful
- Keep improving

WINNING TEAMS HAVE GREAT LEADERS.

Everything rises and falls on leadership. There are two ways you can get others to do what you want: You can compel them to do it or you can persuade them. Compulsion is the method of slavery; persuasion is the method of free men.

Persuading requires an understanding of what makes people tick and what motivates them; that is, a knowledge of human nature. Great leaders possess that knowledge.

In a recent survey, seventy psychologists were asked: "What is the most essential thing for a supervisor to know about human nature?" Two-thirds said that motivation—an understanding of what makes people think, feel, and act as they do—is uppermost.

If you understand what motivated people, you have at your command the most powerful tool for dealing with them.

People Management has been studying the personal histories of tens of thousand of people since 1961. They found that, without exception, people repeat a pattern of behavior every time they accomplish something they think they do well and find deeply satisfying. They also found that excellent leaders underscore this behavior in the following ways.

Excellent Leaders Create the Right Environment.

They believe in their team. This creates an environment for success. The best way to gain and hold the loyalty of your personnel is to show interest in and care for them by your words and actions. Sam Walton said, "Outstanding leaders go out of the way to boost the self-esteem of their personnel. If people believe in themselves, it's amazing what they can accomplish."

Excellent Leaders Know Basic Human Needs.

Paul "Bear" Bryant, the legendary football coach at the University of Alabama, said there are five things winning team members need to know:

1. What is expected from each one.

2. That each will have an opportunity to perform.

3. How each one is getting along.

4. That guidance will be given where each needs it.

5. That each will be rewarded according to his contribution.

Excellent Leaders Keep Control of the "Big 3."

Any leader who wants to play an active role in all areas of the organization may be tempted to take on too many responsibilities. However, three areas are crucial to the leader's authority and success:

1. **Finance:** because the finance staff is a prime means of exercising executive control in any organization.

2. Personnel: because the selection of people will determine the organization.

3. Planning: because the area determines the future of the organization.

Excellent Leaders Avoid the "Seven Deadly sins."

1. Trying to be liked rather than respected.

2. Not asking team members for advice and help.

3. Thwarting personal talent by emphasizing rules rather than skills.

4. Not keeping criticism constructive.

5. Not developing a sense of responsibility in team members.

6. Treating everyone the same way.

7. Failing to keep people informed.

T. Boone Pickens said, "There are many ways to avoid mistakes, but the best way to sidestep the disasters is to be available. You don't have to make every decision, but you should always be accessible. If your people are smart, they will keep you informed, and if you're informed, you're a part of the decision. With that in place, it's easy for you to back your people and that eliminates second guessing."

WINNING TEAMS PICK GOOD PEOPLE.

When building the staff for his newly conceived computer company, H. Ross Perot hired the best people he could find. His motto is, "Eagles don't flock. You have to find them one at a time." He was saying that you can't build a strong team on weak individuals.

Adlai E. Stevenson said that there are only three rules of sound administrators: Pick good people, tell them not to cut corners, and back them to the limits. Picking good people is the most important.

Bobb Biehl says that from 60 to 80 percent of the success of any company or organization is attributable to three factors:

- A clear direction
- The right team of players
- Sound finances

That's why few things are as important as putting the right people in the right places.

Recently I read a humorous article entitled, "Who Not to Hire." It said never hire anyone. . . .

- who is accompanied by his or her (a) slave, (b) attorney with a tape recorder, (c) bodyguard, (d) teddy bear, (e) police escort, (f) mother.

- who brags about being smarter than any three of the jerks he or she has worked for previously.

- whose resume runs longer than forty pages.

- whose resume is printed in crayon.

- who talks more rapidly than the man in the Federal Express commercials.

- who hisses at your questions.

- who occasionally lapses into pig Latin.

- who breaks into wracking sobs when asked to name a personal reference.

- who is unable to decide hair and eye colors.

- who is, by court order, on permanent intravenous sedation.

- who tries to impress you with his or her repertoire of "knock knock" jokes.

- who, under salary requirements, scrawls, "I want it all now!"

While you're laughing, remember that Murphy's Law would seem to conclude that the ideal resume will turn up one day after the position is filled! Still, getting the right people in the right places is crucial to the success of your organization. There are five principles for picking people that will help you get the best candidates on your team.

1. The Smaller the Organization, the More Important the Hiring.

Small organizations often make the mistake of thinking that they can get by with inferior staff members because they are small. The opposite is true. In a firm of one hundred employees, if one is inferior the loss is only 1 percent. But if the organization has a payroll of two and one is inferior, the loss is 50 percent. However, the bright side is that it's much easier to pick one excellent person than a hundred.

2. Know What Kind of Person You Need (Personal Requirements.)

Listed below are the "Top 20" personal requirements I look for in a potential staff member:

1. Positive Attitude—the ability to see people and situations in a positive way.

*2. High Energy Level—strength and stamina to work hard and not wear down.

3. Personal Warmth—a manner that draws people to them.

4. Integrity—trustworthy, good solid character, words and walk are consistent.

5. Responsible—always "comes through," no excuses; job delegated-job done.

6. Good Self-image—feels good about self, others, and life.

*7. Mental Horsepower—ability to keep learning as the job expands.

8. Leadership Ability—has high influence over others.

9. Followership Ability—willingness to submit, play team ball, and follow the leader.

*10. Absence of Personal Problems—personal, family, and business life are in order.

11. People Skills—the ability to draw people and develop them.

12. Sense of Humor—enjoys life, fails to take self too seriously.

*13. Resilience—able to "bounce back" when problems arise.

*14. Track Record—has experience and success, hopefully in two or more situations.

15. Great Desire—hungers for growth and personal development.

16. Self-discipline—willing to "pay the price" and handle success.

17. Creative—ability to see solutions and fix problems.

18. Flexibility—not afraid of change; fluid; flows as the organization grows.

19. Sees "Big Picture"—able to look beyond personal interest and see the total picture.

*20. Intuitive—able to discern and sense a situation without tangible data.

*These things probably cannot be taught. The others can be taught with a proper mentor, environment, and willingness by the staff member. Most of the qualities in the above list can be evaluated with a couple of interviews and tests.

3. Know What the Job Requires.

A job has certain characteristics that require specific skills and personality traits. These ten general questions will help a leader pick the right person. Does the job require . . .

1. An up-front or a behind-the-scenes person?

2. A generalist or a specialist?

3. A producer or a maintainer?

4. A people person or a paper person?

5. A leader or a supporter?

6. A veteran or a rookie?

7. A creative thinker or an abstract thinker?

8. Constant supervision or little supervision?

9. A team player or an individual?

10. Short-term commitment or long-term commitment?

The more you know about the kind of person you need and what the job requires, the greater your odds of hiring the right individual. Kurt Einstren says, "Hiring the wrong persons costs your company at least two years' salary. Many times there is a much higher price that is paid, not in cash, but strained relationships, bad PR, and lack of trust."

Often I am asked in leadership conferences, "How do you know which staff person to hire?" I always laugh and say, "You never know for sure," and my track record underscores that comment! These are some guidelines I have tried to follow when looking for staff:

- Know what you need before you start looking for someone.

- Take time to search the field.

- Call many references.

- Have several interviews.

- Include your associates in some of the interviews and ask for their input.

- Interview the candidates' spouses.

- Check out the candidates' track records.

- If possible, have a trial run to see if the job and the potential staff match.

- Ask hard questions, such as, "Why did you leave?"; "What can you contribute?"; "Are you willing to pay the price?"

- Trust your instincts.

There is only so much you can put on paper. If it looks good on paper but feels bad inside, go slowly. In fact, back off and let an associate take over; them compare conclusions. Personally, I only hire a person if it looks good *and* feels good.

4. Know What the Potential Staff Member Wants.

People work harder, stay longer, and do better on the job when they like what they do. Realizing this truth, I always make sure the potential team player feels good about me as the leader, the other players on the team, and the vision and requirements of the team. I always say to them, "Don't come unless it feels right." I know that no amount of money, attention, privileges, and promises will motivate a staff member who really does not want to be on the team. It is also important that the spouse "feels good" about the job. Positive feelings of a staff member will slowly disappear if the spouse is unhappy.

5. When You Cannot Afford to Hire the Best, Hire the Young Who Are Going to Be the Best.

Then:
> Believe in them—that will encourage risk.
> Show them—that will build respect.
> Love them—that will strengthen relationships.
> Know them—that will personalize development.
> Teach them—that will enhance growth.
> Trust them—that will develop loyalty.
> Expand them—that will provide challenges.
> Lift them—that will insure results.

WINNING TEAMS PLAY TO WIN.

The difference between playing to win and playing to not lose is the difference between success and mediocrity. I grew up in Ohio and became a fan of Big Ten football. Over the years I observed that Big Ten teams usually lost the "big game" every year at the Rose Bowl. Why? Were Pac Ten teams consistently better? No, the margin of victory was not a result of talent. It was a result of how each team approached the game. Big Ten teams played conservatively, trying to lose. Pac Ten teams played wide open, trying to win.

Each time new staff members join our team, I give them each a plaque and ask them to display it on the wall of their offices. The words on the plaque read, "I don't have to survive." At the presentation, I encourage them to be not-survivors. I remind them to take risks, make tough decisions, live on the edge, and make a difference. People who play it safe continually miss opportunities and seldom make progress. It's the same way in baseball—you cannot steal second base with your foot on first! This is a favorite poem of mine. It describes those bland safe people.

> There was a very cautious man
> Who never laughed or played.
> He never risked, he never tried,
> He never sang or prayed.
> And when he one day passed away,
> His insurance was denied.
> For since he never really lived,
> They claimed he never really died.

A recent survey of workers across the United States revealed that nearly 85 percent of those interviewed said they could work harder on the job. More than half claimed they could double their effectiveness "if they wanted to."[1] Winning teams are seldom more talented than losing teams. But they are always more committed. They want to win. They pay the price, and go after victory. The crowd in the bleachers may wonder how they got so lucky, but the team members know they played to win.

WINNING TEAMS MAKE THEIR TEAM MEMBER MORE SUCCESSFUL.

In other words, because of the other members of the team, each player is better than the player would be if he or she played alone. Vince Lombardi, one of the all-time great head coaches , said, "Start by teaching the fundamentals. A player's got to know the basics of the game and how to play his position. Next, keep him in line. That's discipline. The men have to play as a team, not as a bunch of individuals. . . . Then you've got to care for one another. You've got to *love* each other. . . . Most people call it team spirit."[2]

Robert W. Keidel said that trying to change individual and/or corporate behavior without addressing the larger organizational context is bound to disappoint. Sooner or later bureaucratic structures will consume even the most determined of collaborative processes. As Woody Allen once said, "The lion and the lamb may lie down together, but the lamb won't get much sleep."

What to do? Work on the lion as well as the lamb by designing teamwork into the organization. Although the Boston Celtics have won sixteen championships, they have never had the league's leading scorer and never paid a player based on his individual statistics. The Celtics understand that virtually every aspect of basketball requires close collaboration.

There are significant ways to engage in better team-building.

Know the Key to Each Player.

Every individual has a personal agenda, the "real reason" he or she wants to be on the team. That personal agenda is the key to motivating each player.

Map Out a Team Mission.

Lay out the vision. Develop organizational mottos, names, symbols, and slogans. This will encourage pride in team memberships.

Define The Role of Each Player.

This will help avoid unnecessary rivalries by clearly identifying each person's role within the group. This will also avoid the "fairness" issue that is common with staffs. Each player will be appreciated for his or her contribution to the team.

Create a Group Identity.

Establish your groups' worth by examining and promoting its history and values. Create memories together as a group.

Use Liberal Doses of "We" and "Our."

Team building involves getting the members to feel a sense of ownership in what they are doing as a group. When the group has done well, it is important to praise the entire effort without singling out individuals.

Communicate with Everyone.

Don't be a fact hog. Share information with everyone who is affected, not with just the key players. People are usually "down on" what they are not "up on." As a leader, you will know you have succeeded when the members of your team put the interests of the group over their own.

Do you recall when Edmund Hillary and his sherpa guide, Tenzing, made their historic climb of Mt. Everest? Coming down from the peak Hillary suddenly lost his footing. Tenzing held the line taut and kept them both from falling by digging his axe into the ice. Later Tenzing refused any special credit for saving Hillary's life; he considered it a routine part of the job. As he put it, "Mountain climbers always help each other."

WINNING TEAMS KEEP IMPROVING.

Whenever an organization is through improving, it's through! Why is it that a professional football, basketball, or baseball team seldom repeats as the world champion in consecutive years? Mainly, it's because of the temptation to keep all the players, practices, and strategies the same as the previous year. Too many think that if they "stay put" they can stay on top. That's not true. Either the current players must keep growing and improving or potentially better ones must be brought into the organization. Continued success is a result of continued improvement.

The first objective of the leader is to develop people, not to dismiss them.

Studies have shown that day-to-day coaching, rather than comprehensive annual appraisals, is most effective for improving performance. This coaching process has two crucial components: setting specific objectives and holding frequent progress reviews.

Objectives should specify end results, the exact extent of achievement the manager expects, and should be tied to a timetable. How many objectives should the employee be given? In our experience, a few are better than too many. If the subordinate is overloaded, expecting all the objectives to be accomplished is unreasonable. Remember, the objectives are the primary measuring stick.

By *end results*, we mean what should be observably different as a result of the subordinate's performance on the job. All too often employees expect to be evaluated on the basis of how much effort they are putting into the job, rather than what they are accomplishing. This is especially true of weak performers. It is critical that the manager make clear that certain outcomes are expected and the subordinate will be held accountable for them. The manager should make every effort to set mutually acceptable goals. If there is disagreement, however, the manager must unhesitatingly insist upon setting the objectives. Remember: performance, not just effort, is the yardstick for meeting objectives.

Frequent progress reviews accomplish three things. First, they serve as a continual reminder that reaching the objectives is important to the person's career. Second, reviews give the manager a chance to recognize positive movement toward objectives. Third, if progress is not forthcoming, the manager can listen to the reasons for lack of performance and attempt to get the subordinate on track. The review becomes a problem-solving session.

Whether or not the employee makes progress, holding reviews permits the manager or boss to remain in control of the process.[3] If you have more than three people reporting to you right now, chances are you are unhappy with at least one of them. The situation usually has one or more of the elements:

- The person is not doing a top-notch job, but not a terrible one either; so you keep him or her around.

- Finding someone else who can do the job means interviewing, hiring (taking a risk), and then training the new person. You do not have time for that either.

- The person definitely is not dong the job, but you like him or her (or more likely you feel sorry for him or her).

- You don't quite have all the documentation you need to fire this person. Your last review was too flowery and you have not really said how unhappy you are with the individual's work.

The result? Nothing happens. But keep in mind that you and the person who need to be dismissed are not the only two people in the equation. What too many leaders fail to realize is that:

- The situation is well known to other workers in the organization. No one can keep below-par performance a secret.

- Your failure to fire will have a detrimental effect on your career. As a leader, your first and greatest responsibility is to the organization and its highest good. Whenever a person's leadership position puts the personal agenda of himself or herself ahead of the organization, that leader is a liability.

- The morale of the other employees suffers because you keep the below-par performer on the payroll while everyone else is pulling more than enough weight.

Remember, it isn't the people you fire who make your life miserable; it's the ones you don't. If you have serious doubts about a staff member and have worked with him or her without success, it is better to have that person working somewhere else.

How can dismissing a person be handled correctly? Bobb Biehl says the essence of doing it right is in maintaining this perspective: "When you appropriately fire a person from a position in which he is failing, you are actually releasing him from that failure—and freeing him to seek a position in which he can find success. With a proper release, it's even possible to install a person the excitement that comes from anticipating a new adventure."

Obviously the optimum scenario is to interview well, hire well, and then begin to develop your staff to reach their—and your—greatest potential. There are three phases of potential:

1. I maximize my potential (I pour my energy into myself).

2. I maximize the potential of others (I pour my energy into key people).

3. They maximize my potential (they pour their energy into me).

Producers excel only at phase 1.
Leaders excel at phases 1 and 2.
Fortunate leaders excel at phases 1 and 2 and experience phase 3.

Let's take a moment now to stop and consider your strengths as a leader. This evaluation will allow you to review those areas of importance to a leader we've discussed in the pages of this book, while reinforcing the areas you need to emphasize in your development. Just circle the number that corresponds with how you see your ability, right now.

1	2	3	4	5
Mastered	Strong	Satisfactory	Needs growth	Difficult

Common Strengths Outstanding Leaders Share

DREAMING 1 2 3 4 5
Never let go of a dream until you're ready to wake up and make it happen.

In working with leaders, I have often asked myself, "Does the man make the dream, or does the dream make the man?" My conclusion: both are equally true.

GOAL-SETTING 1 2 3 4 5
A goal is a dream with a deadline.

If you don't know what you want and where you are going, you will get next to nothing and end up nowhere.

INFLUENCING 1 2 3 4 5
The very essence of all power to influence lies in getting the other person to participate.

People do not care how much you know until they know how much you care.

PERSONAL ORGANIZATION 1 2 3 4 5
"Organizing is what you do before you do something, so that when you do it, it's not all mixed up."—Christopher Robin in *Winnie the Pooh*.

PRIORITIZING 1 2 3 4 5
"He is a wise man who wastes no energy on pursuits for which he is not fitted; and he is wiser still who, from among the things he can do well, chooses and resolutely follows the best."—William Gladstone

PROBLEM-SOLVING 1 2 3 4 5
"The majority see the obstacles; the few see the objectives; history records the successes of the latter, while oblivion is the reward of the former."—Alfred Armand Montapert

RISK-TAKING 1 2 3 4 5
Risks are not to be evaluated in terms of the probability of success, but in terms of the value of the goal.

DECISION-MAKING 1 2 3 4 5
Your decisions will always be better if you do what is right for the organization rather than what is right for yourself.

CREATIVITY 1 2 3 4 5

There is always a better way . . . your challenge is to find it.

"Man's mind, once stretched by a new idea, never regains its original dimensions."—Oliver Wendall Holmes

HIRING/FIRING 1 2 3 4 5

"There are only three rules of sound administration: pick good [people], tell them not to cut corners, and back them to the limit. Picking good [people] is the most important."—Adlai E. Stevenson

"When you appropriately fire a person from a position in which he is failing, you are actually releasing him from that failure—and freeing him to seek a position in which he can find success."—Bobb Biehl

EVALUATION 1 2 3 4 5

People who reach their potential spend more time asking, "What am I doing well?" rather than "What am I doing wrong?"

The person who knows how will always have a job; but the person who knows why will always be the boss.

If you are strong in or if you have mastered four areas you are on Level #1. If you are strong in or if you have mastered eight you are on Level #2. If you are strong in or if you have mastered every area you are on Level #3, and that means you have a strong support team that has allowed you to grow beyond yourself.

At this point in my life, I am fortunate to be living on the phase 3 level. I've grown beyond my own resources and am multiplying instead of adding because of those closest to me. I will be forever grateful to them. With them I will continue to lead. Because of them I will continue to grow.

Some of these precious people are:

Margaret Maxwell—my wife and best friend. Marrying her is the best decision I ever made.

Stephen F. Babby—my colleague and the wisest person I know.

Dick Peterson—my close friend, whose goal in life is to help me.

Dan Reiland—my executive pastor, whose loyalty and energy are unequaled.

Barbara Brumagin—my personal assistant who had a servant's heart and superior skills.

Melvin Maxwell—my father, who is my hero in life and mentor in leadership.

EPILOGUE

This world needs leaders . . .

Who use their influence at the right times for the right reasons;
Who take a little greater share of the
    blame and a little smaller share of the credit;
Who lead themselves successfully before attempting
    to lead others;
Who continue to search for the best answer,
    not the familiar one;
Who add value to the people and organization they lead;
Who work for the benefit of others and not for personal gain;
Who handle themselves with their heads and handle others
    with their hearts;
Who know the way, go the way, and
    show the way;
Who inspire and motivate rather than
    intimidate and manipulate;
Who live with people to know their
    problems and live with God in order
    to solve them;

> The growth and
> development
> of people is
> the highest
> calling of
> leadership.

Who realize that their dispositions are
    more important than their positions;
Who mold opinions instead of following opinion polls;
Who understands that an institution is
    the reflection of their character;
Who never place themselves above others except in carrying
    responsibilities;
Who will be as honest in small things as
    in great things;
Who discipline themselves so they will
    not be disciplined by others;
Who encounter setbacks and turn them
    into comebacks;
Who follow a moral compass that points
    in the right direction regardless of the trends.

NOTES

INTRODUCTION

1. David Hartley-Leonard, "Perspectives," *Newsweek*, 24 August 1987, 11.
2. Contributed by Doug Lysen, *Reader's Digest*, February 1989.
3. John W. Gardner, "The Nature of Leadership," Leadership Papers #1, Independent Sector, January 1986.
4. Richard Kerr for United Technologies Corp. *Bits and Pieces*, *March 1990*.

CHAPTER 1

1. James C. Georges, ParTraining Corp., Tucker, GA, interviewed in Executive Communications, January 1987.
2. J.R. Miller, *The Building of Character* (New Jersey: AMG Publishers, 1975).
3. Warren Bennis and Burt Nanus, *Leaders* (New York: Harper and Row, 1985), 222.
4. Robert Dilenschneider, *Power and Influence: Mastering the Art of Persuasion* (New York: Prentice Hall, 1990).
5. E.C. McKenzie, *Quips and Quotes* (Grand Rapids: Baker, 1980).

6. Fred Smith, *Learning to Lead* (Waco: Word, 1986), 117.

7. John C. Maxwell, *Be a People Person* (Wheaton: Victor, 1989).

CHAPTER 2

1. R. Earl Allen, *Let It Begin In Me* (Nashville: Broadman Press, 1985).

2. William H. Cook, *Success, Motivation and the Scriptures* (Nashville: Broadman, 1974).

CHAPTER 3

1. Dwight D. Eisenhower, *Great Quotes From Great Leaders*, ed. Peggy Anderson (Lombard: Great Quotations, 1989).

2. CCM *Communicator*, newsletter of the Council of Communication, Spring 1988.

3. Peter Drucker, *Management, Tasks, Responsibilities and Practices* (New York: Harper & Row, 1974).

4. *Newsweek* Magazine, 24 August 1987, 11.

5. Joseph Bailey, "Clues for Success in the President's Job," *Harvard Business Review*, 1983.

6. James Kouzes and Barry Posner, *The Leadership Challenge* (San Francisco: Jossey-Bass, 1987).

CHAPTER 4

1. Quoted in Paul Wharton, *Stories and Parables for Preachers and Teachers* (Mahwah: Paulist, 1986).

2. Howard Hendricks, *Teaching to Change Lives* (Portland: Multnomah, 1987), 32.

3. Robert Lacy, *Ford: The Man and the Machine* (New York: Little Brown, 1986).

4. Bobb Biehl, *Increasing Your Leadership Confidence* (Sisters: Questar Publishers, 1989).

5. Melvin E. Page and H. Leon Abrams, Jr., *Your Body Is Your Doctor* (New Canaan: Keats, 1972).

6. John Maxwell, *The Winning Attitude* (San Bernardino: Here's Life, 1984).

7. Winifield Arn, *Growth Report No. 5., Ten Steps for Church Growth* (New York: Harper & Row, 1977).

8. George F. Trusell, *Helping Employees Cope with Change: A Manager's Guidebook* (Buffalo: PAT Publishers, 1988).

9. Bennis and Nanus, *Leaders*.

10. Trusell, *Helping Employees Cope with Change: A Manager's Guidebook*.

11. R. F. Caldwell, "The Face of Corporate Culture," *Santa Clara Today*, November 1984, 12.

12. Max Depree, *Leadership Is an Art* (New York: Doubleday, 1989), 87.

13. Ron Jenson, ed., *Higher Ground*.

CHAPTER 5

1. F. F. Fournies, *Coaching for Improved Work Performance* (New York: Van Nostrand Reinhold, 1978).

2. Taken from a quotation by MacDonald in *Leaves of Gold*, A. C. Remley (Williamsport: Coslett Publishing, 1948).

3. Adapted from G. W. Target, "The Window," in *The Window and Other Essays* (Mountain View: Pacific Press Publishing Association, 1973), 5–7.

4. Beihl, *Increasing Your Leadership Confidence*.

5. Tom Wujec, *Pumping Ions: Games and Exercises to Flex Your Mind* (New York: Doubleday, 1988).

6. John K. Clemens, *Hartwick Humanities in Management Report* (Oneonta: Hartwick Institute, 1989).

CHAPTER 6

1. Chuck Swindoll, *Improving Your Serve* (Waco: Word, 1981).

2. Nell Mohney, "Beliefs Can Influence Attitudes," *Kingsport Times News*, 25 July 1986,4B.

3. Norman Vincent Peale, *Power of the Plus Factor* (New York: Fawcett, 1988).

4. Anonymous, "Attitude," *Bartlett's Familiar Quotations*, ed. Emily

Morison Beck (Boston: Little Brown, 1980).

5. Viktor Frankl, "Youth in Search of Meaning," *Moral Development Foundations*, Donald M. joy, ed. (Nashville: Abingdon, 1983).

6. C. S. Lewis, *Mere Christianity* (New York: Macmillan, 1952), 86.

7. Donald Robinson, "Mind Over Disease," *Reader's Digest*, March 1990.

CHAPTER 7

1. Thomas Peters and Robert Waterman, *In Search of Excellence* (New York: Warner, 1984), 58.

2. Frankl, "Youth in Search of Meaning."

3. Stephen Ash, " The Career Doctor," cited in Michigan Department of Social Services, *No-Name Newsletter*, Fall 1986.

4. From Richard Huseman and John Hatfield, *Managing the Equity Factor* (New York: Houghton Mifflin, 1989).

5. Henry David Thoreau, *Bartlett's Familiar Quotations*.

6. Ron Watts, La Croix United Methodist Church, Cape Girardeau, Missouri, personal communication.

7. Huseman and Hatfield, *Managing the Equity Factor*.

CHAPTER 8

1. Robert K. Greenleaf, *The Servant as Leader* (Mahwah: Paulist, 1977).

2. Biehl, *Increasing Your Leadership Confidence*.

3. Quoted in "Weekend," *Newsday*, 8, 1990.

4. Harry C. McKown, *A Boy Grows Up* (New York: McGraw-Hill, 1985).

5. George S. Patton, *Great Quotes From Great Leaders*, Peggy Anderson, ed. (Lombard: Great Quotations, 1989).

6. Ralph Waldo Emerson, *Bartlett's Familiar Quotations*.

7. Roger von Oech, *A Kick in the Seat of the Pants* (San Francisco: HarperCollins, 1986).

8. Denis Waitley and Reni L. Witt, *The Joy of Working* (New York: Dodd, Mead & Co., 1985).

CHAPTER 9

1. Harry S. Truman, *Great Quotes from Great Leaders*.
2. Edwin Markham, *Great Quotes from Great Leaders*.
3. Edward Everett Hale, *Bartlett's Familiar Quotations*.
4. Stephen Covey, *The Seven Habits of Highly Effective People: Restoring the Character Ethic* (New York: Simon and Schuster, 1989).

CHAPTER 10

1. Huseman and Hatfield, *Managing the Equity Factor*.
2. Vince Lombardi, *Great Quotes From Great Leaders*.
3. William J. Morin and Lyle Yorks, *Dismissal* (San Diego: Harcourt Brace Jovanovich, 1990).

THE 17 INDISPUTABLE
LAWS OF TEAMWORK

Embrace Them and Empower Your Team

ACKNOWLEDGMENTS

E very book I write is an act of teamwork. And this one is no exception. I'd like to thank the people who helped me to create *The 17 Indisputable Laws of Teamwork:*

The INJOY Team, who helped me to think through and refine the laws.

Margaret Maxwell, my wife, best friend, and number one teammate, who gives good advice.

Linda Eggers, who always takes care of all the details of my life.

Kathie Wheat, who did such wonderful research for the book.

Stephanie Wetzel, who sharpened the manuscript by proofreading and editing every word.

Charlie Wetzel, whose writing extends my influence around the world.

INTRODUCTION

E very day, in some way, you are a part of a team. The question is not, *Will you participate in something that involves others?* The question is, *Will your involvement with others be successful?* You can find the answer to that question in this book.

Everyone knows that teamwork is a good thing; in fact, it's essential! But how does it really work? What makes a winning team? Why do some teams go straight to the top, seeing their vision become reality, while others seem to go nowhere?

These questions don't have simple answers. If they did, sports would have more back-to-back world champions, and the list of Fortune 500 companies would never change year after year.

One of the challenges of learning about teamwork is that even people who've taken a team to the highest level in their field sometimes have a hard time identifying what separates a great team from a collection of individuals who can't seem to get it together. Some will say the key to winning is a strong work ethic. But haven't you known plenty of hardworking individuals who never worked together to reach their potential? Others believe that great teams are the result of chemistry. But they often say, "I can't explain how you create it, but I definitely know it when I see it." How can you get your hands around that and learn from it to build *your* team?

As a communicator who spends countless hours speaking to live audiences every year, I am always looking for straightforward ways to teach people complex truths. That's what a communicator does—he takes something complicated and makes it simple. In 1998, I wrote *The 21 Irrefutable Laws of Leadership*. My desire was to share what I had learned from three decades of leading people. The response was overwhelming. The book landed on bestseller lists of the *New York Times* Business Books, the *Wall Street Journal, Business Week*, and the Christian Booksellers Association (CBA) marketplace. For that I am truly grateful. But more important, during the last several years as I have taught the laws throughout the United States and on five continents, I have had the delight of seeing people connect with the laws, apply them to their lives, and improve their leadership. Learning the laws changed people's lives, and I knew that I had found an effective handle for helping people learn leadership.

My desire is to make team building as simple to grasp, retain, and put into practice as leadership. I want to take the mystery out of it. That's why I've worked hard to identify the Laws of Teamwork. The wonderful thing about a law is that you can depend on it. No matter who you are, what your background is, or what circumstances you face; you can take a law to the bank.

As I teach you the laws, you will find that I often approach the subject of teamwork from a leader's point of view—that makes sense since leaders are the ones who bring teams together and lead them to victory. But you don't have to be a leader to benefit from this book. Just about everything you do depends on teamwork. It doesn't matter whether you are a leader or follower, coach or player, teacher or student, parent or child, CEO or nonprofit volunteer worker. No matter who you are, if you learn and apply the laws, your teamwork capacity will increase. The greater the number of laws that you and your teammates learn, the more likely you are to be transformed from a group of individuals into a winning team.

Teams come in all shapes and sizes. If you're married, you and your spouse are a team. If you are employed by an organization, you and your colleagues are a team. If you volunteer your time, you and your fellow workers are a team. As Dan Devine joked, "A team is a team is a team. Shakespeare said that many times." Although the gifted playwright might not have said exactly that, the concept is nonetheless true. That's why teamwork is so important.

At a recent conference where I was teaching, a young leader who was just getting started in his career came up to me and asked, "John, what's the one thing I need to know about teamwork?"

"One thing?" I replied. "That's not an easy answer to come up with."

He persisted: "But just get me started. I want only the thing that's most important."

"All right, if you insist," I said. "The one thing you need to know about teamwork is that there is more than one thing you need to know about teamwork."

At first he looked at me questioningly. Then he became a bit irritated. But then I could see a sudden understanding in his eyes.

"Oh, I get it," he said. "It's a process. Okay, okay. I'm ready to dive in. I'm willing to take the time to learn."

I want to encourage you to do the same, to devote yourself to the process of learning to be a great team member and team builder. As you read about the Laws of Teamwork and begin to apply them, I think you will find that they have a positive impact on every aspect of your life. As you proceed, also remember this: None of the laws stand alone, but they all stand together really well. The greater number of laws you learn, the better you will become.

Enjoy the process, give it your best, and never forget that no matter what you want to do in life, it takes teamwork to make the dream work.

THE LAW OF SIGNIFICANCE

One Is Too Small a Number to Achieve Greatness

W ho are your personal heroes? Okay, maybe you don't have heroes exactly. Then let me ask you this: Which people do you admire most? Who do you wish you were more like? Which people fire you up and get your juices flowing? Do you admire . . .

- Business innovators, such as Jeff Bezos, Fred Smith, or Bill Gates?

- Great athletes, such as Michael Jordan, Marion Jones, or Mark McGwire?

- Creative geniuses, such as Pablo Picasso, Buckminster Fuller, or Wolfgang Amadeus Mozart?

- Pop culture icons, such as Madonna, Andy Warhol, or Elvis Presley?

- Spiritual leaders, such as John Wesley, Billy Graham, or Mother Teresa?

- Political leaders, such as Alexander the Great, Charlemagne, or Winston Churchill?

- Film industry giants, such as D. W. Griffith, Charlie Chaplin, or Steven Spielberg?

- Architects and engineers, such as Frank Lloyd Wright, the Starrett brothers, or Joseph Strauss?

- Revolutionary thinkers, such as Marie Curie, Thomas Edison, or Albert Einstein?

Or maybe your list includes people in a field I didn't mention.

It's safe to say that we all admire achievers. And we Americans especially love pioneers and bold individualists, people who fight alone, despite the odds or opposition: the settler who carves a place for himself in the wilds of the frontier, the Old West sheriff who resolutely faces an enemy in a gunfight, the pilot who bravely flies solo across the Atlantic Ocean, and the scientist who changes the world through the power of his mind.

THE MYTH OF THE LONE RANGER

As much as we admire solo achievement, the truth is that no lone individual has done anything of value. The belief that one person can do something great is a myth. There are no real Rambos who can take on a hostile army by themselves. Even the Lone Ranger wasn't really a loner. Everywhere he went he rode with Tonto!

Nothing of significance was ever achieved by an individual acting alone. Look below the surface and you will find that all seemingly solo acts are really team efforts. Frontiersman Daniel Boone had companions from the Transylvania Company as he blazed the Wilderness Road. Sheriff Wyatt Earp had his two brothers and Doc Holliday looking out for him. Aviator Charles Lindbergh had the backing of nine businessmen from St. Louis and the services of the Ryan Aeronautical Company, which built his plane. Even Albert Einstein, the

> *The belief that one person can do something great is a myth.*

scientist who revolutionized the world with his theory of relativity, didn't work in a vacuum. Of the debt he owed to others for his work, Einstein once remarked, "Many times a day I realize how much my own outer and inner life is built upon the labors of my fellow men, both living and dead, and how earnestly I must exert myself in order to give in return as much as I have received." It's true that the history of our country is marked by the accomplishments of many strong leaders and innovative individuals who took considerable risks. But those people always were part of teams.

Economist Lester C. Thurow commented on the subject:

> There is nothing antithetical in American history, culture, or traditions to teamwork. Teams were important in America's history—wagon trains conquered the West, men working together on the assembly line in American industry conquered the world, a successful national strategy and a lot of teamwork put an American on the moon first (and thus far, last). But American mythology extols only the individual . . . In America, halls of fame exist for almost every conceivable activity, but nowhere do Americans raise monuments in praise of teamwork.

I must say that I don't agree with all of Thurow's conclusions. After all, I've seen the U.S. Marine Corps war memorial in Washington, D.C., commemorating the raising of the flag on Iwo Jima. But he is right about something. Teamwork is and always has been essential to building this country. And that statement can be made about every country around the world.

THE VALUE OF TEAMWORK

A Chinese proverb states, "Behind an able man there are always other able men." The truth is that teamwork is at the heart of great achievement. The question isn't whether teams have value. The question is whether we acknowledge that fact and become better team players. That's why I assert that *one is too small a number to achieve greatness.* You cannot do anything of *real* value alone. That is the Law of Significance.

> *"There are no problems we cannot solve together, and very few that we can solve by ourselves."*
>
> —LYNDON JOHNSON

I challenge you to think of *one* act of genuine significance in the history of humankind that was performed by a lone human being. No matter what you name, you will find that a team of people was involved. That is why President Lyndon Johnson said, "There are no problems we cannot solve together, and very few that we can solve by ourselves."

C. Gene Wilkes, in his book *Jesus on Leadership,* observed that the power of teams not only is evident in today's modern business world, but it also has a deep history that is evident even in biblical times. Wilkes asserts,

- Teams involve more people, thus affording more resources, ideas, and energy than would an individual.

- Teams maximize a leader's potential and minimize her weaknesses. Strengths and weaknesses are more exposed in individuals.

- Teams provide multiple perspectives on how to meet a need or reach a goal, thus devising several alternatives for each situation. Individual insight is seldom as broad and deep as a group's when it takes on a problem.

- Teams share the credit for victories and the blame for losses. This fosters genuine humility and authentic community. Individuals take credit and blame alone. This fosters pride and sometimes a sense of failure.

- Teams keep leaders accountable for the goal. Individuals connected to no one can change the goal without accountability.

- Teams can simply do more than an individual.

If you want to reach your potential or strive for the seemingly impossible—such as communicating your message two thousand years after you are gone—you need to become a team player. It may be a cliché, but it is nonetheless true: Individuals play the game, but teams win championships.

WHY DO WE STAND ALONE?

Knowing all that we do about the potential of teams, why do some people still want to do things by themselves? I believe there are a number of reasons.

1. Ego

Few people are fond of admitting that they can't do everything, yet that is a reality of life. There are no supermen or superwomen. As Kerry Walls, one of the people on my INJOY Group team, says, "Spinning more plates doesn't increase your talent—it increases your likelihood of dropping a plate." So the question is not whether you can do everything by yourself; it's how soon you're going to realize that you can't.

> *Teamwork is birthed when you concentrate on "we" instead of "me."*

Philanthropist Andrew Carnegie declared, "It marks a big step in your development when you come to realize that other people can help you do a better job than you could do alone." To do something really big, let go of your ego, and get ready to be part of a team.

2. Insecurity

In my work with leaders, I've found that some individuals fail to promote teamwork because they feel threatened by other people. Sixteenth-century Florentine statesman Niccolo Machiavelli probably made similar observations, prompting him to write, "The first method for estimating the intelligence of a ruler is to look at the men he has around him."

I believe that insecurity, rather than poor judgment or lack of intelligence, most often causes leaders to surround themselves with weak people. As I stated in *The 21 Irrefutable Laws of Leadership,* only secure leaders give power to others. That is the Law of Empowerment. On the other hand, insecure leaders usually fail to build teams because of one of two reasons: Either they want to maintain control over everything for which they are responsible, or they fear being replaced by someone more capable. In either case, leaders who fail to promote teamwork undermine their own potential and erode the best efforts of the people with whom they work. They would benefit from the advice of President Woodrow Wilson: "We should not only use all the brains we have, but all that we can borrow."

> *"We should not only use all the brains we have, but all that we can borrow."*
>
> —WOODROW WILSON

3. Naïveté

Consultant John Ghegan keeps a sign on his desk that says, "If I had it to do all over again, I'd get help." That remark accurately represents the feelings of the third type of people who fail to become team builders. They naively underestimate the difficulty of achieving big things. As a result, they try to go it alone.

Some people who start out in this group turn out okay in the end. They discover that their dreams are bigger than their capabilities, they realize they won't accomplish their goals solo, and they adjust. They make team building their approach to achievement. But some others learn the truth too late, and as a result, they never accomplish their goals. And that's a shame.

4. Temperament

Some people aren't very outgoing and simply don't think in terms of team building and team participation. As they face challenges, it never occurs to them to enlist others to achieve something.

As a people person, I find that hard to relate to. Whenever I face any kind of challenge, the very first thing I do is to think about the people I want on the team to help with it. I've been that way since I was a kid. I've

> "People have been known to achieve more as a result of working with others than against them."
>
> —DR. ALLAN FROMME

always thought, *Why take the journey alone when you can invite others along with you?*

I understand that not everyone operates that way. But whether or not you are naturally inclined to be part of a team is really irrelevant. If you do everything alone and never partner with other people, you create huge barriers to your own potential. Dr. Allan Fromme quipped, "People have been known to achieve more as a result of working with others than against them." What an understatement! It takes a team to do anything of lasting value. Besides, even the most introverted person in the world can learn to enjoy the benefits of being on a team. (That's true even if someone isn't trying to accomplish something great.)

A few years ago my friend Chuck Swindoll wrote a piece in *The Finishing Touch* that sums up the importance of teamwork. He said,

Nobody is a whole team . . . We need each other. You need someone and someone needs you. Isolated islands we're not. To make this thing called life work, we gotta lean and support. And relate and respond. And give and take. And confess and forgive. And reach out and embrace and rely . . . Since none of us is a whole, independent, self-sufficient, super-capable, all-powerful hotshot, let's quit acting like we are. Life's lonely enough without our playing that silly role. The game is over. Let's link up.

For the person trying to do everything alone, the game really is over. If you want to do something big, you must link up with others. *One is too small a number to achieve greatness.* That's the Law of Significance.

You Can See the Difference

When you look at the way people conduct their lives, you can tell fairly quickly who recognizes and embraces the truth of the Law of Significance. That is certainly true of Lilly Tartikoff. I don't know whether Lilly always knew the value of teamwork, but I suspect she learned it early since she was once a professional ballet dancer. If dancers don't work together, then their performances never reach the caliber of Lilly's. Beginning at age seven, she spent ten hours a day, six days a week, practicing or performing ballet. As a result she became a member of the New York City Ballet Company and performed with them from 1971 to 1980.

At a tennis party in Los Angeles in 1980, Lilly met Brandon Tartikoff, the newly named president of entertainment for NBC. At that time he was the youngest network president in history at age thirty. They soon became friends. Then they began to see each other romantically. In 1982, they were married. And that started a whole new life for Lilly. She went from a nontelevision watcher to the spouse of a network executive immersed in the L.A. culture of the entertainment industry. But that adjustment was nothing compared to the other challenge she faced that year. For the second time in his life, Brandon was diagnosed with Hodgkin's disease.

Amazing Science

On the advice of a physician friend, Brandon went to see a young oncological researcher at UCLA named Denny Slamon. In August 1982, Dr. Slamon started Brandon on two kinds of treatment, one of which was experimental. Brandon would usually be treated on a

Friday, and afterward Lilly would drive him home and take care of him while he suffered from horrible side effects all weekend. They followed that pattern for a year, and all the while Brandon continued in his role of network president. It was a difficult time for them, but they chose to face the cancer as a team, and in time Brandon recovered.

Out of that ordeal came many things. For one, Brandon's network, NBC, went from worst to first in the ratings. In his autobiography he wrote, "Cancer helps you see things more clearly. The disease, I've found, can actually *help* you do your job, and there's a very simple reason why: There's nothing like cancer to keep you focused on what's important."[1] That focus enabled him to air some of the most popular and groundbreaking shows in television's history: *The Cosby Show, Cheers, Hill Street Blues, Miami Vice, The Golden Girls, The A-Team, St. Elsewhere,* and others.

For Lilly, though, there was a different outcome. Once Hodgkin's disease had been driven from her husband's body, she didn't simply move on.

"Brandon was at the receiving end of some pretty amazing science," she observed. The medical research that had extended Brandon's life intrigued her. So when she had an opportunity to help others benefit from that same science, she couldn't say no. That occurred in 1989 when Dr. Dennis Slamon, the UCLA scientist who had treated Brandon seven years before, asked Lilly for her help.

NOBODY CAN DO IT ALONE

For years Dr. Slamon had been studying breast cancer. He believed he was on the verge of developing a radical new treatment that would not only be more effective in treating the disease than anything previously developed, but he could do it without all the usual side effects of chemotherapy. He had the expertise and skill necessary to do the work, but he couldn't do it alone. He needed someone to help with funding. He thought of Lilly. She was only too happy to agree to assist him.

The plan she developed showed keen insight into teamwork and strategic partnerships. Lilly had once worked as a beauty adviser for Max Factor, formerly connected to Revlon. She sought to get Ronald Perelman, the CEO of Revlon, together with Dr. Slamon. At first that wasn't easy, but once Perelman realized the potential of Slamon's research, he pledged $2.4 million to the scientist's work with no restrictions. It was a partnership unlike anything that had been done before. What resulted was the creation of the Revlon/UCLA Women's Cancer Research Program—and a successful new treatment for cancer was soon saving women's lives.

A Taste of Teamwork

For Lilly, cofounding the research program was just a beginning. She had gotten a taste of what teamwork could do, and she was hungry to do much more. She quickly realized that she could enlist others to her cause. She would build a larger team, and she would use her show business connections to do it. That same year she established an annual Fire and Ice Ball in Hollywood to raise money. A few years later, she enlarged her circle and partnered with the Entertainment Industry Foundation (EIF) and created the Revlon Run/Walk, first in Los Angeles, and then in New York. So far, those events have raised more than $18 million for cancer research. And in 1996, she helped create the National Women's Cancer Research Alliance.

In 1997, her husband Brandon's cancer recurred a third time, and it took his life. He was only forty-eight years old. Despite the personal setback, Lilly continues to build teams to fight cancer. When she met Katie Couric, who had lost her husband to colon cancer, Lilly was again inspired to action. With the help of Couric and the EIF, she formed the National Colorectal Cancer Research Alliance in 2000.

"When I sat down with Katie," said Lilly, "to hear that, with an early diagnosis, you could turn the cancer around, and literally, it's 90 percent curable and preventable. Well, this was like putting a steak in front of a hungry dog . . . I thought, we've got to do this. So I brought in all my partners: the Entertainment Industry Foundation and Dr. Slamon . . . and Dr. Slamon brought together an agenda and a mission . . . So we created the NCCRA [National Colorectal Cancer Research Alliance]. You have no idea how exciting and gratifying it is."[2]

An individual cannot do the incredible, significant task that Lilly Tartikoff and her partners are trying to accomplish. No single person can take on cancer. But that's true of anything worth doing. If it's significant, it takes a team. That's something Lilly realized, put into practice, and now lives by every day. *One is too small a number to achieve greatness.* That is the Law of Significance.

TEAMWORK THOUGHT

You may be good—but you're not *that* good!

BECOMING A BETTER TEAM MEMBER

What major goals are you working toward achieving right now? Write some of them here:

1. _____

2. _____

3. _____

Now, reflect on how you are working toward these goals. What approach have you been taking to achieve them? Are you going it alone? Or are you building a team to accomplish them?

If you're not trying to be part of a team, figure out why. Is it a matter of ego? Are you insecure? Have you misjudged the size of the challenges? Or does your temperament incline you to work alone? If you answer yes to one of these questions, work to overcome the difficulty immediately. The sooner you become a team player, the sooner you will be able to achieve your dreams.

BECOMING A BETTER TEAM LEADER

Think about the greatest dream you have for your life. Now ask yourself,

- "Is it bigger than I am?"

- "Does it benefit others as well as myself?"

- "Is it worth dedicating part of my life to?"

If you answer yes to all of these questions, then think about what kinds of people should join you to achieve that dream. Make a list of the like-minded people you know who might want to join you in the process. Then invite them to take the journey with you. And be on the lookout for others who would benefit from being part of the team.

THE LAW OF THE BIG PICTURE

The Goal Is More Important Than the Role

Years ago, I was invited to participate in an important conference that was being planned by a highly respected national organization. I was one of about a dozen speakers who had been selected to speak to an audience of more than sixty thousand people drawn from all parts of the country. It was for a worthy cause that I valued, and I considered the invitation to be an honor.

Several weeks before the conference was to occur, all the speakers were scheduled to meet together along with the founder of the organization to talk strategy, discuss the topics about which we would speak, and give one another support and suggestions. I was really excited about it because the group included some extraordinary leaders. It promised to be an electric time, but the reality of the meeting turned out to be different from what I expected.

When we all got into a room together, it didn't feel like a strategy-and-support session. As we discussed the upcoming day, a few of the speakers seemed to be jockeying for position. Because they were good communicators, they understood that the speaking order, the time of day, and the amount of time allotted would make a big difference in how their messages would be received. The role each speaker was to play seemed to be of more interest than the goal of the conference.

But I also noticed something else. When one speaker briefly informed us about his topic, I sensed immediately that his speech would be the real hinge pin of the whole conference. All of the other messages would be subordinate to it. Yet the man was not fighting for the best place. He wasn't jockeying. He didn't seem to want any part of that kind of maneuvering.

In that moment when everyone was focusing on himself, I realized that we had lost sight of the big picture of why we were there. So I said to the group about this speaker, "I believe his message will be the difference maker in the lives of the people attending this conference. And I think the audience will receive it better if it's delivered when I am slated to speak. Please," I said to the person who wasn't trying to promote himself, "take my spot."

It was almost as if somebody had struck each person in the room. Suddenly everybody regained perspective. After that, instead of looking out for themselves and protecting turf, all of the speakers were willing to give everything for the common good. We all remembered that the goal was more important than our individual roles. That is the essence of the Law of the Big Picture.

WHAT'S IN IT FOR ME?

In a culture that sings the praises of individual gold medals and where a person fights for rights instead of focusing on taking responsibility, people tend to lose sight of the big picture. In fact, some people seem to believe that they *are* the entire picture: Everything revolves around their needs, their goals, and their desires. I saw a message on a T-shirt that expresses the attitude well: "My idea of a team is a whole lot of people doing what I tell them to do."

A team isn't supposed to be a bunch of people being used as a tool by one individual for selfish gain. Members of a team must have mutually beneficial shared goals. They must be motivated to work together, not manipulated by someone for individual glory. Anyone who is accustomed to pulling together people and using them to benefit only himself isn't a team builder; he's a dictator.

> *If you think you are the entire picture, you will never see the big picture.*

If you want to observe team dynamics in action, look at the world of sports where you can easily see whether people are working together. The outcome of a game is immediate and measurable. For that reason it's easy to see when an individual is thinking only of himself and not the shared goals and values of the team.

To win in sports, members of the team must always keep the big picture in front of them. They must remember that the goal is more important than their role—or any individual glory they may desire. NBA superstar David Robinson remarked, "I think any player will tell you that individual accomplishments help your ego, but if you don't win, it makes for a very, very long season. It counts more that the team has played well."

It's All About the Team

The acclaimed football coach of Oklahoma during the 1950s, Bud Wilkinson, put it this way in *The Book of Football Wisdom:* "If a team is to reach its potential, each player must be willing to subordinate his personal goals to the good of the team."

> *"If a team is to reach its potential, each player must be willing to subordinate his personal goals to the good of the team."*
>
> —BUD WILKINSON

Some sports teams seem to embrace an "everyone-for-himself" mind-set. Others weave the attitude of subordination and teamwork into the fabric of everything they do. For example, football teams such as Notre Dame and Penn State don't put the names of the players on their jerseys. Lou Holtz, former coach of the Fighting Irish, once explained why. He said, "At Notre Dame, we believed the interlocking ND was all the identification you needed. Whenever anyone complained, I told them they were lucky we allowed numbers on the uniforms. Given my druthers, I would have nothing more than initials indicating what position the wearer played. If your priority is the team rather than yourself, what else do you need?"

Winning teams have players who put the good of the team ahead of themselves. They want to play in their area of strength, but they're willing to do what it takes to take care of the team. They are willing to sacrifice their role for the greater goal. That's the Law of the Big Picture.

SEEING THE BIG PICTURE

People who build successful teams never forget that every person on a team has a role to play, and every role plays its part in contributing to the bigger picture. Without that perspective the team cannot accomplish its goal, whether the team's "game" is sports, business, family, ministry, or government.

Leaders at the highest level understand the Law of the Big Picture. They continually keep the vision of the big picture before themselves and their people. An outstanding example involves Winston Churchill. It's said that during World War II when Britain was experiencing its darkest days, the country had a difficult time keeping men working in the coal mines. Many wanted to give up their dirty, thankless jobs in the dangerous mines to join military service, which garnered much public praise and support. Yet their work in the mines was critical to the success of the war. Without coal the military and the people at home would be in trouble.

So the prime minister faced thousands of coal miners one day and told them of their importance to the war effort, how their role could make or break the goal of maintaining England's freedom.

Churchill painted a picture of what it would be like when the war ended, of the grand parade that would honor the people who fought the war. First would come the sailors of the navy, he said, the people who continued the tradition of Trafalgar and the defeat of the Spanish Armada. Next would come the best and brightest of Britain, the pilots of the Royal Air Force who fended off the German Luftwaffe. Following them would be the soldiers who had fought at Dunkirk.

Then last of all would come the coal-dust-covered men in miners' caps. And Churchill indicated that someone from the crowd might say, "And where were you during the critical days of the struggle?"

And the voices of ten thousand men would respond, "We were deep in the earth with our faces to the coal."

It's said that tears appeared in the eyes of those hardened men. And they returned to their inglorious work with steely resolve, having been reminded of the role they were playing in their country's noble goal of preserving freedom for the Western world.

> *"Everybody on a championship team doesn't get publicity, but everyone can say he's a champion."*
>
> —EARVIN "MAGIC" JOHNSON

That's the kind of mind-set it takes to build a team. It takes the courage and the resolve to recognize that *the goal is more important than the role*. It's no small thing for people to do what's best for the team. Often it means sacrificing professional satisfaction, individual statistics, or personal glory. But as NBA star-turned-successful-businessman Earvin "Magic" Johnson says, "Everybody on a championship team doesn't get publicity, but everyone can say he's a champion."

WHAT'S UP WITH BIG PICTURE TEAMS?

So how do people start to become a more unified team? How do individuals make the shift from independent people to team players who exemplify the Law of the Big Picture? It's not something that happens overnight. It takes time. Here is my best take on how to get the process started.

1. Look Up *at the Big Picture*

Everything starts with vision. You need to have a goal. Without one you cannot have a real team. Hall of Fame catcher Yogi Berra joked, "If you don't know where you're going, you'll end up somewhere else." An individual without a goal may end up anywhere. A group of individuals without a goal can go nowhere. On the other hand, if everyone in a group embraces the vision for achieving the big picture, then the people have the potential to become an effective team.

Leaders usually have the role of capturing and communicating vision. They must see it first and then help everyone else to see it. That was what Winston Churchill did when he spoke to the coal miners during the war. That was what Dr. Martin Luther King Jr. did as he spoke to people about his dream from the steps of the Lincoln Monument in Washington, D.C. That was what GE CEO Jack Welch did when he let his people know that a division of GE that couldn't be first or second in its market wouldn't be a part of GE. The people on a team will sacrifice and work together *only* if they can see what they're working toward.

If you are the leader of your team, your role is to do what only you can do: Paint the big picture for your people. Without the vision they will not find the desire to achieve the goal.

2. Size Up *the Situation*

One value of seeing the big picture is that it helps you recognize how far you really are from achieving it. For someone determined to do everything alone, seeing the gulf between what is and what could be is often intimidating. But for people who live to build teams, seeing the size of the task ahead doesn't worry them. They don't shrink from the challenge—they savor the opportunity. They can't wait to put together a team and a plan to accomplish that vision.

At a meeting of all three divisions of The INJOY Group, CEO Dave Sutherland stood before our people and outlined a few of our goals for the coming year. (Some of those goals were huge.) During that process, Dave said, "Some people see the size of the goal, and they get scared. That doesn't bother me a bit. We've already got a great team. To make it to the next level, we just need a few more people like the ones we already have." That's the mind-set of a team builder!

3. Line Up *Needed Resources*

Hawley R. Everhart believes, "It's all right to aim high if you have plenty of ammunition." That's what resources are: ammunition to help you reach a goal. It doesn't matter what kind of team you're on. You cannot make progress without the support of the appropriate equipment, facilities, funds, and so forth—whether your goal is climbing a mountain, capturing a market, or creating a ministry. The better resourced the team is, the fewer distractions the players will have as they try to achieve their goal.

4. Call Up *the Right Players*

When it comes to building a successful team, the players are everything. You can have a distinct vision, a precise plan, plenty of resources, and incredible leadership, but if you don't have the right people, you're not going to get anywhere. (I'll talk more about this in several of the other laws.) You can lose with good players, but you cannot win with bad ones.

5. Give Up *Personal Agendas*

Teams that win have players who continually ask themselves, "What's best for the rest?" They continually set aside their personal agendas for the good of the team. Their motto can be expressed by the words of Ray Kroc, founder of McDonald's, who said, "No one of us is more important than the rest of us."

A remarkable sports story from several years ago was the success of the U.S. Women's Soccer Team. They won the Olympic gold medal and the World Cup in a few brief years. A key player on that team was Mia Hamm. In her book *Go for the Goal,* she gives her perspective on her sport and the attitude a player must bring into the game to achieve the goal of becoming a champion:

> *"No one of us is more important than the rest of us."*
>
> —RAY KROC

> Soccer is not an individual sport. I don't score all the goals, and the ones I do score are usually the product of a team effort. I don't keep the ball out of the back of the net on the other end of the field. I don't plan our game tactics. I don't wash our training gear (okay, sometimes I do), and I don't make our airline reservations. I am a member of a team, and I rely on the team. I defer to it and sacrifice for it, because the team, not the individual, is the ultimate champion.

Mia Hamm understands the Law of the Big Picture. And by doing whatever it took to help her team—including washing the gear—she demonstrated that the goal was more important than the role.

6. Step Up *to a Higher Level*

Only when players come together and give up their own agendas can a team move up to a higher level. That's the kind of sacrifice required for teamwork. Unfortunately some people prefer to cling to agendas and pursue the paths of their own inflated egos instead of letting go of them to achieve something greater than themselves.

It's just as philosopher Friedrich Nietzsche said: "Many are stubborn in pursuit of the path they have chosen, few in pursuit of the goal." And that's a shame because people who think only of themselves are missing the big picture. As a result their potential goes untapped, and the people who are depending on them are bound to be let down.

SUBORDINATE ROLE FOR THE TEAM'S SUCCESS

President Abraham Lincoln once remarked, "Nearly all men can stand adversity, but if you want to test a man's character, give him power." Few people have more power than an American president. Being the so-called leader of the free world can certainly go to a person's head. But not to Jimmy Carter's. If you review his career— from the time he was a school board official to his term in the White House and beyond—you can see that he was willing to take on nearly any role to achieve a goal he believed in. He has always embraced the importance of the big picture.

There is possibly no more vivid example of the Law of the Big Picture in Carter's life than his work with Habitat for Humanity. Habitat was officially founded by Millard and Linda Fuller in 1976, though the two had been exploring the idea for many years before that, first in the U.S. and then overseas. The goal of the organization is a huge one—to eliminate poverty-level housing and homelessness from the world.

In the late seventies and early eighties, they began their bold venture. After six years they had built houses internationally in Mexico, Zaire, and Guatemala. And in the U.S., they had affiliates building houses in San Antonio, Texas; Americus, Georgia; Johns Island, South Carolina; and other locations in Florida and Appalachia. Groundwork was being laid for them to build in many other cities, but the process was a struggle. They had found a successful formula for their goal: Offer home ownership to the neediest people able to make a house payment, build low-cost housing using volunteer labor, involve the future home owner in the building process, and create no-interest loans to finance the houses. It was an inspired idea, and it was catching on. To reach the world as they desired, however, the Fullers knew they would have to take Habitat to a whole new level.

From their headquarters in the town of Americus in southern Georgia, the Fullers saw a possibility. Ten miles away in the tiny town of Plains was a man who might be able to help them: Jimmy Carter. The former U.S. president had spoken at a couple of Habitat functions. Following Carter's speaking in 1983, Millard Fuller got the idea to approach Carter about helping the project along. And in early 1984 they made contact. When Carter said he was very interested in Habitat for Humanity, Fuller decided to boldly propose a list of fifteen possible roles the former president could take, hoping he would agree to one or two. His list included serving on Habitat's board, making media contacts, helping to raise money, doing a thirty-minute video, and working on a building crew for a day.

To Fuller's surprise, Carter did not agree to do one or two items on the list. He agreed to do *everything* on it. Ironically the task that captured the attention of the public most was Carter's willingness to serve on a building crew and swing a hammer to help construct a house. At first people thought Carter would just stop by for brief publicity photos. But the former president put together a work crew, traveled with them via Trailways bus to the Brooklyn, New York, building site, worked tenaciously every day for a week, and slept in a church basement along with everyone else. That first time was in 1984. Carter has raised a team and served in similar fashion every year since then. And his dedicated service has attracted people from every walk of life to serve in similar roles.[1]

A Shared Goal

Habitat for Humanity is the brainchild of the Fullers, and its success is the result of the efforts of hundreds of thousands of people from around the globe. But Jimmy Carter is the one who put it on the map. His selfless service inspired people rich and poor, famous and obscure, powerful and not so powerful to see the huge goal of helping people at the lowest level of society by providing them with a decent place to live. And he inspired them to get involved.

So far Habitat and its volunteers have built more than 100,000 houses sheltering more than a half million people all over the world.[2] Why? Because they, like Carter, wanted to be part of something bigger than themselves. They understood that the goal was more important than the role. They embraced the truth of the Law of the Big Picture.

Teamwork Thought

When you see the big picture correctly,
you serve the team more quickly.

Becoming a Better Team Member

What goal in your life is bigger than you are? Are you currently participating in something greater than yourself? If not, set aside some time to spend alone reflecting on your goals and priorities. If you are trying to accomplish something big, then ask yourself what you are willing to do to accomplish it. Are you willing to take a subordinate role if necessary for the good of the team, as President Carter did? If not, you may become a hindrance to the success of the team.

BECOMING A BETTER TEAM LEADER

Think about a team you are currently part of (preferably one with a big goal). What kind of attitude do team members have when it comes to the big picture? Are they team players who desire to do whatever it takes for the team to succeed? Or do they desire to benefit only themselves?

Begin to foster a team mind-set in others by modeling a willingness to serve the big picture rather than yourself. Then think about ways you can help your teammates to embrace the Law of the Big Picture. Motivate people by painting the big picture. Publicly honor team play. And give rewards to people who sacrifice for the good of the team.

THE LAW OF THE NICHE

All Players Have a Place Where They Add the Most Value

On January 26, 2001, the United States experienced a historic first: An African-American assumed the post of secretary of state, the highest cabinet post in the United States government. The man who took that position was Colin Powell. Columnist Carl Rowan remarked of the appointment, "To understand the significance of Powell's elevation to this extremely difficult and demanding post, you must realize that only a generation ago it was an unwritten rule that in the foreign affairs field, blacks could serve only as ambassador to Liberia and minister to the Canary Islands."

Powell's appointment was remarkable, but not just because it was groundbreaking. It was significant because, to put it simply, Colin Powell was the best individual in all of the United States to take on the role of secretary of state. George W. Bush, the president who appointed him, stated, "In this cause, I know of no better person to be the face and voice of American diplomacy than Colin Powell," citing his "directness of speech, his towering integrity, his deep respect for our democracy, and his soldier's sense of duty."[1] Bush recognizes that *all players have a place where they add the most value.* Powell's is running the State Department. That's the Law of the Niche.

A PLACE FOR HIM

A soldier's sense of duty has been a vital part of the character of Colin Powell since he was in his early twenties. Something of a late bloomer, Powell entered college uncertain of what he wanted to do with his life. But it didn't take him long to find his identity: in an ROTC unit called the Pershing Rifles at the City College of New York. It was there that he discovered real teamwork for the first time in his life. In *My American Journey*, Powell wrote:

> My experience in high school, on basketball and track teams, and briefly in Boy Scouting had never produced a sense of belonging or many permanent friendships. The Pershing Rifles did. For the first time in my life I was a member of a brotherhood . . . The discipline, the structure, the camaraderie, the sense of belonging were what I craved. I became a leader almost immediately. I found a selflessness among the ranks that reminded me of the caring atmosphere within my family. Race, color, background, income meant nothing. The PRs [Pershing Rifles] would go the limit for each other and for the group. If this was what soldiering was all about, then maybe I wanted to be a soldier.[2]

As he got closer to graduation from college, there was no doubt in his mind. He gladly chose military life.

No Ordinary Journey

In the army Powell seemed to achieve success everywhere he went and quickly rose in rank. His love was commanding troops, and when he received those assignments, he did well. Yet he was constantly tapped for special jobs and responsibilities. When that happened again and again, keeping him from leading soldiers in the field, he became frustrated. But a mentor, General John Wickham, wisely told him, "You're not going to have a conventional army career. Some officers are just not destined for it."

Wickham was right. Powell's career did turn out to be unusual. And it ultimately prepared him for a cabinet post, sharpening his gifts and giving him broad experience. As an infantry officer who did tours around the globe (including two in Vietnam), Powell learned command and leadership. His work with soldiers also taught him to communicate and connect with people. As a White House Fellow, he got his first exposure to American politics and world governments. Besides his interaction with high-level U.S. officials, he met with leaders of Japan, the Soviet Union, China, Poland, Bulgaria, and West Germany.

Powell moved to a whole new level in his post at the Pentagon during the Carter and Reagan administrations. It was there that he learned how to work with civil servants and he expanded his understanding of government and military politics. As the senior military assistant to Secretary of Defense Caspar Weinberger, Powell traveled the world and attained in-depth comprehension of the complex relationships between the United States and foreign powers.

But in the office of the national security adviser, Powell stepped into the big leagues. As the deputy assistant to the president for national security affairs, he gained valuable experience in foreign policy. In fact, he was so adept that when his boss, Frank Carlucci, was asked to be secretary of defense, Powell stepped into Carlucci's former position as national security adviser. There he not only advised President Reagan, but Powell worked side by side with Secretary of State George Shultz as the statesman negotiated nuclear missile treaties with the USSR, organized summits between heads of state, and worked with Soviet President Mikhail Gorbachev to end the cold war.

COMMAND PERFORMANCE

How does someone like Colin Powell top off a successful term as the nation's first African-American national security adviser? By achieving the military's highest rank of four stars, and then by becoming the youngest chairman of the Joint Chiefs of Staff in the history of the nation. (He was also that position's first African-American and first ROTC graduate.) And once again, Powell shone in his position. Les Aspin, former secretary of defense, commented about Powell following a meeting in the Clinton White House, "It was so clear to all of us that he could do any job in the room, up to and including president."[3]

When President-elect Bush approached him about becoming a cabinet member, there was only one logical place for him to serve, the place where he would add the most. At a town hall meeting on January 25, 2001, Powell remarked,

I didn't know I would be coming back into government when I left the Army seven years ago and went into private life . . . But when Governor Bush asked me to consider it, I was ready for it. I was anxious to see if I could serve again. I think I have something to contribute still. And when he specifically said, I would like you to go to the State Department, it was almost as if I had been preparing for this in one way or another for many, many years. My work in the Pentagon, my work as a Deputy National Security Adviser, National Security Adviser, Chairman of the Joint Chiefs of Staff, and seven years in private life watching the world change, suggested to me this is something I should do.[4]

President Bush, his cabinet, and everyone in the country have a lot to gain from Powell. Not only is he the best person for the job, but he has given the newly elected president and his team greater credibility with a constituency inclined not to trust them. Powell's appointment is tangible proof of Bush's claim to inclusiveness. But that's the power of the Law of the Niche. When the right team member is in the right place, everyone benefits.

Good things happen to a team when a player takes the place where he adds the most value. Great things happen when all the players on the team take the role that maximizes their strengths—their talent, skill, and experience. That's the power of the Law of the Niche.

WHEN PEOPLE ARE IN THE WRONG PLACE

Just about everyone has experienced being on some kind of team where people had to take on roles that didn't suit them: an accountant forced to work with people all day, a basketball forward forced to play center, a guitarist filling in on keyboard, a teacher stuck doing paperwork, a spouse who hates the kitchen taking on the role of cook.

What happens to a team when one or more of its members constantly play out of position? First, morale erodes because the team isn't playing up to its capability. Then people become resentful. The people working in an area of weakness resent that their best is untapped. And other people on the team who know that they could better fill a mismatched position on the team resent that their skills are being overlooked. Before long, people become unwilling to work as a team. Then everyone's confidence begins to erode. And the situation just keeps getting worse. The team stops progressing, and the competition takes advantage of the team's obvious weaknesses. As a result the team never realizes its potential. When people aren't where they do things well, things don't turn out well. That's the Law of the Niche.

Having the right people in the right places is essential to team building. A team's dynamic changes according to the placement of people:

The Wrong Person in the Wrong Place	=	Regression
The Wrong Person in the Right Place	=	Frustration
The Right Person in the Wrong Place	=	Confusion
The Right Person in the Right Place	=	Progression
The Right People in the Right Places	=	Multiplication

It doesn't matter what kind of team you're dealing with, the principles are the same. David Ogilvy was right when he said, "A well-run restaurant is like a winning baseball team. It makes the most of every crew member's talent and takes advantage of every split-second opportunity to speed up service."

I was reminded of the Law of the Niche by something I did a few years ago. I had been asked to write a chapter for a book called *Destiny and Deliverance,* which was tied to the DreamWorks movie *The Prince of Egypt.* It was a wonderful, delightful experience. During the writing process, I was invited to go to California and view parts of the movie while it was still in production. That made me want to do something I had never done before: attend a movie premiere in Hollywood.

My publisher managed to get me a pair of tickets for the premiere, and when the time arrived, my wife, Margaret, and I flew out to the movie capital. Movie stars and moviemakers, along with many other people in the industry, attended the high-energy event. Margaret and I enjoyed the movie—and the whole experience—immensely. In short, we had a blast.

Now, anybody who's gone to a movie, show, or sporting event with me knows my pattern. As soon as I am pretty certain about the outcome of a ball game, I hit the exit to beat the crowds. When the Broadway audience is giving the ovation, I'm gone. And the second the credits begin to roll in a movie, I'm out of my seat. As *The Prince of Egypt* came to a close, I started to get up, but not a person in the theater moved. And then something really surprising happened. As the credits rolled, people began to applaud the lesser-known individuals whose names appeared on the screen: the costume designer, the gaffer, the key grip, the assistant director. It was a moment I'll never forget—and a distinct reminder of the Law of the Niche: *All players have a place where they add the most value.* When each person does the job that's best for him, everybody wins.

PUT PEOPLE IN THEIR PLACE

NFL champion coach Vince Lombardi observed, "The achievements of an organization are the results of the combined effort of each individual." That is true, but creating a winning team doesn't come just from having the right individuals. You may have a group of talented individuals, but if each person is not doing what adds the most value to the team, you won't achieve your potential as a team. That's the art of leading a team. You've got to put people in their places—and I mean that in the most positive way!

To be able to put people in the places that utilize their talents and maximize the team's potential, you need three things:

You Must Know the Team

You cannot build a winning team or organization if you don't know its vision, purpose, culture, or history. If you don't know where the team is trying to go—and why it's trying to get there—you cannot take the team to the height of its potential. You've got to start where the team actually is; only then can you take it somewhere.

You Must Know the Situation

Even though the vision or purpose of an organization may be fairly constant, its situation changes constantly. Good team builders know where the team is and what the situation requires. For example, when a team is young and just getting started, the greatest priority is often to gather good people. But as a team matures and the level of talent increases, fine-tuning becomes more important. At that time a leader must spend more time matching the person to the position.

You Must Know the Player

It sounds obvious, but you must know the person you are trying to position in the right niche. I mention it because leaders tend to want to make everyone else conform to their image, to approach their work using the same skills and problem-solving methods. But team building is not working on an assembly line.

As you work to build a team, evaluate each person's experience, skills, temperament, attitude, passion, people skills, discipline, emotional strength, and potential. Only then will you be ready to help a team member find his proper place.

START BY FINDING THE RIGHT PLACE FOR YOU

Right now you may not be in a position to place others on your team. In fact, you may be thinking, *How do I find my niche?* If that's the case, then follow these guidelines:

- *Be secure.* My friend Wayne Schmidt says, "No amount of personal competency compensates for personal insecurity." If you allow your insecurities to get the better of you, you'll be inflexible and reluctant to change. And to grow, you must be willing to change.

- *Get to know yourself.* You won't be able to find your niche if you don't know your strengths and weaknesses. Spend time reflecting on and exploring your gifts. Ask others to give you feedback. Do what it takes to remove personal blind spots.

- *Trust your leader.* A good leader will help you start moving in the right direction. If you don't trust your leader, look to another mentor for help. Or get on another team.

- *See the big picture.* Your place on the team makes sense only in the context of the big picture. If your only motivation for finding your niche is personal gain, your poor motives may prevent you from discovering what you desire.

- *Rely on your experience.* When it comes down to it, the only way to know that you've discovered your niche is to try what seems right and learn from your failures and successes. When you discover what you were made for, your heart sings. It says, *There's no place like this place anywhere near this place, so this must be the place!*

> *When you discover your place, you will say, "There's no place like this place anywhere near this place, so this must be the place!"*

A PLACE FOR EVERYONE AND EVERYONE IN HIS PLACE

One organization that strives to match its people to the right places is the U.S. military. That is particularly true now that it employs an all-volunteer force. If each function in a military command doesn't work at top efficiency (and interact well with all the other parts), then terrible—and sometimes deadly—breakdowns occur.

Nobody is more keenly aware of that than a combat pilot. Take, for example, Charlie Plumb, who retired as a captain of the U.S. Navy. A graduate of Annapolis, he served in Vietnam in the mid-1960s, flying seventy-five missions from the aircraft carrier USS *Kitty Hawk.*

An aircraft carrier is a place where you can readily observe how all the pieces of the military puzzle come together to support each other. A carrier is often described as being like a floating city with its crew of 5,500 people, a population greater than that of some towns in which its crew members grew up. It must be self-sustaining, and each of its seventeen departments must function as a team accomplishing its mission.

Every pilot knows of the team effort required to put a jet in the air. It takes hundreds of people utilizing dozens of technical specialties to launch, monitor, support, land, and maintain an aircraft. Even more people are involved if that plane is armed for combat. Charlie Plumb undoubtedly recognized that many people worked tirelessly to keep him flying. But despite the efforts of the best-trained air support group in the world, Plumb found himself in a North Vietnamese prison as a POW after his F-4 Phantom jet was shot down on May 19, 1967, during his seventy-fifth mission.

Plumb was held prisoner for nearly six grueling years, part of the time in the infamous Hanoi Hilton. During those years, he and his fellow prisoners were humiliated, starved, tortured, and forced to live in squalid conditions. Yet he didn't let the experience break him. He now says, "Our unity through our faith in God and in our love for country were the great strength which kept us going through some very difficult times."

TURNING POINT

Plumb was released from his imprisonment on February 18, 1973, and continued his career in the navy. But an incident years after his return to the United States marked his life as surely as his imprisonment. One day he and his wife, Cathy, were eating in a restaurant when a man came to the table and said, "You're Plumb. You flew jet fighters in Vietnam."

"That's right," answered Plumb. "I did."

"It was fighter squadron 114 on the *Kitty Hawk*. You were shot down. You parachuted into enemy hands," the man continued. "You spent six years as a prisoner of war."

The former pilot was taken aback. He looked at the man, trying to identify him, but couldn't. "How in the world did you know that?" Plumb finally asked.

"I packed your parachute."

Plumb was staggered. All he could do was struggle to his feet and shake the man's hand. "I must tell you," Plumb finally said, "I've said a lot of prayers of thanks for your nimble fingers, but I didn't realize I'd have the opportunity of saying thanks in person."[5]

What if the navy had put the wrong person in the position of parachute rigger, the anonymous and the rarely thanked job that man performed during the Vietnam War? Charlie Plumb wouldn't have known about it until it was too late. And we wouldn't even know where the breakdown had occurred because Plumb wouldn't have lived to tell the tale.

Today, Charlie Plumb is a motivational speaker to Fortune 500 companies, government agencies, and other organizations. He often tells the story of the man who packed his parachute, and he uses it to deliver a message on teamwork. He says, "In a world where downsizing forces us to do more with less, we must empower the team. 'Packing others' parachutes' can mean the difference in survival. Yours and your team's!"[6]

That's just another way of communicating the Law of the Niche. Are you packing parachutes for your teammates? Or are you functioning at less than 100 percent? *All players have a place where they add the most value.* I want to encourage you to make sure you've found yours.

TEAMWORK THOUGHT

You are most valuable where you add the most value.

BECOMING A BETTER TEAM MEMBER

Have you found your niche? As you fulfill your responsibilities, do you find yourself thinking something like, *There's no place like this place anywhere near this place, so this must be the place*? If so, then stay the course and keep growing and learning in your area of expertise. If not, you need to get on track.

If you know what your niche is but aren't working in it, start planning a transition. It could be as simple as a change in duties or as complex as a change of career. No matter whether it will require six weeks or six years, you need a transition plan and a timetable for completing it. Once you're certain of your course, have the courage to take the first step.

If you have no idea what you should be doing, you need to do some research. Talk to your spouse and close friends about your strengths and weaknesses. Ask for your leader's assessment. Take personality or temperament tests. Look for recurring themes in your life. Try to articulate your life purpose. Do whatever it takes to find clues concerning where you should be. Then try new things related to your discoveries. The only way to find your niche is to gain experience.

BECOMING A BETTER TEAM LEADER

A sign of a great team leader is the proper placement of people. Use the guidelines in the chapter—know your team, the situation, and the players—to begin improving your placement process. And remember this: To help people reach their potential and maximize their effectiveness, stretch them out of their comfort zones, but never out of their gift zones. Moving people outside their gifts leads to frustration, but motivating people out of their comfort zones leads to fulfillment.

> *A sign of a great team leader is the proper placement of people.*

```
┌─────────┐
│         │
│    4    │
│         │
└─────────┘
```

THE LAW OF MOUNT EVEREST

As the Challenge Escalates, the Need for Teamwork Elevates

I n 1935, twenty-one-year-old Tenzing Norgay made his first trip to Mount Everest. He worked as a porter for a British team of mountaineers. A Sherpa born in the high altitudes of Nepal, Tenzing had been drawn to the mountain from the time that Westerners began visiting the area with the idea of climbing to the mountain's peak. The first group had come in 1920. Fifteen years later, climbers were still trying to figure out how to conquer the mountain.

The farthest this expedition would go was up to the North Col, which was at an altitude of 22,000 feet. (A col is a flat area along a mountain's ridge between peaks.) And it was just below that col that the climbing party made a gruesome discovery. They came across a wind-shredded tent. And in that tent was a skeleton with a little frozen skin stretched over the bones. It was sitting in an odd position, with one boot off and the laces of the other boot between its bony fingers.

HARSHEST PLACE ON THE PLANET

Mountain climbing is not for the faint of heart because the world's highest peaks are some of the most inhospitable places on earth. Of course, that hasn't stopped people from attempting to conquer mountains. In 1786, the first climbers made it to the summit of Europe's highest mountain, Mont Blanc in France. That was quite a feat. But there's a big difference between climbing the highest of the Alps at 15,771 feet and climbing Everest, the world's highest peak at 29,035 feet, especially in the days before high-tech equipment. Everest is remote, the altitude incapacitates all but the hardiest and most experienced climbers, and the weather is ruthlessly unforgiving. Experts believe that the bodies of 120 failed climbers remain on the mountain today.[1]

The body Tenzing and the others found in 1935 was that of Maurice Wilson, an Englishman who had sneaked into Tibet and tried to climb the mountain secretly, without the permission of the Tibetan government. Because he was trying to make the ascent quietly, he had hired only three porters to climb the mountain with him. As they approached the North Col, those men had refused to go any farther with him. Wilson decided to try to make the climb on his own. That decision killed him.

MEASURE THE COST

Only someone who has climbed a formidable mountain knows what it takes to make it to the top. For thirty-two years, between 1920 and 1952, seven major expeditions tried—and failed—to make it to the top of Everest. Tenzing Norgay was on six of those expeditions, as well as many other high climbs to other mountains. His fellow climbers joked that he had a third lung because of his ability to climb tirelessly while carrying heavy loads. He became respected, and he learned a lot. The greatest lesson was that no one should underestimate the difficulty of the climb. He had seen people do it at the ultimate cost to themselves.

On one climb, for example, when conditions became difficult, Tenzing and the other Sherpas put on their crampons (spikes that attach to climbing boots). But George Frey, an experienced mountaineer, decided not to wear his because he thought he didn't need them. He slipped and fell one thousand feet to his death below. Tenzing regretted the man's death, but his view was realistic. He wrote of careless climbers, "Like so many men before them—they had held a great mountain too lightly, and they had paid the price."[2]

NOT A CASUAL STROLL

In 1953, Tenzing embarked on his seventh expedition to Everest with a British group led by Colonel John Hunt. By then, he was respected not only as a porter who could carry heavy loads at high altitudes, but also as a mountaineer and full-fledged expedition member, an honor unusual at that time for a Sherpa. The year before he had climbed to a height of 28,250 feet with a Swiss team. Up to then, that was the closest any human being had come to the top of the mountain.

Tenzing was also engaged to be the British group's sirdar for the trip, the Sherpa leader who would hire, organize, and lead the porters for the journey. That was no small task. To hope to get just two people from base camp up to the summit, the team brought ten high-altitude climbers, including a New Zealander named Edmund Hillary. Altogether, the men would require two and a half *tons* of equipment and food. Those supplies couldn't be trucked or air-lifted to the base of the mountain. They had to be delivered to Kathmandu and *carried* on the backs of men and women 180 miles up and down Himalayan ridges and over rivers crossed by narrow rope-and-plank bridges to the base camp. Tenzing would have to hire between two and three hundred people just to get the supplies in the vicinity of the mountain.

Supplies needed by the party above the base camp would have to be carried up the mountain by another forty porters, each a Sherpa with extensive mountain experience. The best third of that team would continue working higher up the mountain, carrying up the 750 pounds of necessary equipment in 30-pound loads. Only Tenzing and three other porters would have the strength and skill to go to the high camps near the summit.

IT TAKES A TEAM

For each level that the climbers reached, a higher degree of team-work was required. One set of men would exhaust themselves just to get equipment up the mountain for the next group. Two-man teams would work their way up the mountain, finding a path, cutting steps, securing ropes. And then they would be finished, having spent themselves to make the next leg of the climb possible for another team. Of the teamwork involved, Tenzing remarked,

> You do not climb a mountain like Everest by trying to race ahead on your own, or by competing with your comrades. You do it slowly

and carefully, by unselfish teamwork. Certainly I wanted to reach the top myself; it was the thing I had dreamed of all my life. But if the lot fell to someone else I would take it like a man, and not a cry-baby. For that is the mountain way.[3]

The team of climbers, using the "mountain way," ultimately made it possible for two pairs to make an attempt at reaching the summit. The first consisted of Tom Bourdillon and Charles Evans. When they tried and failed, the other team got its chance. That team consisted of Tenzing and Edmund Hillary. Tenzing wrote of the first team:

> They were worn-out, sick with exhaustion, and, of course, terribly disappointed that they had not reached the summit themselves. But still . . . they did everything they could to advise and help us. And I thought, Yes, that is how it is on a mountain. That is how a mountain makes men great. For where would Hillary and I have been without the others? Without the climbers who had made the route and the Sherpas who had carried the loads? Without Bourdillon and Evans, Hunt and Da Namgyal, who had cleared the way ahead? Without Lowe and Gregory, Ang Hyima, Ang Tempra, and Penba, who were there only to help us? It was only because of the work and sacrifice of all of them that we were now to have our chance at the top.[4]

They made the most of their chance. On May 29, 1953, Tenzing Norgay and Edmund Hillary accomplished what no other human being ever had: They stood on the summit of Mount Everest, the world's highest peak!

Could Tenzing and Hillary have made it alone? The answer is

no. Could they have made it without a great team? Again, the answer is no. Why? Because *as the challenge escalates, the need for teamwork elevates.* That's the Law of Mount Everest.

WHAT IS YOUR EVEREST?

You may not be a mountain climber, and you may not have any desire to reach the summit of Everest. But I bet you have a dream. I say that with confidence because deep down everybody has one— even the people who haven't figured out what theirs is yet. If you have a dream, you need a team to accomplish it.

How do you approach the task of putting together a team to accomplish your dream? I think the best way to start is to ask yourself three questions:

1. *"What Is My Dream?"*

It all starts with this question because your answer reveals *what could be.* Robert Greenleaf remarked, "Nothing much happens without a dream. For something really great to happen, it takes a really great dream."

What lies in your heart? What do you see as a possibility for your life? What would you like to accomplish during your time on this earth? Only a dream will tell you such things. As Harlem Renaissance poet Langston Hughes wrote:

> Hold fast to dreams for if dreams die,
> Life is a broken-winged bird that cannot fly.
> Hold fast to dreams for when dreams go,
> Life is a barren field frozen with snow.

If you want to do something great, you must have a dream. But a dream is not enough. You can fulfill a dream only if you are part of a team.

2. "Who Is on My Team?"

This second question tells you *what is*. It measures your current situation. Your potential is only as good as your current team. That's why you must examine who is joining you on your journey. A mountain climber like Maurice Wilson, who had only three halfhearted companions, was never able to accomplish his dream of climbing the mountain. However, someone like Tenzing Norgay, who always climbed Everest with the best mountaineers in the world, was able to make it to the top. A great dream with a bad team is nothing more than a nightmare.

3. "What Should My Dream Team Look Like?"

The truth is that your team must be the size of your dream. If it's not, then you won't achieve it. You simply cannot achieve an ultimate number ten dream with a number four team. It just doesn't happen. If you want to climb Mount Everest, you need a Mount Everest–sized team. There's no other way to do it. It's better to have a great team with a weak dream than a great dream with a weak team.

> *Your team must be the size of your dream.*

FOCUS ON THE TEAM, NOT THE DREAM

One mistake I've seen people repeatedly make is that they focus too much attention on their dream and too little on their team. But the truth is that if you build the right team, the dream will almost take care of itself.

Every dream brings challenges of its own. The kind of challenge determines the kind of team you need to build. Consider a few examples:

> *Many people focus too much attention on their dream and too little on their team.*

Type of Challenge	Type of Team Required
New Challenge	Creative Team
Controversial Challenge	United Team
Changing Challenge	Fast and Flexible Team
Unpleasant Challenge	Motivated Team
Diversified Challenge	Complementary Team
Long-term Challenge	Determined Team
Everest-sized Challenge	Experienced Team

If you want to achieve your dream—I mean really do it, not just imagine what it would be like—then grow your team. But as you do so, make sure your motives are right. Some people gather a team just to benefit themselves. Others do it because they enjoy the team experience and want to create a sense of community. Still others do it because they want to build an organization. The funny thing about these reasons is that if you're motivated by *all* of them, then your desire to build a team probably comes from wanting to add value to everyone on the team. But if your desire to build the team comes as the result of only one of these reasons, you probably need to examine your motives.

How to Grow a Team

When the team you have doesn't match up to the team of your dreams, then you have only two choices: Give up your dream, or grow up your team. Here is my recommendation concerning how to do the latter.

> *When the team you have doesn't match up to the team of your dreams, then you have only two choices: Give up your dream, or grow up your team.*

1. Develop Team Members

The first step to take with a team that's not realizing its potential is to help individual team members to grow. If you're leading the team, then one of your most important responsibilities is to see the potential that people don't see in themselves and draw it out. When you accomplish this, you're doing your job as a leader.

Think about the people on your team, and determine what they need based on the following categories:

- Enthusiastic beginner—needs direction

- Disillusioned learner—needs coaching

- Cautious completer—needs support

- Self-reliant achiever—needs responsibility

Always give the people who are already on your team a chance to grow and bloom. That's what early British explorer Eric Shipton did with a young, inexperienced kid named Tenzing in 1935, and his country was rewarded eighteen years later with a successful climb of the world's highest peak.

2. Add Key Team Members

Even if you give every person on your team a chance to learn and grow, and all of them make the most of the opportunities, you may find that you still lack the talent needed to accomplish your dream. That's when it's time to recruit that talent. Sometimes all the team needs is one key person with talent in an area to make the difference between success and failure. (I'll talk more about this in the Law of the Bench.)

3. Change the Leadership

Various team challenges require different kinds of leadership. If a team has the right talent but still isn't growing, sometimes the best thing you can do is to ask someone from the team who has previously been a follower to step into a leadership role. That transition may occur only for a short season, or it may be more permanent.

> *The challenge of the moment often determines the leader for that challenge.*

The challenge of the moment often determines the leader for that challenge. Why? Because every person on the team has strengths and weaknesses that come into play. That was the case for the Everest team as they faced every stage of the journey. Colonel Hunt chose the climbers and led the expedition, casting vision, modeling unselfish service, and making critical decisions about who would take which part. Tenzing chose the porters, leading, organizing, and motivating them to build the camps at each stage of the mountain. And the climbing teams took turns leading, cutting the trail up the mountain so that Hillary and Tenzing could make the final climb to the summit. When a particular challenge emerged, so did a leader to meet it. And everyone worked together, doing his part.

If your team is facing a big challenge, and it doesn't seem to be making any progress "up the mountain," then it might be time to change leaders. There may be someone on the team more capable for leading during this season. (Learn more by reading the myths of the head table and the round table in the Law of the Edge.)

4. Remove Ineffective Members

Sometimes a team member can turn a winning team into a losing one, either through lack of skill or a poor attitude. In those cases you must put the team first and make changes for the greater good.

Tenzing faced that situation during the Everest expedition of 1953. During early days of travel, there were continual flare-ups between the porters and the British team of climbers, and as sirdar, Tenzing was constantly stuck in the middle trying to work things out. After repeatedly negotiating the peace between the two parties, Tenzing discovered that the source of the problem was two Sherpas who were stirring up dissension. He promptly fired them and sent them home. Peace was quickly restored. If your team keeps breaking down or falling short, you may need to make changes in your team.

Growing a team is demanding and time-consuming. But if you want to achieve your dream, you have no other choice. The greater the dream, the greater the team. *As the challenge escalates, the need for teamwork elevates.* That is the Law of Mount Everest.

NOT EVERY CHALLENGE IS A DREAM

The challenges that our teams face are not always ones we select. Sometimes they are thrust upon us, and we have no choice but to do the best we can with the team we have, or give up and suffer the consequences. That was certainly the case for the crew and support team for Apollo 13.

If you saw the movie *Apollo 13* starring Tom Hanks (or remember some of the coverage on television during the actual flight as I do), then you know the basic story. On April 13, 1970, at 10:07 P.M. EST, an oxygen tank in the service module of the *Odyssey* spacecraft exploded, causing the ship to lose its oxygen supply and all normal power. In addition, the ship's main engine was rendered nonfunctional. Since the ship was 200,000 miles away from earth and on a course that would put it into a permanent orbit around the moon, it was a potentially disastrous—and possibly fatal—challenge.

The astronauts in the *Odyssey*, James Lovell, John Swigart Jr., and Fred Haise, would not be able to make it back to earth on their own. Their survival depended on teamwork at a level that the space program had never experienced—and it was used to having people work together like a well-oiled machine.

TEAMWORK AT A NEW LEVEL

The flight control team on the ground immediately instructed the command crew to shut down the ailing command capsule and move into the lunar module (LM) *Aquarius* for their safety. That put the crew out of harm's way for the moment. But they still faced two major challenges:

1. Getting the command module, *Odyssey*, and the lunar module, *Aquarius*, on the quickest course home.

2. Conserving the "consumables" that kept the astronauts alive: power, oxygen, and water.

Accomplishing both would severely test everyone's abilities and know-how.

During a typical Apollo mission, Houston's mission control employed four teams of controllers, each designated by a color: white, black, gold, and maroon. Each team had technicians responsible for various specific areas required to keep the ship on course. The usual procedure was for each team to take a six-hour shift under the guidance of one of three flight directors. But with the lives of three astronauts on the line, every member of every team jumped in to help. And one team was pulled from the usual rotation by Gene Kranz, the lead flight director, and dubbed the Tiger Team. Those fifteen men worked as a crisis management team.

As Kranz gathered them together, he told them,

> For the rest of the mission, I'm pulling you men off console. The people out in that room [the other teams] will be running the flight from moment to moment, but it's the people in this room who will be coming up with the protocols they're going to be executing . . . For the next few days we're going to be coming up with techniques and maneuvers we've never tried before. I want to make sure we know what we're doing.[5]

In addition, NASA promptly sent word out to contractor representatives, such as the people at Grumman Aerospace, who had built the lunar module. (And when word got out that there was trouble with Apollo 13, virtually *everyone* in the organization showed up at the facility in the middle of the night to pitch in.) They also pulled in every top specialist and experienced astronaut they had, quickly building a coast-to-coast network of simulators, computers, and experts. NASA records state:

Astronauts Alan Shepard and Ed Mitchell operated one of the LM simulators at the Manned Spacecraft Center in Houston, and Gene Cernan and David Scott worked in the other. At Cape Kennedy, Astronaut Dick Gordon simulated emergency procedures in a third LM. One team of simulator specialists worked around the clock without a break. No procedure, no maneuver instruction, no checklist was relayed to the crew that hadn't been thoroughly proved out.[6]

As Easy As One, Two, Three

The team's first task was to figure out how to get the lunar module, which had been designed to support two men for 49.5 hours, to sustain three men for 84 hours. They did that by determining how to get the ship to run using the bare minimum number of systems, which would use less than one-fourth of its normal power.

Next, they had to get the spacecraft on a course that would return it to earth. That was no simple task since they would have to use the lunar module's tiny engine, and the guidance systems were off-line. But between the efforts of the crew, the expertise of the lunar module's manufacturer, and the calculations of Tiger Team, they were able to do it. And they also boosted the craft's speed to shorten the flight time. That would preserve precious water and energy.

The third major challenge the team faced was making the air that the crew was breathing safe. Oxygen was not a problem because the small lunar module was well supplied. But carbon dioxide was building up to dangerous levels because the small craft intended to land on the moon had not been designed to remove so much of it.

The crew on the ground worked out a clever way to adapt the lithium hydroxide filters from the command module so that they would work with the lunar module's noncompatible system.

Each time NASA's massive team faced an obstacle that threatened to leave the crew stranded in space, their pooled ingenuity, inherent tenacity, and incredible cooperation enabled them to overcome it. As a result, on April 17, 1970, the crew of the *Odyssey* made it safely home. NASA likes to call the mission a "successful failure." I call it a lesson in the Law of Mount Everest. *As the challenge escalates, the need for teamwork elevates.*

Putting men on the moon is an incredible challenge. But getting them home when things go wrong 200,000 miles away from earth is an even greater one. Fortunately for those men, the dream team was already in place when they got in trouble. And that is one of the lessons of Apollo 13. The time to build your team is not in the midst of a life-or-death challenge, but long before one can happen. If you haven't already, start building today so that when a formidable challenge occurs, you and your team will be ready.

TEAMWORK THOUGHT

The size of your dream should determine the size of your team.

BECOMING A BETTER TEAM MEMBER

What is your natural first reaction when a challenge becomes more difficult? Do you go off alone to think? Do you try to solve the problem alone? Do you stay away from other people to avoid the pressure? Or do you lean on your teammates and let them lean on you?

If you don't already do it, teach yourself to rally with your teammates. You cannot win a great challenge alone. As Tenzing asserted, "On a great mountain, you do not leave your companions and go to the top alone."[7]

BECOMING A BETTER TEAM LEADER

What kinds of adjustments do you need to make to create your dream team, one that can meet the challenges ahead? Do you need to spend more time developing your people? Do you need to add key team members? Or should you make changes to the leadership? And don't forget that you, too, need to keep growing. What's true for a teammate is also true for the leader: If you don't grow, you gotta go.

THE LAW OF THE CHAIN

The Strength of the Team Is Impacted by Its Weakest Link

O n March 24, 1989, the news broke that an environmental disaster had occurred in Alaska's Prince William Sound. The oil tanker *Exxon Valdez* had run aground on the Bligh Reef, damaging the hull of the ship and rupturing eight of the vessel's eleven cargo tanks. As a result, 10.8 million of the ship's approximately 53 million gallons of oil poured out of the ship and into the sea.

The negative impact on the area was immense. Fishing and tourism came to a halt, harming the local economy. The environment suffered. Experts estimate wildlife losses at 250,000 seabirds, 2,800 sea otters, 300 harbor seals, 250 bald eagles, 22 killer whales, and billions of eggs for food-fish species such as salmon and herring. Though it wasn't the largest oil spill on record, experts consider it to be the worst spill in history in terms of the damage done to the environment.[1]

Of course, Exxon, the company that owns the ship, also paid a price. The company's representatives estimate that the incident cost Exxon $3.5 *billion:*

- $2.2 billion in cleanup costs

- $300 million in claims paid

- $1 billion in state and federal settlements[2]

But that's not all. In addition to what Exxon has already paid, the company stands to lose an additional $5 billion in punitive damages, a judgment it is still attempting to reverse through the appellate process more than a decade after the incident. What was the cause of such an expensive and far-reaching accident? The answer can be found in the Law of the Chain.

THE BROKEN CHAIN

When the *Exxon Valdez* cast off from the Alyeska Pipeline Terminal on the evening of March 23, the voyage began routinely. An expert ship's pilot guided the vessel through the Valdez Narrows and then returned control of the ship to its captain, Joe Hazelwood. The captain ordered that the ship be put on a particular course, turned control over to Third Mate Gregory Cousins, and left the bridge. Thirty-five minutes later, the *Exxon Valdez* was stranded on a reef and leaking tons of oil into the sea.

Investigation following the accident painted an ugly picture: neglect of safety standards, indifference to company policy, and unwise decision making. The ship's captain had been drinking in the hours before he took command of the ship. One officer, rather than the required two, remained in the wheelhouse as the tanker navigated the Valdez Narrows and again after the pilot left the ship. (And that officer, Cousins, had been so overworked that fatigue is thought to have contributed to the navigation error that followed.) Nor was a lookout always present on the bridge while the vessel was under way.

There were also discrepancies between what Captain Hazelwood told the Vessel Traffic Center he was doing and the orders he actually gave on the ship. At 11:30 P.M., the captain radioed that he would take a course of 200 degrees and reduce speed to wind his way through the icebergs that sometimes float in the shipping lanes. Yet the engine logs showed that the ship's speed kept increasing. Nine minutes after that, the captain ordered that the ship take a course of 180 degrees and be put on autopilot, but he never informed the traffic center of the change. Then at 11:53, he left the bridge.

At four minutes after midnight, the ship was on the reef. For almost two hours, first Cousins and then Hazelwood tried to get the ship free, all the while leaking oil into the sea. In the first three hours, it's estimated that 5.8 million gallons poured from the distressed tanker. By then, the damage was done, and the weak link had caused the "chain" to break. Alaska's coastline was a mess, Hazelwood's career as a ship's captain was over, and Exxon was stuck with a public relations nightmare—and massive financial obligations.

As much as any team likes to measure itself by its best people, the truth is that *the strength of the team is impacted by its weakest link.* No matter how much people try to rationalize it, compensate for it, or hide it, a weak link will eventually come to light. That's the Law of the Chain.

Your Team Is Not for Everyone

One of the mistakes I often made early in my career as a team leader was that I thought everyone who was on my team should remain on the team. That was true for several reasons. First, I naturally see the best in people. When I look at individuals with potential, I see all that they can become—even if they don't see it. And I try to encourage and equip them to become better. Second, I truly like people. I figure the more who take the trip, the bigger the party. Third, because I have vision and believe my goals are worthwhile and beneficial, I sometimes naively assume that everyone will want to go along with me.

But just because I wanted to take everyone with me didn't mean that it would always work out that way. My first memorable experience with this occurred in 1980 when I was offered an executive position at Wesleyan World Headquarters in Marion, Indiana. When I accepted the position, I invited my assistant to come with me to be a part of the new team I was building. So she and her husband considered my offer and went to Marion to look around. I'll never forget when they came back. As I excitedly talked about the coming challenges and how we could begin to tackle them, I began to realize from the expressions on their faces that something was wrong. And that's when they told me. They weren't going.

That statement took me completely by surprise. In fact, I was sure that they were making a mistake and told them so, doing my best to convince them to change their minds. But my wife, Margaret, gave me some very good advice. She said, "John, your problem is that you want to take everybody with you. But not everyone is going to go on the journey. Let it go." It was a hard lesson for me to learn—and sometimes it still is.

From that experience and others I've had since then, I've discovered that when it comes to teamwork . . .

1. Not Everyone Will Take the Journey

Some people don't want to go. My assistant and her husband wanted to stay in Lancaster, Ohio, where they had built relationships for many years. For other people the issue is their attitude. They don't want to change, grow, or conquer new territory. They hold fast to the status quo. All you can do with people in this group is kindly thank them for their past contributions and move on.

2. Not Everyone Should Take the Journey

Other people shouldn't join a team because it's a matter of their agenda. They have other plans, and where you're going isn't the right place for them. The best thing you can do for people in this category is wish them well, and as far as you are able, help them on their way so that they achieve success in their venture.

3. Not Everyone Can Take the Journey

For the third group of people, the issue is ability. They may not be capable of keeping pace with their teammates or helping the group get where it wants to go. How do you recognize people who fall into this category? They're not very hard to identify.

- They can't keep pace with other team members.
- They don't grow in their area of responsibility.
- They don't see the big picture.
- They won't work on personal weaknesses.
- They won't work with the rest of the team.
- They can't fulfill expectations for their area.

If you have people who display one or more of those characteristics, then you need to acknowledge that they are weak links.

That's not to say that they are necessarily bad people. In fact, some teams exist to serve weak links or help them become stronger. It depends on the team's goals. For example, when I was a senior pastor, we reached out to people in the community with food and assistance. We helped people with addictions, divorce recovery, and many other difficulties. Our goal was to serve them. It's good and appropriate to help people who find themselves in those circumstances. But putting them on the team while they are still broken and weak doesn't help them, and it hurts the team—even to the extent of making the team incapable of accomplishing its goal of service.

What can you do with people on your team who are weak links? You really have only two choices: You need to train them or trade them. Of course, your first priority should always be to try to train people who are having a hard time keeping up. Help can come in many forms: giving people books to read, sending them to conferences, presenting them with new challenges, pairing them with mentors. I believe that people often rise to your level of expectations. Give them hope and training, and they usually improve.

But what should you do if a team member continually fails to meet expectations, even after receiving training, encouragement, and opportunities to grow? My father used to have a saying: "Water seeks its own level." Somebody who is a weak link on your team might be capable of becoming a star on another team. You need to give that person an opportunity to find his level somewhere else.

THE IMPACT OF A WEAK LINK

If you are a team leader, you cannot avoid dealing with weak links. Team members who don't carry their own weight slow down the team, and they have a negative effect on your leadership. Several things may happen when a weak link remains on the team:

1. The Stronger Members Identify the Weak One

A weak link cannot hide (except in a group of weak people). If you have strong people on your team, they always know who isn't performing up to the level of everyone else.

2. The Stronger Members Have to Help the Weak One

If your people must work together as a team to do their work, then they have only two choices when it comes to a weak teammate. They can ignore the person and allow the team to suffer, or they can help him and make the team more successful. If they are team players, they will help.

3. The Stronger Members Come to Resent the Weak One

Whether strong team members help or not, the result will always be the same: resentment. No one likes to lose or fall behind consistently because of the same person.

4. The Stronger Members Become Less Effective

Carrying someone else's load in addition to your own compromises your performance. Do that for a long time, and the whole team suffers.

5. The Stronger Members Question the Leader's Ability

Anytime the leader allows a weak link to remain a part of the team, the team members forced to compensate for the weak person begin to doubt the leader's courage and discernment. You lose the respect of the best when you don't deal properly with the worst.

Many team members may be able to avoid the hard decision of dealing with subpar members, but leaders can't. In fact, one of the differences between leaders and followers is action. Followers often know what to do, but they are unwilling or unable to follow through. But know this: If

> *You lose the respect of the best when you don't deal properly with the worst.*

other people on the team make decisions for you because you are unwilling or unable to make them, then your leadership is being compromised, and you're not serving the team well.

STRENGTHENING THE CHAIN

Weak team members always take more of the team's time than strong ones. One reason is that the more competent people have to give their time to compensate for those who don't carry their share of the load. The greater the difference in competence between the more accomplished performers and the less accomplished ones, the greater the detriment to the team. For example, if you rate people on a scale from 1 to 10 (with 10 being the best), a 5 among 10s really hurts the team where an 8 among 10s often does not.

Let me show you how this works. When you first put together a group of people, their talents come together in a way that is analogous to addition. So visually a 5 among 10s looks like this:

$$10 + 10 + 10 + 10 + 5 = 45$$

The difference between this team and great ones with five 10s is like the difference between 50 and 45. That's a difference of 10 percent. But once a team comes together and starts to develop chemistry, synergy, and momentum, it's analogous to multiplication. That's when a weak link really starts to hurt the team. It's the difference between this:

$$10 \times 10 \times 10 \times 10 \times 10 = 100,000$$

and this:

$$10 \times 10 \times 10 \times 10 \times 5 = 50,000$$

That's a difference of 50 percent! The power and momentum of the team may be able to compensate for a weak link for a while, but not forever. A weak link eventually robs the team of momentum—and potential.

Ironically, weak links are less aware than stronger members of their weaknesses and shortcomings. They also spend more time guarding their turf, saving their positions, and holding on to what they have. And know this: When it comes to interaction between people, the weaker person usually controls the relationship. For example, someone with a good self-image is more flexible than a person with a poor self-image. An individual with a clear vision acts more readily than someone without one. A person with superb ability and high energy accomplishes more and works longer than an individual with lesser gifts. If the two people journey together, the stronger member must constantly work with and wait on the weaker one. That controls what happens on the journey.

If your team has a weak link who can't or won't rise to the level of the team—and you've done everything you can to help the person improve—then you've got to take action. When you do, heed the advice of authors Danny Cox and John Hoover. If you need to remove somebody from the team, be discreet, be clear, be honest, and be brief. Then once the person is gone, be open about it with the rest of the team while maintaining respect for the person you let go.[3] And if you start to have second thoughts before or afterward, remember this: As long as a weak link is part of the team, everyone else on the team will suffer.

No Weak Links!

Nobody particularly wants to have a weak link on a team, someone who causes the team to fail at its objectives. Yet we've all had to work with weaker team members. And sometimes good experiences have come out of it. There is rich personal reward to be reaped by helping a teammate go from being a weak link to a solid team member—and sometimes even to becoming a star player. But for good or bad, dealing with subpar performers is an inevitable part of being on any team, right? There's no such thing as a team that has no weak links, is there?

As I already mentioned, the goal of the team often determines how well it can work with a weak link. Sometimes the stakes for a team are so high that its members cannot afford to have a weak link. And that is the case for the U.S. Navy SEALs. The jobs they do are so demanding that a weak person on the team will get everyone on the team killed.

In recent years the SEALs have generated a lot of popular interest. They've been the subject of numerous novels and movies. They've captured people's imaginations because they are considered the best of the best. As one former SEAL remarked, "No group of men is closer to perfection in their chosen field."

The SEALs were first commissioned by President John F. Kennedy in 1962. They evolved from the underwater demolition teams who were developed during World War II to clear the amphibious landing areas of obstacles in such locations as Omaha and Utah Beaches in Normandy and later on the islands of the Pacific. Like all the special operations forces in the various branches of the U.S. military, they are experts in weapons, hand-to-hand combat, and demolition, and they have trained to parachute from airplanes. But their expertise is in operations based on and in water. That's the origin of their name: SEALs indicates that they are capable of operating in the SEa, from the Air, and on Land.

FORGING THE CHAIN

The key to the success of the SEALs is their training—the real emphasis of which is not learning about weapons or gaining technical skills; it's about strengthening people and developing teamwork. Weapons change, and so do methods of conducting operations, but the intense mental and physical training has remained much the same for all the years that the SEALs have been in existence. Peter J. Schoomaker, commander in chief of U.S. Special Operations Command, says, "Everything but our core values are on the table; we have to be ready to change anything but those values to get the job done. The core value for a SEAL Team is the people."[4]

Having the right people on the team starts with the selection process. Only a certain kind of person will even apply to go through SEAL training. And of those who apply, only one in ten is accepted. (The navy recommends that candidates be running at least thirty miles a week and swimming long distances *before* they apply.) Those who do make it into the program then undergo twenty-six weeks of intense physical, psychological, and mental stress. The physical and emotional rigors of that training make marine boot camp look like a picnic. John Roat, who went through the training, was one of the first members of the newly formed SEAL teams in 1962. He said that more than 1,300 men tested to get into the training, but the program accepted only 134. The bar for physical training was so high that people began dropping out the first day. And he saw that as a good thing. He explained:

> There were still some 130 guys when the instructors broke us up into ten-man boat crews and gave us our boats . . . The men of each crew carried their boat on their heads, and until a crew got its ducks in a row, everyone in it suffered. There was no chance of a boat crew's learning how to work as a team until it got rid of the men who didn't belong in training. Until they were gone, they were just an added harassment factor. Sounds cold, but that's life.[5]

For the first five weeks, the training is torturous and the physical demands incredible. Then comes Hell Week, five days of constant physical and mental challenges where the trainees are kept awake and training for all but four or five hours during the entire week. It's the trial that eliminates remaining weak links and at the same time forges the class into a real team. Roat described the impact of that part of the training:

> Each training class still learns the same things during Hell Week: You can go farther than you ever thought possible, but you can't do it alone, and everyone left standing belongs there. Hell Week has changed less than any part of training, for one simple reason: The instructors cannot find a better way. You can't pick the ones who can

hack it by their looks. No written test will find out if a man is a Team player. If it was possible to get good operators by letting some shrink interview trainees and say yea or nay, the navy would love it. The big problem is, the psychologists can't predict who will survive five-plus days of no sleep, with constant harassment, and impossible physical demands with an easy way out. That's still the test.[6]

SEAL training is so intense that there have been classes from which *no one* completed the training. In the end, 49 of the 134 people who started training with Roat graduated. The hearts of those who made it through the stress and pain can be represented by the words of one of Roat's classmates: "I couldn't quit; I would have let my classmates down. I just couldn't do it."

Many people consider the Navy SEALs to be the elite among the already elite company of special operations forces in the U.S. military. Their interaction is the definition of teamwork, and they depend upon each other at a level that most people cannot understand and will never experience. Their survival depends on it. And for that reason, they cannot afford to have any weak links.

Although you may never have to face the pressures that SEALs do, you can be sure of this: *The strength of the team is impacted by its weakest link.* No matter what kind of team you're on, that's always true. That's the Law of the Chain.

TEAMWORK THOUGHT

The team cannot continually cover up its weakness.

BECOMING A BETTER TEAM MEMBER

Most people's natural inclination is to judge themselves according to their best qualities while they measure others by their worst. As a result, they point to areas where their teammates need to grow. But the truth is that every person is responsible for his own growth first.

Take a hard look at yourself. Using the criteria from the chapter, examine yourself to see where you may be hindering the team. Mark the box under the word *Self* for any issue that applies to you. And if you have real courage, ask your spouse or a close friend to evaluate you by marking the boxes listed under the word *Friend*.

Evaluated by		Possible Issues
Self	*Friend*	
❑	❑	*Have trouble keeping pace with other team members.*
❑	❑	*Am not growing in my area of responsibility.*
❑	❑	*Have a hard time seeing the big picture.*
❑	❑	*Have difficulty seeing my personal weakness.*
❑	❑	*Have a tough time working with the rest of the team.*
❑	❑	*Consistently fail to fulfill expectations in area of responsibility.*

If you (or the other person who evaluated you) checked more than one box, you need to put yourself on a growth plan so that you don't hinder your team. Talk to your team leader or a trusted mentor about ways you can grow in any weak area.

BECOMING A BETTER TEAM LEADER

If you're a team leader, you cannot ignore the issues created by a weak link. For the various kinds of teams, different solutions are appropriate. If the team is a family, then you don't simply "trade" weak people. You lovingly nurture them and try to help them grow, but you also try to minimize the damage they can cause to other family members. If the team is a business, then you have responsibilities to the owner or stockholders. If you've offered training without success, then a "trade" might be in order. If the team is a ministry and training has made no impact, then it might be appropriate to ask the weak people to sit on the sidelines for a while. Or they might need some time away from the team to work on emotional or spiritual issues.

No matter what kind of situation you face, remember that your responsibilities to people come in the following order: to the organization, to the team, and then to the individual. Your own interests—and comfort—come last.

6

THE LAW OF THE CATALYST

Winning Teams Have Players Who Make Things Happen

Most teams don't naturally get better on their own. Left alone, they don't grow, improve, and reach championship caliber. Instead, they tend to wind down. The road to the next level is always uphill, and if a team isn't intentionally fighting to move up, then it inevitably slides down. The team loses focus, gets out of rhythm, decreases in energy, breaks down in unity, and loses

> *Catalysts are get-it-done-and-then-some people.*

momentum. At some point, it also loses key players. And it's only a matter of time before it plateaus and ultimately declines into mediocrity. That's why a team that reaches its potential always possesses a catalyst.

THE DEFINITION OF A CATALYST

Catalysts are what I call get-it-done-and-then-some people. The most outstanding one I've ever had the privilege of seeing in action is Michael Jordan. In the opinion of many people (including me), he is the greatest basketball player ever to play the game, not only because of his talent, athleticism, and understanding of the game, but also because of his ability as a catalyst. His résumé as an amateur, and as a professional with the Chicago Bulls attests to that ability:

- Won NCAA Division I Championship (1982)

- Named the *Sporting News* College Player of the Year twice (1983, 1984)

- Received the Naismith and Wooden Awards (1984)

- Won 2 Olympic gold medals (1984, 1992)

- Won 6 NBA world championships (1991, 1992, 1993, 1996, 1997, 1998)

- Selected NBA Rookie of the Year (1985)

- Selected to the NBA All-Rookie Team (1985)

- Selected for All-NBA First Team a record 10 times (1987, 1988, 1989, 1990, 1991, 1992, 1993, 1996, 1997, 1998)

- Holds the NBA record for highest career scoring average (31.5 points per game)

- Holds the NBA record for most seasons leading the league in scoring (10)

- Holds the NBA record for most seasons leading the league in field goals made (10) and attempted (10)

- Ranks 3rd in NBA history in points (29,277), 3rd in steals (2,306), and 4th in field goals made (10,962)

- Voted NBA Defensive Player of the Year (1985; after being criticized that he was "only" an offensive player)

- Selected to the All-NBA Defensive First Team 8 times (1988, 1989, 1990, 1991, 1993, 1997, 1998)

- Named NBA MVP 5 times (1988, 1991, 1992, 1996, 1998)

- Named NBA Finals MVP 6 times (1991, 1992, 1993, 1996, 1997, 1998)

- Named 1 of the 50 greatest players in NBA history

Statistics make a strong statement about Jordan, but they really don't tell the whole story. For that, you had to see him in action. When the Bulls needed to get the team out of a slump, the ball went to Jordan. When a player needed to take the last shot to win the game, the ball went to Jordan. Even if the team needed to get things going in practice, the ball went to Jordan. No matter what the situation was on the court, Jordan was capable of putting the team in the position to win the game. That's always the case for championship teams. *Winning teams have players who make things happen.* That's the Law of the Catalyst.

STILL MAKING THINGS HAPPEN

As you know, Michael Jordan has retired from basketball as a player. But he is still in the game. In early 2000, Jordan became part owner and president of basketball operations of the Washington Wizards. Only a week after becoming part of the organization, Jordan put on a number 23 Wizards jersey and joined the team for a practice.

Wizards forward Tracy Murray, who guarded Jordan during some drills, remarked afterward, "He's definitely moving the same way . . . dunking the ball, shooting a jump shot, fade away. Still got the same game, hasn't gone anywhere."

Nobody expected his talent to be diminished, especially not just two years after his retirement. But his ability as a catalyst hadn't diminished either. Murray continued, "And as soon as he sets foot in that gym, he starts talking trash, so of course the intensity is going to pick up."

Every catalyst brings intensity to the table. One commentator remarked of Jordan's visit to the court, "By being himself, he turned a Wizards practice into something it hasn't been in a while—energetic and fun."

"Which is what we should expect every day," was Jordan's reaction. "Actually, I told them they shouldn't have to wait for me to come out to show the energy that they had today. I just tried to keep them focused, challenge them, say whatever I have to say. If they can play hard against me, they can play hard against anybody. It was fun."[1]

That's the way it always is for a catalyst. Having fun. He loves stirring up the team, making things happen, doing whatever it takes to push the team to the next level. When a catalyst does that consistently, the team becomes expectant, confident, elevated, and ultimately amazed. That's the Law of the Catalyst. *Winning teams have players who make things happen!*

THREE KINDS OF PLAYERS

When crunch time comes, a catalyst becomes critical, whether it's the salesperson who hits the impossible goal, the ballplayer who makes the big play, or the parent who gets a child to believe in himself at a critical moment in life. A team can't reach big goals or even break new ground if it doesn't have a catalyst.

My experience with teams has taught me that what is true for sports is also the case for business, ministry, and family relationships. When the clock is running down and the game is on the line, there are really only three kinds of people on a team:

1. People Who Don't Want the Ball

Some people don't have the ability to come through for the team in high-pressure situations, and they know it. As a result, they don't want the responsibility of carrying the team to victory. And it shouldn't be given to them. They should be allowed to play in their areas of strength.

2. People Who Want the Ball But Shouldn't

A second group contains people who can't carry the team to victory. The problem is that *they don't know* that they can't. Often the cause is that these players' egos are greater than their talent. These people can be dangerous to a team.

3. People Who Want the Ball and Should

The final group, which is by far the smallest, consists of people who want to be "go to" players at crunch time and who can actually deliver. They are able to push, pull, or carry the team to new levels when the going gets tough. They are the catalysts.

Every team needs catalysts if it wants to have any hope of winning consistently. Without them, even a team with loads of talent cannot go to the highest level. I saw an illustration of this in the late 1990s and again in 2000 with the Atlanta Braves. They had the best starting pitchers in baseball. They had strong hitters, Gold Glove fielders, and talent in the bull pen. They possessed team members who had been league MVP or rookie of the year. But they lacked the catalytic players they needed to become World Series champions.

CHARACTERISTICS OF A CATALYST

It's easy to point out a team's catalyst after he has made an impact on the group and spurred the members on to victory, especially in the world of sports. You can point to particular moments when the person went to a whole new level and took the team there at the same time. But how do you recognize a catalyst *before* the fact? How do you look for catalytic people for your current team?

No matter what kind of "game" you're playing or what kind of team you're on, you can be sure that catalysts have certain characteristics that make them different from their teammates. I've observed that these nine are often present in the catalysts with whom I've interacted. They are . . .

1. Intuitive

Catalysts sense things that others don't sense. They may recognize a weakness in an opponent. They may be able to make an intuitive leap that turns a disadvantage into an advantage. They are able to use whatever it is they sense to help the team succeed.

For different kinds of teams, the way the intuition plays out changes. That makes sense because the goal of the team determines what the team values. Another reason is that people are most intuitive in their areas of natural strength. So for a small business, the catalyst may be an entrepreneur who can smell an opportunity when no one else is aware of it. For a ministry or other nonprofit organization, the catalyst may be a person who intuitively recognizes leadership and can recruit talented volunteers. For a football team, it may be a quarterback who senses that a defense isn't adjusting well and calls the play that wins the game. In each case the situation is different, but the result is the same: A catalyst senses an opportunity, and as a result, the team benefits.

2. Communicative

Catalysts say things that other team members don't say in order to get the team moving. Sometimes they do it to share with their teammates what they have sensed intuitively so that they will be better prepared to meet the challenge. Other times their purpose is to inspire or incite other team members. And they usually know the difference between when a teammate needs a boost—and when he needs a boot.

Anytime you see a team of people suddenly turn around or crank their play up to another level, you'll see someone on the team talking, directing, inspiring others. You'll see it, too, with strong political leaders. People such as Churchill, Roosevelt, and Kennedy changed the world with their words. They were catalysts, and catalysts communicate.

3. Passionate

Catalysts feel things that others don't feel. They are passionate about what they do, and they want to share that love with their teammates. Sometimes the passion explodes as a controlled fury to achieve goals in their area of passion. Other times it manifests itself as a contagious enthusiasm. But however it comes out, it can inspire a team to success.

Legendary baseball player Pete Rose of the Cincinnati Reds has experienced his share of problems, but he was certainly one of the great catalysts of his sport in the twentieth century. He was once asked which goes first on a baseball player: his eyes, his legs, or his arm. Rose's response was telling. He said, "None of these things. It's when his enthusiasm goes that he's through as a player." And he's also through as a catalyst.

4. Talented

Catalysts are capable of doing what others cannot do because their talent is as strong as their passion. People rarely become catalysts outside an area of expertise and gifting. That's the case for two main reasons. First, talent knows what it takes to win. You can't take the team to the next level when you haven't mastered the skills it takes to succeed on a personal level. It just doesn't happen.

The second reason people must have talent in an area where they desire to be a catalyst is that part of being a catalyst is influencing other team members. You can't do that if you have no credibility with them because of your own poor performance. Part of being a catalyst is sharing your gift with others to make them better. You can't give what you don't have.

5. Creative

Another quality commonly found in catalysts is creativity. Catalysts think things that others do not think. While most team members may do things by rote (or by rut), catalysts think differently from their teammates. They are constantly looking for fresh, innovative ways to do things.

Business and sports team consultant Carl Mays asserts that "creativity involves taking what you have, where you are, and getting the most out of it." Sometimes what they come up with can change the tempo of a game. Other times their ability to rewrite the rules changes the whole way the game is actually played.

6. Initiating

I enjoy creative people, and I've worked with many through the years. In fact, I consider myself to be creative, especially in the areas of writing and teaching. But my experience with creative people has taught me something about them: While all creative people have more than enough ideas, not all of them are good at implementing those creative thoughts.

Catalysts don't have this problem. They do things that others cannot do. Not only are they creative in their thinking, but they are disciplined in their actions. They delight in making things happen. That initiative can take almost any form: a baseball manager arguing with an umpire to stir up his players, a parent changing jobs or moving the family to help a struggling child, or a business owner putting up financial incentives for employees to break through barriers. So they initiate. And as a result they move the team as they move themselves.

7. Responsible

Catalysts carry things that others do not carry. My friend Truett Cathy, the founder of Chick-Fil-A, has a saying: "If it's to be, it's up to me." That could very well be the motto for all catalysts.

Not long ago a commercial appeared on television that showed a pair of consultants giving a company's CEO advice on how he could take his business to the next level. They explained how the company's computer system should be overhauled, how the distribution system could be improved, and how marketing channels could be changed to make the company much more effective and profitable.

The CEO listened carefully to everything they had to say, and finally he smiled and said, "I like it. Okay, do it."

The consultants looked confused for a moment, and one of them stammered, "We don't actually *do* what we recommend."

Catalysts are not consultants. They don't recommend a course of action. They take responsibility for making it happen.

8. Generous

Catalysts give things that others don't give. A true mark of people's taking responsibility is their willingness to give of themselves to carry something through. Catalysts display that quality.

> *Catalysts are not consultants. They don't recommend a course of action. They take responsibility for making it happen.*

They are prepared to use their resources to better the team, whether that means giving time, spending money, or sacrificing personal gain.

A vivid example of someone giving of himself for the team can be found in the life of New York businessman Eugene Lang. On June 25, 1981, Lang stood before sixty-one graduating sixth graders in P.S. 121, the East Harlem elementary school from which he had graduated decades before. He knew that statistically, 75 percent of the children would probably drop out of school during the next six years and would never graduate from high school. And he wanted to try to do something to change that.

He began by encouraging them to work hard, telling them that if they did, success would follow. But then on the spur of the moment, Lang moved from consultant to catalyst. He promised those kids that if they would stick with it and graduate from high school, he would provide each of them with scholarship money for college. That promise was the start of what became the "I Have a Dream" program.

Four years later, all 61 students were still in school. Six years later, 90 percent of the 54 kids who remained in touch with Lang graduated from high school, and two-thirds of them went on to college. Today, I Have a Dream sponsors 160 projects in 57 cities, and it touches the lives of 10,000 kids—all because Lang decided to become a catalyst.[2]

9. Influential

Catalysts are able to lead teammates in a way that others cannot. Team members will follow a catalyst when they won't respond to anyone else. In the case of a highly talented team member who is not especially gifted in leadership, he may be an effective catalyst in an area of expertise. But people with natural leadership ability will have influence far beyond their own team.

Michael Jordan, once again, is a wonderful example. Obviously he had influence with his teammates in Chicago. But his influence stretched far beyond the Bulls. I got a taste of that firsthand at the NBA 2001 All-Star Game. I had the pleasure of speaking at the chapel for players and officials before the game, and later I got to spend time with the referees who had been picked to officiate. During my talks with them, I asked what player they respected the most in terms of his honesty. Their answer was Michael Jordan.

One ref then recounted that in a close game, Danny Ainge, whose team was playing against the Bulls, made a shot near the three-point line. The officials had given Ainge only two points for the basket since they were not sure whether he was outside the three-point line. During the timeout immediately after the shot, one of the refs asked Jordan whether his opponent's score had been a valid three-point shot. Jordan indicated that it was. They gave Ainge the three points. Jordan's integrity—and influence—caused them to reverse their call.

When you see many of those nine qualities in someone on your team, then take heart. When crunch time comes, he is likely to step up to a whole new level of performance and attempt to take the team there too.

My Own Go-to Guy

At my company, The INJOY Group, a number of team members are catalysts within the organization. But none are stronger than Dave Sutherland, the CEO.

Dave came on board in 1994 as the president of ISS, the division of The INJOY Group that helps churches with fund-raising through capital campaigns. Just prior to his coming on board, I had given serious thought to shutting down that arm of the organization. ISS wasn't supporting itself financially, it was draining time and re-sources from other more productive areas of the company, and it wasn't having the positive influence I had hoped for. But I believed that Dave Sutherland's leadership could make a difference. And soon after I hired him, I began seeing progress at ISS.

The second year that Dave was with me, the company had some pretty aggressive goals. That year the company's goal had been to partner with eighty churches, more than twice as many as it had the previous year. And each partnership could come only after a personal presentation to a church's board and their acceptance of our offer to help.

One day during the first week of December, I stopped by Dave's office and spoke to his wife, Roxine, who works with Dave as his assistant. I hadn't seen Dave in a while, and I asked where he was.

"He's on the road making a presentation," she said.

I thought that was a little odd because the company had several key people whose job it was to make the presentations to churches.

"On the road? When will he be back?" I asked.

"Well, let's see," said Roxine, "when he left the Monday after Thanksgiving, we still needed twenty-four more churches to reach our goal. Dave said he won't be home until we reach it."

And reach it he did. Dave was on the road until December 19. But that was no great surprise. My writer, Charlie Wetzel, told me that in a sales and marketing career that spans three decades, Dave has *never* missed a goal. Not once.

His tenacity and ability serve Dave well. But they also serve the team well. By reaching that goal, Dave made every person on the team a winner that year. And everyone in the company used the momentum he created to take ISS to a whole new level. A year later, ISS became the second largest company of its type in the world. And by the end of the year 2000, it had helped more than one thousand churches across America raise more than $1 billion.

When you have a Michael Jordan or a Eugene Lang or a Dave Sutherland, your team always has a chance to win. They are get-it-done-and-then-some people. Why is that important? Because *winning teams have players who make things happen*. Without them, a team will never reach its potential. That is the truth of the Law of the Catalyst.

TEAMWORK THOUGHT

Games are won by get-it-done-and-then-some people.

BECOMING A BETTER TEAM MEMBER

How are you when it comes to crunch time on your team? Do you want the ball, or would you rather it was in someone else's hands? If there are more talented and effective catalysts on your team, then you should not want to be the go-to player in a pinch. In those cases, the best thing you can do is get an "assist" by helping to put those people into position to benefit the team. But if you avoid the spotlight because you are afraid or because you haven't worked as hard as you should to improve yourself, then you need to change your mind-set.

Start to put yourself on the road to improvement by doing the following things:

1. *Find a mentor.* Players become catalysts only with the help of people better than themselves. Find someone who makes things happen to help you along the way.

2. *Begin a growth plan.* Put yourself on a program that will help you develop your skills and talents. You cannot take the team to a higher level if you haven't gotten there.

3. *Get out of your comfort zone.* You won't know what you're capable of until you try to go beyond what you've done before.

If you follow these three guidelines, you still may not become a catalyst, but you will at least become the best you can be—and that's all that anyone can ask of you.

BECOMING A BETTER TEAM LEADER

If you lead a team, you need catalysts to push the team to its potential. Use the list of qualities in the chapter to begin identifying and enlisting people who can get it done and then some. If you see that potential in some of your current teammates, encourage them to take initiative and become positive influencers on the team. If the people on the team can't or won't step up to that level of play, then start recruiting people from outside the team. No team can go to the highest level without a catalyst. *Winning teams have players who make things happen.*

THE LAW OF THE COMPASS

Vision Gives Team Members Direction and Confidence

F or nearly a hundred years, IBM has been a rock of American business standing firm in a stream of competition. Even during the Great Depression of the 1930s, while thousands of companies were disappearing, IBM kept growing. The source of its strength was business and technological innovation.

INTRODUCING TECHNOLOGY

For a half century, IBM continually broke ground in the area of computers, beginning in the 1940s with its Mark I. In the 1950s and 1960s, the firm introduced innovation after innovation. By 1971, IBM was receiving $8 billion in annual revenues and employed 270,000 people. When people thought of blue-chip companies, IBM is likely the first one they pictured.

But for all its history of advances, by the late 1980s and early 1990s, the company was struggling. For a decade IBM had been slow to react to technological changes. As a result, by 1991, it suffered $8 billion in *losses* every year. And even though IBM fought to regain ground technologically, consumers' favorable perceptions of the company were at an all-time low. Where IBM had once been seen as dominant, people looked upon it as hopelessly behind the times—a slow-moving dinosaur among new companies that moved like cheetahs. If something didn't change, IBM was going to be in big trouble.

Then in 1993, IBM got a new CEO, Lou Gerstner. He quickly began recruiting key members for his team, IBM's executive committee. Perhaps the most important addition was Abby Kohnstamm, whom he invited to be IBM's senior vice president of marketing.

INTRODUCING . . . A COMPASS

Kohnstamm was eager to get started. She believed the company's products were strong enough, but its marketing was weak. When she arrived at IBM, what she found was much worse than she had expected. Not only was IBM failing to reach customers effectively; when it came to the marketing department, employees weren't even sure who did what or why. For example, when Kohnstamm asked how many employees were in the marketing area, she couldn't get the same answer from any two employees. Greg Farrell of *USA Today* described the situation: "The company was a fragmented, decentralized organization with more than a dozen quasi-autonomous businesses, and 70 ad agency partners worldwide."[1]

Kohnstamm immediately dismissed all those agencies and hired one to replace it: Ogilvy & Mather Worldwide. Her desire was to give the entire IBM team a single unifying theme for the hardware, software, and services they had to offer. Before long, she had found it. The company adopted the concept of e-business. Kohnstamm asserts, "E-business is the single focal point for the company, and is the single largest marketing effort ever undertaken by IBM."[2]

The vision seems to be working. Steve Gardner, an ad agency owner who once promoted Compaq, says, "The most stunning thing about e-business was that it transformed IBM from perceived laggard to leader in the Internet space without any real change in its lines of products or services. That's an astonishing achievement."[3]

Where once IBM was struggling, it now has renewed direction and confidence. Bill Etherington, senior vice president and group executive over sales and distribution, notes that the marketing focus has had an incredibly positive effect on IBM's employees. And he should know. He's been with IBM for thirty-seven years. He says, "We all had enthusiasm for this wonderful campaign. It had an edge to it and portrayed the company in a much more modern light."[4] Maureen McGuire, vice president of marketing communications, agrees: "The campaign has galvanized employees. We're trying to get all those people to sing the same song, read from the same book." For a company that hadn't sung for a long time, that's a momentous achievement. And it just goes to show you, *vision gives team members direction and confidence*. That's the power of the Law of the Compass.

Don't Get Lost

Have you ever been part of a team that didn't seem to make any progress? Maybe the group had plenty of talent, resources, and opportunities, and team members got along, but the group just never *went* anywhere! If you have, there's a strong possibility that the situation was caused by lack of vision.

Great vision precedes great achievement. Every team needs a compelling vision to give it direction. A team without vision is, at worst, purposeless. At best, it is subject to the personal (and sometimes selfish) agendas of its various teammates. As the agendas work against each other, the team's energy and drive drain away. On the other hand, a team that embraces a vision becomes focused, energized, and confident. It knows where it's headed and why it's going there.

> *Great vision precedes great achievement.*

Field Marshal Bernard Montgomery, a leader of troops during World War II who was called a "soldier's general," wrote that "every single soldier must know, before he goes into battle, how the little battle he is to fight fits into the larger picture, and how the success of his fighting will influence the battle as a whole." People on the team need to know why they're fighting. Otherwise, the team gets into trouble.

THE LEADER'S RESPONSIBILITY

Field Marshal Montgomery was adept at connecting with the soldiers on his team and casting vision for their battles. That ability brought him and them success. He understood that leaders must be vision casters. Author Ezra Earl Jones points out,

> Leaders do not have to be the greatest visionaries themselves. The
> vision may come from anyone. The leaders do have to state the

vision, however. Leaders also have to keep the vision before the people and remind them of the progress that is being made to achieve the vision. Otherwise, the people might assume that they are failing and give up.

If you lead your team, then you are responsible for identifying a worthy and compelling vision and articulating it to your team members. However, even if you are not the leader, identifying a compelling vision is still important. If you don't know the team's vision, you can't perform with confidence. You can't be sure you and your teammates are going in the right direction. You can't even be sure that the team you're on is the right one for you if you haven't examined the vision in light of your strengths, convictions, and purpose. For everyone on the team, the vision needs to be compelling.

CHECK YOUR COMPASS!

How do you measure a vision? How do you know whether it is worthy and compelling? You check your compass. Every team needs one. In fact, every team needs several. A team should examine the following six "compasses" before embarking on any journey.

A team's vision must be aligned with:

1. A Moral Compass (Look Above)

Millionaire philanthropist Andrew Carnegie exclaimed, "A great business is seldom if ever built up, except on lines of strictest integrity." That holds true for any endeavor. There's only one true north. If your compass is pointing in any other direction, your team is headed the wrong way.

A moral compass brings integrity to the vision. It helps all the people on the team to check their motives and make sure that they are laboring for the right reasons. It also brings credibility to the leaders who cast the vision—but only if they model the values that the team is expected to embrace. When they do, they bring fuel to the vision, which keeps it going.

2. An Intuitive Compass (Look Within)

Where integrity brings fuel to the vision, passion brings fire. And the true fire of passion and conviction comes only from within.

In *The Leadership Challenge,* James Kouzes and Barry Posner explain that "visions spring forth from our intuition. If necessity is the mother of invention, intuition is the mother of vision. Experience feeds our intuition and enhances our insight." A vision must resonate deep within the leader of the team. Then it must resonate within the team members, who will be asked to work hard to bring it to fruition. But that's the value of intuitive passion. It brings the kind of heat that fires up the committed—and fries the uncommitted.

> *"A great business is seldom if ever built up, except on lines of strictest integrity."*
>
> —ANDREW CARNEGIE

3. A Historical Compass (Look Behind)

There's an old saying that I learned when I lived in rural Indiana: "Don't remove the fence before you know why it's there." You never know: There might be a bull on the other side! A compelling vision should build on the past, not diminish it. It should make positive use of anything contributed by previous teams in the organization.

Anytime you cast vision, you must create a connection between the past, the present, and the future. You must bring them together. People won't reach for the future until they have touched the past. When you include the history of the team, the people who have been in the organization a long time sense that they are valued (even if they are no longer the stars). At the same time, the newer people receive a sense of security, knowing that the current vision builds on the past and leads to the future.

> *People won't reach for the future until they have touched the past.*

What is the best way to do that? You tell stories. Principles may fade in people's minds, but stories stick. They bring relationships to the vision. Tell stories from the past that give a sense of history. Tell stories about the exciting things that are happening now among team members. And tell the story of what it will be like the day that the team fulfills the vision. Stories are like thumbtacks that help to keep a vision in front of people.

4. A Directional Compass (Look Ahead)

Poet Henry David Thoreau wrote, "If one advances confidently in the direction of his dreams, and endeavors to live the life which he has imagined, he will meet with a success unexpected in common hours." As I already mentioned, vision provides direction for the team. Part of that direction comes from a sense of purpose. Another comes from having goals, which bring targets to the vision.

A goal motivates the team. NFL referee Jim Tunney commented on this when he said, "Why do we call it a goal line? Because eleven people on the offensive team huddle for a single purpose—to move the ball across it. Everyone has a specific task to do—the quarterback, the wide receiver, each lineman, every player knows exactly what his assignment is. Even the defensive team has its goals too—to prevent the offensive team from achieving its goal."

5. A Strategic Compass (Look Around)

A goal won't do the team much good without steps to accomplish it. Vision without strategy is little more than a daydream. As Vince Abner remarked, "Vision isn't enough—it must be combined with venture. It is not enough to stare up the steps; we must step up the stairs."

The value of a strategy is that it brings process to the vision. It identifies resources and mobilizes the members of the team. People need more than information and inspiration. They need instruction in what to do to make the vision become reality and a way to get there. A strategy provides that.

6. A Visionary Compass (Look Beyond)

The vision of the team must look beyond current circumstances and any obvious shortcomings of current teammates to see the potential of the team. A truly great vision speaks to what team members can become if they truly live out their values and work according to their highest standards.

If you are your team's leader, getting people to reach their potential means challenging them. As you know, it's one thing to have team members show up. It's another to get them to grow up. One of the things about having a far-reaching vision is that it brings "stretch" to the team.

> *"You must have a long-range vision to keep you from being frustrated by short-range failures."*
>
> —CHARLES NOBLE

Without a challenge many people tend to fall or fade away. Charles Noble observed, "You must have a long-range vision to keep you from being frustrated by short-range failures." That's true. Vision helps people with motivation. That can be especially important for highly talented people. They sometimes fight lack of desire. That's why a consummate artist like Michelangelo prayed, "Lord, grant that I may always desire more than I can accomplish." A visionary compass answers that prayer.

Someone said that only people who can see the invisible can do the impossible. That shows the value of vision. But it also indicates that vision can be an elusive quality. If you can confidently measure the vision of your team according to these six "compasses," and you find them all aligned in the right direction, then your team has a reasonably good chance at success. And make no mistake. Not only can a team fail to thrive without vision—it cannot even survive without it. The words of King Solomon of ancient Israel, reputed to be the wisest man who ever lived, are true: "Where there is no vision, the people perish."[5] *Vision gives team members direction and confidence,* two things they cannot do without. That is the critical nature of the Law of the Compass.

COFFEE MAGIC

Some people capture a vision, as Abby Kohnstamm did at IBM, and they use it to focus their teams. Others are captured *by* a vision, and the power of it changes the courses of their lives.

That was certainly the case for Howard Schultz, the man who bought Starbucks Coffee Company in 1987.

Schultz was no stranger to Starbucks. In 1982, just six years out of Northern Michigan University, he had walked away from a great job as vice president in charge of U.S. operations at Hammarplast, a Swedish company that specializes in housewares, to join Starbucks. He had discovered the Seattle coffee retailer when he saw that their four stores sold more of Hammarplast's drip coffeemakers than Macy's in New York.

Schultz remembers the vision he had for Starbucks the day after his first visit to the company:

> It was like a shining jewel . . . There was something magic about it, a passion and authenticity I had never experienced in business. Maybe, just maybe, I could be part of that magic. Maybe I could help it grow. How would it feel to build a business? . . . How would it feel to own equity, not just collect a paycheck? What could I bring to Starbucks that could make it even better than it was?[6]

Schultz was captivated by a vision to expand Starbucks beyond Seattle, perhaps even across the entire country. When he began working for Starbucks as their director of retail operations and marketing, he started helping them to expand. But after Schultz had been with Starbucks for about a year, his vision for the coffee business itself also began to expand.

MAKE MINE A GRANDE!

After a visit to Italy, Schultz saw the huge potential of putting a coffee bar with espresso drinks in each Starbucks location. He believed that move held the greatest promise for the company, but he couldn't convince the owners to buy in to his vision. Since its inception in 1971, Starbucks had been a retailer of fresh whole coffee beans, not a seller of coffee by the cup.

Despite his love for Starbucks, Schultz left after three years to start his own company, which he made into a success. But two years later, when the owners of Starbucks let him know they wanted to sell the company, Schultz jumped at the chance. In 1987 the two companies merged and became the Starbucks Corporation.

Two factors drove Howard Schultz as he began the work of expanding Starbucks. The first was his love of coffee. The second was his desire to create a workplace that valued people and treated them with respect and dignity. That mattered to him greatly after a childhood of seeing his father struggle to support his family. Schultz says,

> I have a lot of respect for my dad. He never finished high school, but he was an honest man who worked hard. He sometimes had to take two or three jobs just to put food on the table. He cared a lot about his three kids, and played ball with us on weekends . . . But he was a beaten man. In a series of blue-collar jobs—truck driver, factory worker, cab driver—he never made as much as $20,000 a year, never could afford to own his own home. I spent my childhood in the Projects, federally subsidized housing in Canarsie, Brooklyn, [New York] . . . He had tried to fit into a system, but the system had crushed him.[7]

When it came to the coffee part of his vision, Schultz didn't worry about Starbucks. However, the working environment was another matter. In the two years he had been away from the company, the employees at Starbucks had become demoralized. Schultz says, "People were cynical and wary, beaten down and unappreciated. They felt abandoned by previous management and anxious about me. The fabric of trust and common vision that Starbucks had when I first joined had frayed badly." [8]

RECASTING THE VISION

Schultz began to address the issues immediately—starting with this statement to employees:

> Five years ago, I changed my life for this company. I did it because I recognized in it your passion. All my life I have wanted to be part of a company and a group of people who share a common vision. I saw that here in you, and I admire it.
>
> I'm here today because I love this company. I love what it represents . . . I know you're scared. I know you're concerned. Some of you may even be angry. But if you would just meet me halfway, I promise you I will not let you down. I promise you I will not leave anyone behind.[9]

Schultz had cast the vision. And in the coming months, he proved that he still valued great coffee. But he also went further. He began doing things that showed he valued the team. He called the people working for Starbucks "partners," and he backed it up with how he ran the company. He created a health plan that covered everyone, including part-timers. He clarified the company's mission and put into place a system in which hourly employees could hold management accountable to them. He even offered stock options to everyone, right down to the hourly employee who worked twenty hours a week making cappuccinos.

Schultz was trying to create the kind of company that people wanted to work for, the kind of place where someone like his father could have worked with dignity and respect. And he did it while making the company highly profitable. Starbucks is now a publicly traded company worth over $6 billion.[10] It serves more than 20 million people each week in more than 5,000 stores around the globe with plans to keep growing.[11] And it ranks high on the Forbes list of the best companies to work for.

Schultz sums up his role at Starbucks this way:

> I started off as a dreamer . . . Then I moved to entrepreneur . . . Then I had to become a manager, as the company grew larger and I needed to delegate more and more decisions. Today, my role is to be Starbucks' leader, its visionary, cheerleader, and keeper of the flame. [12]

Today Starbucks' customers, partners, and stockholders can clearly see the company's direction and have confidence in it. That's what vision does for a team. That's the power of the Law of the Compass.

TEAMWORK THOUGHT

When you see it, you can seize it.

BECOMING A BETTER TEAM MEMBER

What is the vision for your team? You'd be surprised how many individuals are part of a group that works together but isn't clear about why. For example, that was the case when I became the leader of Skyline Church in the San Diego area. The church's board was comprised of twelve people. When I asked each member to articulate the church's vision the first time we met, I got eight different answers. A team can't move forward in confidence if it has no compass!

As a member of your team, you need a clear understanding of its vision. If the team doesn't have one, then help it to develop one. If the team has already found its compass and course, then you need to examine yourself in light of it to make sure there is a good match. If there isn't, you and your teammates are going to be frustrated. And everyone will probably be best served by a change.

BECOMING A BETTER TEAM LEADER

If you are the leader of your team, then you carry the responsibility for communicating the team's vision and keeping it before the people continually. That's not necessarily easy. Jack Welch, CEO of General Electric, observed, "Without question, communicating the vision, and the atmosphere around the vision, has been, and is continuing to be, by far, the toughest job we face."

I have found that people need to be shown the team's compass clearly, creatively, and continually. Whenever I endeavor to cast vision with the members of my team, I use the following checklist. I try to make sure that every vision message possesses . . .

❏ *Clarity:* brings understanding to the vision (answers what the people must know and what I want them to do)

❏ *Connectedness:* brings the past, present, and future together

❏ *Purpose:* brings direction to the vision

❏ *Goals:* bring targets to the vision

❑ *Honesty:* brings integrity to the vision and credibility to the vision caster

❑ *Stories:* bring relationships to the vision

❑ *Challenge:* brings stretching to the vision

❑ *Passion:* brings fuel to the vision

❑ *Modeling:* brings accountability to the vision

❑ *Strategy:* brings process to the vision

The next time you prepare to communicate vision to your people, use this checklist. Make sure you include each component, and I believe your team members will find the vision more accessible and will more readily buy into it. And if they do, you will see that they have greater direction and confidence.

8

THE LAW OF THE BAD APPLE

Rotten Attitudes Ruin a Team

Growing up, I loved basketball. It all started for me in the fourth grade when I saw a high school basketball game for the first time. I was captivated. Soon after that my dad poured a cement driveway along the side of our house and put a goal up on the garage for me. From that day until I went to college, I could usually be found practicing my shooting and playing pickup games on that small home court.

By the time I got to high school, I had become a pretty good player. I started on the junior varsity team as a freshman, and when I was a sophomore, our JV team had a 15-3 record, which was better than that of the varsity. We were proud of that—maybe a little too proud. I say that because of something that happened during my sophomore year.

One of the traditions on the team was that our coach, Don Neff, would give Ohio State basketball tickets to some of the players who had performed especially well during the season. Those players were almost always seniors, and they were always on the varsity. But that year I was one of the players offered Buckeye tickets. What was my response? Was I grateful and humbled by Coach Neff's recognition? No, I told him I thought he should let the JV play the varsity for *all* the tickets. Needless to say, he never allowed that game to be played.

The next year, critics who followed high school basketball in Ohio thought our team had a chance to win the state championship in our division. I guess they looked at the players who would return as seniors from the previous year's varsity team and saw the talent that would be moving up from the JV, and they figured we would be a powerhouse. And we did have a lot of talent. How many high school teams in the late 1960s could say that all but a couple of players on the team could dunk the ball? But the season turned out far different from everyone's expectations.

FROM BAD TO WORSE

From the beginning of the season, the team suffered problems. There were two of us juniors on the varsity who had the talent to start for the team: John Thomas, who was the team's best rebounder, and me, the best shooting guard. We thought playing time should be based strictly on ability, and we figured we deserved our place on the team. The seniors, who had taken a backseat to the previous year's seniors, thought we should be made to pay our dues and wait.

What began as a rivalry between the JV and varsity the year before turned into a war between the juniors and the seniors. When we scrimmaged at practice, it was the juniors against the seniors. In games the seniors wouldn't pass to the juniors and vice versa. We judged our success not by whether the team won or lost, but by whether the juniors' stats were better than those of the seniors. If we outshot, outpassed, and outrebounded the seniors, then we thought we had "won" the game, regardless of the outcome against our opponent.

The battles became so fierce that before long, the juniors and the seniors wouldn't even work together on the court during games. Coach Neff had to platoon us. The seniors would start, and when a substitution became necessary, he'd put not one but *five* juniors in the game. We became two teams on one roster.

I don't remember exactly who started the rivalry that split our team, but I do remember that John Thomas and I embraced it early on. I've always been a leader, and I did my share of influencing other team members. Unfortunately, I have to confess that I led the juniors in the wrong direction.

What started as a bad attitude in one or two players made a mess of the situation for everyone. By the time we were in the thick of our schedule, even the players who didn't want to take part in the rivalry were affected. The season was a disaster. In the end, we finished with a mediocre record and never came close to reaching our potential. It just goes to show you, *rotten attitudes ruin a team*. That's the Law of the Bad Apple.

TALENT IS NOT ENOUGH

From my high school basketball experience I learned that talent is not enough to bring success to a team. Of course, you need talent. My friend Lou Holtz, the outstanding college football coach, observed, "You've got to have great athletes to win . . . You can't win without good athletes, but you can lose with them." But it also takes

> *Good attitudes among players do not guarantee a team's success, but bad attitudes guarantee its failure.*

much more than talented people to win.

My high school teammates were loaded with talent, and if that were enough, we could have been state champions. But we were also loaded with rotten attitudes. You know which won the battle between talent and attitude in the end. Perhaps that is why to this day I understand the importance of a positive attitude and have placed such a strong emphasis on it for myself, for my children as they were growing up, and for the teams I lead.

Years ago I wrote something about attitude for *The Winning Attitude*. I'd like to share it with you:

> Attitude . . .
>
> It is the "advance man" of our true selves.
>
> Its roots are inward but its fruit is outward.
>
> It is our best friend or our worst enemy.
>
> It is more honest and more consistent than our words.
>
> It is an outward look based on past experiences.
>
> It is a thing which draws people to us or repels them.
>
> It is never content until it is expressed.
>
> It is the librarian of our past.
>
> It is the speaker of our present.
>
> It is the prophet of our future.[1]

Good attitudes among players do not guarantee a team's success, but bad attitudes guarantee its failure.

The following five truths about attitudes clarify how they affect a team and teamwork.

1. Attitudes Have the Power to Lift Up or Tear Down a Team

In *The Winner's Edge* Denis Waitley stated, "The real leaders in business, in the professional community, in education, in government, and in the home also seem to draw upon a special cutting edge that separates them from the rest of society. The winner's edge is not in a gifted birth, in a high IQ, or in talent. The winner's edge is in the attitude, not aptitude."

Unfortunately, I think too many people resist that notion. They want to believe that talent alone (or talent with experience) is enough. But plenty of talented teams out there never amount to anything because of the attitudes of their players.

Various attitudes may impact a team made up of highly talented players:

Abilities	+	Attitudes	=	Result
Great Talent	+	Rotten Attitudes	=	Bad Team
Great Talent	+	Bad Attitudes	=	Average Team
Great Talent	+	Average Attitudes	=	Good Team
Great Talent	+	Good Attitudes	=	Great Team

If you want outstanding results, you need good people with great talent and awesome attitudes. When attitudes go up, so does the potential of the team. When attitudes go down, the potential of the team goes with it.

2. An Attitude Compounds When Exposed to Others

Several things on a team are not contagious. Talent. Experience. Willingness to practice. But you can be sure of one thing: Attitude is catching. When someone on the team is teachable and his humility is rewarded by improvement, others are more likely to display similar characteristics. When a leader is upbeat in the face of discouraging circumstances, others admire that quality and want to be like her. When a team member displays a strong work ethic and begins to have a positive impact, others imitate him. People become inspired by their peers. People have a tendency to adopt the attitudes of those they spend time with—to pick up on their mind-set, beliefs, and approaches to challenges.

The story of Roger Bannister is an inspiring example of the way attitudes often "compound." During the first half of the twentieth century, many sports experts believed that no runner could run a mile in less than four minutes. And for a long time they were right. But then on May 6, 1954, British runner and university student Roger Bannister ran a mile in 3 minutes 59.4 seconds during a meet in Oxford. Less than two months later, another runner, Australian John Landy, also broke the four-minute barrier. Then suddenly dozens and then hundreds of others broke it. Why? Because the best runners' attitudes changed. They began to adopt the mind-set and beliefs of their peers.

Bannister's attitude and actions compounded when exposed to others. His attitude spread. Today, every world-class runner who competes at that distance can run a mile in less than four minutes. Attitudes are contagious!

3. Bad Attitudes Compound Faster Than Good Ones

There's only one thing more contagious than a good attitude—and that's a bad attitude. For some reason many people think it's chic to be negative. I suspect that they think it makes them appear smart or important. But the truth is that a negative attitude hurts rather than helps the person who has it. And it also hurts the people around him.

A wise baseball manager once remarked that he never allowed the positive players to room with the negative ones on the road.

When he created the team's room assignments, he always put the negative ones together so that they couldn't poison anyone else.

To see how quickly and easily an attitude or mind-set can spread, just think about this story from Norman Cousins. Once during a football game, a doctor at the first aid station treated five people for what he suspected might be food poisoning. Since their symptoms were similar, he tried to track down what they had in common. He soon discovered that all five people had bought drinks from a particular concession stand at the stadium.

There's only one thing more contagious than a good attitude—and that's a bad attitude.

The physician wanted to do the responsible thing, so he requested that the game's announcer advise people in the stadium to avoid buying drinks from the particular vendor because of the possibility of food poisoning. Before long, more than two hundred people complained of food poisoning symptoms. Nearly half the people's symptoms were so severe that they were taken to the hospital.

The story doesn't end there, however. After a little more detective work, it was discovered that the five original victims had eaten tainted potato salad from one particular deli on the way to the game. When the other "sufferers" found out that the drinks in the stadium were safe, they experienced miraculous recoveries. That just goes to show you, an attitude spreads very quickly.

4. Attitudes Are Subjective, So Identifying a Wrong One Can Be Difficult

Have you ever interacted with someone for the first time and suspected that his attitude was poor, yet you were unable to put your finger on exactly what was wrong? I believe many people have that experience.

The reason people doubt their observations about others' attitudes is that attitudes are subjective. Someone with a bad attitude may not do anything illegal or unethical. Yet his attitude may be ruining the team just the same.

People always project on the outside how they feel on the inside. Attitude is really about how a person is. That overflows into how he acts. Allow me to share with you common rotten attitudes that ruin a team so that you can recognize them for what they are when you see them.

An inability to admit wrongdoing. Have you ever spent time with people who *never* admit they're wrong? It's painful. Nobody's perfect, but someone who thinks he is does not make an ideal teammate. His wrong attitude will always create conflict.

Failing to forgive. It's said that Clara Barton, the founder of modern nursing, was once encouraged to bemoan a cruel act inflicted on her years earlier, but Barton wouldn't take the bait.

"Don't you remember the wrong that was done to you?" the friend goaded.

"No," answered Barton, "I distinctly remember forgetting that."

Holding a grudge is never positive or appropriate. And when unforgiveness occurs between teammates, it's certain to hurt the team.

Petty jealousy. An attitude that really works against people is the desire for equality that feeds petty jealousy. For some reason the people with this attitude believe that every person deserves equal treatment, regardless of talent, performance, or impact. Yet nothing could be farther from the truth. Each of us is created uniquely and performs differently, and as a result, we should be treated as such.

The disease of me. In his book *The Winner Within,* highly successful NBA coach Pat Riley writes about the "disease of me." He says of team members who have it, "They develop an overpowering belief in their own importance. Their actions virtually shout the claim,

'I'm the one.'" Riley asserts that the disease always has the same inevitable result: "The Defeat of Us."[2]

A critical spirit. Fred and Martha were driving home after a church service. "Fred," Martha asked, "did you notice that the pastor's sermon was kind of weak today?"

"No, not really," answered Fred.

"Well, did you hear that the choir was flat?"

"No, I didn't," he responded.

"Well, you certainly must have noticed that young couple and their children right in front of us, with all the noise and commotion they made the whole service!"

"I'm sorry, dear, but no, I didn't"

Finally in disgust Martha said, "Honestly, Fred, I don't know why you even bother to go to church."

When someone on the team has a critical spirit, everybody knows it because everyone on the team can do no right.

A desire to hog all the credit. Another bad attitude that hurts the team is similar to the "disease of me." But where the person with that disease may simmer in the background and create dissension, the credit hog continually steps into the spotlight to take a bow—whether he has earned it or not. His attitude is opposite that of NBA Hall of Fame center Bill Russell, who said of his time on the court, "The most important measure of how good a game I played was how much better I'd made my teammates play."

> *Most bad attitudes are the result of selfishness.*

Certainly there are other negative attitudes that I haven't named, but my intention isn't to list every bad attitude—just some of the most common ones. In a word, most bad attitudes are the result of selfishness. If one of your teammates puts others down, sabotages teamwork, or makes himself out to be more important than the team, then you can be sure that you've encountered someone with a bad attitude.

5. Rotten Attitudes, Left Alone, Ruin Everything

Bad attitudes must be addressed. You can be sure that they will always cause dissension, resentment, combativeness, and division on a team. And they will never go away on their own if they are left unaddressed. They will simply fester and ruin a team—along with its chances of reaching its potential.

Because people with bad attitudes are so difficult to deal with and because attitudes seem so subjective, you may doubt your gut reaction when you encounter a bad apple. After all, if it's only your *opinion* that he has a rotten attitude, then you have no right to address it, right? Not if you care about the team. *Rotten attitudes ruin a team.* That is always true. If you leave a bad apple in a barrel of good apples, you will always end up with a barrel of rotten apples.

President Thomas Jefferson remarked, "Nothing can stop the man with the right mental attitude from achieving his goal; nothing on earth can help the man with the wrong mental attitude." If you care about your team and you are committed to helping all of the players, you can't ignore a bad attitude. If you do, you will find out the hard way about the Law of the Bad Apple.

YOUR BEST FRIEND OR WORST ENEMY

Attitude colors everything someone does. It determines how an individual sees the world and interacts with other people. A person's attitude—positively if it's good, negatively if it's not—always impacts his performance, regardless of talent, track record, or circumstances.

One of the most remarkable stories I've ever read that illustrates the Law of the Bad Apple came out of the San Francisco Bay area. Evidently the principal of a school called in three teachers to inform them of an experiment that the district would be conducting.

"Because you are the finest teachers in the system," she said, "we're going to give you ninety selected high-IQ students. We're going to let you move these students through this next year at their pace and see how much they can learn."

The faculty and students were delighted. During the next year, they had a wonderful experience. By the end of the last semester, the students had achieved 20 to 30 percent more than any other group of students in the area.

After the year was completed, the principal called in the teachers and told them, "I have a confession to make. I have to confess that you did not have ninety of the most intellectually prominent students. They were run-of-the-mill students. We took ninety students at random from the system and gave them to you."

The teachers were pleased. If the students were only average, that showed that the teachers had displayed exceptional skill and expertise.

"I have another confession," the principal continued. "You're not the brightest of the teachers. Your names were the first three names drawn out of a hat."

If the students and the teachers had been picked at random, then what had enabled them to make greater progress than any other group in the system? It was the attitudes of the people involved. Because the teachers and students expected to succeed, they increased their potential for success. Attitude had made all the difference.

If you want to give your team the best chance for success, then practice the Law of the Bad Apple. Trade your bad apples for good ones and you have a chance, because *rotten apples ruin a team.*

TEAMWORK THOUGHT

Your attitude determines the team's attitude.

BECOMING A BETTER TEAM MEMBER

The first place to start when it comes to attitude is yourself. How are you doing? For example, do you . . .

- ❏ Think the team wouldn't be able to get along without you?
- ❏ Secretly (or not so secretly) believe that recent team successes are really attributable to your personal efforts, not the work of the whole team?
- ❏ Keep score when it comes to the praise and perks handed out to other team members?
- ❏ Have a hard time admitting when you make a mistake? (If you believe you're not making mistakes, you need to check this!)
- ❏ Bring up past wrongs from your teammates?
- ❏ Believe that you are being grossly underpaid?

If you could place a check next to any of them, then you need to check your attitude.

Talk to your teammates, and find out if your attitude is doing damage to the team. Talk to your leader. And if you really think your pay is inequitable, you need to talk it out with your employer and find out where you stand. Anytime a relationship is unequal, it cannot last—whether you are giving more than you get or getting more than you deserve. In either case, the relationship will break down.

> *Anytime a relationship is unequal, it cannot last—whether you are giving more than you get or getting more than you deserve.*

Warning! I have one word of caution: If you leave your position because you believe you are undervalued, and you don't succeed in your new situation, then you most likely overestimated your value or underestimated what the organization was doing to help you succeed.

BECOMING A BETTER TEAM LEADER

If you think you have a bad apple on your team, you need to take the person aside and discuss the situation with him. Doing it the right way is important. Take the high road: As you approach him, share what you have observed, but give him the benefit of the doubt. Assume that your perception might be wrong and you want clarification. (If you have several people with bad attitudes, start with the ringleader.) If it truly is your perception and the team is not being hurt, then you haven't done any damage, and you have smoothed the relationship between you and the other person.

However, if it turns out that your perception was correct and the person's attitude is the problem, give him clear expectations and an opportunity to change. Then hold him accountable. If he changes, it's a win for the team. If he doesn't, remove him from the team. You cannot allow him to remain because you can be sure his *rotten attitude will ruin the team.*

THE LAW OF COUNTABILITY

Teammates Must Be Able to Count on Each Other When It Counts

One of the many strong points of Atlanta, Georgia, where I moved my family and my companies in 1997, is that it's a sports town. I don't get the chance to go to a lot of games, but there are few things I like better than attending a sporting event with all of the energy and excitement. Watching a team with a friend or two is a joy, whether it's the Braves (baseball), the Hawks (basketball), the Falcons (football), or the Thrashers (hockey).

When the announcement was made that Atlanta would be getting a hockey team, plans were set in motion to build the team a new arena. The old Omni, where the Hawks had played since the early 1970s, was slated to be demolished and replaced on the same site by the Philips Arena. It would be an 18,000-seat state-of-the-art entertainment complex with box seating, which could host not only hockey and basketball but also concerts and other events.

Tearing down the Omni wasn't going to be a routine process. First, it needed to be done quickly so that construction could begin on the new arena. Second, because the old structure had a cantilevered roof, taking the building apart in opposite order from the way it was constructed was out of the question. It would be far too dangerous for the demolition crews. That left only one choice: blowing it up.

Explosive Family Business

When demolition crews need help blowing up a building—or more accurately imploding a building—they inevitably turn to the Loizeaux family, the people who pioneered the safe demolition of buildings using explosives. They are owners and founders of Controlled Demolition Incorporated (CDI). The company was founded by Jack Loizeaux who had started a company in the 1940s removing tree stumps with dynamite. In 1957, he blasted his first building. And in the 1960s, he began CDI. Since that first demolition—an apartment building in Washington, D.C., his company has demolished more than seven thousand structures worldwide.

CDI is a family operation. Jack and his wife, Freddie, ran the business in the beginning. It wasn't long before they were joined by their sons, Mark and Doug. When Jack retired in 1976, his sons took over the operation. Today, they are joined by several of Mark's children, including his daughter Stacey, in her early thirties, who has worked in the field since age fifteen and is already an expert in her own right.

LIKE THREADING A NEEDLE

When the Loizeauxs were contacted for the job, they quickly discovered that the demolition wouldn't be easy because of the Omni's proximity to other buildings. On one side was the World Congress Center, which is used for conventions. On another side was a station for MARTA (Atlanta's mass-transit rail system). On the third was the CNN Center from which cable and radio programming broadcasts twenty-four hours a day. And CNN Plaza was a mere thirteen feet away from the Omni! A mistake could damage the MARTA line and shut it down at one of its busiest stations. Or it could put CNN news service temporarily out of business. And of course in a worst-case scenario, the Omni could topple in the wrong direction and take down the CNN building itself. It would take every bit of the Loizeauxs' expertise and fifty years of experience to do the task right.

Using explosives to take down a building is always a dangerous undertaking. Each project is different and requires a custom-made strategy. Holes are drilled in strategic places in many parts of the structure, such as in columns, and filled with appropriate amounts of explosive material. Then those blast points are often wrapped in chain-link fence (to catch the big pieces upon detonation) and wrapped in a special fabric that helps contain the explosion. "It allows the concrete to move, but it keeps the concrete from flying," says Stacey Loizeaux. "We also sometimes put up a curtain around the entire floor, to catch stuff that gets through these first two layers. That's really where your liability is."[1] Often, earthen berms are also erected around the building to protect nearby people and structures.

Obviously there is risk anytime someone works with explosives. But the greatest danger comes in the way explosives are rigged to go off. To get the building to fall in on itself, the Loizeauxs and their crew have to precisely sequence the charges, often using delays that differ from one another by the tiniest fractions of a second. That was the case for the Omni, where first the roof needed to fall straight down, then three of the walls would need to fall inward, and then the fourth wall outward. And on July 26, 1997, at 6:53 A.M., that's exactly the way it happened. The demolition took ten seconds.

When it comes to blowing up a building the way the Loizeauxs do, everything has to go right—from analyzing the building, to planning the demolition, to transporting the explosives, to rigging the devices, to preparing the building for the safety of the surrounding area. If anyone on the crew fails to get his part right and lets the other members of the team down, not only does the CDI team fail in its objective, but it also puts a lot of people and property in danger. *Teammates must be able to count on each other when it counts.* That's the Law of Countability.

HOLDING EACH OTHER ACCOUNTABLE

The importance of the Law of Countability is clearest when the stakes are high. But you don't have to be in an explosive situation for the law to come into play. The person running a business who is trying to get out a product on schedule depends on her vendors to deliver on their promises during crunch time. The waiter trying to please his customer counts on the kitchen staff to prepare the food properly. The mom getting ready for a job interview has to know that her baby-sitter will show up as promised. If there is a breakdown in countability, then the account is lost, the customer goes away unhappy, and the job goes to some other candidate. *Teammates must be able to count on each other when it counts.*

I was reminded of how often we encounter examples of the Law of Countability, even in small things, when I was on a trip to South Africa. I was there to teach at a conference sponsored by EQUIP, my nonprofit organization. I was waiting in the hotel lobby for my ride to the conference, and I was having some trouble with a cough. That's usually no big deal, but when you're preparing to speak for five or six hours straight, it's not a great way to start the day. As the conference team and I got

> *"We don't work for each other; we work with each other."*
>
> —STANLEY C. GAULT

under way, Erick Moon, a member of the team, pulled a Ricola cough drop (my brand) out of his pocket and handed it to me. When he saw my surprise, he said simply, "We're all carrying them for you, just in case."

Stanley C. Gault asserted, "We don't work for each other; we work with each other." That is the essence of countability—it's the ability and desire for teammates to work together toward common goals. But that doesn't happen on its own. Nor is countability a given. It has to be earned. Team members who can depend on each other only during the easy times have not developed countability.

THE FORMULA FOR COUNTABILITY

I believe that there is a formula for countability. It's not complicated, but its impact is powerful. Here it is:

Character + Competence + Commitment +

Consistency + Cohesion =

Countability

When every team member embraces each of these five qualities, within himself and with others, the team can achieve the countability that is necessary to succeed.

1. Character

In *The 21 Irrefutable Laws of Leadership*, I wrote about the Law of Solid Ground, which says that trust is the foundation of leadership. That law is really about character. In the book I state, "Character makes trust possible. Trust makes leadership possible. That is the Law of Solid Ground."[2]

> *"There is no substitute for character. You can buy brains, but you cannot buy character."*
>
> —ROBERT A. COOK

In a similar way, countability begins with character because it is based on trust, which is the foundation for all interaction with people. If you cannot trust someone, you will not count on him. As Robert A. Cook remarked, "There is no substitute for character. You can buy brains, but you cannot buy character."

Anytime you desire to build a team, you have to begin by building character in the individuals who make up the team. For example, my friend Lou Holtz, who coaches football at the University of South Carolina, introduces the players on his team to a list of twelve covenants at the beginning of the season to help them understand the team culture he is trying to create. Here are the covenants:

USC—12 Covenants

1. We will accomplish what we do together. We share our success, and we never let any one of us fail alone.

2. We are all fully grown adults. We will act as such, and expect the same from the people around us.

3. We will not keep secrets. Information that affects us all will be shared by all of us, and we will quickly and openly work to separate fact from fiction.

4. We will not lie to ourselves or to each other. None of us will tolerate any of us doing so. We will depend on each other for the truth.

5. We will keep our word. We will say what we mean, and do what we say. We trust the word of others to be good as well.

6. We will keep our head. We will not panic in the face of tough times. We will always choose to roll up our sleeves rather than wring our hands.

7. We will develop our abilities and take pride in them. We will set our own standards higher than our most challenging opponent, and we will please our fans by pleasing ourselves.

8. We will treat our locker room like home and our teammates like friends. We spend too much time together to allow these things to go bad.

9. We will be unselfish and expect that everyone else will exhibit this same quality. We will care about each other without expectations.

10. We will look out for each other. We truly believe that we are our brother's keeper.

11. We are students at USC, and as such we will strive to graduate. We take pride in our grade point average and expect our teammates to do the same.

12. Losing cannot and will not be tolerated in anything we do. Losing to us is to be shamed, embarrassed, and humiliated. There is no excuse for losing a football game at USC.

When you read through the twelve points, did you notice anything? Most of them touch on issues of character. Holtz knows that if he doesn't lay a solid foundation of character within the young men on his team, he can't build anything of value on top of it.

Barry Gibbons, in his book *This Indecision Is Final*, asserted, "Write and publish what you want, but the only missions, values, and ethics that count in your company are those that manifest themselves in the behavior of all the people, all the time."[3]

> *"Write and publish what you want, but the only missions, values, and ethics that count in your company are those that manifest themselves in the behavior of all the people, all the time."*
>
> —BARRY GIBBONS

2. Competence

I spent over twenty-five years as a pastor, so I know the church world very well, and I have seen people in the religious community who act as if character is the only thing that matters. I don't think that's true. What you do is also important, as Scripture makes clear.[4] Character is the most important thing, but it's not the only thing.

If you have any doubts about that, consider this. If you had to go into surgery because of a life-threatening illness, would you be happier having a good surgeon who was a bad person or a good person who was a bad surgeon? That puts it in perspective, doesn't it? Competence matters. And if the person is going to be on the same team with you, you want competence *and* character.

3. Commitment

Having fair-weather team members doesn't make for a very pleasant team experience. When times are tough, you want to know that you can count on your teammates. You don't want to be wondering whether they're going to hang in there with you.

Dan Reiland, who is a vice president at The INJOY Group, shared with me the table on the next page that indicates the commitment of various team members.

Teams succeed or fail based on teammates' commitment to one another and the team. My friend Randy Watts, who pastors a church in Virginia, sent me a note after a conference where I taught the Law of Countability. He wrote:

Years ago, a friend of mine attended the Virginia Military Institute, known for its rugged physical, mental, and emotional training. He told me that all the incoming freshmen are separated into companies. One of their training obstacles is to race up House Mountain, which is very steep and more than a challenge. The motivation for climbing: If you finish last, you run again. Not you, but your whole company! This makes for team commitment. If a person in your company twists an ankle or breaks a leg, other members of his company carry him! It is not enough to be the first man on top of the mountain; everyone on the team has to make it.

Real teamwork requires that kind of commitment. When team-mates can't make it, you carry them the rest of the way for the sake of the team.

Level	Type of Teammate	Description
1. Green Beret Colonel	Committed Team Leader	*Dedicated to the cause. Focused on the big picture. Has a whatever-it-takes attitude.*
2. First Lieutenant	Team Achiever	*Buys into the spirit and culture of the organization. Is self-motivated and productive.*
3. OCS Graduates	Genuine Team Player	*Has passion and enthusiasm. Arrives early and stays late. Is not yet a proven leader.*
4. Private	Formal Team Member	*Enjoys being on the team. Wants to stay. Serves out of duty. Not yet a high achiever.*
5. Boot Camp Recruit	Begrudging Follower	*Will work, but only with a kick in the seat of the pants.*
6. Deserter	Nonfollower	*Won't do anything. Needs to be court-martialed.*
7. Sniper	Dangerous Follower	*Works, but makes life difficult for team. Will shoot teammates if given the chance.*

4. Consistency

Every once in a while somebody comes along who defines consistency for the rest of his teammates. In the case of the Atlanta Braves, I believe that person is Greg Maddux. If you follow baseball, then you probably know about him. Maddux is a first-rate pitcher, and he has the awards—and statistics—to prove it. He has won more than 200 games, including 176 games in the 1990s, the most of any pitcher in major-league baseball. He is the only pitcher besides Cy Young and Gaylord Perry to have won 15 or more games in 13 consecutive seasons. He is the only pitcher in baseball's history to have won the Cy Young Award four years in a row (1992–95).

For all of Maddux's awards for pitching and noteworthy stats, do you know what has been his most remarkable honor? He has been recognized as the National League's best fielder in his position by receiving a Gold Glove *ten years in a row!*

Many great pitchers are not known for their fielding. When a difficult ball is hit to a pitcher, or when the pitcher has to cover first base on a tough play to the right side of the infield, many times the other players on the team hold their collective breath. If anyone on the field is likely to make a fielding mistake, it's the pitcher. But not Maddux. He works at his fielding with the same fantastic work ethic that has made him an outstanding pitcher. The result is a career that has seen only fourteen errors in fifteen years (with two seasons of error-free fielding).

If you want your teammates to have confidence in you, to know they can count on you day in and day out, then use someone like Maddux as your example. Consistency is key.

5. Cohesion

Teammates need to develop cohesion. That's the ability to hold together, no matter how difficult the circumstances become. Navy SEAL John Roat describes cohesion this way:

Unit cohesion is one of those terms that everyone thinks they understand. In truth, most people don't have a clue. It is definitely not about everybody liking each other or being nice. It means you have a pride in the ability of your group to function at a higher level than possible for the individual. The unit doesn't shine because you're a member, you shine because you're good enough to be a member.[5]

There's an old saying when it comes to teams: Either we're pulling together or we're pulling apart. Without cohesion people aren't really a team because they're not pulling together. They're merely a group of individuals working for the same organization.

> *There's an old saying when it comes to teams: Either we're pulling together or we're pulling apart.*

Novelist and civil rights activist James Baldwin asserted, "The moment we break faith with one another, the sea engulfs us and the light goes out." When it comes down to it, countability is being able to have faith in your teammates, no matter what happens. When the chips are down, you can turn to the people on your team. Let's face it: You can't do anything that counts unless you have countability. *Teammates must be able to count on each other when it really counts.*

BROKEN TRUST

When you see a major example of broken trust that destroys countability on a team, you know it instantly. When parents run out on their children, a spouse is guilty of infidelity, or children callously deceive their parents, it is a violation of countability in the family. When employees embezzle money, or leaders abuse the power entrusted to them by people in their organization, it undermines countability in a business. And when an officer in a government agency is guilty of espionage, it not only hurts his teammates; it breaks trust with the people in an entire nation.

When the news broke in early 2001 that an FBI agent had been caught passing highly classified national security information to Russia and the former Soviet Union, the first thing I thought of was the Law of Countability. The man in this case was Robert Philip Hanssen, a counterintelligence agent who had made a career with the FBI.

Hanssen is suspected of having given the KGB (and the organization that replaced it called the SVR) sensitive information on more than twenty occasions. That information totaled more than six thousand pages of material, including counterintelligence investigative techniques, sources, methods, and operations.[6] And just as in the case of Aldridge Ames, the CIA counterintelligence officer convicted of espionage in 1994, the information illegally passed by Hanssen is believed to have precipitated the deaths of field agents working for the U.S. government.[7]

Nobody likes a traitor. In fact, in America, the name Benedict Arnold is still associated with treachery and betrayal, even though his actions occurred more than two hundred years ago. (And few remember that Arnold was a brilliant military leader.) But what makes Hanssen's case especially distasteful is that the betrayer was a member of a team that maintains high standards of conduct because of the trust given to it by the people. The FBI identifies its core values as "rigorous obedience to the Constitution of the United States; respect for the dignity of all those we protect; compassion; fairness; and uncompromising personal and institutional integrity."[8] FBI Director Louis J. Freeh said of Hanssen:

A betrayal of trust by an FBI agent, who is not only sworn to enforce the law but specifically to help protect our nation's security, is particularly abhorrent. This kind of criminal conduct represents the most traitorous action imaginable . . . It also strikes at the heart of everything the FBI represents—the commitment of over 28,000 honest and dedicated men and women in the FBI who work diligently to earn the trust and confidence of the American people every day.[9]

In other words, *teammates must be able to count on each other when it counts.* Robert Hanssen broke the trust that makes countability possible. And it may be decades before we find out how much damage he did to the country. That's a terrible thought, but that's the price that sometimes has to be paid when someone breaks the Law of Countability.

TEAMWORK THOUGHT

The greatest compliment you can receive is being counted on.

BECOMING A BETTER TEAM MEMBER

People often say that imitation is a compliment. In regard to teamwork I believe the highest compliment you can receive is trust from your teammates when it really counts.

How do your teammates feel about you? In Chapter 6 we talked about how catalysts step up to a higher level of play when crunch time comes. You may or may not be the type of player who can make things happen and then some when the game is on the line. That's okay. But can you be depended on to do *your* part, whatever that is, when your teammates need you? Do you perform and follow through in such a way that the team considers you someone they can count on? How are you doing in each of the areas examined in the chapter?

- Is your integrity unquestioned (character)?

- Do you perform your work with excellence (competence)?

- Are you dedicated to the team's success (commitment)?

- Can you be depended on every time (consistency)?

- Do your actions bring the team together (cohesion)?

If you are weak in any of these areas, talk to a mentor or trusted friend to get suggestions concerning how you can grow in that area.

BECOMING A BETTER TEAM LEADER

Developing countability and cohesion among team members is not always an easy task. And it takes time. If you are responsible for leading your team, use the suggestions of William A. Cohen in *The Art of the Leader* for building a team that is able to count on each member when it counts:

1. Develop pride in group membership.

2. Convince your group that they are the best.

3. Give recognition whenever possible.

4. Encourage organizational mottos, names, symbols, and slogans.

5. Establish your group's worth by examining and promoting its history and values.

6. Focus on the common purpose.

7. Encourage your people to participate in activities together outside of work.[10]

The more of these activities you embrace, the greater countability you will develop.

THE LAW OF THE PRICE TAG

The Team Fails to Reach Its Potential When It Fails to Pay the Price

On December 28, 2000, one of the nation's oldest retailers, Montgomery Ward and Company, announced that it would be filing Chapter 7 bankruptcy and closing its doors forever. That announcement saddened the people of Chicago, for Ward had been an institution in that city for more than a century. What's even sadder is that the company's failure might have been avoided if leaders had learned and practiced the Law of the Price Tag before it was too late.

The retailing chain's early history is really quite remarkable. The company was founded in 1872 by Aaron Montgomery Ward, a young salesman who had worked for various dry goods merchants throughout the Midwest and South. While he was working in rural areas far from cities or large towns, he discovered that many consumers in remote areas were at the mercy of local merchants who often overcharged them for merchandise. That gave him an idea. Railroads and mail service were improving by that time. What if he bought dry goods directly from manufacturers for cash and sold them for cash via mail order to rural consumers, thus eliminating the middlemen who were gouging those customers?

Paying the First Price

In 1871, Ward saved enough money from his work as a salesman to purchase some merchandise and print a one-page price list that he planned to mail out to a bunch of farmers who belonged to a fraternal organization. But before he could follow through with his plan, the devastating Chicago fire of 1871 destroyed his stock and price sheets. The setback didn't stop Ward. He convinced two sales colleagues to join him as partners, began rebuilding his stock, and reprinted the price sheet, which would become the world's first general merchandise mail-order catalog. And in 1872, at age twenty-eight, Ward opened for business.

At first, Ward was only moderately successful. In fact, a year into the business, his two partners got cold feet and asked to be bought out. Ward paid them off, then took his friend George Thorne into the business as a full partner. Together they worked hard, taking orders and shipping out merchandise by rail. Meanwhile, in 1875, Ward and Thorne came up with a novel idea. They decided to include a new credo in their catalog. It said, "Satisfaction Guaranteed or Your Money Back." And the business took off.

Ward's tenacity and willingness to pay the price twice for starting his own business came to fruition less than a decade later. The company that had begun with $1,600 of capital in 1872 had sales of

$300,000 in 1878. Nine years after that, the company's sales rose to $1 million. By the turn of the century, Montgomery Ward and Company's catalog, which would come to be known as the "Wish Book," grew to five hundred pages and was being mailed to more than a million people every year. And the company's headquarters was a new building on Michigan Avenue in Chicago—the biggest skyscraper west of New York City.[1]

STOPPING PAYMENT

Then in 1901, Montgomery Ward retired in order to spend the final years of his life working to make Chicago a better place. During the first two decades of the new century, the company continued to thrive. But in the late 1910s, things began to change. Ward's success had prompted the start of another Chicago-based company in 1886: Sears, Roebuck, and Co. It, like Montgomery Ward and Company, was a catalog-based merchant that catered to rural customers. Back when both companies began business, most of the U.S. population lived in rural areas. But the country was changing. Cities were filling up. When the 1920 census was completed, it showed that for the first time in the nation's history, the majority of the population lived in urban centers—and shopping habits were changing as a result.

Robert E. Wood, a former army quartermaster general, was brought in to run Montgomery Ward in 1919, and he saw the coming boom in retail sales. He wanted to begin opening stores in cities where people could shop in person, but the owners were unwilling to go along with the idea.[2] They simply would not pay the price to make the change.

PASSED BY

Knowing where the future lay in the business, Wood left Ward. In 1924, he went on staff at Sears as vice president. He convinced the people who ran Sears to take a chance on retail store sales. They agreed to open one store in Chicago as a test the following year. It was an immediate success. Two years later, Sears had opened 27 stores. By 1929, the company had built more than 300. Even during the depression, Sears continued to expand, and in 1931, Sears retail store sales surpassed catalog sales.[3] Wood became the company's chairman, a position he held until 1954, and Sears became the most successful department store chain in the country.

Montgomery Ward and Company never really recovered from that early error. It opened some retail stores, but it wasn't aggressive enough to overtake Sears. *The team fails to reach its potential when it fails to pay the price.* Time after time, Ward failed to pay the price. During the depression, the company hoarded cash and stopped expansion while Sears gained more ground. After World War II when other stores began moving to the suburbs, Ward failed to seize the opportunity to try to get back on top. Each time the market changed, the company's leaders didn't pay the price necessary to win a market. For the last twenty-five years of the twentieth century, they struggled to keep their doors open. Finally, after 128 years in business, Montgomery Ward closed. That's what can happen when people violate the Law of the Price Tag.

PRICE POINTS

If a team doesn't reach its potential, seldom is ability the issue. It's rarely a matter of resources either. It's almost always a payment issue. Montgomery Ward and Company had plenty of resources, and it had the talent it needed, including the leader who could move the team forward. The problem was that the company's owners were unwilling to get out of their comfort zone, take a risk, and try to break new ground.

One of the reasons teams fail to pay the price to reach their potential is that they misunderstand the Law of the Price Tag. They honestly don't know how it works. Allow me to give you four truths about this law that will help to clarify it in your mind.

1. The Price Must Be Paid by Everyone

In *Straight Talk for Monday Morning,* Allan Cox observed:

> You have to give up something to be a member of a team. It may be a phony role you've assigned to yourself, such as the guy who talks too much, the woman who remains silent, the know-it-all, the know-nothing, the hoarder of talented subordinates, the non-sharer of some resource such as management information systems (MIS), or whatever. You give up something, to be sure, such as some petty corner of privilege, but gain authenticity in return. The team, moreover, doesn't quash individual accomplishment; rather it empowers personal contributions.[4]

> *If everyone doesn't pay the price to win, then everyone will pay the price by losing.*

People who've never had the experience of being on a winning team often fail to realize that *every* team member must pay a price. I think some of them think that if others work hard, they can coast to their potential. But that is never true. If everyone doesn't pay the price to win, then everyone will pay the price by losing.

2. The Price Must Be Paid All the Time

Many people have what I call destination disease. I describe it in my book *The 21 Indispensable Qualities of a Leader.*

> Some people mistakenly believe that if they can accomplish a particular goal, they no longer have to grow. It can happen with almost anything: earning a degree, reaching a desired position, receiving a particular award, or achieving a financial goal.
>
> But effective leaders cannot afford to think that way. The day they stop growing is the day they forfeit their potential—and the potential of their organization. Remember the words of Ray Kroc: "As long as you're green, you're growing. As soon as you're ripe, you start to rot."[5]

Destination disease is as dangerous for a team as it is for any individual. It makes us believe that we can stop working, stop striving, stop paying the price—yet still reach our potential. But as Earl Blaik, former football coach at the United States Military Academy, observed, "There is no substitute for work. It is the price of success." That truth never goes away. That's why President Dwight D. Eisenhower remarked, "There are no victories at bargain prices." If you want to reach your potential, you can never let up.

> *"There are no victories at bargain prices."*
>
> —DWIGHT D. EISENHOWER

3. The Price Increases If the Team Wants to Improve, Change, or Keep Winning

As I mentioned in the introduction of this book, there are few back-to-back champions in sports. And few companies stay at the top of *Forbes* magazine's lists for a decade. Becoming a champion has a high price. But remaining on top costs even more. And improving upon your best is even more costly. The higher you are, the more you have to pay to make even small improvements. World champion sprinters improve their times not by seconds, but by hundredths of a second.

No one can move closer to his potential without paying in some way to get there. If you want to change professions, you have to get more education, additional work experience, or both. If you want to run a race at a faster pace, you must pay by training harder and smarter. If you want to increase earnings from your investments, you put in more money or take greater risks. The same principle applies to teams. To improve, change, or keep winning, as a group the team must pay a price, and so must the individuals on it.

4. The Price Never Decreases

Most people who quit don't give up at the bottom of the mountain; they stop halfway up it. Nobody sets out with the purpose of losing. The problem is often a mistaken belief that a time will come when success will suddenly get cheaper. But life rarely works that way.

Maybe that kind of thinking was the problem with Montgomery Ward and Company. In 1919, when the decision

> *Most people who quit don't give up at the bottom of the mountain; they stop halfway up it.*

makers had the chance to make Ward one of the first big companies to open a chain of retail stores, they probably evaluated what it would cost them—in terms of time, money, effort, change—and they thought that it was too great a price to pay. So they passed on the opportunity.

A few years later when Sears began to breeze past Ward, the cost to compete was even higher. The company paid to get into retail store sales, yet it was still behind. That price continued to go up year after year, especially as Sears beat Ward in securing prime locations. Even as late as the 1970s and 1980s, Ward paid more and more to improve, yet fell farther and farther behind. The company dabbled in various niches, trying to compete against Wal-Mart, Target, and Circuit City, but it kept getting clobbered. The leaders thought the price would be less the next time—but it kept going up and up.

> *When it comes to the Law of the Price Tag, I believe there are really only two kinds of teams who violate it: those who don't realize the price of success, and those who know the price but are not willing to pay it.*

When it comes to the Law of the Price Tag, I believe there are really only two kinds of teams who violate it: those who don't realize the price of success, and those who know the price but are not willing to pay it. No one can force a team member to have the will to succeed. Each person must decide in his own heart whether the goal is worth the price that must be paid. But every person ought to know what to expect to pay in order for a team to succeed.

THE PRICE OF TEAMWORK

For that reason, I offer the following observations about the cost of being part of a winning team. To become team players, you and your teammates will have at least the following required of you:

Sacrifice

There can be no success without sacrifice. James Allen observed, "He who would accomplish little must sacrifice little; he who would achieve much must sacrifice much." When you become part of a team, you may be aware of some of the things you will have to give up. But you can be sure that no matter how much you expect to give for the team, at some point you will be required to give more. That's the nature of teamwork. The team gets to the top only through the sweat, blood, and sacrifice of its team members.

Time Commitment

Teamwork does not come cheaply. It costs you time—that means you pay for it with your life. It takes time to get to know people, to build relationships with them, to learn how you and they work together. Teamwork can't be developed in microwave time. Teams grow strong in a Crock-Pot environment.

Personal Development

Your team will reach its potential only if you reach your potential. That means today's ability is not enough. Or to put it the way leadership expert Max DePree did: "We cannot become what we need to be by remaining what we are." That desire to keep striving,

> *Your team will reach its potential only if you reach your potential.*

to keep getting better, is a key to your ability, but it is also crucial for the betterment of the team. That is why UCLA's John Wooden, a marvelous team leader and the greatest college basketball coach of all time, said, "It's what you learn after you know it all that counts."

Unselfishness

People naturally look out for themselves. The question "What's in it for me?" is never far from their thoughts. But if a team is to reach its potential, its players must put the team's agenda ahead of

> *"When you give your best to the world, the world returns the favor."*
>
> —H. JACKSON BROWN

their own. Some people see the big picture more easily than others do and realize that they will receive more if they give more. For others, that is more difficult—especially if they already have a track record of high achievement. But H. Jackson Brown's Boomerang Theory is true: "When you give your best to the world, the world returns the favor." And if you give your best to the team, it will return more to you than you give, and together you will achieve more than you can on your own. *I buy it but Yet to see this....*

Certainly there are other prices individuals must pay to be part of a team. You can probably list several specific ones you've paid to be on a team. The point is that people can choose to stand on the sidelines of life and try to do everything solo. Or they can get into the game by being part of a team. It's a trade-off between independence and interdependence. The rewards of teamwork can be great, but there is always a cost. You always have to give up to go up.

About a month ago I was teaching the 17 Laws of Teamwork to a group of businesspeople in Atlanta, and after I taught the Law of the Price Tag, Virgil Berry came up to me and slipped me a note. It said, "John, the price tag for failure is greater than the price of success. The price for accepting failure is poverty, depression, dejection, and a downtrodden spirit." The people at Montgomery Ward know that all too well. *The team fails to reach its potential when it fails to pay the price.*

WHAT PRICE FOR A NATION?

Paying a high price does not always guarantee victory. Many teams sacrifice dearly, only to fall short of their goals. But sometimes great sacrifice is rewarded with great results. That was the case for the Revolutionary Army of the newly formed United States and its commander, George Washington, during the winter of 1777 in Valley Forge, Pennsylvania.

The year 1777 was not a particularly successful one for General Washington and his troops. Following defeats at Brandywine, Paoli, and Germantown and the loss of Philadelphia to the British, Washington and eleven thousand soldiers straggled into Valley Forge on December 19 of that year. The troops were demoralized, and they were facing the prospect of a bitter winter with minimal shelter and comforts.

What those men probably wanted most was to go home and forget about the war for freedom. But if they did, the cost would be high. Positioned as they were, they could keep an eye on the British troops under General Howe in Philadelphia. More important, they were in a place where they could defend York, Pennsylvania, to which the Continental Congress had fled when the capital fell to the British. If the men at Valley Forge didn't pay the price, the government would fall, the army would be disbanded, and the Revolutionary War would be lost.

Conditions were horrible. The men were ill-equipped and poorly supplied. A few days after their arrival, Washington wrote to the Continental Congress, saying, "2,898 men were unfit for duty because they were barefoot or otherwise naked [insufficiently clothed for the harsh weather]." Things were so bad that sentries had to stand on their hats to ward off frostbite in their feet. By February 1, 1778, only 5,000 men were available for service.[6]

PAYING THE PRICE—AND THEN SOME

Miraculously, the troops didn't give up. They bore the brunt of the difficult winter. But they did more than just hang on and survive. They took the time to become better soldiers. Prior to their stay at Valley Forge, they were disorganized and untrained. To remedy that, General Washington employed the talents of a former officer in the Prussian army, Baron von Steuben.

First, von Steuben imposed organization on the camp and introduced improved sanitation. Then, under his instruction, one company of men was transformed into a crack team of soldiers. They in turn helped to train the other companies of men. Von Steuben also standardized the military maneuvers throughout the army so that the men could work better as a team, no matter which officers commanded them. By the time the army mobilized in June of 1778, it was a match for any group of soldiers, even the British, who were considered by some to be the best in the world.

Washington's army went on to win battles against a British army with far superior numbers. And his soldiers fought in the Battle of Yorktown, the decisive battle that turned the war in favor of the newly formed country. Those of us who live in the United States are grateful to them, for the price they paid more than two hundred years ago paved the way for us to live in a country of great freedom and opportunity. While it's true that *the team fails to reach its potential when it fails to pay the price*, it's also true that when the price *is* paid, the rewards can be abundant. That's the blessing of the Law of the Price Tag.

TEAMWORK THOUGHT

You seldom get more than you pay for.

BECOMING A BETTER TEAM MEMBER

If you are an achiever, then you probably have lots of dreams and goals. Write down some of the things you desire to accomplish in the next one to five years:

1. _____

2. _____

3. _____

4. _____

5. _____

6. _____

7. _____

8. _____

9. _____

10. _____

Now, which of them are you willing to give up? You always need to be ready to ask yourself that question when you are part of a team. When your personal goals conflict with the greater goals of your team, you have three choices:

1. Put down the goal (because the team is more important).

2. Put off the goal (because it's not the right time).

3. Part with the team (because it's better for everyone).

The one thing you have no right to do is to expect the team to sacrifice its collective goals for yours.

BECOMING A BETTER TEAM LEADER

If you lead a team, then you must convince your teammates to sacrifice for the good of the group. The more talented the team members, the more difficult it may be to convince them to put the team first.

Begin by modeling sacrifice. Show the team that you are . . .

- Willing to make financial sacrifices for the team.

- Willing to keep growing for the sake of the team.

- Willing to empower others for the sake of the team.

- Willing to make difficult decisions for the sake of the team.

Once you have modeled the willingness to pay a price for the potential of the team, you have the credibility to ask others to do the same. Then when you recognize sacrifices that teammates must make for the team, show them why and how to do it. Then praise their sacrifices to their teammates.

THE LAW OF THE SCOREBOARD

The Team Can Make Adjustments When It Knows Where It Stands

I n the previous chapter, you read about Montgomery Ward and Company, an American business that fell on hard times because it failed to heed the Law of the Price Tag. For a couple of decades, it looked as if another American institution was headed for a similar disaster: Walt Disney Productions.

THE MOUSE THAT ROARED

The company was founded by Walt Disney and his brother, Roy, in the 1920s. They began doing silent animation shorts and grew the company into one of the most loved and respected entertainment companies in the world. They continually broke new ground. They produced the first talking cartoon and the first color cartoon, both featuring Mickey Mouse, who has since become an American icon. *Snow White,* the first feature-length animated movie ever, was a radically innovative idea. While it was being made, many called it "Disney's folly." When it was released in 1937, it became the most successful film ever made up to that time. (Some say it's the most successful of all time!)

During the next two decades, Walt Disney Productions made wonderful movies that became classics. It expanded into television production. And it opened the world's first theme park. The name Disney became synonymous with creative family entertainment.

THE COMPANY THAT WHIMPERED

But after Walt died in 1966, the company started down a very bumpy road. Where Walt Disney Productions had once stood for innovation, it came to be marked by imitation—of its own past successes. Don Bluth, who left Disney in 1979, commented, "We felt like we were animating the same picture over and over again, with the faces changed a little."[1]

Instead of trying to look forward and break ground, Card Walker, who oversaw movie production, always asked himself, "What would Walt have done?" People at the studio began to joke morbidly, "We're working for a dead man."[2] The company cranked out more formula movies that didn't make a profit, and revenues continued to shrink. In 1981 the film division had an income of $34.6 million. In 1982 its income had fallen to $19.6 million. In 1983 it incurred a loss of $33.3 million. And the value of Disney stock was plummeting.

During that period, many American corporations were becoming victims of hostile takeovers, where Wall Street raiders would gain control of the company, cut it into pieces, and sell off its parts at a profit for themselves and their backers. Since Disney's stock value was down and it carried little debt, it became ripe for a hostile takeover.

In 1984, Disney narrowly avoided one takeover attempt and was facing the threat of yet another when its board of directors finally took a realistic look at where Disney stood. They decided that if the company was to survive, it would require radical changes, including something it had never done in its history—bringing in someone from outside Disney to run the company.

GETTING BACK INTO THE GAME

The people selected to turn around Disney were Michael Eisner as chairman and CEO and Frank Wells as president and COO. Concerning their challenging task, Eisner remarked,

> Our job wasn't to create something new, but to bring back the magic, to dress Disney up in more stylish clothes and expand its reach, to remind people why they loved the company in the first place . . . A brand is a living entity, and it is enriched or undermined cumulatively over time, the product of a thousand small gestures.[3]

Eisner was writing about his work on the Disney brand, but his remarks describe the approach he and Wells took to revitalizing the entire company. That involved a variety of strategies.

For one thing, they changed the name of the organization from Walt Disney Productions to the Walt Disney Company, reflecting the diversity of its interests. They brought together all of the organization's corporate executives and division heads for a weekly lunch to promote cohesiveness and to share ideas across divisions. They also hired key leaders, such as Jeffrey Katzenberg, to run their movie and television operations.

GOAL!

In a matter of a few years, Disney once again became a vital player in the entertainment industry. The almost-dead television division produced hits such as *The Golden Girls* and *Home Improvement.* The movie division, which had recently produced few movies and lost so much money, produced more movies in greater volume, with twenty-seven of its first thirty-three turning a profit. Before long, the company had four movie divisions: Disney, Touchstone, Hollywood Pictures, and Miramax. In late 1987, Disney became the number one studio at the box office for the first time in its history. And the animation division once again set the pace for the industry by creating films such as *The Little Mermaid, Beauty and the Beast, Aladdin,* and *The Lion King.*

Eisner and Wells expanded the company's efforts into new areas. They increased land development and built numerous new hotels at Walt Disney World. In 1987 they also opened retail stores in malls for the first time. Four years later, Disney owned 125 stores, which were generating $300 million in annual revenue. And of course, they improved the theme parks through expansion, innovation, and strategic partnerships with people such as George Lucas and Steven Spielberg. When they took over the company in 1984, the parks generated income of $250 million. By 1990, their income reached $800 million.

In 2000, the Walt Disney Company had revenues of $25.4 billion with $2.9 billion in net income (more than double the figures from 1984).[4] Disney has done more than just turn itself around. It has become an entertainment giant and one of the most powerful corporations in the world. For many of the years when the company was struggling, its team members looked at its history and the memory of its dead founder to gauge what to do. What they needed to do was to look at the scoreboard. *The team can make adjustments when it knows where it stands.* Eisner and Wells brought that ability to the company. They understood and implemented the Law of the Scoreboard.

UNDERSCORING THE SCOREBOARD

Every "game" has its own rules and its own definition of what it means to win. Some teams measure their success in points scored; others in profits. Still others may look at the number of people they serve. But no matter what the game is, there is always a scoreboard. And if a team is to accomplish its goals, it has to know where it stands. It has to look at itself in light of the scoreboard.

> *If a team is to accomplish its goals, it has to know where it stands.*

Why is that so important? Because teams that succeed make adjustments to continually improve themselves and their situations. For example, think about how a football team approaches a game. Before the competition starts, the team spends a tremendous amount of time planning. Players study hours of game film. They spend days figuring out what their opponent is likely to do, and they decide the best way to win. They come up with a detailed game plan.

As the game begins, the game plan is very important, and the scoreboard means nothing. But as the game goes on, the game plan means less and less, and the scoreboard becomes more and more significant. Why? Because the game is constantly changing. You see, the game plan tells what you *want* to happen. But the scoreboard tells what *is* happening.

WHY THE SCOREBOARD?

No team can ignore the reality of its situation and win. For years, Disney clung tenaciously to an out-of-date game plan while the world and the entertainment industry kept changing around it. The Disney team never really gave a hard look at the scoreboard. As a result they kept losing. That's what happens when you ignore the Law of the Scoreboard.

For any kind of team, the scoreboard is essential in the following ways:

1. The Scoreboard Is Essential to Understanding

In sports, players, coaches, and fans understand the importance of the scoreboard. That's why it is so visible at every stadium, arena, and ball field. The scoreboard provides a snapshot of the game at any given time. Even if you arrive at a game halfway into it, you can look at the scoreboard and assess the situation well.

> *The scoreboard provides a snapshot of the game at any given time.*

I'm often surprised by how many people outside sports try to succeed without a scoreboard. Some families operate their households without budgets, yet wonder why they are in debt. Some small-business owners go year after year without tracking sales or creating a balance sheet and wonder why they can't grow the business. Some pastors busy themselves with worthy activities, but never stop to measure whether they are reaching people or performing according to biblical standards.

2. The Scoreboard Is Essential to Evaluating

I believe that personal growth is a key to success. That's why I've taught lessons on growth at conferences and in books for more than twenty years. A key principle I teach is this:

$$Growth = Change$$

This sounds overly simple, doesn't it? But people sometimes lose sight of the fact that they cannot grow and remain the same at the same time. Most people are in a position that could be described by something Coach Lou Holtz once said: "We aren't where we want to be; we aren't where we ought to be; but thank goodness we aren't where we used to be."

But when it comes to growth, change alone is not enough. If you want to become better, you have to change in the right direction. You can do that only if you are able to evaluate yourself and your teammates. That is another reason for the scoreboard. It gives you continual feedback. Competing without a scoreboard is like bowling without pins. You may be working hard, but you don't really know how you're doing.

3. The Scoreboard Is Essential to Decision Making

Once you've evaluated your situation, you're ready to make decisions. In football, the quarterback uses information from the scoreboard to decide what play to call. In baseball, the scoreboard helps the manager know when to bring in a relief pitcher. In basketball, it can be used to determine whether to call a timeout.

That was the case at Disney. First Eisner looked at the company to understand its overall position. Then he evaluated individual areas for their effectiveness. Only then was he able to make sound decisions concerning how to get Disney back into the game.

4. The Scoreboard Is Essential to Adjusting

The higher the level on which you and your team are competing, the smaller the adjustments become to achieve your best. But making key adjustments is the secret to winning, and the scoreboard helps you to see where the adjustments need to be made.

One of the people on my staff is employing a unique scoreboard to help him make the adjustments required to go to the next level. That person is Kevin Small, the president of INJOY. Kevin is a real go-getter with high energy and enthusiasm. Being a young leader, he also has weak areas he needs to work on. To help him with that, he has engaged a personal coach to advise him, to help him read the scoreboard in his life, and to hold him accountable for growth. And it's really helping him. The small adjustments Kevin is making are taking him to another level and moving him closer to fulfilling his already tremendous potential.

5. The Scoreboard Is Essential to Winning

In the end, nobody can win without the scoreboard. How do you know when the game is on the line without the scoreboard? How do you know when time is running out unless you check the scoreboard? How will you know if it's cruise time or crunch time unless you have the scoreboard as a measuring device? If your desire is to take a leisurely drive with some friends, then you don't need to worry about a thing. But if you're trying to win the Indy 500, then you and your team *must* know how you're doing!

Some organizations view the scoreboard as a necessary evil. Others try to ignore it—something they cannot do for long and still do well in their profession. And some organizations make checking the scoreboard such an integral part of their culture that they are continually able to recognize and seize opportunities leading to huge success.

HIGH TOUCH IN A HIGH-TECH WORLD

That is certainly the case for eBay. I'm not a technical person. I don't have a computer—I don't even know how to use one—so I have not used eBay. I first heard about it from friends who are collectors. They talked about being able to find things they wanted through auctions held on the Internet. They seemed to be having fun with it, but to tell the truth I didn't pay much attention. Then I started seeing articles about eBay in the financial pages, and I read about the company's president and CEO, Meg Whitman.

Ebay is an e-commerce company that specializes in connecting buyers and sellers of goods on-line. It was founded by Pierre Omidyar in his San Jose, California, living room in September of 1995 with the idea of helping people find used, rare, or collectible items. The idea took off and became so successful that Omidyar soon recognized that he was in over his head. That's when he hired Meg Whitman, who had an MBA from Harvard and tremendous leadership experience as a general manager at Hasbro, president and CEO of FTD, and senior vice president of the Walt Disney Company.

An article in *Time* magazine explains eBay's success this way:

> As an online middleman between buyers and sellers, eBay is building an empire that bricks and mortar could not have touched. "If Buy.com goes down, you can still go to Circuit City," says Meg Whitman, . . . CEO of eBay. But if eBay crashes, there's nowhere else to go. And because eBay's job is connecting people—not selling them things—it isn't lumbered with a traditional retailing cost structure . . . "Ebay is the only e-tailer that really fulfills the promise of the Web," says Faye Landes, an e-commerce analyst at Sanford C. Bernstein & Co.[5]

The real genius of eBay is its mastery of the Law of the Scoreboard. It constantly makes adjustments because it knows where it stands, and that is what keeps it ahead. In the case of eBay, the scoreboard is the desires and interests of its customers—and potential customers. Sensing that many people are uneasy with conducting monetary transactions on the Internet, eBay made trust, safety, and privacy hallmarks of the company. Knowing that people wanted to get specific feedback on the individuals selling merchandise on the site, eBay created a unique rating system that allows subscribers to exchange information. The company even created a special Consumer Insights Group to track what people want.

LEARNING FROM THE CUSTOMER

Over the last three years, eBay has learned everything it can about its users and what they want while keeping its finger on the pulse of larger consumer trends. The company has expanded from being a place to trade Beanie Babies to a multifaceted auction service that offers among other services:

- Special local trading for difficult-to-ship items

- Global auction service that covers 150 countries (including a strong presence in Europe)

- A business-to-business exchange for products and services

- An automobile auction site

- Real estate services

And in 2000, when eBay saw that a new start-up company called Half.com was thriving by selling used CDs, books, movies, and video games at set prices, eBay bought the company and added it to its holdings.[6]

The result is that eBay has received highly favorable recognition and hundreds of awards, including *Business Week* Entrepreneur of the Year, E-Retailer of the Year Award from *E-Retailer*, and a place on the list of *Forbes* magazine's one hundred most dynamic companies in America. In 2000, it had 22.5 million registered users, controlled 80 percent of the on-line auction market, and had revenues of $430 million (up 92 percent from 1999).

While other Internet-based companies are struggling to survive and searching for ways to finally make a profit, eBay seems poised to keep growing—and winning. Why? Because the eBay team always has an eye on the scoreboard. And *the team can make adjustments when it knows where it stands.* That's the Law of the Scoreboard.

TEAMWORK THOUGHT

When you know what to do, then you can do what you know.

BECOMING A BETTER TEAM MEMBER

What is the scoreboard in your business or field? How do you measure your progress? Is it the bottom line? Is it the number of people you reach? Is it the level of excellence or innovation with which you do your work? How do you keep score?

> *When you know what to do, then you can do what you know.*

Take some time to identify how your team keeps score. Write the criteria here:

_____

_____

_____

_____

Now think about how you should be measuring yourself individually. What should you be keeping track of to make sure you are doing your best? Write the criteria here:

_____

_____

_____

_____

BECOMING A BETTER TEAM LEADER

If you lead the team, you have primary responsibility for checking the scoreboard and communicating the team's situation to its members. That doesn't necessarily mean you have to do it all by yourself. But you do need to make sure that team members continually evaluate, adjust, and make decisions as quickly as possible. That's the key to winning.

Do you have a system to make sure that happens? Or do you generally rely on your intuition? Using intuition is fine—as long as you have some fail-safe backups to make sure you don't let the team down.

Evaluate how consistently and effectively you consult your scoreboard. If you're not doing it as well as you should, then create a system that helps you to do it or empowers the leaders on your team to share the responsibility.

12

THE LAW OF THE BENCH

Great Teams Have Great Depth

Have you ever heard the expression "It's not over until the fat lady sings," or Yogi Berra's famous comment, "It ain't over till it's over"? Would you be surprised to know that sometimes it *is* over before it's over—and you can know when that is if you know the Law of the Bench?

Let me give you an example. One Saturday in September of 2000, I went to a football game with some friends: Kevin Small, the president of INJOY; Chris Goede, who used to play professional ball; and Steve Miller, my wonderful son-in-law. We were looking forward to an exciting game between the Georgia Tech Yellow Jackets and the Florida State Seminoles, even though FSU was a very strong favorite. There's an intense rivalry between all Georgia and Florida college teams, so the teams can get pretty pumped up.

And on that day, we weren't disappointed. The teams were battling, and the score was close. Tech was playing its heart out.

ONLY A MATTER OF TIME

But as the third quarter came to a close, I said, "Come on, guys. This one is over." I sometimes leave games early because I hate to be stuck in traffic. Of course, if a game is really close or is likely to have some historic significance (such as a no-hitter in baseball), I stay to the end. On that day, the guys were surprised by my desire to leave, especially since the game was close and Tech had finally pulled ahead, 15 to 12.

"You don't want to see the end of the game?" asked Chris, a little curious.

"No, this game is over," I said. "Let's go to the car."

On our way back, we talked about it. It's true that Tech was hanging in there against FSU, especially when it came to the way the Yellow Jackets were playing defense. That was no easy task because the Seminoles had a powerful offense. But I had noticed throughout the course of the game that while Tech's starters were still in the game, FSU had been substituting many players from the bench—

> *A great starter alone is simply not enough if a team wants to go to the highest level.*

and the team's level of play had not been negatively affected. Because of that, I knew it was only a matter of time before Tech's players would be worn down by the powerful bench of FSU. And sure enough, the final score was 26 to 21 with FSU on top. That's the impact of the Law of the Bench. *Great teams have great depth.*

THE ROLE OF THE BENCH

It's not difficult to see the importance of having well-trained, capable reserve players who sit on the bench in sports. In major-league baseball, the teams who win championships do so because they have more than just a good pitching rotation and solid field-ing. They possess a bull pen with strong players who can substitute or pinch-hit off the bench. In the NBA, players and fans have long recognized the impact of the bench by talking about the all-impor-tant sixth man, the person who makes a significant contribution to the team's success yet isn't one of the five starters on the basketball court. And today's professional football coaches express the need to have two highly skilled quarterbacks capable of winning games on their teams. A great starter alone is simply not enough if a team wants to go to the highest level.

Any team that wants to excel must have good substitutes as well as starters. That's true in any field, not just sports. You may be able to do some wonderful things with a handful of top people, but if you want your team to do well over the long haul, you've got to build your bench. A great team with no bench eventually collapses.

DEFINING THE BENCH

In sports, it's easy to define which people are the starters and which make up the bench. But how do you define them in other fields? I want to suggest the following definitions:

Starters are frontline people who directly add value to the organi-zation or who directly influence its course.

The bench is made up of the people who indirectly add value to the organization or who support the starters.

A team's starters are the people most often in the spotlight, and as a result, they get most of the credit, and the people on the bench are liable to be neglected or overlooked. In fact, the people most likely to discount or discredit the contribution of the bench may be the starters. Some key players enjoy reminding the substitutes that they are "riding the pine." But any starter who minimizes the contribution of the bench is self-centered, underestimates what it takes for a team to be a success, and doesn't understand that *great teams have great depth.*

A leader who truly understood the Law of the Bench was UCLA's John Wooden, the "Wizard of Westwood," whose teams won ten college basketball national championships. Coach Wooden valued every person on his teams and the contribution that each person made. No coach did a better job of keeping his teams playing at the highest level over the long haul than Wooden. He observed, "Unselfishness is a trait I always insisted upon. I believed that every basketball team is a unit, and I didn't separate my players as to starters and subs. I tried to make it clear that every man plays a role, including the coach, the assistants, the trainer and the managers."[1]

THE BENCH IS INDISPENSABLE

Every human being has value, and every player on a team adds value to the team in some way. These truths alone should be enough to make team members care about the bench players. But there are also more specific reasons to honor and develop the players who may not be considered starters. Here are several:

1. Today's Bench Players May Be Tomorrow's Stars

Rare are the people who begin their careers as stars. And those who do sometimes find that their success is like that of some child actors. After a brief flash in the pan, they are never able to recapture the attention they got early on.

Most successful people go through an apprenticeship or period of seasoning. Look at someone like quarterback Joe Montana, who was inducted into the NFL Hall of Fame in 2000. He spent two years on the bench as a backup before being named the San Francisco 49ers starter. And as he was breaking records and leading his team to numerous Super Bowls, the person who sat on the bench as a backup to him was Steve Young, another top-notch quarterback.

> *Every human being has value, and every player on a team adds value to the team in some way.*

Some talented team members are recognized early for their positive potential and are groomed to succeed. Others labor in obscurity for years, learning, growing, and gaining experience. Then after a decade of hard work, they become "overnight successes." With the way people like to move from job to job today—and even from career to career—good leaders should always keep their eyes open for emerging talent. Never be in a hurry to pigeonhole anyone on your team as a nonstarter. Given the right encouragement, training, and opportunities, nearly anyone who has the desire has the potential to emerge someday as an effective player.

2. The Success of a Supporting Player Can Multiply the Success of a Starter

When every team member fulfills the role that best suits his talents, gifts, and experience and excels in that role, then the team really hums. The achievement of the whole team makes the starters flourish, and the achievement of the starters makes the team flourish. The whole team really is greater than the sum of its parts. Or to put it the way John Wooden did: "The main ingredient of stardom is the rest of the team."

> *"The main ingredient of stardom is the rest of the team."*
>
> —JOHN WOODEN

You have probably seen teams led by people who don't understand this truth. For example, they have million-dollar salespeople spending half of their time bogged down in paperwork rather than making calls on potential clients. If the organization would hire someone who enjoyed administrative tasks, not only would the salespeople be happier and more productive, but the gains in sales would more than make up for the cost of that support person.

We follow this rule at ISS, my company that provides consulting to churches for fund-raising. We employ consultants whose skills and backgrounds are truly one in a million. They work with hundreds of individual churches out in the field every year, and that is where they need to be to use their strengths. However, each consulting job requires numerous letters, instruction manuals, and other printed materials. And to accomplish that, ISS employs a team of talented support people who do a fabulous job with that work. When each person is allowed to work in an area of strength, the entire team wins.

3. There Are More Bench Players Than Starters

If you read through the roster of any successful team, you will see that the starters are always outnumbered by the other players on the team. In professional basketball, twelve people are on the team, but only five start. Major-league baseball teams start nine but carry forty players. In pro football, twenty-two people start on offense and defense, but each team is allowed to have fifty-three players in all. (College teams often have more than one hundred!)

You find similar situations in every field. In the entertainment industry, the actors are often known, but the hundreds of crew members necessary to make a movie aren't. In ministry, everyone recognizes the people up front during a worship service, but it takes scores of people working behind the scenes to bring that service together. For any politician or corporate executive or big-name fashion designer that you know about, there are hundreds of people toiling quietly in the background to make the person's work possible. Nobody can neglect the majority of the team and hope to be successful.

4. A Bench Player Placed Correctly Will at Times Be More Valuable Than a Starter

I think if you asked most people how they would classify administrative assistants as team members, they would tell you that they consider them to be bench players since their primary role is support. I would agree with that—although in some cases, administrative people have direct influence on an organization.

Take, for example, my assistant, Linda Eggers. Over the years, Linda has done just about everything at INJOY. She has been the company's bookkeeper. She used to run our conferences. She did marketing and product development. She is a very talented person. I think Linda is capable of doing just about anything. But she has chosen to take a supporting role as my assistant. And in that position, she makes a huge impact. Today my company has more than two hundred employees. I respect and value all of them. But if I lost everything tomorrow and I could keep only five or six people with whom to start over from scratch, Linda would be one of the people I would fight to keep. Her value as a support person makes her a starter.

5. A Strong Bench Gives the Leader More Options

When a team has no bench, the only option of its leader is moving the starters around to maximize their effectiveness. If a starter can't perform, the team is out of luck. When a team has a weak bench, the leader has a few options, but

> *When a team has a great bench, the options are almost endless.*

they are often not very good. But when a team has a great bench, the options are almost endless.

That's why someone like Bobby Bowden, the coach at FSU, was able to wear down Georgia Tech. If one of his players got hurt, he had someone to replace him. If his opponent changed defenses, he had offensive players in reserve to overcome the challenge. No matter what kind of situation he faced, with a strong bench he had options that would give the team a chance to win.

6. The Bench Is Usually Called Upon at Critical Times for the Team

When an army is in trouble, what does it do? It calls up the reserves. That's the way it is in every area of life. You don't need the bench when things are going well; you need it when things aren't going well. When the starter gets hurt and the game is in jeopardy, a substitute steps in. That person's effectiveness often determines the team's success.

If your team is experiencing a tough time, then you know the importance of having a good bench. But if you are experiencing a smooth period, then now is the time to develop your backup players. Build the bench today for the crisis you will face tomorrow.

TODAY'S ACTIONS BUILD TOMORROW'S TEAM

As you think about the starters and the bench players on your team, recognize that the future of your team can be predicted by three things:

1. Recruitment: Who Is Joining the Team?

Adlai E. Stevenson offered this advice: "There are only three rules of sound administration: Pick good men, tell them not to cut corners, and back them to the limit; and picking good men is the most important." You cannot build a winning team without good players.

When it comes to recruiting, there are really only two kinds: You find the player for the position, or you find the position for the player. In the first situation, you have a position open, and you look for someone to fill that position. That is the typical way most recruiting works. But sometimes even when you don't have a position open, you find a potential player who is so good that you simply cannot pass up the opportunity to get him on the team.

I was in the second situation last year. When I discovered that John Hull might be interested in coming to work for The INJOY Group, I didn't have a specific position for him. But he is such a high-impact player that I brought him aboard. And in a matter of a few months, he became the president of EQUIP, the nonprofit organization I founded, when its original president, Ron McManus, desired to lead another department for me. If I hadn't asked John to come aboard when I did, the team might have missed out on a wonderful leader.

2. Training: Are You Developing the Team?

You cannot solve tomorrow's problems with today's solutions. If you want the team to succeed as it meets new challenges, you have to prepare it. That means helping starters to maximize their potential and training the people on the bench to become starters when their time comes.

> *You cannot solve tomorrow's problems with today's solutions.*

If you have leadership responsibility for your team, then take the initiative to make sure everyone on the team is growing and improving.

3. Losses: Who Is Leaving the Team?

The only place that never loses people is the cemetery. Losing team members is inevitable. But the good news is that you can choose the members you lose. If you keep nonproductive people, the productive ones become frustrated and leave. If you remove the people who don't add value, then the whole team gets better. It's just like trimming trees: If you don't cut the deadwood, eventually the whole tree falls. But if you remove the deadwood, the tree becomes healthier, the healthy branches produce more, and there's room for productive new branches on the tree.

The best way to describe how to grow and improve the team

and its bench is what I call the revolving door principle. Here's the way it works: A team will always have gains and losses. People are constantly coming into an organization while others leave it. The key to its future success is gaining a more effective person with each loss.

Let's say, for example, that you can rate every person's effectiveness on a scale of 1 to 10, with 10 as the highest. As the revolving door turns, if your team is losing 4s but gaining 8s, then your future looks bright. If you're losing 8s and gaining 4s, then the future looks bleak. And if you're losing 4s and gaining other 4s, then you're wearing your team out with activity but making no progress.

Phases of an Organization and
Its Revolving Door

Any team that is avoiding stagnation by trying to improve will go through changes, and as the revolving door moves, different kinds of people will come and go during various phases. For example, when an organization is new and just getting started, it recruits strongly. It has no one to lose and is glad to gain anyone. The good news is that as people come on board, a team is being formed. The bad news is that the people the team is gaining are not always good.

When a team asks for commitment, some team members leave the team. But that's good. Commitment drives away the uncommitted, while it makes those who stay even stronger in the commitment they already possess.

Once the team has a committed core and begins to grow, it again gains people. The people who join the team are often attracted to it because of the level of commitment they see in existing players. That

Type of Team	Gain or Loss	Nature of Loss or Gain
New Team	More Gains Than Losses	Gains Are Not Always Positive
Committed Team	More Losses Than Gains	Losses Are Positive
Growing Team	More Gains Than Losses	Gains Are Positive
Successful Team	More Losses Than Gains	Losses Are Not Positive
Legacy Team	More Gains Than Losses	Gains Are Positive

builds the team's ability and drives it to achieve—and leads to its success.

However, once a team becomes successful, some members will want to leave to try to find greater success on their own. That's a critical time for a team. If you can give people intriguing challenges and share both responsibilities and rewards with them, you may be able to persuade them to stay. (If you can't, you'll probably have to rely on your backup players, and then you'll find out what kind of bench you've built!)

If you can sustain growth in the midst of success and repeat the process while continually building your bench, then you can create a legacy team. That's what organizations such as General Electric, Disney, and Home Depot have done. Their sustained growth and reputations for success continue to draw good people to them.

WHO IS YOUR MVP?

The key to making the most of the Law of the Bench is to continually improve the team. As you bring on better players, first improve your starters. Then build your bench. Do that long enough and you will build a great team because *great teams have great depth*. That's the Law of the Bench.

Building a great team is a process that takes a tremendous amount of work, and the bigger the organization gets, the harder the task becomes. I'm acutely aware of that because in the last three and a half years, The INJOY Group has grown from less than fifty people to more than two hundred! When you're experiencing that kind of explosive growth, your HR person may be your MVP.

Let me tell you about the person most responsible for keeping the revolving door moving in the right direction in my company. Her name is Stacy Buchanan. Two and a half years ago, an acquaintance of hers who was a headhunter directed her to The INJOY Group. At the time, we were looking for a senior accountant, and Stacy had an extensive background in accounting, having done much of the groundwork to become a CPA. She had also worked for six years at an internationally known nonprofit organization and spent several years teaching.

> *The key to making the most of the Law of the Bench is to continually improve the team.*

BOLD MOVE

Stacy believed with all her heart that she belonged at The INJOY Group, and she really wanted to work with us. So she came in and interviewed with us. But the last thing in the world she wanted to do was go back into accounting. Christine Johnson, a longtime INJOY employee who was functioning as our HR manager at the time, was interviewing Stacy. Christine could tell that she was an "eagle" and didn't want her to get away. So she introduced Stacy to the COO, Dick Peterson. As they talked, he, too, could tell she was a tremendous catch. Finally he asked her, "What do you want to do?"

Stacy gathered her courage and replied, "To tell you the truth, Dick, I want Christine's job: recruiting."

That was music to Christine's ears. She was dutifully recruiting new employees, but she didn't really enjoy it—nor did it utilize her greatest strengths. She and Dick were happy to create a position for Stacy as a recruiter, thus freeing Christine to focus on administration and management. In the thirty months since then, Stacy has hired nearly two hundred people for the company—both starters and bench players. And she does a fantastic job.

"I know I am going to sound like a preacher with my six Ps," says Stacy, "but this will give you an idea of how I place people. I analyze the following areas:

1. *Personality:* I use the DISC test, a diagnostic tool that indicates whether someone's personality is driving, influencing, supporting, or calculating.

2. *Passion:* I find out what motivates them—results, relationships, money, recognition, affirmation, impact, or security.

3. *Pattern:* I look for patterns in their successes and their failures. I figure out whether they work best alone or on a team.

4. *Potential:* I try to see what they might accomplish given the

right direction, motivation, coaching, and leadership. I particularly gauge whether they are maintainers or builders.

5. *Profile:* I gauge whether they will fit our culture and whether they are really INJOY material.

6. *Placement:* Finally I try to measure where they fit—which team will both benefit from them and add value to them.

Stacy has done a wonderful job of building our team through recruiting. And now she has expanded her role into the area of training. She has played an instrumental role in starting the nine mentoring groups that are currently in place at The INJOY Group. Stacy summarizes her work by saying, "My desire is to see people play the music that is contained in their souls."

If you want your team to become the very best it can be, then you need to concentrate on the people you're gaining, the ones you're losing, and the ones you're developing. That's the only way to build a great team. It has to be solid at every level. And never lose sight of the Law of the Bench. Remember, *great teams have great depth.*

Teamwork Thought

Better players make you a better player.

Becoming a Better Team Member

How would you define yourself: a bench player or a starter? If you are on the bench, then your job is to do two things: Help the starters to shine, and prepare yourself to be a starter in the future. You can do that by cultivating an attitude of service and teachability, and by doing whatever you can to learn and grow.

If you are a starter, then you should perform at your best for the sake of the team, and you should honor the people on the bench. You do that by acknowledging the value of their contribution and by helping prepare them to start someday. If you are not already mentoring a teammate on the bench, start doing so right away.

Becoming a Better Team Leader

If you lead your team, you are responsible for making sure the revolving door moves in such a way that the players who are joining the team are better than those who are leaving. One way you can facilitate that is to place high value on the good people already on the team.

Every team has three groups of players. In this chapter I described the *starters,* who directly add value to the organization or who directly influence its course, and the *bench players,* who indirectly add value to the organization or who support the starters. The third group is a core group within the starters that I call the *inner-circle members.* Without these people the team would fall apart. Your job is to make sure each group is continually developed so that bench players are able to step up to become starters, and starters are able to step up to become inner-circle members.

If you're not sure who the inner-circle members are on your team, then try this exercise: Write the names of the people on your team who are starters. Now determine the people you could most easily do without. One by one, check off the names of the people whose loss would hurt the team least if they left. At some point you will end up with a smaller group of people without whom the team would be dead. That's your inner circle. (You can even rank the remaining people in order of importance.)

It's a good exercise to remind you of the value of people on the team. And by the way, if your treatment of those people doesn't match their value, you run the risk of losing them and having your revolving door work against you.

13

THE LAW OF IDENTITY

Shared Values Define the Team

A t least one day a year, I try to bring together everyone in my organization. Early in INJOY's history, that was easy. Back in 1985 when we founded the company, Dick Peterson, who is now the company's COO, and I could get together on a moment's notice with his mother-in-law, Erma (our only employee), and the four or five volunteers who helped us (two of whom were our wives). Even ten years later we were still a fairly small outfit. The entire company could meet around one large conference table.

Today things are different. Now we have to rent a hall to accommodate all of our employees, but we still make the effort to get together. In fact, it's more important for us to do that now than it ever was before. Because of our size and the diversity of operations, the people on our team have a tendency to get disconnected from one another. And it becomes increasingly difficult for the leaders in the organization to maintain a personal connection with everyone.

DEFINING THE TEAM

Maybe you've experienced the disconnectedness that often accompanies rapid growth in an organization. Granted, with slightly more than two hundred employees, ours is not a large company, but it is big enough to experience growing pains. Where the team was once defined almost entirely through relationships, it now needs something more to keep it together. That's where the Law of Identity comes into play: *Shared values define the team.* Even if some members of a team don't share common experiences or have a personal relationship with one another, they can possess a cohesiveness that defies the size of the team. What it takes is a common vision (the Law of the Compass) and shared values. If everyone embraces the same values, team members can still have a connection to one another and to the larger team.

> *Just as personal values influence and guide an individual's behavior, organizational values influence and guide the team's behavior.*

We've all seen teams that have a common goal yet lack common values. Everyone on the team has different ideas about what's important. The result is chaos. Eventually the team breaks down if everyone tries to do things his own way. That's why team members need to be on the same page. Just as personal values influence and guide an individual's behavior, organizational values influence and guide the team's behavior.

THE VALUE OF VALUES

Values can help a team to become more connected and more effective. Shared values are like . . .

Glue

When difficult times come—and they do for every team—values hold people together. Look at a marriage, for example. It's easy for a couple to stay together when they are feeling the flush of love and everything is going smoothly. But eventually the passion that drew them together fades. And adversity comes. What keeps the people who stay married together? It's their values. Their values are more important than their feelings. They value their marriage so highly that they are willing to fight *for* the relationship. If two people don't have that mind-set going into the wedding, then their chances of staying together are pretty slim.

The same is true for any other team. If the players don't know what their values are—and live them out—their chances of working as a unit and reaching their potential are very small.

A Foundation

All teams need stability to perform well and to grow. Values provide a stable foundation that makes those things possible. This is true for just about any kind of relationship to grow. For example, if you are trying to build a relationship with someone from another culture, you begin by looking for the things you have in common. If you are trying to make a sale with a new customer, you look for common ground. The same is true when it comes to team building. You need something to build on, and values make the strongest foundation.

A Ruler

Values also help set the standard for a team's performance. In the corporate world, the values are often expressed in a mission statement or set of guidelines for doing business. But sometimes a company's stated values and its real values don't match up.

Author and management expert Ken Blanchard emphasizes, "Lots of companies claim they have a set of core values,

> *Values help set the standard for a team's performance.*

but what they mean is a list of generic business beliefs that everyone would agree with, such as having integrity, making a profit, and responding to customers. Such values have meaning only when they are further defined in terms of how people actually behave and are rank-ordered to reveal priority." And they function as a measure of expectations and performance when they are genuinely embraced.

A Compass

Do you remember the television show *Dallas* from the 1980s? The main character was J. R. Ewing, a notoriously dishonest businessman. His character code for living can be summarized by something he said in an episode of the show: "Once you give up your ethics, the rest is a piece of cake." To a person with no values, anything goes.

I think we live in a time when people are searching for standards to live by. When individuals embrace strong values, they possess a moral compass that helps them make decisions. The same is true for people in an organization. When the team identifies and embraces a set of values, then in a month, a year, or a decade, no matter how much circumstances change or what challenges present themselves, people on the team still know it's moving in the right direction and make good decisions.

A Magnet

A team's values attract people with like values to the team. Think about some of the teams we've examined in previous chapters. What kinds of people are drawn to Habitat for Humanity? People who want to see substandard housing eliminated. What kinds of people are attracted to Enron? People who value innovation and organizational flexibility.

In *The 21 Irrefutable Laws of Leadership*, the Law of Magnetism states, "Who you are is who you attract." That law is as true for teams as it is for leaders. People attract other like-minded people.

An Identity

Values define the team and give it a unique identity—to team members, potential recruits, clients, and the public. What you believe identifies who you are.

THE VALUES OF THE INJOY GROUP

When I brought together all of the employees of The INJOY Group for our annual meeting this year, I wanted to emphasize our values. I think our team members see them acted out every day, but I wanted to give everyone a common language for the values to help ensure our alignment with them. To do that, I taught a lesson on those values.

Communication of the team's values is the place to start with the Law of Identity. A team cannot share values if the values have not been shared with the team. Allow me to acquaint you with the six core values that I shared with The INJOY Group so that you have a sense of what I mean.

1. The Personal Growth of Each Team Member

I am a strong believer in potential. Every day I work to develop my own, and I encourage everyone in my sphere of influence to do the same. How do people work to develop their potential? They start by making personal growth a priority.

Personal growth has been a major theme of my life. When I was a kid, my father used to pay me and my siblings to read books that would improve us. He also sent us to con-
ferences. As I got older, reading books, listening to instructional tapes, and attending conferences became regular practices for me. Later, as I sought the key to organizational growth, I discovered another reason to promote personal growth because I found that the way to grow any organization is to grow the people in that organization.

> *A team cannot share values if the values have not been shared with the team.*

To promote personal growth in my organization, we encourage people to become members of a mentoring group. We also send people to our own conferences and to other types of training. We provide books, tapes, and other personal-growth tools. And I personally spend time every month mentoring and developing the top leaders of the organization. When we or an employee discovers that the person would flourish in a different position or division of the company, we encourage him to explore new possibilities and make a change. You can't stand in the way of your employees' growth and still hope to grow your organization.

2. The Priority of Adding Value to Others

The INJOY Group exists to add value to people. That is our primary mission. First, we do that with the people in our own organization. But we also do it for our customers and clients. It's the reason we develop and provide consulting, training, and resources to organizations and individuals across the country and around the world. The day we can't add value to people is the day we close our doors.

3. The Power of Partnership

One of my favorite quotes comes from Mother Teresa, who observed, "You can do what I cannot do. I can do what you cannot do. Together we can do great things." That's a succinct way to describe partnership.

> "You can do what I cannot do. I can do what you cannot do. Together we can do great things."
>
> —MOTHER TERESA

It took me almost forty years to discover that I can't do everything. (You probably learned that sooner than I did; my high energy, low IQ, and endless optimism got the better of me for years!) That's when I realized the power of partnership. Over the years, our organization has learned more and more about working with others. Now partnership is the way we choose to accomplish our mission.

Dave Sutherland, the CEO of The INJOY Group, likes to remind everyone, "Partnership begins the moment that a leader realizes we add value to him, and it ends when his vision is accomplished."

In recent years, we have expanded our partnership to include strategic alliances with other organizations. These partnerships have enabled The INJOY Group to train thousands of leaders in nearly a dozen countries overseas and to give away tens of thousands of books every year to people in developing countries.

I've come up with an acronym that describes what partnership means to me. As your partner, we promise to . . .

Put your needs first in every situation.

Add value to your personal leadership.

Recognize we serve a common goal.

Tailor our services to meet your need.

Never take for granted the trust placed in us.

Embody excellence in everything we do.

Respect everyone's uniqueness.

As individuals and as an organization, we can be good partners if we can remember each element.

4. The Practice of Raising Up and Developing Leaders

Everything rises and falls on leadership. That's why I have dedicated the past twenty years of my life to teaching leadership. That's also why I spend so much time finding and developing leaders. The single greatest way to impact an organization is to focus on leadership development. There is almost no limit to the potential of an organization that recruits good people, raises them up as leaders, and continually develops them.

> *The single greatest way to impact an organization is to focus on leadership development.*

5. The Proper Stewardship of the Organization

Any organization that wants to continue fulfilling its mission must learn to be a good steward of its resources. There are three primary ways we do that in our company: managing our assets to get the most out of them, placing our people strategically so they can give and receive as much as possible, and giving of ourselves to worthy causes. If we can do all three of these things, then we are maximizing the use of all the resources we have.

6. The Purpose of Glorifying God

The INJOY Group is an organization made up primarily of Christians, and our roots are in helping churches and pastors to reach their potential. Because of our heritage and our strong convictions, we believe that everything we do should honor God.

Undoubtedly the values of your organization will be different from ours. And that's as it should be. Your values should reflect the people on the team and their leader. What's important is that you go through the discovery process and embrace the team's values. Once you do, you will better understand your team, its mission, and its potential. Never forget that *shared values define the team.* That's the Law of Identity.

VALUES ADD VALUE TO YOUR TEAM

If you've never really thought about how your team's values can reveal its identity and increase its potential, go through the following process with your team:

- *Articulate the values.* Spend some think time or bring together a group of key team members to articulate the team's values. Then put them on paper.

- *Compare values with practices.* Then watch the team in action. You want to make sure the values you identify match the ones you're living. The alignment of the stated values and the behavior of team members boosts the team's energy and effectiveness. But if they are out of alignment, then the team will suffer.

- *Teach the values.* Once you settle what the right values are, you need to teach them to everyone on the team. Do it clearly, creatively, and continually.

- *Practice the values.* Values have no value if you don't put them into practice. If you discover teammates whose actions don't match the team's values, help them to make the changes necessary to align themselves with the rest of the team.

- *Institutionalize the values.* Weave the team's values into the fabric of the team. For example, my friend Bill Hybels, senior pastor of Willow Creek Community Church, identifies "community" as one of the core values of his church. To reinforce that value, the first third of every leadership meeting—whether it is staff, elders, or the board—is dedicated to building and maintaining the personal relationships among the members of that group.

- *Publicly praise the values.* The most fundamental management truth I've ever learned is that what gets rewarded gets done. If you praise and honor the people who epitomize the values of the team, those values get embraced and upheld by other members of the team. There is no better reinforcement.

If you are the leader of your team, it is especially important that you take your team through this process. Left to themselves, with no help to embrace the values you know to be fundamental, team members will create an identity of their choosing. For better or worse, the values of the most influential people on the team will become the team's values. However, by implementing each of the steps I outlined and continuing to repeat them over time, you will find that the culture of your organization will begin to change, and your people will embrace a new identity that you help them find. And once they develop a common team identity, they will work together better, even as the organization grows and changes.

> *The most fundamental management truth I've ever learned is that what gets rewarded gets done.*

NO PLACE LIKE HOME

When I moved to Atlanta, I became acquainted with an organization that has developed its unique identity and fosters a strong sense of teamwork despite being a huge company. That organization is Home Depot.

Now, I am not a do-it-yourselfer. What's the opposite of handy? Handless? Manually challenged? Whatever it is, that describes me. Then there's my son, Joel Porter. He never met a tool he didn't like, and if a thing can be fixed, he will find a way to do it. When he was thirteen years old, we let him create a workshop in a room adjacent to our garage. He put in a workbench, installed fixtures, and wired the room. A friend of ours who used to be a contractor said Joel had put enough power in that small room to light up an entire house!

After our arrival in Atlanta, Joel found himself a job at Home Depot, and he couldn't have been happier. Every day he would come home and tell us about the company, what he did that day, and the values the company held dear.

Intrigued, I did some research of my own. I discovered that the company was founded by Bernie Marcus and Arthur Blank. They opened their first store in Atlanta in June of 1979 after both men had been fired fourteen months earlier from Handy Dan, a home improvement chain located in the western part of the United States. For years, Marcus, a man with considerable retail experience and leadership talent, had possessed a vision for a national chain of huge one-stop home improvement stores. His idea was to offer the widest selection of products at the lowest prices with the best customer service possible.

BUILDING HOME DEPOT

Getting the company off the ground required the two men to keep plugging away, slowly expanding the business, opening more stores, and attracting first-rate people. Marcus said, "We are only as good as our people—especially the men and women working in our stores every day . . . That's why we believe a sure way of growing this company is to clearly state our values and instill them in our associates."[1]

The right leaders with the right values have attracted the right people to make the company a blockbuster. In 1979, they started with four stores. In 1999, Home Depot had 775 stores, 160,000 employees, and $38.4 billion in annual sales.[2]

Values truly are at the heart of Home Depot's success. Marcus explained,

> A set of eight values has been our bedrock for the past twenty years. Although they were not put in writing until 1995, these values—the basis for the way we run the company—enabled us to explode across the North American landscape and will be the vehicle for reaching our ambitious goals in the international marketplace . . .

- *Excellent customer service.* Doing whatever it takes to build customer loyalty.

- *Taking care of our people.* The most important reason for The Home Depot's success.

- *Developing entrepreneurial spirit.* We think of our organizational structure as an inverted pyramid: Stores and customers are at the top and senior management is on the bottom.

- *Respect for all people.* Talent and good people are everywhere, and we can't afford to overlook any source of good people.

- *Building strong relationships with associates, customers, vendors and communities.*

- *Doing the right thing, not just doing things right.*

- *Giving back to our communities as an integral part of doing business.*

- *Shareholder return.* Investors in The Home Depot will benefit from the money they've given us to grow our business.[3]

These values have made the company a great place for people to work. For example, from the day Home Depot opened, the company has offered employees stock options rather than bonuses. That kind of treatment has made more than one thousand of its employees millionaires!

Joel Porter has since left his job at Home Depot. He now works for The INJOY Group in a technical capacity as our studio production manager. But he will always have a heart for Home Depot. Why? Because the company has an identity he respects. It has *shared values, and the values define the team.* That's the impact their organization had on him, and that's the impact the Law of Identity can have on you and your team.

TEAMWORK THOUGHT

If your values are the same as the team's, you become
more valuable to the team.

BECOMING A BETTER TEAM MEMBER

If you want to add value to your team and help it reach its potential, then you need to share in its values. First, make sure that you know what they are. Then, examine your values and goals in comparison to them. If you can wholeheartedly buy into the team's values, commit yourself to aligning yourself with them. If you can't, then your misalignment will be a constant source of frustration to you and your teammates. And you might want to think about finding a different team.

BECOMING A BETTER TEAM LEADER

As the leader of an organization, you have responsibilities when it comes to the team's values. I recommend that you proceed by following these steps:

- Know the values that the team should embrace.

- Live the values.

- Communicate the values to the team.

- Obtain buy-in of the values through aligned behavior among teammates.

Remember, the process takes time. Getting your people to buy in can be especially difficult. But the better leader you are, the more quickly they will buy into you. And the more quickly they buy into you, the more rapidly they will buy into the values you communicate. (To explore this leadership concept in more depth, read the Law of Buy-In in *The 21 Irrefutable Laws of Leadership*.)

14

THE LAW OF COMMUNICATION

Interaction Fuels Action

Whan Gordon Bethune took over Continental Airlines in 1994, the company was a mess. It had suffered through ten changes in leadership in ten years. It had gone through bank- ruptcy proceedings twice. Its stock value was at a pitiful $3.25 a share. It had not made a profit in a decade. Customers were flock- ing away from the airline, and those who did use Continental were rarely happy because in the words of Bethune, their planes "came and went as they happened to" with no predictability. That's not what business travelers and vacationers are looking for in an airline!

TRYING TIMES FOR THE TEAM

In his book, *From Worst to First*, Bethune described the state of Continental when he arrived:

In the years leading up to 1994, Continental was simply the worst among the nation's 10 biggest airlines . . . For example, DOT [the Department of Transportation] measures those 10 largest airlines in on-time percentage . . . *Continental was dead last.* It measures the number of mishandled-baggage reports filed per 1,000 passengers. *Continental was worst.* It measures the number of complaints it receives per 100,000 passengers on each airline. Continental was last. And not just last—in 1994, *Continental got almost three times as many complaints as the industry average* and more than 30 percent more complaints than the ninth-best airline, the runner-up in lousy service. We had a real lock on last place in that category . . . We weren't just the worst big airline. *We lapped the field.*[1]

When a company is that bad, the employees can't help being affected. Morale at Continental was abysmal. Cooperation was non-existent. Communication was at an all-time low. Employees had been lied to so often and so thoroughly that they didn't believe anything they were told. According to Bethune, they had learned one survival strategy: Duck. "That's what I joined in 1994," commented Bethune, "a company with a lousy product, angry employees, low wages, a history of ineffective management, and, I soon learned, an incipient bankruptcy, our third, which would probably kill us."[2]

TRYING TO TURN AROUND THE TEAM

Bethune's goal was to save Continental, but he knew that to do it, he would have to change the culture of the company. The key would be communication. He knew that positive interaction could turn the company around. If he could win the communication battle, he believed he could get the employees to work together again for the good of the team, the customers, and the stockholders.

His first step was to open up the executive offices to the rest of the team. When he began working for Continental, the twentieth-floor suite occupied by top management in Houston was like a fortress. Its doors were locked, the area was surveyed by lots of security cameras, and nobody could enter the area without a proper ID. It wasn't exactly inviting. Bethune literally propped open the doors and hosted open houses for employees to break down the intimidation factor between leaders and the rest of the team.

The next thing he did was to work to break the old bureaucracy that had developed over the years. At Continental, rules and manuals had taken the place of communication and the use of judgment. The chief symptom of that mind-set was the nine-inch-thick book of rules for employees that had come to be known as the "Thou Shalt Not" book. It was so detailed that it dictated what color pencil an agent was supposed to use on a boarding pass. In a significant gesture, CEO Bethune, along with Continental President Greg Brenneman, gathered employees in the parking lot, dropped the manual in a trash can, doused it with gasoline, and burned it![3] The message was clear. Everything at Continental was going to change.

COMMUNICATION CULTURE

Continental didn't change overnight. In fact, as Bethune and Brenneman laid out their "Go Forward Plan," employees were skeptical. But the leaders kept meeting with the people, committed themselves to being honest with them, and maintained their patience. If the news was good, they told the people. If the news was bad, they still told them. They put up bulletin boards in every employee area that showed two things: (1) their ratings for the last year according to the Department of Transportation rating guidelines; and (2) daily news updates from the company. They created a weekly voice-mail message to everyone on the team. They also put lots of communication in writing, using a monthly employee newsletter called *Continental Times and Continental Quarterly*, which they mailed to every employee's home. They put news wire–style LED displays by every coffee and soda machine. They even created 800-number hot lines for questions and information that could be accessed by any employee from anywhere in the world.

> *Bethune's communication policy was—and is—simple: "Unless it's dangerous or illegal for us to share it, we share it."*

A company that had been characterized by distrust and lack of cooperation became a place where communication was pervasive. Bethune's communication policy was—and is—simple: "Unless it's dangerous or illegal for us to share it, we share it."[4] It took time, but eventually the company began to turn. Employees started to trust their leaders. They began to work with and trust one another. And for the first time in more than a decade, the employees of Continental functioned as a team.

Today, Continental's service is among the best in its industry. Employee morale is high. And the company is profitable. In 1994, the year Bethune took over, the company *lost* $204 million. In 1995, it made a *profit* of $202 million. The next year it doubled. As of April 2001, Continental had posted twenty-four consecutive profitable quarters in an industry where many of its competitors are struggling to stay in the black. The company's stock has split twice, and each share is worth more than ten times the value it had in 1994.

What's in a Word?

Communication wasn't the entire reason for Continental's success. But without good communication, the company most likely would have continued on autopilot right into its third (and final) bankruptcy. Creating positive change in an organization requires communication. *Interaction fuels action.* That is the power of the Law of Communication.

> *Effective teams have teammates who are constantly talking to one another.*

Only with good communication can a team succeed—it doesn't matter whether that team is a family, a company, a ministry, or a ball club. Effective teams have teammates who are constantly talking to one another. Communication increases commitment and connection; they in turn fuel action. If you want your team to *perform* at the highest level, the people on it need to be able to talk to and listen to one another.

Communication Matters

When people don't communicate effectively, the result can often be comical. Years ago, I came across the following illustration that conveys what I mean. It is made up of a series of memos on a college campus:

President to Academic V.P.: Next Thursday Halley's Comet will appear over this area. This is an event which occurs only once every 75 years. Call the Division Heads and have them assemble their professors and students on the athletic field and explain this phenomenon to them. If it rains, then cancel the observation and have the classes meet in the gym to see a film about the comet.

Academic V.P. to Division Chairmen: By order of the President, next Thursday Halley's Comet will appear over the athletic field. If it rains, then cancel classes and report to the gym with your professors and students where you will be shown films, a phenomenal event which occurs only once every 75 years.

Division Chairman to Professors: By order of the Phenomenal President, next Thursday Halley's Comet will appear in the gym. In case of rain over the athletic field the President will give another order, something which occurs every 75 years.

Professor to Students: Next Thursday the President will appear in our gym with Halley's Comet, something which occurs every 75 years. If it rains the President will cancel the comet and order us all out to our phenomenal athletic field.

Student Writing Home to Parents: When it rains next Thursday over the school athletic field, the phenomenal 75-year-old President will cancel all classes and appear before the whole school in the gym accompanied by Bill Halley and the Comets.

Scott Adams, the creator of the Dilbert comic strip, has masterfully described an organization where everyone does his best to undermine communication. The boss sends an employee to work for a year on a project that has been canceled, then later demotes the person for wasting so much time. Members of the marketing department continually think up harebrained products and promote them to the public; then they ask the engineers to produce them on an impossible timetable. The higher up in the organization people are, the more clueless they are. Thinkers are punished, the lazy are rewarded, and every decision is arbitrary. The comic strip is hilarious. What's sad is that too many American workers identify with it.

If you've ever been on a team where teammates never let one another know what's going on, then you know how frustrating poor communication can be. The team gets stuck because nobody knows what the real agenda is. Important tasks remain uncompleted because each of two team members believes the other one is taking care of it—or people duplicate others' work. Departments within the organization fight because each believes it is being sabotaged by the other.

In the book *Empowered Teams,* authors Richard Wellins, William Byham, and Jeanne Wilson state, "Communication refers to the style and extent of interactions both among members and between members and those outside the team. It also refers to the way that members handle conflict, decision making, and day-to-day interactions."

A Different Picture of Communication

An excellent example of the complexity—and importance—of good communication can be seen by watching a professional football team in the half minute prior to a play. When one play ends, the offensive team has only forty seconds to get itself ready for the next play. In that time, the quarterback first decides if there is enough time for the team to huddle. If there is, he calls the team members together and gives them the play. If there isn't, he communicates that he will call the play using a code at the line of scrimmage.

For many plays at the professional level, the team will line up with players in one formation and then move them around before the play to try to confuse the defense. If time is short, the quarterback will communicate to the players that they should skip the extra steps and just line up in the formation that will be used to run the play.

As the eleven offensive players approach the line, each is doing two things: assessing what the defense is doing, and paying attention to teammates for communication cues. The linemen who will be blocking pay attention to what kinds of players the other team has in the game and where they are positioned. The center, who hikes the ball to the quarterback, is usually responsible for calling out the blocking scheme to his teammates based on the defense.

Meanwhile, the quarterback is assessing the defense. If he thinks the play he has called in the huddle will fail against the defense, he is likely to use a few words to call an alternate play at the line of scrimmage. If the defense is lined up in such a way that the original play will work, but the blocking scheme of the running backs behind him is likely to fail, then he can change their blocking assignments.

At the same time, the quarterback, the running backs, and the receivers are watching the defense to see if they are about to do anything unusual, such as sending extra players after the quarterback to tackle him in a blitz. If the offensive players do see a blitz coming, then, without a word, the receivers and running backs change their assignments to a predetermined Plan B for that play, and they hope that everyone on the team made the same assessment.

Football is an extremely complex sport. The casual observer has no idea so much communication is going on before every play.

Sometimes it's subtle. Players call out things in code. They use hand signals. One player may simply point and communicate a lot of information to another teammate. And sometimes a quarterback and a receiver will just give each other a look and communicate enough information to make it possible for them to score on the play.

COMMUNICATION ON YOUR TEAM

Communication on your team may not look anything like what happens on a football field. But the success of your team and the ability of your team members to work together are just as dependent on good communication. Allow me to give you some guidelines that will help your team to improve in this area. Every team has to learn how to develop good communication in four areas.

1. From Leader to Teammates

John W. Gardner observed, "If I had to name a single all-purpose instrument of leadership, it would be communication." Perhaps you are familiar with my books on leadership; then you know that I believe everything rises and falls on leadership. What I haven't mentioned before is that leadership rises and falls on communication. You must be able to communicate to lead others effectively.

> "If I had to name a single all-purpose instrument of leadership, it would be communication."
>
> —JOHN W. GARDNER

If you lead your team, give yourself these standards to live by as you communicate to your people:

- *Be consistent.* Nothing frustrates team members more than leaders who can't make up their minds. One of the things that won the team over to Gordon Bethune was the consistency of his communication. His employees always knew they could depend on him and what he said.

- *Be clear.* Your team cannot execute if the members don't know what you want. Don't try to dazzle anyone with your intelligence; impress people with your straightforwardness.

- *Be courteous.* Everyone deserves to be shown respect, no matter what the position or what kind of history you might have with him. By being courteous to your people, you set the tone for the entire organization.

Never forget that because you are the leader, your communication sets the tone for the interaction among your people. Teams always reflect their leaders. And never forget that good communication is never one-way. It should not be top-down or dictatorial. The best leaders listen, invite, and then encourage participation.

2. From Teammates to Leader

Good team leaders never want yes-men. They want direct and honest communication from their people. Even autocratic movie mogul Sam Goldwyn quipped, "I want my people to speak up and be honest, even if it costs them their jobs."

I have always encouraged people on my team to speak openly and directly with me. When we hold meetings, they are often brainstorming sessions where the best idea wins. Often, a team member's remarks or observations really help the team. Sometimes we disagree. That's okay because we've developed strong enough relationships that we can survive conflict. Getting everything out on the table always improves the team. I never want to hear a teammate say, "I could have told you that wouldn't work." If you know it beforehand, that's the time to say it.

Besides directness, the other quality team members need to display when communicating with their leaders is respect. Leading a team isn't easy. It takes hard work. It demands personal sacrifice. It requires making tough and sometimes unpopular decisions. We should respect the person who has agreed to take on that role and show him loyalty.

3. Among Teammates

Author Charlie Brower remarked, "Few people are successful unless a lot of other people want them to be." In a team that desires to experience success, all team members must communicate for the common good. That means exhibiting the following qualities:

- *Being supportive.* Former NBA player Earvin "Magic" Johnson summed up support by paraphrasing President John F. Kennedy: "Ask not what your teammates can do for you. Ask what you can do for your teammates." Communication that is focused on giving rather than getting takes the team to a whole new level.

> *"Ask not what your teammates can do for you. Ask what you can do for your teammates."*
>
> —EARVIN "MAGIC" JOHNSON

- *Staying current.* Teammates who rehash old problems and continually open old wounds don't work together. And if they don't work together, they're sunk. As Babe Ruth remarked, "You may have the greatest bunch of individual stars in the world, but if they don't play together, the club won't be worth a dime."

- *Being vulnerable.* Teams are like little communities, and they develop only when the people in them don't posture with one another. In his book *The Different Drum,* psychiatrist M. Scott Peck observes, "If we are to use the word *community* meaningfully, we must restrict it to a group of individuals who have learned how to communicate honestly with each other, whose relationships go deeper than their masks of composure."

Teams succeed or fail based on the way that team members communicate with one another. Martin Luther King Jr. declared, "We must learn to live together as brothers or perish together as fools." If the interaction is strong, then the action teams take can be strong. *Interaction fuels action.* That's the essence of the Law of Communication.

4. Between the Team and the Public

For most teams, communication within the team isn't the only kind that's important. Most teams interact with outsiders in some way, whether the people are clients, customers, or the concerned public. When approached by people from outside the group, team members must remember three Rs; they need to be *receptive, responsive,* and *realistic.* If they receive communication from others gracefully, always respond in a timely fashion, and are realistic about setting and receiving expectations, they will do just fine. Outsiders will perceive that their concerns are being well received.

On the other hand, when it comes to communicating to people who are not on the team, the most important quality a team can display is unity. The more independent team members are, the more difficult that can be; it's not easy to get eagles to fly in formation. Yet the power of unity is incredible.

An old story that I heard when I lived in the Midwest was about a horse-pull at a country fair. That's an event where various horses compete to see which one can pull a sled with the greatest weight. One year, the champion horse pulled 4,500 pounds. The runner-up pulled 4,400. Wondering what the two stout horses might be able to pull together, a group of men yoked them together. They pulled more than 12,000 pounds—an increase of more than 33 percent over their individual efforts.

There's tremendous power in unity. One of the principles I always tell my team is that when we are brainstorming and planning, I want all the ideas and criticisms out on the table. We need an opportunity to hash things out. But once we leave the room, we must be united— even if we face opposition or criticism. We remain a strong team.

When it comes down to it, you spell cooperation "w-e." Working together means winning together. But no team works together unless it's communicating. It takes *interaction to fuel action.* That's just the way it works. That's the Law of Communication.

> *Working together means winning together.*

HANG TOGETHER OR HANG SEPARATELY

One of the most remarkable stories of communication and teamwork I've ever encountered occurred among the U.S. prisoners of war (POWs) who were detained in Vietnam. As American involvement in the war in Vietnam increased, so did the number of U.S. servicemen who were captured. Ultimately 772 servicemen, mostly pilots, were captured and imprisoned.

Most of the prisoners were held at the Hoa Lo prison, which the men called the Hanoi Hilton. There they suffered unspeakable torture and inhumane conditions. Most of them wasted away. It wasn't unusual for someone over six feet tall to weigh 120 pounds. But the worst part for most of the men was the forced solitude. Former POW Ron Bliss explained, "You get isolated. That's when the trouble begins. You have to communicate at virtually any cost. If you get caught and tortured for a little while, that's just the overhead. But you do it anyway."

The North Vietnamese captors at the Hanoi Hilton tried to defeat the POWs by breaking them physically, crushing their spirits, and keeping them isolated. If a man thought of himself as an abandoned individual, then he would give up hope. Jerry Driscoll, a POW who originally thought he might be released after a few months, was told by a fellow prisoner that it might be two years: "When I finally came to that realization that, my God, that's going to be a long time . . . it just kind of hit me all at once. And I just took my blanket and kind of balled it up and I . . . screamed with all this anguish that it's going to be that long. Two years. And when I was finished, I felt, *Oh, okay. I can do that. I can do two years.* Of course, as it turned out, it was two years, and it was two years after that, and two years after that, until it was about seven years in my case."

TAPS FOR THE PRISONERS

Communication and connection with the other prisoners became necessary for the men to endure and survive. To make that communication possible, the prisoners devised an ingenious system. When four POWs—Carlyle Harris, Phillip Butler, Robert Peel, and Robert Shumaker—were held in the same cell for a time, they devised a tapping code that they could use to spell out words. When they were split up, they used it to communicate, and they taught the code to every prisoner they could. In a matter of months, nearly all of the prisoners knew the code and were using it. "The building sounded like a den of runaway woodpeckers," recalled former POW Ron Bliss.

The men would tap on the walls between cells or push a wire through a wall and tug on it using the code. They would sweep or shovel rhythmically, sending each other messages. They also developed hand signals and other ways of communicating. Ex-POW Thomas McNish observed, "We passed the equivalent of *War and Peace* several times over through different methods of communication."[5]

Even though the prisoners were kept separate from one another—and many men who "talked" all the time never saw the others' faces until they were released—they became a team. They worked together. They shared information. They supported one another. They became such a solid unit that they determined none of them would accept release until all of them could obtain it. The one person who did leave early, Seaman Douglas Hegdahl, accepted release only because he was given a direct order by Lt. Commander Al Stafford to accept it. And he was given the order for one reason: Hegdahl had memorized the 256 names of fellow prisoners, which the men wanted communicated to authorities back home.

Finally in January of 1973, a cease-fire was signed in Paris that made provision for the release of American POWs. They began coming home on February 12, and on March 29, the last prisoners left the

Hanoi Hilton. In all, 462 prisoners were released. That number might have been far fewer if they had not found—and fought for—a way to communicate with one another. But *interaction fuels action*. And their connection with one another fueled their ability to endure and to hold together as a team. That's the value of the Law of Communication.

TEAMWORK THOUGHT

Communication increases connection.

BECOMING A BETTER TEAM MEMBER

How committed are you to communicating with the other members of your team? Are you supportive of everyone, even the people who aren't your friends? Are you open and vulnerable, even if it's not pleasant? Are you holding a grudge against anyone on the team? If you are, you need to clear the air. If there are *any* barriers to good communication standing between you and another team member, you need to remove them. That is your responsibility.

BECOMING A BETTER TEAM LEADER

As the leader of an organization, you set the tone for communication. In this chapter, I mention that a leader's communication must be consistent, clear, and courteous. But leaders must also be good listeners. When leaders don't listen . . .

- They stop gaining wisdom.

- They stop "hearing" what isn't being said.

- Team members stop communicating.

- Their indifference spreads to other areas.

Ultimately, poor listening leads to hostility, miscommunication, and a breakdown of team cohesion.

Give yourself a 360-degree review. Ask for feedback concerning your listening skills from your boss or mentor, your colleagues, and your subordinates. If you don't get high marks from all of them, then quiet down, listen up, and work to become a better communicator.

15

THE LAW OF THE EDGE

The Difference Between Two Equally Talented Teams Is Leadership

Teams are always looking for an edge. I'm sure you've seen it. A ball team recruits new talent or develops new plays to beat a tough opponent—or even develops a whole new system to turn around a legacy of losing. Businesses invest in the latest technology, hoping to improve their productivity. Companies fire their ad agencies and hire new ones to launch a campaign, desiring to make gains on major competitors. Corporations cycle through the latest management fads like channel surfers through television reruns. Everyone is seeking the magic formula that will lead to success. The more competitive the field, the more relentless the search.

What is the key to success? Is it talent? Hard work? Technology? Efficiency? To be successful, a team needs all of these things, but it still needs something more. It needs leadership.

- *Personnel* determine the potential of the team.

- *Vision* determines the direction of the team.

- *Work ethic* determines the preparation of the team.

- *Leadership* determines the success of the team.

Everything rises and falls on leadership. If a team has great leadership, then it can gain everything else it needs to go to the highest level.

FINDING THE EDGE

Look at any team that has achieved great success, and you will find that it has strong leadership. What enabled General Electric to gain the respect of the corporate world? The leadership edge of Jack Welch. What sealed the victory of the United States in the Persian Gulf War? The leadership edge of Generals Norman Schwarzkopf and Colin Powell. What powered the Chicago Bulls to win six NBA championships? The leadership edge of Phil Jackson and Michael Jordan. That's why I say *the difference between two equally talented teams is leadership.* That's the Law of the Edge.

> *Look at any team that has achieved great success, and you will find that it has strong leadership.*

To get a clearer picture of the difference that leadership can make, think of the same players on the same team with different leadership. The Los Angeles Lakers are a notable example. During the late 1990s, they struggled despite having a very talented group of players, including Kobe Bryant, who many hoped would be the next Michael Jordan, and Shaquille O'Neal, the best center in the game. Both players were acquired in 1996, yet they continued to have major problems and never clicked as a team. In 1999, teammate Eddie Jones remarked, "Something isn't right with this team. We're all struggling to keep it together and with a team that has that much talent, this shouldn't be going on."[1]

The next year, the team brought in Phil Jackson, the man who had led the Chicago Bulls to six championships, to coach the Lakers. He kept the same team intact with few changes because he knew talent was not the issue. Of his three key players, O'Neal, Bryant, and Glen Rice, Jackson remarked,

I think we have three of maybe the most talented players since the time of Kareem and Worthy and Magic. However, Baylor, West and Chamberlain [on the 1968–71 Lakers] outshone even those people. They were three of the greatest scorers in the game, and yet they couldn't win a championship. So yeah, we got the talent, we got the show, we got everything else—but how do you make all the pieces complement each other? That's really what my specialty is as a coach, to try to bring that to bear. And this team is learning that.[2]

Leadership is all about understanding players, bringing them together, and getting them to work together as a team to reach their potential. And Jackson provided it. In only one season, the team came together. In 2000, the Lakers won the NBA championship that everyone had believed they had the potential to win. They did it in the same city working under the same conditions and with the same players they'd had in previous years. The only thing that had changed was the leadership. That gave them the edge. *The difference between two equally talented teams is leadership.* That is the Law of the Edge.

NEED A LIFT?

With good leadership, everything improves. Leaders are lifters. They push the thinking of their teammates beyond old boundaries of creativity. They elevate others' performance, making them better than they've ever been before. They improve their confidence in themselves and each other. And they raise the expectations of everyone on the team. While managers are often able to maintain a team at its current level, leaders are able to lift it to a higher level than it has ever reached before. The key to that is working with people and bringing out the best in them.

- *Leaders transfer ownership for work to those who execute the work.* For a team to succeed, responsibility must go down deep into the organization, down to the roots. Getting that to happen requires a leader who will delegate responsibility and authority to the team. Stephen Covey remarked, "People and organizations don't grow much without delegation and completed staff work, because they are confined to the capacities of the boss and reflect both personal strengths and weaknesses." Good leaders seldom restrict their teams; they release them.

- *Leaders create an environment where each team member wants to be responsible.* Different people require different kinds of motivation to be their best. One needs encouragement. Another needs to be pushed. Another will rise to a big challenge. Good leaders know how to read people and find the key that will make them take responsibility for their part on the team. They also remember that they are responsible *to* their people, not *for* them.

- *Leaders coach the development of personal capabilities.* The team can reach its potential only if each individual on the team reaches his potential. Effective leaders help each player do that. For example, Phil Jackson is well known for giving his players books to read that will help them improve themselves, not just as basketball players, but as people.

- *Leaders learn quickly and encourage others to learn rapidly.* Leaders lift themselves to a higher level first; then they lift the others around them. Modeling comes first, then leadership. If everyone is improving, then the team is improving.

If you want to give a team a lift, then provide it with better leadership. The Law of the Edge works every time.

THE LAWS OF LEADERSHIP IMPACT THE TEAM

Leadership can improve a team and give it an edge in many ways, and the 21 laws from my book on leadership provide a useful summary. Good leaders . . .

1. Do not limit an organization as others do. (The Law of the Lid)

2. Have greater influence than others do. (The Law of Influence)

3. Value the process of developing people more than others do. (The Law of Process)

4. Prepare the team for the journey better than others do. (The Law of Navigation)

5. Communicate more effectively than others do. (The Law of E. F. Hutton)

6. Create momentum and lift the team to a higher level than others do. (The Law of the Big Mo)

7. Stand on a foundation of trust that is more solid than others' is. (The Law of Solid Ground)

8. Command greater respect than others do. (The Law of Respect)

9. Work on leadership issues earlier than others do. (The Law of Intuition)

10. Draw more leaders to themselves than others do. (The Law of Magnetism)

11. Connect with people better than others do. (The Law of Connection)

12. Bring stronger key people around them than others do. (The Law of the Inner Circle)

13. Reproduce more leaders than others do. (The Law of Reproduction)

14. Empower team members more than others do. (The Law of Empowerment)

15. Win with teams more than others do. (The Law of Victory)

16. Sell themselves and their vision to a greater degree than others do. (The Law of Buy-In)

---

17. Establish priorities more effectively than others do.
(The Law of Priorities)

18. Understand and use timing more effectively than others do.
(The Law of Timing)

19. Give up their personal agendas more than others do.
(The Law of Sacrifice)

20. Grow leaders and organizations faster than others do.
(The Law of Explosive Growth)

21. Leave a legacy that lasts longer than others do.
(The Law of Legacy)

Good leaders do things just a little bit better than others do. The result is usually victory. That's the Law of the Edge.

TURNING THE TABLE ON THE TABLES

Leadership is the key to the Law of the Edge, but I don't want you to get the idea that the responsibility for leadership always falls on one person. Although most teams have a designated leader who is ultimately responsible for the oversight of the team, the actual leadership of the team is usually shared.

I find that when it comes to leadership, many people tend to see it in one of two ways. The first I call *the myth of the head table*. It's the notion that on a particular team, one person is always in charge in every situation. It's the idea that this particular individual permanently occupies the "head table" in the organization and that everyone else always takes a subordinate role to him. For example, here is an illustration that might have been written by someone who subscribes to the myth of the head table:

> As everyone knows, an executive has practically nothing to do except . . .
>
> To decide what is to be done;
>
> To tell somebody to do it;
>
> To listen to reasons why it should not be done, why it should be done by somebody else, or why it should be done in a different way;
>
> To follow up to see if the thing has been done, only to discover that it has not;
>
> To inquire why;
>
> To listen to excuses from the person who should have done it;
>
> To follow up again to see if the thing has been done, only to discover that it has been done incorrectly;
>
> To point out how it should have been done;
>
> To conclude that as long as it has been done, it may as well be left where it is;
>
> To wonder if it is not time to get rid of a person who cannot do a thing right;
>
> To reflect that the person probably has a spouse and large family, and that certainly any successor would be just as bad—or maybe worse;
>
> To consider how much simpler and better the thing would have been done if one had done it oneself in the first place;
>
> To reflect sadly that one could have done it right in twenty minutes, and as things turned out, one has had to spend two days to find out why it has taken three weeks for somebody else to do it wrong.

The idea that one person is always doing all the leading is false. The same person should not always lead the team in every situation. The challenge of the moment often determines the leader for that challenge because every person on the team has strengths that come into play. Let me illustrate this point. Even though I lead The INJOY Group as its founder, I don't always lead the team. Other people on the team have gifts, skills, and abilities that I do not possess. When we moved our offices—along with the employees, their equipment, our supplies and computers, our information and communication systems—the job required sophisticated navigating and incredible planning skills.

The most obvious person to lead the team was Frank Hartman, a logistical thinker, exceptional planner, and detailed administrator. Frank created the plan for the move. He had the authority and responsibility of managing the process—and of leading all of the people, including the CEO and other officers of the organization. And he did a wonderful job. We didn't lose a single day of productivity at the office during the move. Nobody else on our team could have pulled it off as effectively. I handed the ball off to Frank, and he successfully led us—and fulfilled the Law of the Edge.

> *Everyone is important, but everyone isn't equal.*

The other misconception about leadership takes the opposite extreme. I call it the *myth of the roundtable*. It's the belief that everyone on the team is equal, all opinions count the same, and a team can function without leadership. That isn't true either. A team that tries to function like a democracy never gets anything done.

Everyone is important, but everyone isn't equal. The person with greater experience, skill, and productivity in a given area is more important to the team in that area. GE CEO Jack Welch's opinion carries more weight than the person who packs boxes on the assembly line. The NBA's Michael Jordan is worth more money than the guard who sits on the bench. That's the way it is. That doesn't mean that Jack and Michael have more value as *human beings*. In the eyes of God, everyone is loved equally. But when it comes to leading the team, somebody needs to step forward.

GIVING THE TEAM A HEAD START

In essence, leadership is like a running head start for the team. Leaders see farther than their teammates. They see things more quickly than their teammates. They know what's going to happen and can anticipate it. As a result, they get the team moving in the right direction ahead of time, and for that reason, the team is in a position to win. Even an average runner can win a 100-meter race against a world-class sprinter if he has a 50-meter head start.

The greater the challenge, the greater the need for the many advantages that leadership provides. And the more leaders a team develops, the greater the edge from leadership. If you want to win and keep winning for a long time, train players on the team to become better leaders.

The edge gained from good leadership is quite evident in sports, but the power of leadership carries over into every field. The business that is run by a top-notch leader often finds its market niche first and outperforms its rivals, even if the rivals possess greater talent. The nonprofit organization headed by strong leaders recruits more players, equips them to lead, and serves a greater number of people as a result. Even in a technical area such as engineering or construction, leadership is invaluable in ensuring the team is successful.

GOLDEN OPPORTUNITY

The Law of the Edge was at work in one of the most extraordinary feats of engineering in the world: the Golden Gate Bridge. Completed in 1937, the bridge had the longest main span of any suspension bridge in the world until the construction of the Verrazano Narrows Bridge was finished in New York City in 1964. If you've been to San Francisco, then you've seen how beautiful and impressive the Golden Gate Bridge is. But the story of its construction is even more impressive.

The concept of a bridge spanning the Golden Gate—the opening to San Francisco's bay—was proposed as early as 1872, although nobody thought it was really possible. The idea wasn't brought up again and taken seriously until 1916. The reason people wanted a bridge was simple: San Francisco's growth and expansion were being hindered by its location since it was surrounded on three sides by water. Plenty of open land lay to the north, but getting to it was hard. Even though Marin County lay only about a mile north across the strait, getting there required a circuitous drive of one hundred miles around San Francisco's huge bay area. The only other alternative was to take a ferry across the gap, but at peak times, drivers had to wait in line for hours to catch the ferry.

Building a bridge across the Golden Gate Strait looked as if it would never happen. The physical and technological challenges of the project were overwhelming. The entrance of the bay experienced strong ocean currents and battering winds. The depth of the channel, which reached more than three hundred feet at points, would make construction very difficult. On top of that, any bridge that would be built had to be high enough to allow large ships to navigate beneath it. Engineers from around the country estimated that a bridge would cost as much as $250 million. (At that time, the value of every piece of property in the entire city of San Francisco totaled only $375 million!)

ENTER A LEADER

Then along came Joseph B. Strauss. He was the owner of an engineering firm that had built more than four hundred bridges. But more important than his experience were his astonishing vision and powerful leadership. He believed he could build a bridge spanning the Golden Gate for $25 million. In 1921, Strauss put together preliminary designs for a bridge and began to gather support for the project among the leaders of the counties adjoining San Francisco. He promoted the bridge tirelessly. In the beginning, his influence was unofficial. But in time, after the formation of the Golden Gate Bridge and Highway District, he was named chief engineer of the proposed project.

If it hadn't been for a leader like Strauss, the bridge never would have been built. For twelve years, he fought every imaginable obstacle and opponent to the project. When the San Francisco political machine (including the city's chief engineer, Michael O'Shaughnessy) opposed him, he met with leaders and citizens in every county to raise grassroots support. When the Army Corps of Engineers and the War Department (which controlled the land on both sides of the strait) threatened to withdraw approval, Strauss went to Washington and persuaded the secretary of war to guarantee the government's cooperation. When the Golden Gate Bridge and Highway District experienced a severe cash flow problem, Strauss met with Amadeo P. Giannini, founder of Bank of America. In just a few hours he was able to persuade Giannini to buy bonds immediately to keep the project going—

and commit to buy more the next time they were offered. Strauss overcame powerful special interest groups, environmentalists, labor problems, and the ravages of the Great Depression, which hit in the middle of the process. His energy and influence were astounding.

A Leader Who Didn't Get in His Own Way

One of Strauss's greatest strengths was his ability to attract good leaders and engineers. To make the project successful, he brought in the best bridge designers in the world. When he realized that his original design for the bridge was inadequate and could endanger the project, he abandoned it and relied on his leaders to create something better. "Strauss had an unusual ability," remarked author John Van der Zee, "to locate and draw to him men of greater abilities than his own, men who would accept his leadership."[3]

Strauss was a leader's leader, and no matter what difficulty was thrown at him, he handled it. He was a natural leader who understood how to influence others. Van der Zee observed, "Strauss was, if anything, stronger at marketing and promoting ideas than he was at conceiving them. He seemed to know instinctively whom to reach, whom to get to and persuade, who were the decision makers, the people who mattered in any given situation."[4]

Finally Breaking Ground

In 1933, construction finally began on the bridge. Again, Strauss hired the best engineers he could find to oversee construction.

That was no small task. The team who built the bridge put in 25 million hours of work on it.[5] But the actual construction of the bridge seemed almost easy by comparison to what had been necessary before the process could begin. When the bridge was completed, Strauss remarked that it had taken him two decades to convince people that the bridge was feasible, but only four years to actually build it! And he completed it just in time. He died at age sixty-eight—the year after the bridge was finished.

Look behind the scenes of any major undertaking, and you will always find a strong leader. If Joseph Strauss hadn't taken personal responsibility for the creation of the Golden Gate Bridge—and dedicated himself to it wholeheartedly—then it wouldn't have been built. That's the reality of the Law of the Edge. It takes a leader if a team wants to realize its potential and reach its goals. That's why I say that *the difference between two equally talented teams is leadership.*

TEAMWORK THOUGHT

Everything rises and falls on leadership.

BECOMING A BETTER TEAM MEMBER

You don't have to be *the* leader to be *a* leader on your team. Begin the process of improving your leadership skills today. Do the following:

- Acknowledge the value of leadership.
- Take personal responsibility for your leadership growth.

• Put yourself on a leadership development program.

• Find a leadership mentor.

Once you have added value to yourself, you will be able to add value to—and influence—others to help your team.

BECOMING A BETTER TEAM LEADER

If you are *the* leader of your team, then the best thing you can do for your teammates is to follow the example of Joseph Strauss. Add other leaders to the team.

You can do that in two ways. First, attract the best leaders you can—people whose talent and potential are greater than your own. Second, develop the people already on the team. The stronger the leadership of the team, the greater the team's potential for success. Never forget: Everything rises and falls on leadership.

16

THE LAW OF HIGH MORALE

When You're Winning, Nothing Hurts

It's an image most Americans will never forget: gymnast Kerri Strug being carried in the arms of Coach Bela Karolyi to the podium to receive her gold medal along with her six teammates in the 1996 Summer Olympic Games in Atlanta. It was a landmark moment. It was the first time the women's gymnastics team from the United States had won the gold medal, but that isn't why people will remember it. Although it was a stick-in-your-mind image—the tiny eighty-seven-pound Strug being cradled by a big bear of a man who is considered the greatest gymnastics coach in history—it will be remembered primarily because it is the perfect picture of the Law of High Morale.

A First for the Team

Even if you didn't see it on television as I did, you probably know the story. In a sport dominated by the Russian and Romanian teams, the United States team was actually ahead during the Olympic Games. The Russians had opened strong, but after the first rotation of events, the Americans were in first place. As the athletes competed in each event, the U.S. team's lead continued to grow—not by a lot but steadily. As the teams went into the final event—the floor exercise for the Russians and the vault for the Americans—all the U.S. team had to do was to finish solidly, and the gold medal would be theirs.

The second to last vaulter for the U.S. was Dominique Moceanu, usually a smooth performer. Much to everyone's surprise, on her first attempt she landed on her bottom instead of her feet, which gave her a very low score. Fortunately, in women's vault, each athlete gets a second attempt, and only the better of the two scores counts. But, unbelievably, Moceanu missed her second attempt with the same results.

Although Moceanu's performance was unexpected, the situation wasn't desperate. The U.S. still had one athlete left: Kerri Strug, who had received the highest scores in the vault during U.S. Olympic trials. One good vault from her, and the gold medal would belong to the team. When Strug tried to land her first vault, however, her feet weren't positioned quite right. She, too, slipped and fell. Worse yet, she injured herself, and she still needed to complete another vault for the team.

The situation was desperate. After the fact, some commentators remarked that the U.S. could have won without Strug's second vault. But at that moment, Russian gymnast Rozalia Galiyeva was still to compete in the floor exercise. U.S. coach Bela Karolyi was concerned that a high score by the Russian would cost the Americans their hard-fought victory.

Strug knew what she had to do. She needed to land her vault—the final attempt of the final event of the women's team competition. "Give me one last vault," Karolyi encouraged her. "Give me one last good vault."

NOT A FIRST FOR STRUG

Every athlete who makes it to the highest levels knows what it means to play through pain. Kerri Strug was no different. Besides all the normal strains, sprains, and bruises, in the past she had recovered from a torn stomach muscle and a serious back injury received in a fall on the uneven parallel bars. Karolyi said of her, "She is just a little girl who was never the roughest girl . . . always a little shy, always standing behind someone else. But sometimes this is the person with the biggest ggrrrrr."[1]

A gymnast has only thirty seconds to complete her second vault after the scores from the first one have been tabulated. In those moments, Strug focused herself. She later remembered, "I knew something was wrong with me. I heard something snap. I kept telling myself not to fall on the vault or the gold would slip away and all that hard work and effort would fall apart in a few seconds. I just said a little prayer and asked God to help me out."[2]

PAIN OR GAIN?

What Strug didn't know then was that two ligaments in her left ankle had torn during her first vault. But that didn't matter. She flew down the runway, hit the beat-board, sprang off the vault with her hands, and went flying through the air. Miraculously, she landed solidly on both feet. Then, she felt excruciating pain. Standing on one foot, she quickly saluted the judges, then crumpled to the floor. She landed her vault, she got her score, and the entire team received its gold medal.

After that, the girl who had always been in the background, who had never been the star of her gym, became the star of the Olympic team. Everyone seemed to appreciate the sacrifice she made. Sports journalist E. M. Swift wrote,

> All she knew, beyond the certainty of the gold medal, was that she had injured herself too badly to compete in the individual all-around competition two days later, a goal she'd clung to for the past four years. This was her moment of greatest triumph, also her moment of greatest disappointment. Her will had found a way to block out the pain for a few crucial seconds, but it had exacted a punishing price. She had literally sacrificed herself for the team.[3]

Strug's own words were direct and simple: "When you do well, you think it's worth it. When you sacrifice so much and you finally do well, it feels really good."[4] In other words, *when you're winning, nothing hurts.* That is the Law of High Morale.

TAKING THE TEAM HIGHER

The Law of High Morale may ring a bell with you because the phrasing of the law was inspired by the words of Joe Namath, the quarterback who helped the New York Jets win the Super Bowl in 1969.

Like any champion, he understood that there is an exhilaration that comes from winning. That feeling can be so strong that it sustains you through the discipline, pain, and sacrifice required to perform at the highest level.

That's what Kerri Strug felt. As she faced that final vault, she knew that her performance would help her team win. And that knowledge empowered her to come through for the team when it mattered most. Perhaps that's why George Allen, who coached the Washington Redskins in the early 1970s, said, "Every time you win, you're reborn; when you lose, you die a little." It's ironic, but if you play hurt, you can put the team in the position to win. And if you win, nothing hurts.

> *It's ironic, but if you play hurt, you can put the team in the position to win. And if you win, nothing hurts.*

Really high morale helps the team to perform at its best. High morale can be a crucial difference maker. When a team has high morale, it doesn't just have to deal with whatever circumstances get thrown at it. It creates its own circumstances.

- The *fund-raiser* knows that under the right circumstances, people love to give.

- The *teacher* knows that under the right circumstances, students love to grow.

- The *leader* knows that under the right circumstances, people love to follow.

- The *coach* knows that under the right circumstances, players are able to win.

High morale is one of the essentials to creating the right circumstances for any team to perform at the highest level.

HIGH MORALE IS GREAT . . .

If the team is winning, then morale is high. And if morale is high, then the team is in a position to win. So which comes first: high morale or winning? I believe that high morale usually comes first. Why? Because high morale magnifies everything positive that is happening for a team.

1. High Morale Is the Great Exaggerator

When an entire team is positive and all the players feel good about themselves, *everything* seems good. Preparation seems to proceed more smoothly. Every break seems to go your way. The small victories seem sweet, and the big ones make you feel almost invincible. The stars of the team deliver at crunch time, and even the bench players seem to be playing beyond their usual capabilities.

Some people call such a time a winning streak or a stretch of good luck. But it's really just high morale. In sports, during times of high morale, everybody jumps onto the bandwagon as a fan. In big business, people buy the company's stock. In entertainment, magazines and television networks ask for interviews—and producers pay top dollar for the team's services. Has the team changed from talentless to talented overnight? Is the team really as good as its press? Probably not. The team is enjoying the great exaggerator at work.

2. High Morale Is the Great Elevator

When a team possesses high morale, the performance of its people goes to a whole new level. The team focuses on its potential, not its problems. Team members become more committed. And everyone finds it easier to be unselfish. Team members are confident, and that confidence helps them to perform at a higher level.

When a team is losing, the opposite effect occurs. Players focus on their problems. Everyone's level of commitment goes down. The team repels others rather than attracts them. And everyone starts to look out for himself rather than his teammates. When you're losing, everything hurts.

3. High Morale Is the Great Energizer

High morale gives a team energy. Players become like the Energizer bunny: They keep going and going. No mountain seems too high. No project seems too difficult. No race seems too long. Their enthusiasm builds along with their energy, and the team develops a momentum that is almost unstoppable.

4. High Morale Is the Great Eliminator

Because of the momentum and energy that come with it, high morale also becomes the great eliminator. While a team that is losing and experiencing poor morale can be hurt by even the most minor problem, a team with high morale will keep right on going even when faced with a huge obstacle or otherwise disabling setback. Problems just seem to disappear—no matter how big they are.

5. High Morale Is the Great Emancipator

Something else that high morale does for a team is to free it up. Winning creates breathing room. A good team with high morale will use that breathing room to take risks and try out new ideas, new moves, new concepts that it otherwise wouldn't. It stops to ask questions that it otherwise might not. And doing these things yields creativity and innovation. In the end, high morale releases the team to reach its potential.

THE FOUR STAGES OF MORALE

You may be saying, "Okay, I agree. *When you're winning, nothing hurts.* High morale is great for the team. How in the world do we get it?" Let me tell you. If you are a player, then you need to have a good attitude, always give your best, and support the people on the team—players and leaders alike. If you have little influence, then exert what influence you have by modeling excellence.

However, if you're one of the team's leaders, then you have more extensive responsibilities. You need to model excellence, but you also need to do more. You need to help the people you lead to develop morale and momentum to create a winning team. The key to knowing what to do can be found in the four stages of morale.

Stage 1: Poor Morale–The Leader Must Do Everything

Nothing is more unpleasant than being on a team when nobody wants to be there. When that is the case, the team is usually negative, feels lethargic, or has no hope. That is often the atmosphere found in a team that is losing.

If you are in that situation, then do the following:

- *Investigate the situation.* Start by addressing what the team is doing wrong. Begin by fixing what's broken. That alone won't give the team high morale, but it will stop giving players reasons to have poor morale.

- *Initiate belief.* A team will change only when people believe in themselves. As the leader, you must initiate that belief. Show people you believe in yourself and them.

- *Create energy.* The desire to change without the energy to change just frustrates people. To bring a greater level of energy to the team, you need to be energetic. Work with energy long enough, and someone on the team will eventually come alongside you and join you. Then another person will. Eventually the energy will spread.

- *Communicate hope.* The deepest need of players at this stage is hope. As Napoleon Bonaparte said, "Leaders are dealers in hope." Help them to see the potential of the team.

> *"Leaders are dealers in hope."*
>
> —NAPOLEON BONAPARTE

In stage one, the only way to get the ball rolling is to start pushing it yourself. As the leader, you can't wait for anyone else to do it.

Stage 2: Low Morale—The Leader Must Do Productive Things

In the beginning, any movement is a noteworthy victory. But to create positive morale, you need to pick up some speed. You need to be productive. After all, you can't steer a parked car! Get the team moving.

- *Model behavior that has a high return.* People do what people see. The best way for them to learn what you expect of them is to model it yourself.

- *Develop relationships with people of potential.* To get any team going in the right direction, you need players who can produce. At this stage, your team may have some producers. If it does, develop relationships with them. If it doesn't, then find the people who have the potential to be productive, and start with them. Don't ask too much of them too soon. Leaders touch a heart before they ask for a hand. That's why you want to begin by building relationships.

- *Set up small victories and talk teammates through them.* Nothing helps people grow in skill and confidence like having some wins under their belts. That's what you want to give the people on your team. Once again, begin with the people who have the most potential. Their small victories will help less talented team members to gain confidence and succeed.

- *Communicate vision.* As I've already explained in the Law of the Compass, vision gives team members direction and confidence. Keep the vision before your team continually.

Once you've got the team really moving, then you can begin to steer.

Stage 3: Moderate Morale—The Leader Must Do Difficult Things

Do you remember what it was like when you first got your driver's license? Maybe before you received it, you enjoyed just sitting in the driver's seat of a car and imagining what it would be like to drive. Later, when you had your license and you were allowed to take out the car, just going for a drive was probably a thrill. It didn't really matter where you went. But as you got older, just driving wasn't enough. Having a destination became significant.

The same is true with a team. Getting the team together and moving add up to an accomplishment. But where you're going matters. To change from simply *moving the team* to *moving the team in the right direction,* you must do the difficult things that help the team to improve and develop high morale. You need to . . .

- *Make changes that make the team better.* You already understand the Law of the Chain. Just remember that leaders are responsible for minimizing the damage any team member can do because of weakness or attitude, and for maximizing the effectiveness of all team members by placing them in their proper niches. Often these actions require tough decisions.

- *Receive the buy-in of team members.* It's one thing to cast vision to the team. It's another to get your teammates to buy in. Yet to build higher morale, you must do that. The teammates must buy into you as a leader, embrace the values and mission of the team, and align themselves with your expectations. If you can do all of that, you will be able to take the team where it needs to go.

- *Communicate commitment.* Part of the process of getting people to buy in comes from showing them your commitment. The Law of Buy-In from *The 21 Irrefutable Laws of Leadership* says that people buy into the leader, then the vision. If you have consistently demonstrated high competence, good character, and strong commitment, you have laid the foundation for your people to buy in.

- *Develop and equip members for success.* Nothing builds morale like success. Most people are not capable of achieving success on their own. They need help, and that is one of the primary reasons for anyone to lead them. If you invest in your teammates, then you help them and the team succeed.

The two toughest stages in the life of the team are the first stage, when you are trying to create movement in a team that's going nowhere, and the third stage, when you must become a change agent. These are the times when leadership is most needed. And stage three is the make-or-break time for a leader. If you can succeed in stage three, then you will be able to create high morale on your team.

Stage 4: High Morale–The Leader Must Do Little Things

In stage four, your job as a leader is to help the team maintain high morale and momentum.

- *Keep the team focused and on course.* High morale leads to winning, and winning maintains morale. That's why it's important to keep team members focused. If they lose focus or get off course, then they'll stop winning. And remember, the farther you intend to go, the greater the impact of an error in direction. If you want to cross a street, being a degree or two off course doesn't hurt you. If you want to cross the ocean, miscalculating by a few degrees can get you into a lot of trouble.

- *Communicate successes.* Knowing what they're doing right helps people stay on track. You can indicate that by communicating the team's successes. Nothing boosts morale like winning and then celebrating it.

- *Remove morale mashers.* Once the team is rolling in the right direction, keep it rolling. The Law of the Big Mo from *The 21*

Irrefutable Laws of Leadership says that momentum is a leader's best friend. Leaders see before others do, so they need to protect the team from the things that will hurt the team.

- *Allow other leaders to lead.* A leader who prepares other team members to lead and then turns them loose to do it accomplishes two things. First, he uses the momentum the team already has to create new leaders for the team. It's easier to make new leaders successful if they are part of a successful team. Second, he increases the leadership of the team. And that makes the team even more successful. A leader who continually does that can create a cycle of success that feeds the team's high morale.

The process of building high morale takes strong leadership, and it takes time. When I think of someone who was a master at that process, I think of Ronald Reagan. When he took office as president of the United States in 1981, morale in the country was at the lowest it had been since the Great Depression. People had lost faith in the American government following Watergate. The threat of nuclear war with the Soviet Union was never far from people's thinking. Inflation was out of control. Oil prices were up. And interest rates were off the charts. People could not have been more discouraged.

Ronald Reagan helped people to

> *Four Stages of Morale:*
> *1. Poor Morale—The leader must do everything.*
> *2. Low Morale—The leader must do productive things.*
> *3. Moderate Morale—The leader must do difficult things.*
> *4. High Morale—The leader must do little things.*

believe in the country again. Under his presidency, the economy revived, the cold war ended, the Berlin Wall fell, and people believed in themselves and their country again.

HIGH MORALE AT HOME

You don't need to have the power of a president or the ability of an Olympic athlete to practice the Law of High Morale. You can apply the principle to your business, your volunteer service, or even your family. In fact, when the Law of High Morale is working at its best, the leader boosts the morale of the team, and the team boosts the morale of the leader. That's the way it should be. *When you're winning, nothing hurts.*

> *When the Law of High Morale is working at its best, the leader boosts the morale of the team, and the team boosts the morale of the leader.*

Let me tell you about a team where the members continually inspire one another and build up one another to such an extent that their morale is high and they keep winning despite the pain they feel. They are the father-and-son team of Dick and Rick Hoyt.

When Rick Hoyt was born in 1962, his parents possessed the typical excited expectations of first-time parents. But then they discovered that during Rick's birth, his umbilical cord had been wrapped around his neck, cutting off the oxygen to his brain. Later, Rick was diagnosed with cerebral palsy. "When he was eight months old," his father, Dick, remembers, "the doctors told us we should put him away—he'd be a vegetable all his life."[5] But Rick's parents wouldn't do that. They were determined to raise him like any other kid.

AN UPHILL BATTLE

Sometimes that was tough. Rick is a quadriplegic who cannot speak because he has limited control of his tongue. But Rick's parents worked with him, teaching him everything they could and including him in family activities. When Rick was ten, his life changed; engineers from Tufts University created a device that enabled him to communicate via computer. The first words he slowly and painstakingly punched out were, "Go Bruins." That's when the family, who had been following the NHL's Boston Bruins in the play-offs, found out Rick was a sports fan.

In 1975, after a long battle, the family was finally able to get Rick into public school, where he excelled despite his physical limitations. Rick's world was changing. It changed even more two years later. When Rick found out that a fund-raising 5K race (3.1 miles) was being put on to help a young athlete who had been paralyzed in an accident, he told his father that he wanted to participate.

Dick, a lieutenant colonel in the Air National Guard (who has since retired), was in his late thirties and out of shape. But he agreed to run and push his son in a modified wheelchair. When they crossed the finish line (second to last), Dick recalls, Rick flashed "the biggest smile you ever saw in your life." After the race, Rick wrote out this simple message: "Dad, I felt like I wasn't handicapped." After that day, their lives would never be the same again.

WORKING TOGETHER

What does a father do when his son, who has never been out of a wheelchair, says that he loves to race? He becomes his boy's hands and feet. That's the day "Team Hoyt" was born. Dick got Rick a more sophisticated racing chair. Then the quadriplegic teenager and the out-of-shape dad began running together—and not casually. Before long, they were training seriously, and in 1981, they ran in their first Boston Marathon together. Since then, they haven't missed a Boston Marathon in twenty years.

After four years of running marathons, the two decided that they were ready for another challenge: triathlons, which combine swimming, cycling, and running. That was no small challenge, especially since Dick would have to learn how to swim! But he did. Dick explained, "He's the one who has motivated me because if it wasn't for him, I wouldn't be out there competing. What I'm doing is loaning Rick my arms and legs so he can be out there competing like everybody else."[6]

Of all the races in the world, one is considered the toughest—the Ironman Triathlon in Hawaii. The race consists of three back-to-back legs: a 2.4-mile swim, a 112-mile bike race, and a full marathon run of 26.2 miles. It's an excruciating test of stamina for any individual. In 1989, Dick and Rick competed in the race together. For the swimming portion, Dick towed a small boat with Rick in it. Then he biked for the 112 miles with Rick in a seat on his bicycle's handlebars. By the time they got to the running leg, Dick was exhausted.

But it's in such situations that the Law of High Morale kicks in. All Dick had to do was to think of the words of his son:

When I'm running, my disability seems to disappear. It is the only place where truly I feel as an equal. Due to all the positive feedback, I do not feel handicapped at all. Rather, I feel that I am the intelligent person that I am with no limits.[7]

When you're winning, nothing hurts. By continuing to run, Dick would be winning for his son, and that's what makes all the training and pain worthwhile. Dick loaded Rick into his running chair, and off they went to finish the Ironman. The pair finished the race in a little over thirteen hours and forty-three minutes—a very strong time.

Since then, Rick has earned his college degree, and he works at Boston University helping to design computer systems for people with disabilities. And of course, he still competes with his father, who is now more than sixty years old. As of March 2001, Team Hoyt had completed a total of 731 races. They had run 53 marathons and 135 triathlons, including 4 races at Ironman distances. And they will keep running. "There is nothing in the world that the both of us can't conquer together," says Dick.[8] He should know. For almost twenty-five years, he and his teammate have been reaping the rewards of the Law of High Morale.

TEAMWORK THOUGHT

When you do good, you feel good—when you
feel good, you do good.

BECOMING A BETTER TEAM MEMBER

If you want to reap the rewards of the Law of High Morale, you can't wait until your morale is high to begin performing. You need to act your way into feeling, not feel your way into acting. Begin by performing at a level of excellence appropriate for someone who is experiencing a winning season. Your dedication and enthusiasm will help your performance—and will inspire some of your teammates.

BECOMING A BETTER TEAM LEADER

If you are a leader on your team, then you need to figure out what kind of morale your team is currently experiencing:

- *Poor morale:* The team is dead in the water and negative.

- *Low morale:* The team is making some progress, but it is not cohesive and confident.

- *Moderate morale:* The team is experiencing some wins and beginning to believe in itself, but some hard decisions need to be made to take it to the next level.

- *High morale:* The team is performing close to its potential, it's winning, and it just needs to be kept on track.

Once you've determined the stage of your team, then apply the guidelines in the chapter so that you can take the team (or your area of it) to the next stage.

┌─────┐
│ **17** │
└─────┘

THE LAW OF DIVIDENDS

Investing in the Team Compounds Over Time

H e's one of the greatest team builders in all of sports, yet you've probably never heard of him. Here is a list of these impressive accomplishments:

- Forty consecutive basketball seasons with at least twenty wins

- Five national championships

- Number one ranking in his region in twenty of the last thirty-three years

- Lifetime winning percentage of .870

His name is Morgan Wootten. And why have most people never heard of him? Because he is a *high school* basketball coach!

When asked to name the greatest basketball coach of all time, most people would respond with one of two names: Red Auerbach or John Wooden. But do you know what John Wooden, the UCLA coach called the Wizard of Westwood, had to say about Morgan Wootten? He was emphatic in his appraisal: "People say Morgan Wootten is the best high school coach in the country. I disagree. I know of no finer coach at any level—high school, college or pro. I've said it elsewhere and I'll say it here: I stand in awe of him."[1]

That's a pretty strong recommendation from the man who won ten NCAA national championships and coached some of the most talented players in the game, including Kareem Abdul-Jabbar. (By the way, when Kareem was in high school at Power Memorial Academy, his team lost only one game—to Morgan Wootten's team!)

No Plan to Be a Team Builder

Morgan Wootten never planned to coach a team. He was a decent athlete in high school, but nothing special. However, he was an excellent talker. When he was growing up, his ambition was to be an attorney. But when he was a nineteen-year-old college student, a friend tricked him into accepting a job coaching baseball, a game he knew little about, to kids from an orphanage. The team had no uniforms and no equipment. And despite working hard, the boys lost all sixteen of their games.

During that first season, Wootten fell in love with those kids. When they asked him to come back and coach football, he couldn't refuse them. Besides, he had played football in high school, so he knew something about it. The orphanage team went undefeated and won the Washington, D.C., Catholic Youth Organization (CYO) championship. But more important, Wootten began to realize that he wanted to invest his time in children, not in court cases.

Even that first year he made a difference in the lives of kids. He remembers one boy in particular who had started stealing and kept being brought back to the orphanage by the police. He described the boy as having "two and a half strikes against him already." Wootten let the boy know he was headed for trouble. But he also took the boy under his wing. Wootten recalled,

> We started spending some time together. I took him to my house and he'd enjoy Mom's meals. He spent weekends with us. He became friends with my brother and sisters. He's still in Washington today and doing quite well and known to a lot of people. Anyone would be proud to call him their son. He was bound for a life of crime and jail, however, and maybe a lot worse, until someone gave him the greatest gift a parent can give a child—his time.

Giving of himself to the people on his teams is something Wootten has done every year since then. NCAA basketball coach Marty Fletcher, a former player and assistant under Wooten, summarized his talent this way: "His secret is that he makes whomever he is with feel like the most important person in the world."[2]

CREATING A DYNASTY

It wasn't long before Wootten was invited to become an assistant coach at a local powerhouse high school. Then with a couple of years' experience under his belt, he became head coach at DeMatha High School.

When he started at the school in 1956, Wootten was taking over a bunch of losing teams. He called together all of the students who wanted to play sports at DeMatha, and he told them:

> Fellas, things are going to change. I know how bad DeMatha's teams have been during these last few years, but that's over with. We're going to win at DeMatha and we're going to build a *tradition* of winning. Starting right now . . . But let me tell you how we're going to do it. We're going to outwork every team we ever play . . . With a lot of hard work and discipline and dedication, people are going to hear about us and respect us, because DeMatha will be a winner.[3]

That year, the football team won half of its games, which was quite an accomplishment. In basketball and baseball, they were division champions. His teams have been winning ever since. DeMatha has long been considered a dynasty.

On October 13, 2000, Wootten was inducted into the Naismith Basketball Hall of Fame in Springfield, Massachusetts. At that time, his teams had amassed a record of 1,210–183. Over the years, more than 250 of his players have won college scholarships. Twelve players from his high school teams went on to play in the NBA.[4]

It's Not About Basketball

But winning games and honors isn't what excites Wootten most. It's investing in the kids. Wooten says,

> Coaches at every level have a tendency to lose sight of their purpose at times, especially after success arrives. They start to put the cart

before the horse by working harder and harder to develop their teams, using their boys or girls to do it, gradually forgetting that their real purpose should be to develop the kids, using their teams to do it.[5]

Wootten's attitude reaps rewards not only for the team, but also for the individuals on the team. For example, for a twenty-six-year stretch, every single one of Wootten's seniors earned college scholarships—not just starters but bench players too. Penn State assistant coach Chuck Swenson observed, "Even if you know a kid isn't a great player, if he's a DeMatha player, he'll help your program. With Morgan, you know you're getting a quality kid, who will make good grades and work hard for you."[6] Gary Williams, head coach of the University of Maryland, agreed about the quality of the players: "His players are so fundamentally sound, do so many things right, that they may not improve as much as kids in another program who haven't been as well coached . . . These aren't raw talents: They're refined ones."[7] What's remarkable is that these comments describe *high school* students, not college players or pros.

Investing in the team compounds over time. Morgan Wootten invests in his players because it is the right thing to do, because he cares about them. That practice has made his players good, his teams successful, and his career remarkable. He is the first basketball coach to have won 1,200 games at any level. Developing people pays off in every way. That is the power of the Law of Dividends.

GREAT INVESTORS

Throughout the chapters of this book, you've read about people who have dedicated themselves to investing in the people on their teams. And those investments pay all kinds of rich dividends. Gordon Bethune's investment of trust has paid off by keeping Continental in business and saving the jobs of its fourteen thousand employees. The investment of Bernie Marcus and Arthur Blank is paying dividends to the employees who own Home Depot stock, including one thousand employee-millionaires. The investment of Jeff Skilling at Enron is paying dividends in the formation of new industry initiatives by leaders in the company. And Lilly Tartikoff's investment in people is paying dividends in cancer research. Usually the time, money, and effort required to develop team members don't change the team overnight, but developing them always pays off. *Investing in the team compounds over time.*

> *The time, money, and effort required to develop team members don't change the team overnight, but developing them always pays off.*

HOW TO INVEST IN YOUR TEAM

I believe that most people recognize that investing in a team brings benefits to everyone on the team. The question for most people isn't *why,* but *how.* Allow me to share with you ten steps you can take to invest in your team. You can implement these practices whether you are a player or coach, employee or employer, follower or leader. There is always someone on the team who can benefit from what you have to offer. And when everyone on the team is investing, then the benefits are like those of compound interest. They multiply.

Here is how to get started:

1. Make the Decision to Build a Team . . . This Starts the Investment in the Team

It's said that every journey begins with the first step. Deciding that people on the team are worth developing is the first step in building a better team. That requires *commitment*.

> *Deciding that people on the team are worth developing is the first step in building a better team.*

2. Gather the Best Team Possible . . . This Elevates the Potential of the Team

As I've previously mentioned, the better the people on the team, the greater the potential. There's only one kind of team that you may be a part of where you *shouldn't* go out and find the best players available, and that's family. You need to stick with those teammates through thick and thin. But every other kind of team can benefit from the recruitment of the very best people available.

3. Pay the Price to Develop the Team . . . This Ensures the Growth of the Team

When Morgan Wootten extended himself to benefit the kid who had two-and-a-half strikes against him, he and his family had to pay a price to help that boy. It wasn't convenient or comfortable. It cost them in energy, money, and time.

It will cost you to develop your team. You will have to dedicate time that could be used for personal productivity. You will have to spend money that could be used for personal benefit. And sometimes you will have to set aside your personal agenda. But the benefit to the individuals—and the team—is worth the price. Everything you give is an investment.

4. Do Things Together as a Team . . . This Provides Community for the Team

I once read the statement, "Even when you've played the game of your life, it's the feeling of teamwork that you'll remember. You'll forget the plays, the shots, and the scores, but you'll never forget your teammates." That is describing the community that develops among teammates who spend time doing things together.

> *Even when you've played the game of your life, it's the feeling of teamwork that you'll remember.*

The only way to develop community and cohesiveness among your teammates is to get them together, not just in a professional setting but in personal ones as well. There are lots of ways to get yourself connected with your teammates, and to connect them with one another. Many families who want to bond find that camping does the trick. Business colleagues can socialize outside work (in an appropriate way). The *where* and *when* are not as important as the fact that team members share common experiences.

5. Empower Team Members with Responsibility and Authority . . . This Raises Up Leaders for the Team

The greatest growth for people often occurs as a result of the trial and error of personal experience. Any team that wants people to step up to a higher level of performance—and to higher levels of leadership—must give team members authority as well as responsibility. If you are a leader on your team, don't protect your position or hoard your power. Give it away. That's the only way to empower your team.

6. Give Credit for Success to the Team . . . This Lifts the Morale of the Team

Mark Twain said, "I can live for two months on one good compliment." That's the way most people feel. They are willing to work hard if they receive recognition for their efforts. That's why Napoleon Bonaparte observed, "A soldier will fight long and hard for a bit of colored ribbon." Compliment your teammates. Talk up their accomplishments. And if you're the leader, take the blame but never the credit. Do that and your team will always fight for you.

> *"I can live for two months on one good compliment."*
>
> —MARK TWAIN

7. Watch to See That the Investment in the Team Is Paying Off . . . This Brings Accountability to the Team

If you put money into an investment, you expect a return—maybe not right away, but certainly over time. How will you know whether you are gaining or losing ground on that investment? You have to pay attention to it and measure its progress.

The same is true of an investment in people. You need to observe whether you are getting a return for the time, energy, and resources you are putting into them. Some people develop quickly. Others are slower to respond, and that's okay. The main outcome you want to see is progress.

8. Stop Your Investment in Players Who Do Not Grow . . . This Eliminates Greater Losses for the Team

One of the most difficult experiences for any team member is leaving a teammate behind. Yet that is what you must do if someone on your team refuses to grow or change for the benefit of teammates. As I mentioned in the Law of the Chain, that doesn't mean that you love the person less. It just means you stop spending your time trying to invest in someone who won't or can't make the team better.

9. Create New Opportunities for the Team . . . This Allows the Team to Stretch

There is no greater investment you can make in a team than giving it new opportunities. When a team has the possibility of taking new ground or facing new challenges, it has to stretch to meet them. That process not only gives the team a chance to grow, but it also benefits every individual. Everyone has the opportunity to grow toward his or her potential.

10. Give the Team the Best Possible Chance to Succeed . . . This Guarantees the Team a High Return

James E. Hunton says, "Coming together is a beginning. Keeping together is progress. Working together is success." One of the most essential tasks you can undertake is to clear obstacles so that the team has the best possible chance to work toward success. If you are a team member, that may mean making a personal sacrifice or helping others to work together better. If you are a leader, that means creating an energized environment for the team and giving each person what he needs at any given time to ensure success.

> *Where there's a will there's a way; where there's a team, there's more than one way.*

Investing in a team almost guarantees a high return for the effort because a team can do so much more than individuals. Or as Rex Murphy, one of my conference attendees, told me: "Where there's a will there's a way; where there's a team, there's more than one way."

My Personal Investment—and Return

Once you have experienced what it means to invest in your team, you will never be able to stop. Thinking about my team—about how the teammates add value to me as I add value to them—brings me abundant joy. And just like my investment and their return, my joy continues to compound.

I value everyone on my team, and if I could, I would tell you about every person. But since that isn't possible, I want to at least acquaint you with key players in my inner circle:

- Larry Maxwell (fifty-four years). He loves me unconditionally. He has taken The INJOY Group to a whole new level. Asks great questions. Keeps our team focused. Protects me. He's my big brother!

- Margaret Maxwell (thirty-seven years). My wife. She knows me so well, loves me so much. Her partnership has allowed me to go to a higher level. Our journey together is my greatest joy.

- Dan Reiland (nineteen years). He was my executive pastor for many years. Now as a consultant, he helps pastors with my heart and experience plus his wisdom and perspective. He is a pastor's best friend and mine!

- Dick Peterson (eighteen years). He follows up on all the details of my company. I open the door, and he closes it. I start a sentence, and he finishes it!

- Tim Elmore (fifteen years). He teaches my leadership material better than I do. He gives me leadership material better than my own.

- Linda Eggers (fourteen years). She knows my strengths and weaknesses. Represents me so well. Answers the team's questions better than I would and much more quickly.

- Charlie Wetzel (eight years). He shapes the lives of more people than anyone else on my team. He takes my ideas, lessons, and outlines and turns them into books. From there, they multiply.

- Dave Johnson (seven years). He stewards The INJOY Group's resources to extend its impact around the globe. He is a financial wizard who loves and understands me.

- Kevin Small (seven years). He has unlimited energy and unlimited potential. Sees an opportunity a mile away. I love pouring myself into him. The return is huge!

- Dave Sutherland (seven years). He is my number one guy. He's the man. A great thinker. He can grow the company without me. When I give him the ball, it's always a touchdown.

- Kirk Nowery (five years). He represents me so well and loves pastors and local churches. Every night he tells the story of how we can add value through ISS. Every night we get that opportunity.

- Doug Carter (five years). He loves to share the mission of EQUIP (my nonprofit organization) with others. He helps businesspeople go from success to significance. He has taken me to a whole new level.

At this stage of my life, everything I do is a team effort. When I first started teaching seminars, I did everything. Certainly there were other people pitching in, but I was just as likely to pack and ship a box as I was to speak. Now, I show up and teach. My wonderful team takes care of everything else. Even the book you're reading was a team effort.

My team is my joy. I would do anything for the people on my team because they do everything for me:

> My team makes me better than I am.
>
> My team multiplies my value to others.
>
> My team enables me to do what I do best.
>
> My team gives me more time.
>
> My team represents me where I cannot go.
>
> My team provides community for our enjoyment.
>
> My team fulfills the desires of my heart.

If your current team experiences are not as positive as you would like, then it's time to increase your level of investment. Building a team for the future is just like developing a financial nest egg. It may start slowly, but what you put in brings a high return—similar to the way that compound interest works with finances. Try it and you will find that the Law of Dividends really works. *Investing in the team compounds over time.*

TEAMWORK THOUGHT

Is the team's investment in you paying off?

Becoming a Better Team Member

Are you giving a good return for what your teammates are investing in you? Think about the opportunities you have received and the positive learning experiences to which you've been exposed. Have you seized all of them enthusiastically, or have you allowed many of them to slip by?

If you've been lackadaisical about pursuing growth opportunities, then change your attitude today. Grow all you can, and determine to give the team a good return on its investment in you.

Becoming a Better Team Leader

As a leader, you, more than anyone else, determine the environment of your organization and whether your people are investing in others. Begin by institutionalizing investment and making it a part of your organization's culture. Encourage growth. Set aside time and money for investment in the team. And take on the responsibility for investing in your core leaders. The more leaders you have on the team and the further developed they are, the greater the dividends.

AFTERWORD

A lot of people talk about team chemistry. You hear it often in sports. Analysts will say, "That team certainly had the talent, but they weren't able to develop the chemistry. That's why they didn't perform the way everyone expected."

You may have noticed that there is no Law of Chemistry in this book, and that may have been a disappointment to you. But let me tell you why that concept isn't one of the 17 Indisputable Laws of Teamwork.

Chemistry isn't something you can create with one skill or implementation of a single technique. Chemistry develops when you are able to implement *all* of the Laws of Teamwork. The more laws you put into practice, the greater the chemistry your team will develop. Each time a player finds his niche on the team, it helps to create positive chemistry. Each time a weak link is replaced by a better player from the bench, it creates better chemistry. When a catalyst steps up to the plate and makes something happen for the first time, or when a leader finds a way to help the team perform at a higher level, it creates good chemistry. When players finally count on one another, it makes the chemistry better. Every time another law comes to life for the team, the chemistry gets that much better—and the team gets that much stronger.

I hope you have enjoyed learning about the Laws of Teamwork. More important, I hope they will help you develop the team of your dreams. Embrace them and you will empower your team. That is my promise to you!

NOTES

Chapter 1

1. Brandon Tartikoff and Charles Leerhsen, *The Last Great Ride* (New York: Turtle Bay Books, 1992), 60.
2. "OncoLink: An Interview with Lilly Tartikoff," <www.oncolink.upenn.edu>.

Chapter 2

1. Frye Gaillard, *If I Were a Carpenter: Twenty Years of Habitat for Humanity* (Winston-Salem, NC: John F. Blair, 1995).
2. "The History of Habitat," <www.habitat.org>.

Chapter 3

1. "Bush Nominates Powell as Secretary of State," 17 December 2000.
2. Colin Powell with Joseph E. Persico, *My American Journey* (New York: Random House, 1995), 28.

3. Michael Hirsh and John Barry, "Leader of the Pack," *Newsweek* <www.newsweek.com>, 25 December 2000.

4. "Town Hall Meeting: January 25, 2001," <www.state.gov>.

5. "Packing Parachutes," audiotape excerpt, <www.charlieplumb.com>.

6. "Charlie Plumb's Speech Content," <www.charlieplumb.com>.

Chapter 4

1. "Mount Everest History/Facts," <www.mnteverest.com>.

2. James Ramsey Ullman, *Man of Everest: The Autobiography of Tenzing* (London: George G. Harrap and Co., 1955), 178.

3. Ibid., 250.

4. Ibid., 255.

5. Jim Lovell and Jeffrey Kluger, *Lost Moon: The Perilous Voyage of Apollo 13* (Boston: Houghton Mifflin, 1994), 159–60.

6. W. David Compton, *Where No Man Has Gone Before: A History of Apollo Lunar Exploration Missions* (Washington DC: NASA SP-4214, 1989).

7. Ullman, *Man of Everest*, 227.

Chapter 5

1. "Quick Answers to the Most Frequently Asked Questions," <www.oilspill.state.ak.us/history>.

2. "Exxon's Appeal of the Valdez Oil Spill $5 Billion in Punitive Judgement," <www.exxon.mobil.com>.

3. Danny Cox with John Hoover, *Leadership When the Heat's On* (New York: McGraw-Hill, 1992), 69–70.

4. John Carl Roat, *Class-29: The Making of U.S. Navy SEALs* (New York: Ballantine Books, 1998), 192.

5. Ibid., 7.

6. Ibid., 223.

Chapter 6

1. "The President Suits Up for Practice,"
   <www.cbs.sportsline.com>.

2. "The History of the 'I Have a Dream' Program,"
   <www.ihad.org>.

Chapter 7

1. Greg Farrell, "Building a New Big Blue," <www.usatoday.com>,
   23 November 1999.

2. "IBM Wants Business Partners to Focus on Growth,"
   <www.findarticles.com>, 2 March 1999.

3. Farrell, "Building a New Big Blue."

4. Michelle Marchetti, "IBM's Marketing Visionary," *Sales and
   Marketing Management,* September 2000, 55.

5. Proverbs 29:18 KJV.

6. Howard Schultz and Dori Jones Yang, *Pour Your Heart into It:
   How Starbucks Built a Company One Cup at a Time,* (New York:
   Hyperion, 1997), 36-37.

7. Ibid., 3-4.

8. Ibid., 102.

9. Ibid., 101.

10. Alex Frew McMillan, "Starbucks' Schultz on Being Big in
    Japan," <www.cnn.com>, 10 October 2001.

11. "Howard Schultz," *BusinessWeek,* <www.businessweek.com>, 14
    January 2002.

12. Schultz and Jones Yang, 200.

Chapter 8

1. John C. Maxwell, *The Winning Attitude* (Nashville: Thomas Nelson, 1993), 24.
2. Pat Riley, *The Winner Within* (New York: Berkley Publishing Group, 1994), 41, 52.

Chapter 9

1. "Interview with Stacey Loizeaux."
2. John C. Maxwell, *The 21 Irrefutable Laws of Leadership: Follow Them and People Will Follow You* (Nashville: Thomas Nelson, 1998), 58.
3. Barry J. Gibbons, *This Indecision Is Final: 32 Management Secrets of Albert Einstein, Billie Holiday, and a Bunch of Other People Who Never Worked 9 to 5* (Chicago: Irwin Professional Publishing, 1996).
4. Colossians 3:23–24.
5. Roat, *Class-29: The Making of U.S. Navy SEALs*, 135–36.
6. "Statement of FBI Director Louis J. Freeh on the Arrest of FBI Special Agent Robert Philip Hanssen," <www.fbi.gov>, 20 February 2001.
7. Walter Pincus and Brooke A. Masters, "U.S. May Seek Death Penalty Against Accused Spy Hanssen," <www.washingtonpost.com>, 28 March 2001.
8. "Core Values," <www.fbi.gov>, 30 March 2001.
9. "Statement of FBI Director Louis J. Freeh on the Arrest of FBI Special Agent Robert Philip Hanssen."
10. William A. Cohen, *The Art of the Leader* (Englewood Cliffs, NJ: Prentice Hall, 1994).

Chapter 10

1. Stephen Franklin, "Founder a Force in Retail, Civic Affairs," <www.chicagotribune.com>, 29 December 2000.

2. "End of the Line," <www.nytimes.com>, 29 December 2000.

3. "Historical Chronology—1925: Opening Retail Stores,"
   <www.sears.com>, 15 March 2001.

4. Allan Cox, *Straight Talk for Monday Morning* (New York: John
   Wiley & Sons, 1990).

5. John C. Maxwell, *The 21 Indispensable Qualities of a Leader:
   Becoming the Person Others Will Want to Follow* (Nashville: Thomas
   Nelson, 1999), 144–45.

6. Robert Newall, "History Comes Alive in Valley Forge,"
   <www.vaportrails.com>, 11 March 2001.

Chapter 11

1. Michael D. Eisner with Tony Schwartz, *Work in Progress* (New
   York: Random House, 1998), 171.

2. John Taylor, *Storming the Magic Kingdom: Wall Street Raiders and
   the Battle for Disney* (New York: Knopf, 1987), 14.

3. Eisner, *Work in Progress*, 235.

4. "The Walt Disney Company Annual Report 2000: Financial
   Review," <www.disney.go.com>, 28 March 2001.

5. Adam Cohen, "eBay's Bid to Conquer All," *Time*, 5 February
   2001, 48.

6. "Company Overview," <pages.ebay.com>, 12 March 2001.

Chapter 12

1. John Wooden with Jack Tobin, *They Call Me Coach* (Chicago:
   Contemporary Books, 1988), 104.

Chapter 13

1. Bernie Marcus and Arthur Blank with Bob Andelman, *Built
   from Scratch: How a Couple of Regular Guys Grew The Home Depot*

from Nothing to $30 Billion (New York: Times Business, 1999), xvi–xvii.

2. "Company Information," <www.homedepot.com>, 11 April 2001.

3. Marcus and Blank, *Built from Scratch*, xvii.

Chapter 14

1. Gordon Bethune with Scott Huler, *From Worst to First: Behind the Scenes of Continental's Remarkable Comeback* (New York: John Wiley and Sons, 1998), 4.

2. Ibid., 6.

3. Thomas A. Stewart, "Just Think: No Permission Needed," *Fortune*, 8 January 2001, <www.fortune.com>.

4. Bethune, *From Worst to First*, 211.

5. "Return with Honor," *The American Experience*, <www.pbs.org>, 22 February 2001.

Chapter 15

1. Mike Kahn, "Harris' Deletion No Surprise," <www.cbs.sport-sline.com>, 24 February 1999.

2. Mike Rowland, *Los Angeles Magazine*, June 2000, <www.findarti-cles.com>.

3. John Van der Zee, *The Gate: The True Story of the Design and Construction of the Golden Gate Bridge* (Lincoln, NE: Backinprint.com, 2000), 50.

4. Ibid., 42.

5. Craig A. Doherty and Katherine M. Doherty, *The Golden Gate Bridge* (Woodbridge, CT: Blackbirch Press, 1995), 17.

Chapter 16

1. Johnette Howard, "True Grit," <sportsillustrated.cnn.com>, 24 July 1996.
2. Ibid.
3. E. M. Swift, "Carried Away with Emotion," <sportsillustrated.cnn.com>, 8 December 1996.
4. "Not Just the Wink of an Eye," <www.strug.com>, 30 March 2001.
5. David Tereshchuk, "Racing Towards Inclusion," <www.teamhoyt.com>, 14 March 2001.
6. "Father-Son Duo Are World Class Competitors, Despite Odds," <www.cnn.com>, 29 November 1999.
7. Ibid.
8. Ibid.

Chapter 17

1. Don Banks, "Teacher First, Seldom Second, Wootten has Built Monument to Excellence at Maryland's DeMatha High," *St. Petersburg Times*, 3 April 1987, <www.dematha.org>.
2. John Feinstein, "A Down-to-Earth Coach Brings DeMatha to New Heights," *Washington Post*, 27 February 1984, <www.dematha.org>.
3. Morgan Wootten and Bill Gilbert, *From Orphans to Champions: The Story of DeMatha's Morgan Wootten* (New York: Atheneum, 1979), 24–25.
4. William Plummer, "Wooten's Way," *People*, 20 November 2000, 166.
5. Wootten and Gilbert, *From Orphans to Champions*, 12–13.
6. Feinstein, "A Down-to-Earth Coach Brings DeMatha to New Heights."
7. Ibid.